INTERNATIONAL DEVELOPMENT IN PRACTICE

Public Investment Management Reference Guide

JAY-HYUNG KIM, JONAS ARP FALLOV, AND SIMON GROOM

WORLD BANK GROUP

1818 H Street NW, Washington, DC 20433
Telephone: 202-473-1000; Internet: www.worldbank.org

1 2 3 4 23 22 21 20

ISBN: 978-1-4648-1529-4
DOI: 10.1596/978-1-4648-1529-4

Cover art: *Cats Two* © Brad Burns / Construction Fine Art. Used with the permission of Brad Burns, ConstructionFineArt.com; further permission required for reuse.
Cover design: Debra Naylor / Naylor Design Inc.

Contents

Boxes

Figures

Tables

Foreword

Public investment management (PIM) is crucial to improving infrastructure outcomes and spurring economic development. Analysis has shown that improvements in the systems, processes, and procedures supporting public investment can significantly increase its quality and efficiency.

Over the past decade, the World Bank has worked extensively to provide guidance to countries and share experiences on how to adopt identified principles of functionality in the design of PIM institutions. A key lesson from the work is that it is tempting but not necessarily wise to seek to emulate high-income countries that may have developed sophisticated management systems compatible with their specific political contexts. Yet, clear management principles exist that should be retained and adapted to lower-capacity contexts. These "must-have" features of a PIM system—features that help to ensure that key risks are appropriately reduced through decision steps and controls—are within most governments' capacity to implement. Since 2008, a World Bank PIM diagnostic framework for assessing the extent to which the must-have principles are reflected in country systems has been applied in more than 70 countries.

World Bank PIM engagements have revealed an increasing demand for practical guidance on how to adapt the must-have principles to country contexts and develop specific reforms in relation to country practices and procedures.

The *Public Investment Management Reference Guide* aims to fill the gap between *what* should be done and the immediate demand for pragmatic guidance from countries on *how* to adapt the implied reforms. It conveys country experiences and good international practices as a basis for decisions on how to address a country-specific PIM reform agenda. The country references are drawn largely from previous diagnostics and technical assistance work of the World Bank.

The *PIM Reference Guide* identifies key reform issues in the following areas: clarification of the definition and scope of public investment and public investment management; establishment of a sound legal, regulatory, and institutional setting for PIM; allocation of roles and responsibilities for key players in PIM across governments; strengthening of appraisal and deepening of appraisal methodologies; integration of strategic planning, project appraisal, and capital budgeting; management of multiyear capital budget allocations and commitments; efforts to address the effective implementation, procurement, and monitoring of projects; strengthening of asset management and ex post evaluation; integration of PIM and public-private partnerships (PPPs) in a unified framework; rationalization and prioritization of the existing nonperforming portfolio of public investment projects; and development of a PIM information system.

The *PIM Reference Guide* provides an overall framework for each of the issues, lists different approaches and experiences across countries, and summarizes actionable reforms. It does not seek to provide definitive answers or detailed templates for replication across countries. Instead, it clarifies the differences and commonalities across countries.

I hope readers will appreciate the experience-based knowledge and practical value of this publication and that it will encourage countries to seek reforms more systematically. PIM is indeed a complex matter, but it is of critical importance if countries want to meet the current and emerging demands of the global economy, reduce poverty, and increase their contribution to global prosperity. In the World Bank, we look forward to working closely with member countries, other development partners, and the private sector to deliver better public investment solutions and achievements.

Edward Olowo-Okere
Director, Governance Global Practice
The World Bank

Acknowledgments

This volume was prepared by a World Bank Governance Global Practice team led by Jay-Hyung Kim (task team leader) and Jonas Arp Fallov, with Simon Groom (international consultant). The team worked under the guidance and direction of James Brumby and Edward Olowo-Okere. The team is grateful to peer reviewers Marianne Fay (former chief economist, Sustainable Development Global Practice and current country director), Cem Dener (lead governance specialist, Governance Global Practice), Jens Kromann Kristensen (head, PEFA Secretariat; lead public sector specialist, Governance Global Practice), Tuan Minh Le (lead economist, Macro, Trade, and Investment Global Practice), David Gentry (former senior economist, Fiscal Affairs Department, International Monetary Fund [IMF]), Rui Monteiro (former senior public-private partnership specialist, Public-Private Partnerships Cross-Cutting Solution Area, World Bank; current technical assistance adviser, Fiscal Affairs Department, IMF), and Onur Erdem (public sector specialist, Governance Global Practice).

The team would like to recognize advice and suggestions received from Bernard Myers, Nicola Smithers, Robert Taliercio, and Hisham Waly at various points during preparation of the volume. The work of Marc Robinson and Andrew Bird (international consultants) provided invaluable source material for chapter 7 and chapter 11, respectively. The background work of Martin Darcy (international consultant) is acknowledged for developing the asset management section of chapter 9 and for framing and strengthening the contents of chapter 10. Background work by Eduardo Talero (international consultant) is also acknowledged for defining the requirements for public investment management (PIM) information systems and enriching the conclusions of chapter 12. Helpful comments were provided by the participants at brown bag seminars organized by the Public Investment Management Community of Practice at the World Bank.

The work on the *PIM Reference Guide* benefited from a valuable partnership with the Korea Development Institute (KDI) and financial support from the Korean Trust Fund Program.

About the Authors

Jonas Arp Fallov is a senior public sector specialist with the World Bank's Europe and Central Asia West Region, specializing in public financial management and public investment management. His experience includes leading projects as well as advisory and analytical work in 18 countries as well as long-term assignments in Bangladesh and Indonesia. Mr. Fallov has served as a steering committee member of the PIM Community of Practice. Before joining the World Bank, Mr. Fallov held several positions in the Danish government, including as head of the Ministry of Finance Budget Reform Secretariat, head of the Division for State Accounts and Reporting under the Ministry of Finance, and head of the Budget Division under the Ministry of Environmental Affairs. Mr. Fallov holds master's degrees in public administration from the Maxwell School of Citizenship and Public Affairs, Syracuse University, and in public managerial economics from Roskilde University.

Simon Groom began his career as an economist working on feasibility studies of public sector transport infrastructure projects, first in the United Kingdom and then internationally. He then became involved in public financial management, focusing on assisting countries such as Albania, Bosnia, and Vietnam to introduce a stronger medium-term perspective and performance orientation to budgeting. Since 2008, he has specialized in advising on public investment management (PIM) reforms, mostly for the World Bank and the International Monetary Fund. This work has involved participating in PIM diagnostic assessments and providing follow-up technical assistance, including drafting of procedures and guidelines and advising on legislative changes. His work in this area has taken him to countries in the European Union (Bulgaria, Cyprus, Ireland, and Romania), Eastern Europe and the South Caucasus (Azerbaijan, Southeast Balkan countries, Belarus, Georgia, Moldova, and Ukraine), and Africa (Botswana, Ethiopia, Ghana, Kenya, Rwanda, Tanzania, and Uganda), as well as to Vietnam. As part of the technical assistance, Mr. Groom has been involved in organizing study visits to the Republic of Korea, Norway, Slovenia, and the United Kingdom. Mr. Groom has a BSc in economics from the London School of Economics and Political Science and an MA in development economics from the University of Sussex.

Jay-Hyung Kim is an adviser in the Governance Global Practice of the World Bank. Since 2012, he has been working in areas of public investment management and public-private partnership (PPP) in various departments and units of the World Bank. He served as co-convenor and steering committee member of the PIM Community of Practice. His country experience includes substantive assignments for advisory and analytical works on Cambodia, Ethiopia, Georgia, Kenya, Mongolia, Romania, Ukraine, Vietnam, and Zimbabwe. Before joining the World Bank, from 2000 to 2003 and from 2006 to 2012, he served as executive director of the PIM/PPP organization of the government of the Republic of Korea, the Public and Private Infrastructure Investment Management Center (PIMAC), which, according to the National Finance Law and the Public Private Partnership Law, is mandated to be responsible for supporting the management and supervision of public and private infrastructure investments of the government. From 2003 to 2005, he was seconded as a senior economist in the Operations Evaluation Department of the World Bank. He has been a fellow of the Korea Development Institute (KDI) since 1994. Dr. Kim holds bachelor's and master's degrees in economics from Seoul National University and a PhD in economics from the University of Chicago.

Abbreviations

FMIS	financial management information system
ICT	information and communication technology
IMF	International Monetary Fund
IPSAS	International Public Sector Accounting Standards
IT	information technology
LOLF	Loi Organique Relative aux Lois de Finance (Organic Budget Law) (France)
MCA	multicriteria analysis
MFD	maximizing finance for development
MTBF	medium-term budgetary framework
MTEF	medium-term expenditure framework
MTFF	medium-term fiscal framework
MTPF	medium-term performance framework
NPC	net present cost
NPV	net present value
OBC	outline business case
OECD	Organisation for Economic Co-operation and Development
PEFA	public expenditure and financial accountability
PIM	public investment management
PIMAC	Public and Private Infrastructure Investment Management Center (Republic of Korea)
PIP	public investment portfolio
PPP	public-private partnership
SCBA	social cost-benefit analysis
SDR	social discount rate
SNG	subnational government
SNI	National Public Investment System (Chile)
SOC	social opportunity cost; strategic outline case
SOE	state-owned enterprise
SRO	senior responsible owner
SRTP	social rate of time preference

TIP	traditionally implemented project
VFM	value for money
WTA	willingness to accept
WTP	willingness to pay

1

Introduction

THE NEED FOR A PIM REFERENCE GUIDE

Public investment management (PIM) is a crucial component of infrastructure investment and economic development. Improvements to PIM are expected to enhance the efficiency and effectiveness of infrastructure investment as well as its contribution to achieving development goals. Analysis has shown that the quality of public governance correlates with public investment and growth outcomes; improving governance arrangements, across levels of government at national and subnational levels, throughout the life cycle of an investment project could therefore achieve significant benefits (OECD 2013). An International Monetary Fund (IMF) study using a scale to measure the difference between one country's efficiency and that of its best-performing peers has shown that countries achieve very different efficiency from their public investments (IMF 2015). In emerging markets, the difference in efficiency is 27 percent on average; in low-income countries, it is 40 percent. The differences become even more pronounced for the bottom quarter of performers, where more than half of the public capital accumulated from public investment does not contribute meaningfully to the delivery of quality infrastructure services.

A World Bank publication, *The Power of Public Investment Management: Transforming Resources into Assets for Growth*, synthesized global knowledge on this topic to provide guidance on how to adopt identified principles of functionality in the design of institutions in order to strengthen PIM (Rajaram et al. 2014). Given a country's institutions, infrastructure, and unique issues, it is tempting but unwise to seek to emulate high-income countries that have evolved sophisticated management systems compatible with their specific political contexts. Yet clear management principles exist that should be retained and adapted to lower-capacity contexts. These principles can be termed the "must-have" features of a PIM system—features that help to ensure that key risks are appropriately reduced through decision steps and controls that are within most governments' capacity to implement. Addressing these issues requires a systemic view and careful diagnostic assessment (Rajaram et al. 2014, 8). Since 2008, a World Bank PIM diagnostic framework for assessing the extent to which "must-have" principles are reflected in country systems was applied in more than 70 country diagnostics, revealing the generally poor quality of systems across the globe.

Introduced in 2015 (IMF 2015) and recently revised (IMF 2018), the IMF's Public Investment Management Assessment (PIMA) framework is another key tool for assessing infrastructure governance over the full investment cycle and for supporting economic institution building in this area. A key motivation for its development has been that strong infrastructure governance is critical for public investment to spur economic growth. PIMAs are used to assess infrastructure governance—that is, the key PIM institutions and processes of a country. More than 50 PIMAs have been conducted to date, revealing much room for strengthening PIM.

These PIM diagnostic assessments often lead to follow-up work by the World Bank, IMF, or other global institutions involving technical assistance and development actions to address recommendations for individual countries. Follow-up work has included support for building PIM institutional frameworks, developing PIM regulations and guidelines, and launching capacity-building programs. The work has been carried out using a variety of instruments, including development policy loans or operations (DPLs or DPOs), reimbursable advisory services (RASs) or technical assistance (TA), investment project financing (IPF), and program for results (PforR) projects. Recent DPLs or DPOs have included PIM components in many country operations, such as in Georgia, Ghana, Iraq, Jamaica, Mongolia, Peru, São Tomé and Príncipe, and Tanzania. PIM RAS or TA projects have been implemented in Belarus, Botswana, China, Colombia, Croatia, Cyprus, Ethiopia, Equatorial Guinea, Georgia, Ghana, Jordan, Kuwait, Libya, Oman, Romania, Ukraine, Vietnam, Zambia, and Zimbabwe. Recently, some IPF or PforR projects have also included PIM components in countries such as Benin and Nigeria or Kenya and Nigeria,[1] respectively.

Unfortunately, a gap remains between the functionality principles presented in the PIM and PIMA diagnostic frameworks and the countries' demand for practical guidance on how to adapt these principles to their country contexts. While the PIM and PIMA diagnostics recommend *"what"* should be done, countries frequently request a provisional reference guide on *"how"* to develop specific reforms in relation to country PIM practices and procedures and how to clarify the roles and responsibilities of key players. Addressing PIM reforms by developing customized institutions and regulations presents a complex challenge, given unique country settings that reflect different political and institutional histories. Country-specific variations in public investment and the underlying institutional, policy, and legal arrangements argue against the development of a standardized set of management rules and guidelines.

The *Public Investment Management Reference Guide* aims to fill the gap between "what" should be done and the immediate demand for pragmatic guidance from countries on "how" to adapt the implied reforms. It provides PIM practitioners with different approaches and experiences and draws attention to any commonalities among them.

The application of the country diagnostics and assessments has revealed the following prioritized agenda when undertaking reform (World Bank 2015):

- Clarification of the definition and scope of public investment and public investment management

- Establishment of a sound legal, regulatory, and institutional setting for PIM, making sure that it is linked to the budget process
- Allocation of roles and responsibilities for key players in PIM across government
- Strengthening appraisal and deepening appraisal methodologies
- Integration of strategic planning, project appraisal and selection, and capital budgeting
- Management of multiyear capital budget allocations and commitments
- Efforts to address the effective implementation, procurement, and monitoring of projects
- Strengthening of asset management and ex post evaluation
- Integration of PIM and public-private partnerships (PPPs) in a unified framework
- Rationalization and prioritization of the existing portfolio of PIM projects
- Development of a PIM database and information technology in the form of a PIM information system.

The *PIM Reference Guide* provides an overall framework for each of the issues, lists different approaches and experiences across countries, and summarizes actionable reforms. It does not seek to provide definitive answers or a detailed template for replication across countries; such a template would be impossible given the diversity of country situations. Instead, it clarifies the differences and commonalities across countries.

WHAT IS IN THIS REFERENCE GUIDE

The *PIM Reference Guide* sets out the reform agenda outlined above and examines the key issues to be addressed. It identifies the most important areas for country-level discussion and provides references that country PIM practitioners can turn to for answers or to enhance their own knowledge. It is arranged into 12 chapters, including this introduction, plus four appendixes. The chapters focus on each of the agendas in turn, aiming to give detailed advice on how to formulate and establish country practices, procedures, and roles and responsibilities in PIM development. Application of the *PIM Reference Guide* will help governments to improve their core public expenditure management functions and capacities, particularly by helping to strengthen the relevant functionalities of the finance ministry (and/or planning ministry), line ministries, and agencies. It draws upon the lessons emerging from comparisons of the systems and practices of high- and low-income countries.

Chapter 2 discusses the agenda of how to deal with the concepts and definitions of public investment and public investment management. It explores how public investment and PIM are conceptualized and how their scope is determined. Defining public investment is important for establishing the boundaries of the PIM system; public investment can be defined too narrowly or too broadly, usually as a result of the context within which it is being defined. A narrow definition may lead to significant expenditures bypassing the PIM system. A broad definition may equate public investment with the general notion of "development" expenditures and could, for example, capture expenditure initiatives relating to human capital formation within a PIM system. Ensuring a precise definition of public investment does not mean that public expenditure proposals falling outside the definition should escape proper planning, scrutiny, and management; rather, the particular characteristics of public investment, appropriately defined, demand the special attention achieved through a dedicated system.

PIM is a regulatory and oversight system that forms a subcomponent of public financial management. As such, there should be no room for interpretation when it comes to its scope. There may be no universally recognized answers to the questions posed here, but each country needs to have its own definitions and conceptual understanding of the scope of PIM within its own jurisdiction. These definitions need to be well established in the legal and regulatory framework to avoid ambiguity. The chapter examines the features of public investment that differentiate it from other types of expenditures and that require a separate regulatory system and distinct management processes. It links public investment management to the broader public financial management system and identifies key features and institutional arrangements for supporting an effective PIM system.

Chapter 3 discusses how to develop a hierarchical legal and regulatory framework for PIM to ensure its proper functioning and to support the consistent application of common standards and methods. The legal tradition and administrative culture in any given country will determine the most suitable approach, but the guiding principle should be to avoid using legal instruments to set down detailed procedural arrangements and methodological guidance. Procedures and methods will almost certainly have to be adapted over time, particularly in the early days of PIM reform, and the more authoritative a legal instrument is, the harder it is to change.

There are three principal points in the design and adoption of a three-tier hierarchical legal and regulatory framework:

1. Legal authority for the PIM system, which is usually established through some form of primary legislation
2. Basic procedural guidelines, high-level decision criteria, roles and responsibilities, and designation of analytical tools
3. Methodological guidance, detailed criteria, standardized parameter values, and procedural documentation, which are generally issued directly by the PIM coordinating agency in the form of manuals, templates, and circulars, under the authority granted to it by the primary legislation.

Within this broad hierarchical framework, chapter 3 demonstrates that there can be much variation from country to country. Despite this variety, the aim should be to preserve as much flexibility as possible so that the agency responsible for coordinating PIM can improve systems on the basis of lessons learned and capacity developed. This agency also needs to be given clear legal authority to enforce the rules of the game.

Chapter 4 discusses and presents lessons on the allocation of roles and responsibilities among the main players, a core part of PIM institutional arrangements. This allocation is important for both the upstream and downstream phases of the PIM system, when assessments, budgeting, and implementation must be carried out and overseen, and formal decisions on whether to proceed further with a project must be made at key control points. Key players in the PIM process may include the finance ministry, the planning ministry or agency, line ministries and their departments and subordinated agencies, an interministerial committee or similar body, and a ministerial committee, made up of finance, planning, and infrastructure ministers, with powers delegated from the council of ministers in the area of major projects. The role of the legislature should not be forgotten, since the legislature has the ultimate decision-making power over project funding through the budget process. Depending on the country context, this role may or may not extend to decisions on individual projects.

Chapter 4 defines four general roles for PIM functions:

- Proposer, who, in response to an identified need or emerging problem, identifies the project concept and initiates the steps that follow
- Appraiser, who performs analysis of the net social worth, affordability, and sustainability of the project as it develops from concept to budget-ready expenditure proposal
- Reviewer, who reviews the quality and robustness of the analysis at each step and advises decision makers accordingly
- Decision maker, who is ultimately responsible for deciding to proceed to the next stage on the basis of the analytical findings and the reviewers' advice.

For each stage of the PIM system, responsibilities related to each role must be clarified. In some cases, the same body may perform different roles; but where this is the case, internal safeguards against conflicts of interest may be required, such as involving disinterested parties within the organization.

Chapter 5 discusses how to establish suitable institutional arrangements and provides supportive guidance for strengthening or developing the project appraisal and selection processes within PIM. As part of the upstream part of the PIM system, quality-at-entry processes ensure that the projects that are implemented have been properly vetted.

Quality-at-entry processes combine rigorous analysis with sequenced and disciplined review and decision making. Although the terms used may vary between countries, four distinct processes are involved in the PIM upstream decision:

1. Preappraisal
2. Appraisal
3. Independent review
4. Project selection.

These processes act as a filtering system, by which projects are passed through finer and finer filters to arrive at projects that are eligible to be considered for funding.

Preappraisal introduces gradualism into the assessment process, creating space to reflect on the merits of the project, its logic, and its coherence with government and sectoral strategic policy priorities. It provides an opportunity to consider alternative solutions to the reference project. The aim should be to produce a short list of a handful of alternatives from a long list for further analysis alongside the reference project.

Appraisal activities create the analytical basis for making an informed decision on whether a project is the most socioeconomically profitable use of public financial resources. This factor is not the only basis for proceeding with a project; appraisal also provides the basis for assessing the long-run sustainability of the project from financial, budgetary, environmental, social, and managerial perspectives.

The main rationale for independent review derives from the problem of systematic optimism bias, which has been shown to beset all major projects, across time, across countries, and across sectors. This function can be performed by the finance ministry or by a designated specialized agency. The chapter discusses the meaning of independence and the coverage, depth, outcomes, and timing of the review.

Project selection is a key decision point and the culmination of the quality-at-entry processes. The decision is made on the basis of appraisal findings and recommendations, usually presented to decision makers in a summary appraisal report together with supporting documentation. Selection ends with a formal decision on a project's socioeconomic viability and sustainability and confirmation of its eligibility to be proposed for budget funding. Selection does not represent a decision to fund a project, which can only be made through the budgetary process.

Chapter 5 also explores issues in relation to the effective design of the project appraisal process and methodology. It envisages key issues in designing an appraisal process, including stepwise appraisal analytics, proportionate appraisal considering the threshold, publication of national methodological guidance, optional or obligatory prefeasibility study, and limitations of quantitative economic analysis, taking into account distributional and environmental sustainability, among other issues. It does not set out a detailed appraisal methodology for governments to adopt; rather, it points out some of the more important design issues to be considered when using social cost-benefit analysis (SCBA) and addresses some of the potential pitfalls. Along with an overview of SCBA, the chapter discusses the choice of approach to estimating nonmarket benefits and costs, the treatment of labor market distortions, the setting of national parameter values, decisions regarding the sophistication of risk analysis, and decisions concerning the setting of the social discount rate. When drawing up national methodologies, governments need to include specific guidance regarding common pitfalls in the application of SCBA, such as double counting benefits, ignoring displacement effects, including job creation effects during construction as benefits, counting multiplier effects as benefits, or ignoring the opportunity cost of public assets. The chapter is supported by appendix B, which explores these issues in depth.

Chapter 6 discusses how to integrate the strategic planning, project selection, and capital budgeting cycles. Upstream PIM processes consist of more than quality at entry. The upstream subsystem, if designed well and working properly, should ensure that strategic planning, quality at entry, and capital budgeting are closely integrated, so that the right infrastructure is provided at the right price and at the right time. This integration is not straightforward, because the strategic planning cycle, the project cycle, and the budgeting cycle are not concurrent and have different planning and implementation horizons. Strategic planning and budgeting have a wider scope than public investment. A functioning PIM system must, however, ensure that the three cycles come together at key points.

The governance structure and procedural and methodological manuals for PIM should be designed with a view to strengthening the integration of the three upstream cycles, while taking account of their differences in timing and scope. At the strategic planning stage, several important linkages need to be considered: strategic planning is the basis for identifying projects for preparation and appraisal, strategic plans are key for prioritization during capital budgeting, and strategic plans have to be fiscally constrained to improve consistency with future capital budgets.

During the quality-at-entry stage (including preappraisal, appraisal, and selection stages), verifying project compliance with the relevant strategic documents is essential. Strategic relevance should therefore be assessed at preappraisal and reviewed again at appraisal. To the extent possible, affordability and fiscal sustainability should also be taken into account during preappraisal and appraisal, making the link (although not direct) with capital budgeting.

At the capital budgeting stage, it is important both to reflect strategic guidance in decisions regarding resource allocation and prioritization of new projects and to respect quality-at-entry decisions. The critical linkages to consider are (a) effective "gatekeeping" to ensure that projects entering the capital budgeting process have been positively appraised and selected beforehand; (b) a medium-term budget framework, possibly supplemented by a longer-term strategic expenditure framework for infrastructure sectors, to provide a conducive environment for linking strategic plans, appraisal, and capital budgets; and (c) an emphasis on strategic prioritization in capital budget decisions.

Chapter 7 tackles how to upgrade the capital budgeting system and processes in order to ensure continuity of funding for ongoing projects and sustainable funding for new projects. In weaker PIM systems, ongoing projects typically compete with new projects for funding and frequently lose out, resulting in them either being "drip-funded" or stalled altogether. When ongoing projects are starved of funding for efficient implementation, costs tend to be higher overall and the realization of benefits is often delayed, eroding social viability.

The chapter examines continuity of funding for ongoing projects by estimating a capital budget baseline as part of the medium-term expenditure framework, with the aim of completing projects before funding is redirected to new projects. It also describes the carryover of unused budget for capital projects, which can help to prevent inefficient bunching of expenditures at the end of a year and avoid having slower-moving projects compete for funding with new priorities in the new budget year.

The adoption of multiannual commitment appropriations for investment projects could help to resolve the problem of having too many "drip-funded" projects. Under this system, an initial multiannual commitment equal to the total approved project cost is made. This appropriation is used each time a legal contract is entered into in relation to implementation of the project. The unused balance of the multiannual appropriation, if any, is then carried forward to subsequent years so as to remain available when further contracts are signed. The multiannual commitment appropriation for a specific investment project is reserved specifically for that project and may not be used for other projects. The advantage of such a system is that it clearly shows the amount required to complete all current projects, thus avoiding the illusion that additional fiscal space is being created by splitting available payment appropriations among more projects.

Chapter 8 is reserved for discussions of project implementation, monitoring, and adjustment. Previous chapters deal mostly with upstream PIM processes and their treatment in the regulatory framework. The downstream stages of the project cycle and the broader PIM system also need to be addressed in the regulatory framework for PIM. Procedural guidelines are required, supported by detailed methodological guidance.

Where aspects of downstream processes are already defined in existing legal and regulatory instruments—for example, budget execution or public procurement—it is not useful to repeat these definitions in the regulatory framework for PIM. Instead, national PIM guidance should refer users to the relevant parts of existing laws and regulations. It is important for PIM procedural guidelines to set out the organizational requirements for managing project implementation. These guidelines may vary in sophistication, depending on the project size, but accountabilities and responsibilities need to be clearly assigned in all cases.

Monitoring should provide early warning of implementation problems and be accompanied by formal procedures to ensure that such warnings are addressed. More sophisticated monitoring after project completion ensures that projects are delivering the intended outcomes—that is, services are being delivered to target beneficiaries with the anticipated positive effects on their welfare. Monitoring provides the raw material for midterm and ex post evaluation exercises.

If a project is so badly off track that it is no longer feasible within reasonable budgetary and time constraints, the possibility of making fundamental adjustments, including closure, should exist.[2]

Chapter 9 envisages ex post evaluation and asset management as integral parts of PIM. On project completion, following formal verification and handover to the user, the basis for proper custodianship should be established by registering the asset in a country's asset management system.

Immediately after project completion, a basic completion review, involving analysis and lesson learning from project implementation, is the minimum requirement for a functioning PIM system. More advanced systems deepen the feedback mechanism by evaluating the impact of a project and assessing whether its objectives have been achieved. The aims of this evaluation are to inform policy design, to develop similar projects in the future, and to strengthen accountability for project results. Such ex post evaluations should examine how the PIM system functions as a whole to provide feedback into system design. The chapter discusses the legal and regulatory framework for these requirements.

Asset registers need to be updated regularly, and asset values need to be recorded. Countries should require their operating agencies to compile balance sheets, where the value of assets created from new fixed capital expenditures can be recorded alongside existing assets. Active asset management helps to ensure that assets serve their purpose throughout their intended life span. This process requires asset quality to be tracked over time. The chapter describes how agencies that are responsible for service delivery should be held accountable for results as an incentive to optimize the economic life of the assets.

Chapter 10 discusses developing a harmonized and integrated PIM-PPP system, focused on achieving the best outcomes at the lowest cost and risk, regardless of the implementation and contracting modality. All public investment projects, whether they are implemented through a PPP modality or through a traditionally implemented project (TIP) modality, should aim to support the creation of viable economic infrastructure—such as roads, airports, and railways—or to provide social infrastructure and public services. In many countries, however, PPPs have been prepared, appraised, selected, budgeted, and monitored separately from TIPs. This disparity has undermined unified public financial management; it has also created undue fiscal risks and lack of clarity, leading to concerns with accounting, reporting, and budgeting, among other processes. Intrinsically, a "PPP project" is simply a way of implementing a public investment project. A bad project will remain a bad project, and a PPP form of implementation cannot transform it into a good one, underlining the need for a harmonized and integrated system.

The chapter develops specific guidance on how to go about framing PIM-PPP harmonization and integration and discusses specific country examples for establishing an integrated regulatory framework for PIM and PPP. All projects should follow the process requested by the PIM system, regardless of whether they are flagged as potential PPPs at the preappraisal stage. A project not flagged as a potential PPP during the preappraisal stage may nevertheless be flagged as such later, at the appraisal stage, if it presents significant PPP potential during the detailed assessment of the project's costs and benefits. The chapter discusses how to examine the rationale for flagging a project as a potential PPP within a unified framework.

Some governments introduce rules to control the fiscal commitment to PPP projects. Defining the types of fiscal commitments to be included and establishing how to aggregate a long-term flow of different types of fiscal commitments presents a challenge. One issue is to determine whether the rule applies only to direct liabilities or whether contingent liabilities are also to be included. Working out how to measure and aggregate these liabilities is challenging. For this reason, the chapter presents relevant examples of safeguards against exposure to risk from PPPs.

Many public authorities are still unfamiliar with PPPs, and it is critical to understand the differences between traditional contracting and PPP methodologies for project implementation rules and practices. The chapter addresses various issues from the perspective of PPPs, including procurement, renegotiation, contract management in operation, asset registers, and ex post evaluation. It encourages authorities to use the same rules and conditions as for PIM.

Chapter 11 examines approaches to rationalizing a severely nonperforming and underfunded portfolio of public investment projects, a common situation in many countries. Portfolios are underfunded when the financing required to deliver public investment projects according to the original implementation schedule significantly exceeds the available funding. An underfunded portfolio is often a legacy of inadequate quality-at-entry processes that lead to exceeding the budget financing during project selection, despite planned fiscal limits for the annual and the medium-term budgets. A dilution of financial resources across too many projects is a symptom of an ineffective gatekeeping mechanism; a central finance agency should be checking that all quality-at-entry requirements have been complied with and that a project's affordability in the context of the wider portfolio has been verified. Faced with a shortage of funds, too many projects, and the fact that ongoing projects tend to compete with new projects for funding, decision makers often feel compelled to spread funds too thinly across the portfolio, rather than prioritizing the projects.

Problems with an oversubscribed portfolio of public investment projects may be resolved by implementing reforms to strengthen quality-at-entry processes, provided these reforms address affordability issues from an early stage. As ongoing projects are completed and fiscal space for new projects gradually builds, reforms of these processes—if successfully implemented—will ensure the necessary quality control of new projects. Reforms should prevent approval of low-quality proposals and unaffordable project commitments. Without such reforms, significant damage to public investment outcomes is likely.

A more effective short- to medium-term option is to initiate a portfolio rationalization, especially in cases where the portfolio is overloaded and implementation performance is chronically affected. Rationalization involves portfolio review, identification of poorly performing projects, and creation of a resolution procedure to restructure or terminate projects.

The chapter describes how rationalization might be designed and organized. It provides an overview of the main features of portfolio rationalization, including the objectives, scope, and main steps of a rationalization program; it details the criteria, indicators, and other aspects of the analytical framework to be used for rationalization; and it offers guidance on managing a rationalization program, including data, legal, institutional, and sustainability issues.

Chapter 12, the final chapter of the *PIM Reference Guide*, addresses the design and implementation of a PIM information system. An efficient and effective PIM system requires diligent management at project and program levels and throughout all stages of the project life cycle. As PIM coincides with several public expenditure management processes, establishing an information system will need to overcome complex information requirements. Comprehensive data handling is needed, which requires collecting, storing, and processing large amounts of data from a variety of sources and making them available in a timely fashion and in easily digestible form at each decision point.

The chapter provides an overview of requirements and options for developing and implementing PIM information systems. It focuses on the following issues: a conceptual description of PIM information systems with regard to objectives, stakeholders, functional scope, and capabilities; the most important issues related to system design; issues and options related to the architecture of a PIM information system, including whether to build the system as a module of another system or as a stand-alone system; and how to plan for implementation.

HOW TO USE THIS REFERENCE GUIDE

The *PIM Reference Guide* is a practical guide to critical PIM reform actions. For each potential reform agenda, it describes different approaches and experiences from around the world, while aiming to find commonalities. It is designed to provide advice on focused and pragmatic actions for dealing with the agenda set out above, providing *"how-to"* advice and relevant references. It encompasses elements of a PIM reform agenda but is not intended to outline a generic PIM reform strategy: it is seen mainly as a resource that countries can dip into once they have identified priorities and outlined their own strategy on the basis of a diagnostic exercise. The *PIM Reference Guide* is intended to help countries to engage in the detailed design of activities within a chosen reform path. For example, if a country prioritizes building a sound legal, regulatory, and institutional framework for PIM, chapter 3 provides detailed references on a three-tier hierarchical legal and regulatory framework for PIM and describes core procedural guidelines. Alternatively, if the priority is to devise a robust project appraisal and selection process, chapter 5 provides detailed references on how to build project preappraisal, appraisal, independent review, and selection plans.

The *PIM Reference Guide* does not suggest that all countries should have all elements of an idealized PIM system in order to benefit. Reflecting on country-specific implications—such as variations in political circumstances, degree of decentralization, and the role of parliament—it aims to help practitioners to understand and implement reform actions *"selectively."* This knowledge will allow countries to highlight more customized reforms and adopt intermediate solutions.

Appropriate sequencing is critical for implementing PIM reforms, although sequencing should not be viewed simply as a technical exercise. The technical specification of reform actions needed to improve the PIM system must be consistent with what is currently possible (implementable) and what is wanted (politically supported). Aligning these dimensions is a crucial factor in successful reforms. The *PIM Reference Guide* does not indicate a preference for a particular reform-agenda sequencing; rather, a country's priorities for PIM reform should guide sequencing. Sequencing decisions should focus on the following three groups of PIM deliverables:

1. Putting controls in place to ensure the development of core legal, regulatory, and institutional settings for the country, mostly referenced in chapters 2–4

2. Establishing and strengthening decision-making mechanisms to improve both upstream and downstream PIM functionalities, referenced in chapters 5–9

3. Other relevant on-demand agendas concerning PIM-PPP integration, rationalizing the existing project portfolio, or developing a basic data and information system to support performance of the PIM system, addressed individually in chapters 10–12.

Hierarchical prioritization will be needed to mainstream the three groups of deliverables. A core level of arrangements for the legal or regulatory framework and procedures as well as the institutional setup for key stakeholders need to be at the top of the hierarchy. A core level of legal and regulatory settings will also help to support performance in PPP management, portfolio rationalization, and data system development. Attempting to leapfrog this hierarchy will likely lead to unsuccessful reforms. For example, attempting to improve analytical methodologies for project appraisal without adequate legal and regulatory settings or with undue instability in the roles and responsibilities of key stakeholders in the appraisal procedure is unlikely to be successful and could even prove counterproductive. The same applies to attempting to upgrade the PIM information system without the core legal, regulatory, and institutional settings.

With this starting platform, subsequent PIM reforms could be sequenced as follows, depending on country circumstances:

1. Further improving the legal, regulatory, and institutional arrangements for PIM (chapters 2–4)

2. Upgrading the upstream project selection and downstream project implementation processes (chapters 5–9)

3. Concentrating on a staged effort to strengthen PIM-PPP integration, portfolio rationalization, or the PIM information system (chapters 10–12).

Country-specific circumstances and preferences will determine the type and depth of reform actions and the pace of reform.

LIMITS TO THIS REFERENCE GUIDE AND CHALLENGES

The *PIM Reference Guide* is meant to be revised and upgraded continually. The current version is termed "Version 1.0," and future versions will be augmented and updated to reflect comments on the organization of the guide and to introduce more examples from country experiences.

Version 1.0 does not cover some important public sector issues, which may have a significant influence over a country's PIM decisions. Such issues include the political economy of PIM, governance of state-owned enterprises (SOEs), coordination with subnational governments (SNGs), procurement practices, and maximizing finance for development (MFD). These issues are closely linked to the traditional PIM framework, procedures, and decision making. Improvements to the PIM system must be consistent with what is supported politically and must accommodate political-economic aspects of PIM. SOEs play critical roles in public investment in many countries, which ties issues of SOE governance to PIM (and public financial management). Countries are unlikely to achieve their public investment aspirations unless SNGs contribute and are involved as stakeholders, funders, and implementers. Inefficiency in the procurement system may also have significant effects on the cost-benefit rationale for investment decisions. The MFD approach is a new finance window that leverages private sector support for infrastructure investment and can have an important place in PIM.

Major challenges exist for connecting each of the currently out-of-scope issues to the traditional PIM guidance and references. Future work will be needed to elaborate the specifics of the many challenges for PIM related to the political economy, SOEs, SNGs, procurement, MFD, and so forth and then to adapt the PIM guidance and references accordingly.

The political economy of PIM

There are concerns about why policies and reforms can be ineffective (World Bank 2017b). It may be that the political will at the national level is missing. Political will plays a critical role in successfully implementing policies and reforms, including in the PIM arena. There is a risk that implementing the right policies could challenge the existing balance of power.

Approaching PIM reforms through the lens of the political economy has enormous potential to strengthen the driving force of reforms and to identify obstacles to reform with an eye to designing more appropriate institutional solutions. Future editions of the *PIM Reference Guide* could address the following issues:

- Who are the actors involved in de facto decisions over the PIM cycle?
- What are their incentives, and how do they affect PIM decisions?
- What are the processes and procedures, both formal and informal, according to which these actors reach decisions for PIM?
- Which institutional reforms would shift the balance of power in favor of those actors who are more likely to make prudent fiscal and investment choices and, at the same time, help to mediate distributional and allocative conflicts?[3]

PIM and state-owned enterprises

SOEs are discussed briefly in chapter 2 in relation to public investment. A reasonably tight definition of "investment" can be formulated, but there is considerable room for variation when defining a system for managing public investment projects in SOEs. A key issue is the extent to which investments by SOEs fall within the remit of the national PIM system. Governance arrangements for SOEs pursuing economic activities, which have been established as part of a government's industrial policy, should be exercised largely through the state's role as shareholder. In exercising its position as shareholder on behalf of the public, the government has a clear interest in ensuring the good governance and sound financial performance of commercial SOEs. This interest may be better exercised separately from PIM, reflecting the distinct legal status of SOEs and the shareholder-management relationship implied by their corporatized status. In countries with more developed systems, SOE investment usually falls outside the scope of PIM.

SOE investment may be included in PIM in certain country cases—for example, if a government is financing investment in pursuit of public policy objectives that are outside the main remit of an SOE or if the SOE investment is established specifically to address public policy. This sort of investment, which fits with the state's role in assuring the provision of welfare and growth-enhancing public services, is considered more appropriately within the scope of PIM.

In countries where SOE governance is still in the early stages of development, there may be a case for governments to have a more hands-on approach to investment, something that would extend the scope of PIM to SOEs. Whether to include budget-funded SOE investment within the scope of the PIM system remains a country's choice and needs to consider workload, capacities, and financial risks.

Further work could be done to develop clear PIM guidance and references for SOEs, especially in countries that are sensitive to governance arrangements, funding mechanisms, regulatory regimes, and public policy objectives.

PIM in subnational governments

Most national and central government PIM systems have linkages to subnational government budgetary and management systems. They may also be affected by such factors as the constitutional position of SNGs in relation to central government. Constitutional issues may prevent the national PIM system from extending to subnational governments or make the system "advisory" only. This situation arises especially in federal states, but it also applies to constitutional arrangements where local governments have significant autonomy. Even when SNG investment is not covered, it would be good for the national PIM system to include any SNG project that benefits from earmarked capital transfers from the central government budget. If the national PIM system cannot be applied to lower levels of government, SNGs should try to replicate it.

All PIM functionalities and references in the *PIM Reference Guide* can be decentralized or performed across levels of government. Regulation—including the setting of legal, regulatory, and institutional frameworks and implementation practices—can be decentralized to SNGs or be concurrent. Different formats exist for connecting the national PIM system with the SNG PIM system and could be considered in more depth in the future. The following are some of the possible formats (Frank and Martínez-Vázquez 2015):

- *National planning and implementation, subnational maintenance.* Public investment can be created by the national government and then transferred to subnational governments for operation and maintenance.
- *National planning, subnational implementation.* Public investment can be planned by the national government and implemented by subnational governments.
- *National goal setting, subnational planning and implementation.* Public investment can be created by subnational governments in line with the national government's planning goals.
- *Devolution.* Subnational governments can define their own public investment priorities and manage the creation and use of infrastructure throughout. However, the central government may have a role in planning and finance.

Decentralized provision of infrastructure requires coordination among levels of government. Project planning and appraisal rules, service standards, and procurement regulations tend to be shared; and even in the most decentralized countries, SNGs are often required to adopt central regulations and standards.

Procurement and PIM

According to Rajaram et al. (2014, 139–40), procurement is often mistakenly conceived as a technical contracting exercise that culminates in the signing of a contract by a successful bidder. This conceptualization has given rise to the need to focus on the contracting process and to define the steps and mechanisms needed to determine the winning bid. Steps and mechanisms are important aspects of a good procurement system, but they provide an incomplete picture and create a potentially costly detachment from the full public investment process. A more integrated and robust understanding of the procurement function stretches from project planning through selection of the appropriate procurement method, contracting process, and contract management. Procurement does not stop when the contract is awarded; it remains relevant during implementation and contract management, particularly for technically complex systems.

The key stages of procurement are planning, method selection, contract planning, tender evaluation and contract award, contract management, review and monitoring, and audit and reporting.[4] Each stage has linkages to aspects of PIM and budgeting that could lower costs and speed up project implementation. Some of the complexity of public investment procurement can be better managed with an approach that links project selection, design, budgeting, and procurement processes. Making better use of information from upstream PIM and budgeting can enhance key stages of procurement and project implementation and contribute to efficiency in public investment. As Rajaram et al. (2014) identify the need for linking procurement processes more strongly to PIM and budgeting processes, more detailed guidance could be developed in this area for future versions of the *PIM Reference Guide.*

PIM and maximizing finance for development

The MFD initiative is a recent World Bank "algorithm" that involves leveraging the private sector and optimizing the use of scarce public resources in a way that is fiscally, environmentally, and socially sustainable. The World Bank has embarked on an effort to help countries to maximize finance for development and to do so responsibly, without pushing the public sector into unsustainable levels of debt and contingent liabilities. This effort will entail pursuing private sector solutions where they can help to achieve development goals and reserving scarce public finance for where it is needed most (World Bank 2017a).

Operations aligned with the MFD approach typically include the following:

- Those that lead to more sustainable private sector solutions—private finance (crowding-in) or private delivery—for development projects
- Those that address binding constraints (for example, physical, operational, regulatory environment) in a way that could open up private solutions where appropriate.

The extent, nature, and relevance of the MFD approach will depend on the nature of the project or program development objectives. The algorithm can be used to weigh the benefits and opportunity costs of deploying public and private resources for individual investments included in a government's overall development plans. The first issue to consider is whether an investment project or program can be financed on commercial terms, while remaining affordable and offering value for money; if this is the case, the investment would not be a priority for the provision of finance on private concessional terms or through public forms of financing.

There is a challenge to using the MFD algorithm: public investment systems for the physical, operational, and regulatory environment are rarely developed enough for the algorithm to be feasible. Without well-established institutional or regulatory frameworks in PIM, public and private parties will be unable to implement the algorithm; therefore, the MFD algorithm will work well under the precondition of a unified and sufficiently developed PIM-PPP framework. The aim should therefore be to provide clear guidance and references for the following question: what are the PIM and PPP preconditions for successful MFD projects? Strengthening governance for integrating PIM and PPP, as presented in chapter 10, may partly answer this question.

NOTES

1. Nigeria has the Kaduna State Economic Transformation PforR as well as an IPF, the Fiscal Governance and Institutions Project, supporting better PIM.
2. If many existing projects are off track and exceed agreed-on tolerance levels, the existing portfolio of PIM projects may be reprioritized. See discussions in chapter 11.
3. These issues comply with the issues discussed in the political economy of public financial management reforms. See Allen, Hemming, and Potter (2013).
4. For more detailed steps in the procurement process, see Viega Malta et al. (2011).

REFERENCES

Allen, R., R. Hemming, and B. Potter, eds. 2013. *The International Handbook of Public Financial Management*. London: Palgrave Macmillan.

Frank, J., and J. Martínez-Vázquez. 2015. *Decentralization and Infrastructure in the Global Economy: From Gaps to Solutions*. Routledge Studies in the Modern World Economy. London: Routledge.

IMF (International Monetary Fund). 2015. "Making Public Investment More Efficient." IMF Policy Paper, IMF, Washington, DC.

——. 2018. "Public Investment Management Assessment—Review and Update." IMF Policy Paper, IMF, Washington, DC.

OECD (Organisation for Economic Co-operation and Development). 2013. *Investing Together: Working Effectively across Levels of Government*. Paris: OECD Publishing.

Rajaram, A., T. M. Le, K. Kaiser, J. H. Kim, and J. Frank, eds. 2014. *The Power of Public Investment Management: Transforming Resources into Assets for Growth*. Washington, DC: World Bank.

Viega Malta, J. N., P. Schapper, O. Calvo-Gonzales, and D. Berroa. 2011. "Old Rules, New Realities: Are Existing Public Procurement Systems Addressing Current and Future Needs?" Public Sector Study 66427, World Bank, Washington, DC.

World Bank. 2015. "Public Investment Management: Status, Opportunities, Challenges." Technical Briefing to the World Bank Board, World Bank, Washington, DC.

——. 2017a. "Maximizing Finance for Development (MFD): Guidance for Applying an MFD Lens." Unpublished paper, World Bank, Washington, DC.

——. 2017b. *World Development Report 2017: Governance and the Law*. Washington, DC: World Bank.

2

Establishing the Concept and Scope of Public Investment Management

OVERVIEW

Before embarking on the design of guidelines, procedures, and methods, it is important to establish the concept and scope of public investment management (PIM). Public investment and public investment management can mean different things to different people in different places. This chapter therefore attempts to address the following questions:

- *What is being managed?* PIM is designed to manage public investment projects, and "public investment" and "project" need to be well defined.
- *Why and how is it being managed?* Public investment is part of public expenditures; governments therefore need to have a clear understanding of why it deserves supplementary processes beyond those required as part of the public financial management system. The basic features of a system for managing public investment projects need to be defined.

PIM is a regulatory and oversight system that forms a subcomponent of public financial management, and there should be no room for interpretation when it comes to its scope. There are no universally accepted solutions to the questions posed above, and each country needs to have its own definitions and conceptual understanding of the scope of PIM within its own jurisdiction. These definitions need to be established in the legal and regulatory framework. The scope of PIM may change over time as reforms evolve, and the regulatory framework must be updated as necessary.

DEFINING PUBLIC INVESTMENT: WHAT IS BEING MANAGED?

Introduction

PIM concerns the management of public investment projects; each part of the term "public investment project" needs to be defined carefully to establish the boundaries of the PIM system. This section considers the possible definitions of "investment," "public investment," and "project," so that users of this guidance may fix the operational scope of their own PIM system. There is reasonable agreement about what constitutes a project, but public investment is subject to different interpretations, particularly the "public" part. Too narrow a definition of public investment can lead to significant expenditures bypassing the PIM system,[1] while too broad a definition can erode the rationale for having a distinct PIM system or overwhelm its capacities. The aim here is to guide users toward a balanced definition appropriate to their country context.

The discussion in this chapter fills a gap in the international reference material. The International Monetary Fund's *Government Finance Statistics Manual* (IMF 2014), the usual reference point for public expenditure terminology, provides some significant insights, but no explicit definitions of the terms to be discussed. The latest public expenditure and financial accountability (PEFA) framework (PEFA Secretariat 2016), which now includes an indicator for public investment management (PI–11), is also silent on what expenditures are captured under the heading of "public investment," except to indicate that they should be delivered in project form.

What is investment?

Generally defined, investment is the acquisition of an asset in the expectation of generating a stream of future benefits. Investment by the public sector can therefore take various forms involving the acquisition of both financial and nonfinancial assets, including fixed assets.[2]

The *PIM Reference Guide* takes the position that the PIM system should be concerned with the acquisition (or major improvement) of fixed assets, which is synonymous with capital expenditures.[3] This does not mean that the acquisition of other assets—that is, financial assets and other nonfinancial assets—should not be subject to proper management and oversight, only that it would be better to keep the acquisition of such assets outside the scope of PIM. Capital expenditures on fixed assets should be the point of departure for PIM, but the scope of PIM processes should also extend to proper planning and management of the whole-life costs of the fixed assets created (see chapters 5 and 7).

In countries with development budgets, care should be taken when defining the scope of PIM. Development budgets often include significant noncapital expenditures, and the "recurrent" budget may include capital expenditures not captured in the development budget.[4] It is suggested that in such cases, the focus of PIM should be on capital expenditures, properly defined, and not on wider developmental expenditures or donor-financed initiatives.

The *Government Finance Statistics Manual* identifies the different categories of fixed assets, as shown in box 2.1. These categories and their finer subcategories are useful when determining the types of expenditures to be considered capital investment.[5]

The definition of capital investment should not be confined to physical fixed assets; hence, the category "other fixed assets" is important. The inclusion of computer software and databases in this category and within the scope of PIM is particularly important. For many countries, investment in information and communication technology (ICT) systems—hardware and software—is an increasingly significant part of public investment and can be a major source of waste, if managed poorly.[6]

Many countries exclude weapons systems from their PIM systems on the grounds of sensitivities relating to national security. This is a legitimate choice.

Other countries—Norway, for example—consider that such a significant investment should be subject to the discipline of the PIM system, as poor planning and management of defense procurement are often a major source of inefficiency.

The *Government Finance Statistics Manual* also distinguishes between expenditures on a major improvement to a fixed asset, classified as capital expenditures, and maintenance and repair, classified as current expenses (see box 2.2). The main difference is that major improvements are discretionary, whereas maintenance and repairs are an obligation of owning an asset.

The distinctions made in box 2.2 can be important when establishing definitions. In some countries, periodic maintenance (or "heavy maintenance") is often considered to be a capital expenditure, and therefore discretionary, which it should not normally be. The regular replacement of the wearing course of a road, for example, is an obligation of asset ownership and should not be a choice. When counted as public capital investment and included under the PIM system, such expenditures are traded off against new investment and risks being underfunded or delayed, when maintenance of the existing asset stock should generally be given the highest priority.[7] In other countries, substantial improvements to fixed

BOX 2.1

Major categories of fixed assets

- Buildings and structures, including all amounts payable for site clearance and preparation and the cost of all fixtures, facilities, and equipment that are integral parts of buildings and structures
- Machinery and equipment (when separate from buildings and structures)
- Other fixed assets, including intellectual property products, such as research and development and computer software and databases
- Weapons systems.

Source: IMF 2014.

BOX 2.2

Distinguishing between major improvement and maintenance

Major improvements cover renovations, reconstructions, and enlargements of existing assets to increase their productive capacity, extend their service life, or both. According to the IMF (2014), they have the following features:

- "The decision to renovate, reconstruct, or enlarge an asset is a deliberate investment decision that may be undertaken at any time and is not dictated by the condition of the asset. Major renovations of ships, buildings, or other structures are frequently undertaken well before the end of their normal service lives.
- The major renovations, reconstructions, or enlargements increase the performance or capacity of existing assets or significantly extend their previously expected service lives. Enlarging or extending an existing road, building, or structure constitutes a major change in this sense, but a complete refitting or restructuring of the interior of a building also qualifies."

Maintenance and repairs are different and have the following features:

- "They are activities that owners or users of assets are obliged to undertake periodically in order to be able to utilize such assets over their expected service lives. They are current costs that cannot be avoided if the fixed assets are to continue to be used. The owner or user cannot afford to neglect maintenance and repairs, as the expected service life may be drastically shortened otherwise.
- They do not change the fixed asset or its performance, but simply maintain it in good working order or restore it to its previous condition in the event of a breakdown. Defective parts are replaced by new parts of the same kind without changing the basic nature of the fixed asset."

assets may be carried out under the guise of "maintenance," without proper planning and scrutiny. Taking the example of a road again, the replacement of a double-surface treatment wearing course with an asphaltic concrete overlay may be classified as periodic maintenance, when, in fact, it would substantially strengthen the pavement and extend its expected life. According to the IMF definitions, such an expenditure should be considered an improvement to a fixed asset and be subject to the discipline of the PIM system.

Rehabilitation is usually considered to be capital investment because the need to rehabilitate the asset arises from a poor maintenance program, to the extent that the planned life or performance of the asset is reduced. Capital investment is therefore required to reestablish the performance or planned life of the degraded asset. The timing of rehabilitation becomes a matter of choice because the asset is no longer subject to a planned maintenance program.

Notwithstanding the distinctions made above, there will always be gray areas where judgment will be necessary to decide whether an expenditure fits within the definition of capital investment. There will be a natural tendency for spending agencies to try to exploit these gray areas if the PIM system forces more rigor on planning and decision making than is required for expenditures not classified as public investment. It would be wise, therefore, for PIM regulations to hand over the final say on what expenditures should fall within the scope of PIM to the relevant oversight authorities (see chapter 4, on roles and responsibilities).

What is infrastructure investment?

A body of evidence confirming the importance of the quantity of infrastructure assets and economic growth has spurred interest in public investment and its management. It is therefore important to see how "infrastructure" fits into the previous discussion of investment.

Despite numerous studies exploring the relationship between infrastructure provision and economic growth, there is no precise definition of infrastructure (Torrisi 2009). Generally speaking, however, infrastructure is taken to be a subset of investment, encompassing the physical assets required to deliver the services needed to support economic activity. As such, IMF (2017) identifies key characteristics that distinguish infrastructure from other types of capital:

> First, infrastructure investments are often large, capital-intensive projects that tend to be "natural monopolies"—it is often more cost-effective for services to be provided by a single entity. Second, they tend to have significant up-front costs, but the benefits or returns accrue over very long periods of time, often many decades; this longevity (and the associated difficulty of ascertaining adequate returns over such a long horizon) can pose a challenge to private financing and provision. Third, infrastructure investments have the potential to generate positive externalities, so that the social return to a project can exceed the private returns it can generate for the operator. This can lead to underprovision of needed investments. For these reasons, infrastructure has historically been provided by the public sector, public-private partnerships, or regulated private entities.

This categorization of infrastructure is consistent with the definition used in Australia, where Infrastructure Australia is responsible for preparing an infrastructure priority list covering transport, water, energy, and telecommunications.[8] The World Bank implicitly uses this definition,[9] which excludes the physical assets required to deliver many public services—such as education, health, and justice—as well as the assets of the public administration. Also excluded are the categories "other fixed assets" and "weapons systems," which are included in box 2.1.

This characterization of infrastructure is not universal, and looser definitions, which include social infrastructure, are possible. Although the United Kingdom, for example, initially adopted a definition of infrastructure that was broadly consistent with the preceding discussion,[10] the most recent National Infrastructure Delivery Plan extends the coverage to include housing and urban regeneration, social infrastructure, and regional infrastructure.[11]

The definition of infrastructure only becomes important if a decision is made to restrict the scope of the PIM system to this narrower class of fixed assets. Otherwise, it is not an issue. The *PIM Reference Guide* takes the position that the wider perspective on investment is more suitable; if a decision is made to limit the scope of PIM, it is important to define what is meant by "infrastructure" in the regulatory framework to avoid any ambiguity.

The IMF quotation above indicates that the private sector may also provide infrastructure, in regulated or unregulated form, depending on the nature of competition. Governments should have policies encompassing national infrastructure as a whole, including the private sector. In general, private provision of infrastructure would be outside the scope of PIM, with some important exceptions. These exceptions include cases where earmarked capital subsidies (direct or contingent) are given to private sector infrastructure providers in order to achieve public policy objectives, such as welfare gains from changes in externalities, and where infrastructure is provided through public-private partnership (PPP) arrangements (discussed later in this chapter).

What is a project?

The PIM system should deal with investment delivered through projects. A project can be defined as follows:

> A group of activities (and associated expenditures) with clearly defined objectives and outputs implemented over a fixed time schedule and within a fixed budget. It should encompass all the activities and resulting outputs required to deliver sustainable benefits to the target beneficiaries.[12]

This definition draws attention to the need to specify project boundaries properly. First, a project needs to have clear beginning and end dates, and its scope needs to be well defined. A frequent mistake is to define the scope of a project too narrowly and omit key activities or to equate projects with "objects" or contracts, when multiple components or contracts may be required to achieve the desired objective. An example would be a bridge forming part of a new city bypass. The bridge cannot deliver benefits to the population without the rest of the investment in road infrastructure; it should not, as a consequence, be planned, analyzed, and managed in isolation from the rest of the investment, even if different contractors, funding sources, and timing are involved.

Equating projects with contracts can underestimate the full scope and cost of projects with multiple contracts. Such underestimates can happen as a result of internal coordination problems within the proposing agency, but they may also be a strategy to hide the full cost of a project, particularly if there are value thresholds above which analytical requirements are more stringent or decisions go to a higher authority.

Adequate safeguards should be put in place, beginning at the preappraisal stage, to ensure that a project is being defined properly in the PIM system so as to avoid fragmentation. A common error is to restrict the project's scope to components that are the responsibility of the proposing agency, omitting components that are the responsibility of another agency and that are critical to the project's success. This error can be the result of problems with interagency coordination or an attempt to keep the apparent costs of a project down and to influence decision makers when funding has been secured. Occasionally, it may be helpful to define a "programmatic project." This is a "composite" project that groups similar, small, site-specific projects with common objectives, implementation arrangements, and management responsibilities (HM Treasury 2003).[13] The PIM system would then focus on the internal management systems for programmatic projects rather than on individual-component projects. This approach can assist high-level management and decision making by focusing on strategic decisions and leaving the day-to-day planning and management of the component projects to the project management team. One representative component project may be analyzed, or the project as a whole may be examined and prioritized; in either case, a programmatic project design should not be used as a smoke screen for poor-quality subprojects.

Variation in the scope of "public" investment: SOEs and subnational government investment

A reasonably tight definition of "investment" can be formulated, but there is considerable variation when defining the scope of a management system for public investment projects. A key issue is the extent to which investments by state-owned enterprises (SOEs) and subnational governments (SNGs) fall within the scope of the national PIM system.

When defining the scope of PIM, countries should consider two principles:

- PIM is a subsystem of public financial management; as such, public investment should have direct implications, actual or potential,[14] for the public finances at some point in time.
- "Public" may be interpreted as indicating a public policy purpose—that is, through the delivery of public services or other welfare-improving effects.

Figure 2.1 looks at the issue from a statistical, or national income accounting, perspective; it distinguishes between public capital expenditures, public investment, and national capital investment. Public investment, as defined in figure 2.1, is investment undertaken by the public sector, and thus extends to investment by SOEs. When the PIM system is defined in line with the first principle above, it would be confined to that part of SOE investment with potential implications for public finance—that is, it would be funded by capital transfers or subject to government guarantees.

Figure 2.1 shows the full-scope model—a PIM system covering all national public sector investment with a potential impact on public finances. In practice, most PIM systems will be narrower in scope, depending on such factors as the constitutional position of subnational government and the framework for SOE governance. A narrower scope for the central PIM system is especially common in federal states, but it also applies to constitutional arrangements where local governments have significant autonomy. Even where subnational government

FIGURE 2.1

Capital expenditures, public investment, and national capital investment

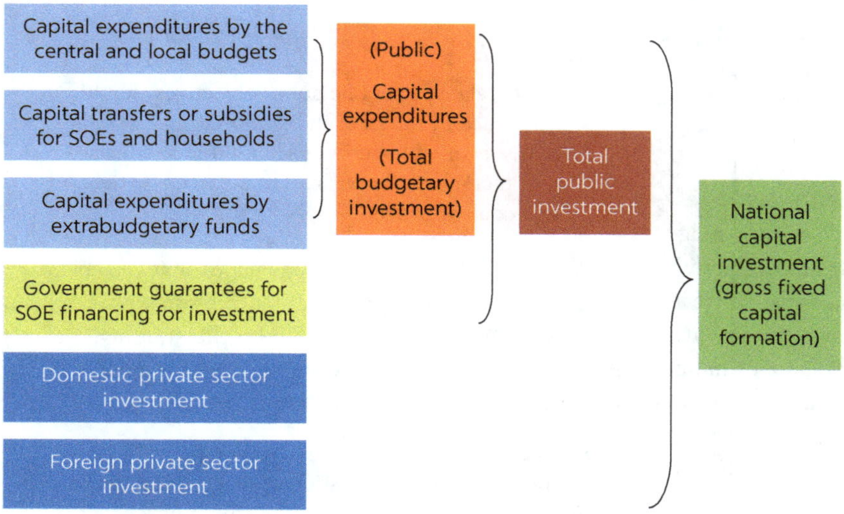

Source: World Bank 2007.
Note: SOE = state-owned enterprise.

investment is not covered, the system usually would include SNG projects receiving earmarked capital transfers from the central government budget. Where constitutional arrangements prevent the national system from applying to lower levels of government, SNGs should replicate the national system at their level. This is the case in the Australian states and in the devolved governments of the United Kingdom.[15]

Ideally, governance arrangements for SOEs pursuing an economic activity,[16] established as part of a government's industrial policy, should be "arm's-length," exercised largely through the state's role as shareholder (see box 2.3). In its position as shareholder on behalf of the public, the government has an undeniable interest in ensuring good governance and sound financial performance of commercial SOEs. This interest is, however, better exercised separately from PIM, reflecting the distinct legal status of SOEs and the intended shareholder-management relationship implied by this status. In countries with more advanced systems, SOE investment generally falls outside the scope of PIM.[17] By contrast, in the Republic of Korea, major budget-funded public investment projects in SOEs are subject to the PIM appraisal system.

SOE investment may be included in PIM in those cases where government investment has public policy objectives that are not the SOE's primary economic activity or where an SOE has been established to achieve public policy objectives that enhance welfare or public services.[18]

In countries where SOE governance is still developing and management is weak, there may be a case for taking a more "hands-on" approach to investment by SOEs engaged in economic activity; this approach would extend the scope of PIM closer to that shown in figure 2.1. In Zimbabwe, for example, all SOE projects should follow the PIM guidelines when requesting capital budgetary funding, imposing recurrent expenditures on the budget, or seeking government guarantees. In the end, inclusion of all budget-funded SOE investment within

BOX 2.3

OECD governance framework for SOEs

The Organisation for Economic Co-operation and Development (OECD) has developed corporate governance guidelines that shed light on the possible scope of PIM with respect to state-owned enterprises—SOEs (OECD 2015). The framework acknowledges that some SOEs may be engaged in economic activity and the pursuit of public policy objectives. However, the presumption is that, as far as economic activities are concerned, the government should adopt a hands-off approach, exercising influence through its position as a majority shareholder. It should not provide finance for investment on favorable terms through the budget. According to OECD guidelines,

- "The government should allow SOEs full operational autonomy to achieve their defined objectives and refrain from intervening in SOE management. The government as a shareholder should avoid redefining SOE objectives in a non-transparent manner.
- The state should let SOE boards exercise their responsibilities and should respect their independence.
- Where SOEs combine economic activities and public policy objectives, high standards of transparency and disclosure regarding their cost and revenue structures must be maintained, allowing for an attribution to main activity areas.
- Costs related to public policy objectives should be funded by the state and disclosed.
- SOEs' economic activities should face consistent market conditions regarding access to debt and equity finance."

As indicated, the framework envisages that the costs of achieving public policy objectives in a mixed-purpose SOE should be funded by the state. OECD guidelines also exclude any SOE engaged primarily in public policy objectives (OECD 2015):

> "The Guidelines are generally not intended to apply to entities or activities whose primary purpose is to carry out a public policy function, even if the entities concerned have the legal form of an enterprise."

The guidelines imply that, where an appropriate corporate governance framework for SOEs exists, the PIM system should only encompass investment related to the achievement of public policy objectives. Where corporate governance deviates from the model, as may be the case in low-income or emerging economies, the scope for PIM might be wider, including expenditures on fixed assets for economic activities, where these expenditures have actual or potential implications for public finances.

the scope of the PIM system, irrespective of the policy purpose, is each country's choice; however, the decision needs to be made in the knowledge of the workload and capacities involved and the relative risks that poor investment management by SOEs will lead to the misallocation of public sector resources.

Public investment through public-private partnerships

Public-private partnerships should fall within the scope of the PIM system because they use public financial resources (even if only over the longer term or on a contingent basis); as such, they should have a public policy rationale.[19] A PPP should be subject to the same preinvestment processes as any other public investment project, plus some additional analytical steps and decisions to determine whether the PPP represents better value for public money than other implementation modalities. The additional analysis should be performed only after the project has been shown to be a good use of public financial resources, irrespective of how it is implemented. Consistent with this approach, PPPs are generally fully integrated into the PIM system of good-practice countries, and there is no dual-track approach. Chapter 10 discusses how to engage PIM and PPP in a unified framework.

WHY DOES PUBLIC INVESTMENT NEED SPECIALLY DESIGNED MANAGEMENT ARRANGEMENTS?

Introduction

Public investment management is a regulatory concept. It should be governed by an appropriate legal and regulatory framework, including agreed-on definitions and scope, and should be supported by comprehensive procedures and methods. For PIM to function effectively, the roles and responsibilities of key players should be clearly established. This section looks at those features that differentiate public investment from other types of expenditures and that necessitate a separate regulatory system and special management processes. It links public investment management to the broader public financial management system.

Special features of public investment requiring a separate regulatory system

Certain technical features set public investment apart from other forms of expenditures and give rise to the need for a dedicated management system with distinct procedures and specialized methods:

- *Multiyear projects.* Public investment usually involves multiyear projects with long gestation periods, long implementation phases, and extended operating lives. The planning and implementation of these projects are difficult to synchronize with the budget cycle or even a medium-term budget. Special arrangements are needed to manage the interfaces between the different planning cycles and to ensure intertemporal consistency.
- *Large and "lumpy" projects.* Capital investment projects tend to be large scale and irreversible; as such, a mistake can be very costly, certainly higher than for current expenditure initiatives, which can be piloted on a small scale before full implementation and reversed if necessary. Processes and methods that support good decision making and help to manage risk are essential.
- *Long forecasting horizons.* The long-term nature of costs and benefits, which usually include intergenerational effects, means that sophisticated forecasting techniques and analytical methods are needed, as are the requisite skills to apply them.
- *Potential impacts on economic growth.* Filling gaps in infrastructure service provision and meeting suppressed demand can provide a significant boost to economic growth, but the provision of excess capacity can be very costly in terms of the opportunity cost of public resources. This opportunity cost suggests a need for taking a considered approach to timing.
- *Systematic planning error.* There is clear evidence that investment planning is subject to systematic excessive optimism concerning the estimation of costs and benefits and the underlying factors critical to project success

(Ansar et al. 2014; Flyvbjerg 2005). This tendency has been referred to as the "iron law of megaprojects"— "over budget, over time, over and over again" (Flyvbjerg 2014)—and requires well-designed arrangements for ensuring greater planning realism and impartial review.

- *Megaprojects.* Extremely large projects, often known as megaprojects, have their own particular set of problems—some of which are a magnified version of the problems besetting major projects, while others are unique to the scale and dynamics (both technical and political) of a megaproject. These problems are summarized in box 2.4.

Public investment management as it relates to public financial management

Public investment is a component of public expenditures, and public investment management is a branch of the wider public financial management system. Therefore, the hierarchy of objectives for public financial management corresponds to those for PIM, as shown in table 2.1.

Some of the important specificities of PIM within the broader public financial management system have been recognized in the recently revised PEFA framework (PEFA Secretariat 2016). A new PEFA indicator, PI–11, has been added, which looks at whether the public financial management system ensures

BOX 2.4

Planning and management of megaprojects: 10 negative characteristics

According to Flyvbjerg (2014), megaprojects often suffer from the following problems:

- "Megaprojects are inherently risky due to long planning horizons and complex interfaces.
- Often, projects are led by planners and managers without domain experience who keep changing throughout the long project cycles that apply to megaprojects, leaving leadership weak.
- Decision making, planning, and management are typically multiactor processes involving multiple stakeholders, both public and private, with conflicting interests.
- Technology and designs are often nonstandard, leading to 'uniqueness bias' among planners and managers, who tend to see their projects as singular, which impedes learning from other projects.
- Frequently there is overcommitment to a certain project concept at an early stage, resulting in 'lock-in' or 'capture," leaving analyses of alternatives weak or absent and leading to escalated commitment in later stages ...
- Due to the large sums of money involved, principal-agent problems and rent-seeking behaviour are common, as is optimism bias.
- The project scope or ambition level will typically change over time.
- Delivery is a high-risk, stochastic activity, with overexposure to so-called 'black swans,' i.e., extreme events with massively negative outcomes. Managers tend to ignore this [risk], treating projects as if they exist largely in a deterministic Newtonian world of cause, effect, and control.
- Statistical evidence shows that such complexity and unplanned events are often unaccounted for, leaving budget and time contingencies inadequate.
- As a consequence, misinformation about costs, schedules, benefits, and risks is the norm throughout project development and the decision-making process. The result is cost overruns, delays, and benefit shortfalls that undermine project viability during project implementation and operations."

TABLE 2.1 **Public financial management objectives and implications for PIM**

LEVEL	OBJECTIVES OF PUBLIC FINANCIAL MANAGEMENT	IMPLICATIONS FOR PUBLIC INVESTMENT MANAGEMENT
Level I: aggregate fiscal discipline	Exercising effective control of the total budget and management of fiscal risks	Aggregate public investment spending planned within realistic resource ceilings and individual projects completed within budget
Level II: strategic allocation of resources	Planning and executing the budget in line with government priorities aimed at achieving policy objectives	Capital investment projects selected and budgeted in accordance with government's strategic priorities to address the most pressing problems or constraints
Level III: efficient service delivery	Using budgeted resources to achieve the best levels of public services within available resources	Capital investment projects evaluated to verify that they represent efficient and effective solutions to identified problems; that they are procured economically, implemented efficiently, and operated as planned

that public investment provides value for money. This indicator falls under pillar III, management of assets and liabilities, and includes the following four dimensions:

- Economic analysis of investment proposals
- Investment project selection
- Investment project costing
- Investment project monitoring.

Common failings indicating that public investment management requires attention

Signs of weak PIM are often apparent to citizens and other stakeholders, mostly in terms of poor public services, but also the low importance given to achieving value for money—that is, vanity projects going ahead when basic services remain unmet or new projects starting while others are visibly stalled.

Short-term political influence that leads to wasteful "white elephant" projects, with limited economic or social value compared with costs, is a serious problem in a weak PIM environment. A tendency to fund new projects rather than to complete ongoing projects efficiently, leading to a backlog of stalled and incomplete projects, may be the result of the search for short-term political gain or a sign of general weakness in multiyear budgeting.

Corrupt procurement practices, often with a political dimension, can lead to higher costs than necessary and to the selection of unsuitable contractors that are unable to meet the necessary standards or worse. In the least robust systems, corruption and poor supervision of contractors during implementation lead to the delivery of substandard assets that are unable to provide the intended quality. General capacity and procedural weaknesses in project planning and management may cause significant delays and cost overruns. Finally, even high-quality assets, delivered on time, on budget, and to specification, will not produce benefits if no provision has been made for sustainable operations and maintenance, which is often the case with donor-funded projects in low-capacity environments (Rajaram et al. 2014).

The common failings of PIM and the resulting consequences are inventoried in table 2.2.

TABLE 2.2 **Potential consequences of PIM failings**

COMMON PROBLEMS	POTENTIAL CONSEQUENCES
• Development plans disconnected from actual budgets or projects • White elephant projects with little socioeconomic value • Lack of pipeline of high-quality projects • Projects awarded to unqualified firms • Opaque resource-for-infrastructure deals without due safeguards for ensuring good value • Corruption or delays in procurement • Delays in land or site acquisition • Cost escalation, time overruns • Contract disputes or abandoned projects • Poor quality of completed projects • Poor operation and maintenance of completed assets • Institutional inertia or no systemic response to problems	• Creation of few valuable public assets • Lack of key public facilities • Stock of decaying infrastructure: power and water shortages, road and railway accidents, crowded hospitals, deteriorating human development index • Failure of investment to spark growth and improve social welfare • Difficulty of countercyclical expansion of investments • Creation of a liability if investment is financed by debt • Burden on citizens and private sector if investment is financed by taxes • Reduction in net wealth if investment is financed by the extraction of finite natural resources • Macroeconomic instability • Political instability • Fiscal pressures and risk

Source: Based on World Bank 2015.

FIGURE 2.2
Systematic framework for public investment management

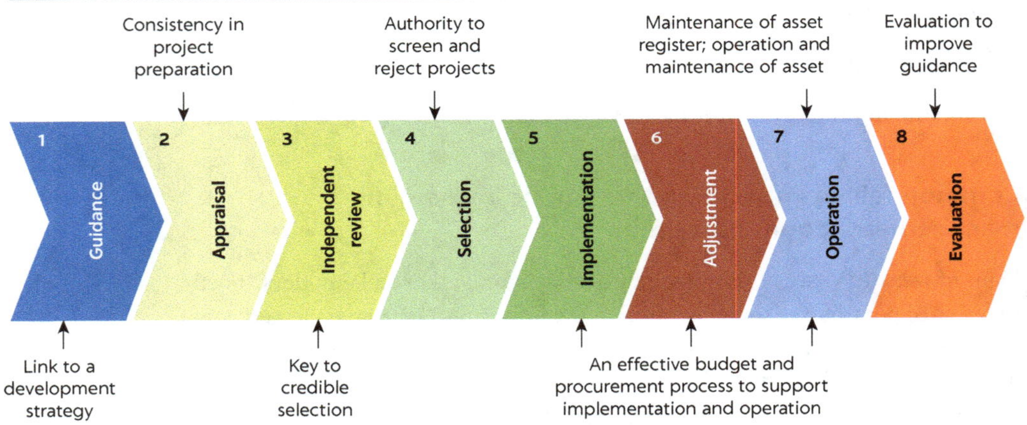

Sources: Rajaram et al. 2010, reproduced in Rajaram et al. 2014.

Main features of an effective public investment management system

A World Bank publication (Rajaram et al. 2014) identifies eight key features for an effective PIM system, as illustrated in figure 2.2. The "must-have" functions associated with these key features can be found in good-practice countries; their division into eight categories is for the purpose of conceptualizing the framework.

In simplified terms, eight must-have functions are key:

1. *Strategic investment guidance, project concept development, and preappraisal screening.* Broad strategic guidance to guide sector-level decision makers and preliminary screening to ensure that project concepts meet minimum criteria

of consistency with the government's strategic objectives and with the economic classification

2. *A formal project appraisal process.* A regulated set of project preparation steps: prefeasibility and feasibility studies, including preliminary design; environmental and social impact assessments that must be completed before a project can be approved for funding; and methods appropriate to the technical capacities and scale and scope of the project.
3. *Independent review of appraisal.* Review by the finance ministry, a planning ministry, or an independent agency to counter optimism bias—overestimation of demand and underestimation of costs
4. *Final decision on project selection and budgeting using a well-managed budget process.* Linking appraisal and selection of public investment projects to the budget cycle, even if the project evaluation cycle is on a different timetable; verification of project eligibility and priority; close scrutiny of forward costs and funding during budgeting
5. *Efficient project implementation.* Scrutiny for implementation realism, including organizational arrangements, procurement planning, and a timetable; adequate monitoring systems; and systems for managing total project costs
6. *Ability to make project adjustments.* Flexibility to allow changes in the disbursement profile—including discontinuation of nonperforming projects—to take account of changes in project circumstances
7. *Provision for sustainable operation of facilities.* Processes to ensure that a new facility is ready for operation and that the intended services can be delivered on a sustainable basis; requires effective handover of management responsibility for operation and maintenance and upkeep of robust and up-to-date capital asset registers
8. *Basic completion review and ex post evaluation.* A systematic review of all projects upon completion to assess whether a project was delivered as specified, on time, and according to budget, and to introduce a more sophisticated ex post evaluation to assess the project's outputs and outcomes against objectives established in the design.

Reforming public investment management

The challenges faced when introducing reform to public investment management are significant and well known; they should not be underestimated. As the common failings and problems presented in table 2.2 illustrate, three facets of public investment present potential obstacles to improving procedures and methods: public investment is highly politicized, it involves a high risk of corruption, and it is in an area demanding a high level of public management.

Public investment is highly politicized because of the discretionary nature of these expenditures, their high visibility, and the fact that they are location-specific. The long life of the assets created is attractive to politicians wishing to leave a "legacy." The corruption risk attached to public investment is well known and comes from the high value of contracts and the vulnerability to manipulation of the procurement process. Corruption can distort investment and implementation decisions and render useless any intended procedural and methodological improvements. In a corrupt environment, strong vested interests can smother PIM reforms in their infancy.

PIM is a highly demanding area of public management, requiring advanced technical capacities and organizational capabilities. Even the key features of a minimally effective system, as identified in figure 2.2, require high levels of skill, farsightedness, and discipline. Given these potential obstacles, there should be no misconceptions about the scale of the challenge of a PIM reform, even for supportive governments.

Ensuring a suitably precise definition of public investment does not mean that public expenditure proposals outside the definition should escape proper planning, scrutiny, and management; all the same, public investment proposals demand the attention of a dedicated system. The procedures and methods for public investment management may be applied to other expenditure proposals or even to regulatory measures. Ireland's 2005 Guidelines for the Appraisal and Management of Capital Expenditure Proposals are now incorporated in the broader Public Spending Code that covers capital and current spending. In the United Kingdom, methodological guidance is applied to capital and current expenditures and to regulatory measures.[20] These examples show the wide applicability of the procedures and methods, but the priority for reforming countries should be to develop a focused PIM system, as the payoff in terms of enhanced growth, improved welfare, and improved efficiency is high (IMF 2015).

NOTES

1. In Ukraine, before 2015 amendments to the Budget Code, only 8.9 percent of public capital investment by value was passing through the regulated PIM system. See Biletska et al. (2012).
2. IMF (2014) defines fixed assets as "produced assets that are used repeatedly or continuously in production processes for more than one year."
3. IMF (2014) adopts the accrual accounting basis and does not define capital expenditure explicitly. Instead, it talks about "transactions in fixed assets" affecting the balance sheet. For the purposes of defining capital investment for PIM, the acquisition of fixed assets and capital expenditures can be taken as equivalent. Capital expenditures should not be confused with the term "capital expenses" as used in the *Government Finance Statistics Manual*.
4. This is often the case in aid-dependent countries, where the development budget represents externally financed projects, both capital and recurrent.
5. The categories are broken down into subcategories in the IMF manual.
6. The notorious project to digitize the United Kingdom's health records is an extreme example of a failed ICT project. Costing as much as £9.8 billion, it failed to yield benefits of anything like the same order as a result of poor planning and implementation. See Parliamentary Public Accounts Committee (2013).
7. Many studies have shown that the return to punctual routine and periodic maintenance is many times the return to new investment, in almost all instances. For example, annual benefit-cost ratios of between 1.4 and 44.8, depending on traffic level, have been estimated for timely road maintenance (World Bank n.d.)
8. Infrastructure Australia is an independent statutory body with responsibility for advising the government on infrastructure policies and priorities.
9. See https://data.worldbank.org/topic/infrastructure.
10. See the first National Infrastructure Plan, adopted in 2010.
11. The full scope of the U.K. National Infrastructure Delivery Plan 2016–21 is roads, rail, airports and ports, energy, digital communications, flood and coastal erosion, water and

waste, science and research, housing and regeneration, social infrastructure, and regional infrastructure.

12. This definition is compatible with international experience. In the United Kingdom, for example, a project is defined as having "definite start and finish dates, a clearly defined output, a well-defined development path, and a defined set of financial and other resources allocated to it" (Office of Government Commerce 2007).

    In the European Union, a project is defined as "a series of works, activities, or services intended to accomplish an indivisible task of a precise economic and technical nature which has clearly identified goals" (Article 100 [Major Projects] of Regulation (European Union) no. 1303/2013).
13. The United Kingdom, for example, defines a program as "a group of related projects" and treats it as a single project. "Program" is not used in the *PIM Reference Guide* to avoid confusion with budgetary programs in a program budgeting system.
14. Potential financial liabilities may be explicit or implicit.
15. See https://www.finance-ni.gov.uk/topics/finance/northern-ireland-guide-expenditure-appraisal-and-evaluation-nigeae.
16. "An economic activity is one that involves offering goods or services on a given market and which could, at least in principle, be carried out by a private operator in order to make profits" (OECD 2015).
17. Before the public sector reforms of the 1980s, investment by commercially oriented SOEs in the United Kingdom fell within the scope of the national PIM system.
18. According to the OECD (2015), "Public policy objectives are those benefitting the general public within the SOE's own jurisdiction. . . . These could include the delivery of public services, such as postal services, as well as other special obligations undertaken in the public interest."
19. A PPP is not the same as a commercial joint venture, which would normally fall outside of PIM.
20. "All new policies, programs, and projects, whether revenue, capital, or regulatory, should be subject to comprehensive but proportionate assessment" (HM Treasury 2003).

REFERENCES

Ansar, A., B. Flyvbjerg, A. Budzier, and S. Linn. 2014. "Should We Build More Large Dams? The Actual Costs of Hydropower Megaproject Development." *Energy Policy* 69 (June): 43–56.

Biletska, N., J. A. Brumby, F. Grigoli, R. Hemming, Y, K. Kang, J. W. Lee, Z. Mills, S. Y. Min, B. Moreno-Dodson, M. Verhoeven, R. Vlaicu, H. T. T. Vu, and L. Zoratto. 2012. *Beyond the Annual Budget: Global Experience with Medium-Term Expenditure Frameworks.* Washington, DC: World Bank.

Flyvbjerg, B. 2005. "Policy and Planning for Large Infrastructure Projects: Problems, Causes, and Cures." Policy Research Working Paper 3781, World Bank, Washington, DC.

——. 2014. "What You Should Know about Megaprojects and Why: An Overview." *Project Management Journal* 45 (2): 6–19.

HM Treasury. 2003. *The Green Book: Appraisal and Evaluation in Central Government.* Amended in 2011. London: HM Treasury.

IMF (International Monetary Fund). 2014. *Government Finance Statistics Manual.* Washington, DC: IMF.

——. 2015. "Making Public Investment More Efficient." IMF Policy Paper, IMF, Washington, DC.

——. 2017. *World Economic Outlook.* Washington, DC: IMF.

OECD (Organisation for Economic Co-operation and Development). 2015. *Guidelines on Corporate Governance of State-Owned Enterprises.* Paris: OECD Publishing.

Office of Government Commerce. 2007. "OGC Gateway Process—Review 2: Delivery Strategy." Office of Government Commerce, London.

Parliamentary Public Accounts Committee. 2013. "Dismantled National Programme for IT in the NHS: Nineteenth Report of Session 2013–14." House of Commons, London.

PEFA Secretariat. 2016. *Framework for Assessing Public Financial Management*. Washington, DC: PEFA Secretariat.

Rajaram, A., T. M. Le, N. Biletska, and J. Brumby. 2010. "A Diagnostic Framework for Assessing Public Investment Management." Policy Research Working Paper 5397, World Bank, Washington, DC.

Rajaram, A., T. M. Le, K. Kaiser, J. H. Kim, and J. Frank, eds. 2014. *The Power of Public Investment Management: Transforming Resources into Assets for Growth*. Washington, DC: World Bank.

Torrisi, G. 2009. "Public Infrastructure: Definition, Classification, and Measurement Issues." MPRA Paper, University Library of Munich.

World Bank. 2007. "Belarus Policy Note: Selected Issues in Capital Budgeting; Improving the Quality of Public Capital Expenditures to Promote Growth." Poverty Reduction and Economic Management Unit, Europe and Central Asia Region, World Bank, Washington, DC, August 17.

———. 2015. "Public Investment Management: Status, Opportunities, Challenges." Technical Briefing to the Board, World Bank, Washington, DC.

———. n.d. "The Impact of Poor Road Maintenance." World Bank, Washington, DC. http://siteresources.worldbank.org/INTROADSHIGHWAYS/Resources/338993-1115316562809/10-poor_rd_maint.pdf.

3

The Legal and Regulatory Framework for PIM

OVERVIEW

Public investment management (PIM) needs to be situated in an appropriate legal and regulatory framework to ensure its proper functioning and to apply common standards and methods in a consistent manner. A country's legal tradition and administrative culture will determine the most suitable approach, but the guiding principle should be to avoid using superior legal instruments for detailed procedural arrangements and methodological guidance, as procedures and methods may have to be adapted over time, particularly in the early days of PIM reform, and a superior legal instrument is less flexible. This principle points to the design and adoption of a hierarchical legal and regulatory framework, consisting of three tiers from top to bottom:

- *Tier 1: legal authority for the PIM system.* Usually established through some form of primary legislation
- *Tier 2: basic procedural guidelines, high-level decision criteria, roles and responsibilities, and designation of analytical tools.* Often established in governmental or ministerial regulations, or the equivalent,[1] issued under the authority of primary legislation, but looser and tighter arrangements may be possible or necessary, depending on country circumstances
- *Tier 3: methodological guidance, detailed criteria, standardized parameter values, and procedural documentation.* Generally issued directly by the PIM coordinating agency (finance ministry or other) in the form of manuals, templates, and circulars, under the authority granted to it by the primary legislation. In some countries such guidance may require a stronger legal basis to give it adequate force.

There can be a lot of variation among countries within this broad hierarchical framework, but the main aim should be to preserve as much flexibility as possible for the PIM coordinating agency to improve systems as lessons are learned and capacity is developed. The agency needs to have sufficient legal authority to enforce the "rules of the game."

This chapter describes some of the options for establishing this hierarchical framework, with some relevant country examples.

LEGAL AUTHORITY FOR PIM: TIER 1

The legal authority for PIM can be established via three models:

- Specific primary legislation: a "PIM law"
- Directly through the budget systems law or fiscal responsibility law (or equivalent)[2]
- Indirectly through the budget and fiscal systems legislation (or equivalent).

The second of these three models combines sufficient legal authority with adequate flexibility and is usually the preferred choice.

The first model is the least common and is associated with reform-oriented, state-planned economies such as those of the Lao People's Democratic Republic and Vietnam, where planning and budgeting for capital investment are separated institutionally from planning and budgeting for current expenditures. Vietnam's Law on Public Investment (2014) runs to 57 pages (in English translation); in addition to establishing the legal authority for PIM, it covers the kind of procedural detail indicated at tier 2. Lao PDR's 2009 law (revised in 2015) is similar in scope and content. Italy used a specific law (Law 144/1999) to establish the concept of the project cycle and place the feasibility study at the center of project preparation and appraisal, which is unusual for countries with more advanced systems (Scandizzo and Napodano 2010).

The third model generally applies to countries with more advanced public financial management systems and may not work where there is an urgency to implement PIM reforms. Australia's Financial Management and Accountability Act (1997),[3] for example, requires heads of spending agencies to promote "proper use" of public resources, defining "proper use" as "efficient, effective, and ethical use" that is "not inconsistent with the policies" of the country. In relation to PIM, the Australian Finance Ministry then issues guidelines connecting different dimensions to the obligations of public sector managers to make "proper use" of public resources. New Zealand and the United Kingdom take a similar approach. South Africa goes marginally further by requiring responsible officers to ensure that their organization maintains "a system for properly evaluating all major capital projects prior to making a final decision on the project,"[4] but provides no further detail at the level of primary legislation; the detail comes in regulatory instruments issued by the Finance Ministry.

Within the preferred second model, a decision must be made concerning the level of detail on PIM contained in the budget systems law. At one end of the spectrum, Kazakhstan includes considerable detail in its already very detailed Budget Code (see box 3.1);[5] at the other end of the spectrum, Croatia has a single article on PIM in its Budget Act, requiring expert assessment of projects and conferring authority on the government to prescribe PIM methodologies (see box 3.2). Generally accepted principles concerning the balance between the budget system law and supporting regulations may help policy makers to determine the appropriate level of detail (see box 3.3). Cyprus's recently adopted Fiscal Responsibility and Budget Systems Law illustrates how this approach could be compatible with the legal and administrative context (see box 3.4).

BOX 3.1

Treatment of public investment management in Kazakhstan's budget systems law

Two chapters of Kazakhstan's Budget Code deal with public investment (although these chapters also address concession arrangements and government shareholdings). Chapter 30 covers budgeting for investment projects, and chapter 31 (not summarized here) deals with project implementation, including project adjustment and ex post evaluation.

Chapter 30 sets out a three-stage upstream PIM process:

1. *Project proposal.* Administrators of budget programs develop investment project proposals in coordination with the drafting of medium-term strategic plans. Investment proposals are subject to scrutiny by the Planning Authority and to approval by the relevant budget committees before being included in the budget for funding the next stage.
2. *Project appraisal.* Detailed feasibility studies are undertaken, reports are prepared, and project viability is appraised. Feasibility studies examine economic feasibility using cost-benefit analysis. Independent review of appraisal results, including review of economic performance and risk analysis, is mandatory. Based on the review, budget program administrators may approve projects.
3. *Project selection via the annual budget process.* Only projects that have a completed feasibility report, a positive appraisal, and a positive decision from the relevant budget committee are eligible for inclusion in the draft budget.

Chapter 30 also authorizes the issuance of secondary legislation:

- The government is authorized to specify the detailed procedures for the development, review, and selection of investment proposals.
- The Planning Authority decides on the requirements of feasibility studies (stage 2).
- The government is authorized by law to specify procedures for submission, selection, monitoring, and evaluation of government investment projects, including those not requiring feasibility studies or those having increased budgets.

Source: Kazakhstan's 2009 Budget Code.

PROCEDURAL GUIDELINES AND METHODOLOGICAL GUIDANCE: TIERS 2 AND 3

Once the legal basis for PIM has been established, it needs to be made operational using a comprehensive regulatory framework that details the PIM system's design and functioning. This second tier of the hierarchy generally covers procedures, roles, and responsibilities; higher-level assessment criteria; and designated analytical methods (it does not provide in-depth guidance on the methods). Depending on the depth of coverage at tier 1, there may be some repetition at tier 2; PIM guidelines should deepen the framework established in the law.

In rare cases, such as Lao PDR and Vietnam, some of the content of tiers 1 and 2 is combined in a single piece of primary legislation.

BOX 3.2

Treatment of public investment management in Croatia's budget systems law

"Assumption of liabilities for investment projects

Article 45

1. State budget users may assume liabilities for investment projects only after expert assessment has been completed, and the investment project's justification and efficiency were evaluated.
2. The provisions of this Article shall apply accordingly to local and regional self-government units.
3. The government shall prescribe the methodology of preparation, evaluation, and execution of investment projects by a decree."

Source: Croatia's 2008 Budget Act.

BOX 3.3

Content of budget system laws versus lower-order instruments

Three criteria provide guidance on whether an issue should be covered by law or by government regulation:

- Public finance areas over which the legislature has final authority should be specified in law, whereas budgetary issues for which the executive has delegated authority should be governed by regulations.
- The responsibilities of the executive to the legislature should be covered in the law, whereas the responsibilities internal to the executive are best specified in regulations or decrees issued by the executive.
- The new budget principles should be durable. Since laws are more difficult to change than regulations, they should not include provisions if there is a strong risk that these provisions will be abrogated or amended one to three years later.

Source: Lienert and Fainboim 2007.

Tier 2 procedural guidelines are generally issued by the government or the responsible finance or planning ministry in the form of secondary legislation,[6] as authorized in the primary legislation. In the United Kingdom and countries with similar political and administrative systems, procedural guidelines issued by the economic and finance ministry (the "Treasury") have the implicit legal force of regulations and are recognized as such because of the superior status of this ministry in the political hierarchy.

Moldova, Ukraine, and Zimbabwe are examples of countries where tier 2 regulations have recently been introduced as a basis for initiating operational PIM systems. In Moldova, under authority of the Law on Fiscal Responsibilities[7]—the tier 1 legislation—the Cabinet of Ministers adopted, by resolution,[8] a regulation governing roles and responsibilities and setting out rules and procedures for a five-stage PIM system. In Ukraine, the Cabinet of Ministers adopted, by resolution, procedures for project appraisal and selection and a regulation on organizational arrangements. This resolution was subsequent to amendments to the Budget Code in 2015, which

BOX 3.4

Treatment of public investment in Cyprus's budget systems law

Part XI of the Fiscal Responsibility and Budget Systems Law deals with the selection and implementation of public investment projects. In eight articles, part XI sets out the basic principles and scope of PIM in Cyprus, establishes a five-stage PIM process, and authorizes the minister of finance to issue regulations or instructions to set out "procedures, methodologies, criteria, and other requirements."

The following are the five stages of Cyprus's PIM process:

1. Preselection of projects
2. Project assessment
3. Project selection
4. Project implementation
5. Monitoring of projects and amendments to contracts.

Under the authority of the law (tier 1 in the hierarchy), the minister of finance has issued a methodological manual covering upstream PIM processes and will shortly issue another for downstream processes. The manuals are equivalent to tier 3 in the hierarchy.

The law also includes a general article giving the Council of Ministers power to issue regulations to improve implementation of the law and regulation of technical matters. This power has allowed the Council of Ministers to issue PIM guidelines delineating PIM procedures, roles, and responsibilities and designating analytical methods. The guidelines are equivalent to tier 2 in the hierarchy.

Source: Cyprus's 2014 Fiscal Responsibility and Budget Systems Law.

were required to give PIM a firm legal footing. In Zimbabwe, the Ministry of Finance and Economic Development adopted in 2017, by a Treasury circular, PIM guidelines that regulate a five-stage PIM procedure for project concept note, prefeasibility study, feasibility study, implementation, monitoring and adjustment, and asset registry, management, and evaluation. The PIM guidelines are a tier 2 regulation under the country's public financial management law. Work is ongoing in all three countries to develop, introduce, and further refine methodological guidance at tier 3.

Tier 2 regulations need to be supported at tier 3 by technical guidance on assessment methodologies, detailed assessment criteria, and templates. This guidance usually consists of overarching methodological guidance, supplemented by sector-specific guidance on how to apply the general guidance in an individual sector or subsector (for example, roads, railways, airports, irrigation, and water supply and sanitation). In the United Kingdom, the general methodological guidance (HM Treasury 2003) is supplemented by various sector-specific knowledge resources, including those for transport[9] and flood defenses.[10] The Republic of Korea has published more than 10 sets of guidance books for subsectors.[11] Chile has perhaps the most extensive sector-specific guidance, with more than 30 sets of guidance for individual subsectors (see box 5.4).

Flexibility is required, as methodological approaches may need to be updated and refined on a regular basis; at the same time, the official status of the guidance needs to be upheld. This is usually done by issuing guidance through a ministerial decision or equivalent. Procedural and methodological templates are issued at tier 3, and they may be subject to more regular revision. In the United Kingdom, templates to present "business cases" for projects are required for decision making at three points in time during the upstream phase of the PIM system. In addition to other information for decision makers, the templates present the findings of assessments carried out according to methods from the *Green Book* (HM Treasury 2003).

Overarching national methodological guidance should be issued by the central financial or planning ministry responsible for coordinating PIM; sector-specific guidelines may be developed and promulgated either by the responsible central financial or planning ministry (as in Chile and Korea) or by line ministries or their subordinated agencies (as in France or the United Kingdom). The first model ensures that sector-specific guidelines are consistent with the overarching national guidelines; the second model has the potential to promote buy-in at the sector level and to use available sector expertise more efficiently. The second model needs to have a mechanism for ensuring that sector guidance is consistent with national guidance. Somewhere between these two models and less common is the example of the Netherlands: national guidelines include light treatment of sector-specific methods, which are then open to further development by line ministries or agencies.

Regularly updated guidance on standardized values for key parameters for economic analysis (for example, discount rate, value of work and personal time, value of a statistical life, value of a ton of carbon dioxide saved) supports the methodological guidance. These values may be subject to more frequent updating than the methods themselves, and are often promulgated through ministerial circulars or research papers. National parameter values are discussed further in chapter 5.

COMPARISON OF COUNTRY LEGAL AND REGULATORY FRAMEWORKS

Table 3.1 illustrates the structures of the legal and regulatory frameworks in three countries. Cyprus and Korea illustrate the most typical choices facing most countries embarking on PIM reform and the hierarchical structure. The Cyprus case has already been described in relation to tier 1 (box 3.4).

Cyprus has a separate chapter on PIM in the Fiscal Responsibility and Budget Systems Law. Korea grants PIM legal authority through the National Finance Act, which confers on the Ministry of Economy and Finance the authority to issue detailed regulations (tier 2) and to support these regulations with methodological guidance, both general and sector specific (tier 3). The case of the United Kingdom, while not unusual, is difficult to replicate if a country does not already have similar political and administrative traditions (which may apply to members of the Commonwealth).

It is interesting to compare tier 2 authority in Cyprus and in Korea; in Cyprus, the Council of Ministers adopts the regulatory framework ("guidelines") proposed by the minister of finance; whereas in Korea, the Ministry of Economy and Finance has this authority. Even though it could be useful for the PIM system to obtain buy-in at the highest political level, leaving tier 2 authority with the government may weaken the momentum of reform. This approach has worked in Cyprus but not in Croatia: the government of Croatia has been unable to reach agreement on the details of the PIM system for many years, and PIM reform has stalled, despite the intentions of the 2008 Budget Systems Law (box 3.2). In Korea, a coalition of the Prime Minister's Office and the Ministry of Economy and Finance was responsible for driving through PIM reforms, with some initial resistance from line ministries. This case illustrates that the political context and

TABLE 3.1 **Comparison of legal and regulatory hierarchies for PIM in three countries**

TIER	UNITED KINGDOM	CYPRUS	KOREA, REP.
Tier 1: legal authority	*Finance Act* and *Managing Public Money* embody the principle of efficiency and require public resources to be used in ways that give value for money.	*Fiscal Responsibility and Budget Systems Law* sets out a five-stage PIM system and authorizes the minister of finance to issue regulations and instructions on procedures, methodologies, and criteria.	*National Finance Act* authorizes the Ministry of Economy and Finance to carry out a preliminary feasibility study of major investment projects and to provide guidelines on the conduct of any study that may be delegated to an independent institution.
Tier 2: procedural guidelines	*Major project approval and assurance guidance* is issued jointly by the Cabinet Office and the Treasury (the economic and finance ministry). *Public sector business cases using the five-case model* is issued by the Treasury.	*PIM guidelines* adopted by the Council of Ministers cover procedures, roles, and responsibilities at each stage and set high-level assessment criteria.	*Operational guidelines for the preliminary feasibility study* and *guidelines for total project cost management* are issued by the Ministry of Economy and Finance.
Tier 3: methodological guidance	*Appraisal and evaluation in central government* (the *Green Book*) and *templates for business cases* are issued by the Treasury. *Sector-specific methodological guidance* is issued by line ministries.	*Methodological manual for preselection and appraisal of public investment projects* is issued under authority of the minister of finance by the Directorate General for European Programmes, Coordination, and Development.	*General and sector-specific guidance on appraisal* is issued by the Ministry of Economy and Finance.

relative power and motivation of the players are important in the design of any legal and regulatory framework.

Vietnam's dedicated PIM law is a rarity and includes elements of both tiers 2 and 3. Parliament is involved in regulating details of the PIM system and in upstream decision making through its power to approve investment decisions for nationally important projects. This legalistic approach reflects the country context but may not be efficient because of its inherent inflexibility.

NOTES

1. Usually referred to as "secondary" legislation.
2. The term "budget law" is often used, but it is not used here to avoid confusion with the annual budget law.
3. Australia is generally recognized as having a well-managed public sector.
4. Public Financial Management Act 1999.
5. The Budget Code extends to 125 pages (in English translation).
6. Government decisions or resolutions for adopting regulations and procedures.
7. Amended in 2013.
8. Government's PIM Resolution no. 1029 (dated December 19, 2013).
9. See https://www.gov.uk/guidance/transport-analysis-guidance-webtag.
10. See https://www.gov.uk/guidance/flood-and-coastal-defence-appraisal-of-projects.
11. For example, roads and railways, seaports, airports, water supplies, industrial complexes, information technology projects, social and cultural projects, environmental facilities, and hospital projects.

REFERENCES

HM Treasury. 2003. *The Green Book: Appraisal and Evaluation in Central Government*. Amended in 2011. London: HM Treasury.

Lienert, I., and I. Fainboim. 2007. "IMF Reforming Budget Systems Laws." PFM Technical Note 2, Fiscal Affairs Department, International Monetary Fund, Washington, DC.

Scandizzo, P., and M. Napodano. 2010. *Public Investment Management: Linking Global Trends to National Experiences*. Saarbrücken: VDM Verlag Dr. Müller, Germany.

4

Allocation of Roles and Responsibilities among Key Players

OVERVIEW

A core part of public investment management (PIM) arrangements should be the clear allocation of roles and responsibilities to key players from government bodies at each stage of the PIM system. This allocation is important for upstream and downstream phases of the system; for assessments, for budgeting and implementation, and for key decisions on whether to proceed further with a project.

The following may be key players in the PIM process:

- Line ministries with their departments and subordinated agencies, where projects originate and are implemented
- The finance ministry, which has a critical role in coordinating capital budgeting for new and ongoing projects and may have an oversight role in quality-at-entry processes
- The planning ministry or agency, which may be an alternative location for overseeing quality-at-entry processes and should have a critical role in coordinating strategic planning
- An interministerial committee (or similar committee), which may have a role in confirming appraisal decisions and selecting projects to compete for budget funding
- A ministerial committee—made up of finance, planning, and infrastructure ministers—with powers delegated from the council of ministers for major projects.

These are the key players on the executive side of government, which is the focus of this chapter. The role of the legislature is also important, however, as it makes the final decisions on project funding through the budget process. Depending on the country, this power may or may not extend to decisions on individual projects.

As indicated in chapter 3, roles and responsibilities should generally be set at tier 1 or tier 2 in the hierarchy of PIM legislation and regulations—that is, through government or ministerial decisions, regulations, or the like. Depending on the depth of PIM coverage in primary legislation, high-level roles and responsibilities may be established at tier 1, but they would still need to be given more substance at tier 2. Cases where roles and responsibilities are fully developed in primary legislation are rare—for example, in Vietnam.

The framework for guidance on roles and responsibilities should follow the eight PIM functions identified in figure 2.2. The first four functions prior to implementation (strategic guidance, appraisal, independent review, and selection) are the upstream processes; the remainder (implementation, adjustment, operation, and evaluation) form the downstream processes.

This chapter focuses on upstream roles and responsibilities because well-informed, structured decision making prior to implementation is essential for a good PIM system. While there is still scope for defining roles and responsibilities for the downstream functions, these downstream roles and responsibilities will already be governed partly through legal and regulatory instruments with wider scope than PIM, such as laws on budget systems, procurement, public accounting, public internal financial control, and state audit. Downstream roles and responsibilities are discussed separately in chapters 8 and 9.

OPTIONS FOR THE ALLOCATION OF ROLES AND RESPONSIBILITIES

Upstream PIM functions

Upstream functions have four general roles:

- *Proposer.* Identifies the project concept in response to an identified need or emerging problem and initiates the steps that follow
- *Appraiser.* Analyzes the project's net social worth, affordability, and sustainability as it develops from concept to budget-ready expenditure proposal
- *Reviewer.* Evaluates the quality and robustness of the analysis at each step and advises decision makers
- *Decision maker.* Makes a decision to proceed to the next stage on the basis of analytical findings and reviewers' advice.

Table 4.1 summarizes the responsibilities related to each stage of the upstream phase of the PIM system. In some cases, the same body may carry out different roles, but this approach will require internal safeguards against conflicts of interest, such as involving disinterested parties within the organization.

Project preappraisal

At the preappraisal stage, it is advisable for the proposer and appraiser to be the same in order to ensure the development of a coherent project concept. The reviewer should be different from the proposer and appraiser. Particularly for major projects, the reviewer should be external to the proposing or appraising organization or will need to come from another part of the same organization. The decision maker should be different from the proposer, at least for major projects; it may be the finance or planning ministry, but such strategic decisions may be made at the central government level, particularly for megaprojects.

Project appraisal and selection

At the appraisal stage, capacity considerations and objectivity requirements usually mean that the proposer and appraiser are different. External consultants and experts may act as appraisers, especially for major projects. In such cases, it is important for the proposer to retain strong oversight. The reviewer also needs to be different from the proposer and appraiser and to have no vested interest in the project. The finance or planning ministry usually performs the role of reviewer (sometimes with assistance from external experts), but an independent agency may also be established.

Smaller projects may be reviewed by the proposing organization, but the review must be undertaken by an independent unit within the organization to preserve some degree of separation between the two roles. It is advisable not to take the selection decision to the government level simply to avoid it becoming politicized.

The minister of finance or planning usually makes the final appraisal decision for major projects; for smaller projects, the head of the proposing body may make the final decision. The selection decision may be escalated to a higher authority for "projects of national significance" or "megaprojects," in which case the decision would fall to the council of ministers or to a committee of ministers with delegated authority.

Capital budgeting

Capital budgets are prepared by line ministry planning and finance units and proposed by the respective minister.

The budget department in the finance ministry is in charge of appraising capital budgets. It is not advisable to split this role between separate finance and planning ministries; separating functions within the finance ministry by the economic nature of expenditures is also not recommended.

The minister of finance, advised by the budget department, will generally be the official reviewer of budget submissions and their capital components. Such reviews usually involve a high-level team from within the finance ministry. The finance minister should have ultimate responsibility for advising colleagues in the council of ministers or cabinet about the outcome of the review process.

The final decision on the draft budget, including its capital component, is made by the council of ministers or cabinet. Any unresolved issues from the finance minister's review should be resolved at this time.

Table 4.1 describes the roles and responsibilities of the executive, but the legislature is the ultimate decision maker for capital budgeting. In some countries—for example, the United States—the legislature can play an active role in choosing individual projects (provided decisions are neutral with respect to the overall size of the budget); in other countries, the legislature can only accept or reject the budget in its entirety. The latter model is recommended. If the first model is constitutionally embedded, the PIM legislation (tier 1) needs to be strong enough to ensure that the legislature can only introduce projects that have passed through disciplined quality-at-entry processes.

Through its recently introduced PIM guidelines, Cyprus has carefully systematized roles and responsibilities using the format set out in table 4.1. Similarly, through its Multi-Year Plan for Infrastructure, Spatial Planning, and Transport (MIRT) Rules, the Netherlands also designates decision makers at clearly defined control points in the upstream phase of the PIM system, as summarized in box 4.1.

TABLE 4.1 **Roles and responsibilities of key players in PIM**

STAGE OR ROLE	PROPOSER	APPRAISER	REVIEWER	DECISION MAKER
Preappraisal	Identifies and develops the project concept in response to an identified need or emerging problem, in discussion with relevant stakeholders Secures funding for appraisal if the ultimate decision is positive	Prepares an assessment (preappraisal) of the project concept and possible alternatives, focusing on strategic relevance, rationale, and long-run fiscal sustainability	Reviews justification for proceeding to project preparation, to identify nonstrategic projects and those likely to be nonviable economically or unaffordable (especially "white elephants") Advises decision makers accordingly	Decides if, on balance, there is a strong enough case for proceeding to project preparation, taking account of the preappraisal findings and reviewer's advice
Appraisal and selection	Initiates the preliminary design, feasibility study, and any necessary impact studies for the project Secures funding for detailed design and tender preparation if the decision is positive	Prepares a feasibility study to determine whether the risk-adjusted net social worth of the project is positive, if the social and environmental impacts are acceptable, and if the fiscal consequences are sustainable	Reviews the feasibility findings and tests their robustness, with an eye to identifying excessive optimism concerning costs and benefits and inattention to risks and deliverability	Decides if, in principle, the project represents good value for public money (that is, is likely to be efficient and effective) Decides if a major project is a priority for public funding, given competition from other projects Decides if a project may be proposed for budget funding
Capital budgeting	Prepares the capital budget proposal, including new projects that have been selected; ensures consistency with guidance from the finance ministry on financial constraints and government priorities	Analyzes the capital budget proposal to check that individual projects have all the necessary decisions and that none has circumvented earlier PIM stages; that new projects are deliverable in the planned time frame and within budgets; that proposed funding for new projects does not compromise the implementation of ongoing projects; and that the proposal supports the government's declared policy priorities, fitting within previously specified fiscal limits Identifies any competing claims for funding of new capital projects	Reviews capital budget proposals to verify alignment with government priorities, deliverability of new projects in the budgetary planning horizon, and aggregate fiscal sustainability, taking account of the appraisers' findings Prepares advice for the ultimate decision maker on resolving any competing claims for funding that cannot be resolved bilaterally	Approves capital budget proposals, having resolved all competing claims In so doing, decides to fund the full implementation of new projects included therein

DIFFERENT APPROACHES TO DECISION RIGHTS ACCORDING TO PROJECT SIZE, SECTOR, AND LEVEL OF GOVERNMENT

Bearing in mind the scarcity of key decision makers' time and variations in the riskiness of different sectors, the allocation of roles and responsibilities may differ according to project size, sector, level of government, or all three. This ensures that only "significant" or "major" projects are escalated to the highest levels of scrutiny. This process is illustrated in box 4.2 with reference to the

BOX 4.1

The Netherlands's MIRT rules: Strict definition of roles and responsibilities

The Netherlands's MIRT Rules regulate the project cycle from identification to completion.[a] They describe the roles and responsibilities of the parties involved and the decision-making requirements for the government to reach a decision on a possible financial grant. The rules establish four key decision points corresponding to stages of the project cycle:

1. *Start decision.* A formal declaration is made by the relevant minister that there is a problem that needs to be addressed; a decision is made to begin the explorative study.
2. *Preferred decision.* The preferred option for detailed study is identified on the basis of the explorative study, and a decision is made by the relevant minister to begin the project study.
3. *Project decision.* The decision to proceed with implementation is made on the basis of a detailed study.
4. *Handover decision.* The project is completed and is ready to begin delivering services or benefits as planned.

At each decision point, the aim is to set out the basis for the decision, what the decision involves, and what the possible follow-up process is. To support the decision, information must be supplied in a standard format at each decision point, covering (a) the challenge or problem analysis, (b) solutions, (c) stakeholders, (d) financing, (e) decision making, and (f) follow-up approach.

Apart from the handover decision, the flow of a project from one stage to the next does not happen automatically; an explicit decision must be made regarding whether or not to take the project to the next stage.

Source: World Bank 2014.
a. Rules for the Multiannual Program for Infrastructure, Spatial Development, and Transport (Spelregels van het Meerjaren programma Infrastructuur, Ruimte en Transport).

United Kingdom, where the Treasury becomes involved in decision making for projects above specified thresholds of investment cost. These thresholds vary by sector and level of government, with lower thresholds for local government and for sectors deemed to be risky. Similar arrangements are contained in Vietnam's 2014 Law on Public Investment, which categorizes projects into a four-group hierarchy (nationally important projects and groups A–C) by investment cost, sector, and potential for significant environmental or social impacts. It then specifies a corresponding hierarchy of decision rights from the national assembly down to the people's committees at lower levels of government. Both of these systems may be too elaborate for many countries, but most countries will need to have some degree of hierarchy in the designation of roles and responsibilities.

Based on this discussion, a simple structure of value thresholds for defining a "significant" or "major" project that requires a deeper review and high-level decision making may look like the following:

- A threshold above which a project should be subject to independent review by a body external to the proposing or appraising organization
- A threshold above which the ultimate decision maker for project selection should be the finance or planning minister; for simplicity's sake, this threshold could be the same as in the previous bullet

BOX 4.2

Variations in review and decision making by project size, sector, and level of government in the United Kingdom

In the United Kingdom's public financial management system, the Economic and Finance Ministry (the Treasury) has ultimate responsibility for all expenditure decisions but delegates this authority (by means of a formal letter) to spending ministries for decisions below a certain monetary value. This value varies by ministry and by sector or subsector, according to the Treasury's assessment of the performance of the ministry and the riskiness of the sector or subsector.

Major projects are defined as those costing in excess of the delegated authority's remit, requiring them to be reviewed formally and approved by the Treasury. The definition of a major project can be extended to cover projects that could potentially breach ministry expenditure limits, that set potentially expensive precedents, or that are especially novel or contentious.

Major projects are subject to scrutiny and approval by the Treasury at key control points, known as Treasury approval points (TAPs) during preparation. These TAPs are (a) the strategic outline case, (b) the outline business case, and (c) the full business case.

Delegated limits, and hence the definition of a major project, vary by implementing organization, sector, and subsector. In the transport sector, for example, national road projects are subject to TAP when capital costs exceed £500 million; local government transport projects have a lower threshold of £50 million. In the health sector, capital investment or property transactions above £50 million require Treasury approval. For defense, the figure is £100 million, whereas for foreign affairs, it is only £15 million.

Ministries themselves must establish their own delegated limits for public agencies (arm's-length bodies) coming under their responsibility. Above these limits the ministry itself will scrutinize and approve investment proposals, whereas below the limits responsibility is delegated to the agency proposing the investment. The Health Ministry, for example, requires investment above £35 million to be approved by the ministry, investment of £10 million to £35 million to be approved by the Board of the National Health Service for England, investment of £3 million to £10 million to be approved by the agency's Finance and Investment Committee, and investment of up to £3 million to be approved by a senior officer of the agency.

Megaprojects that are especially large or complex are subject to a different and more intense review by the Major Projects Review Group. Projects are selected for scrutiny according to one or more of the following criteria:

- Projects that have a whole-life cost over £1 billion
- Projects that are high risk and complex in their procurement and delivery of benefits
- Projects that set a precedent or are highly innovative
- Other projects "of concern" (as agreed on by the chair of the Major Projects Review Group or recommended by the Treasury or Major Projects Authority).

Source: World Bank 2014.

- A threshold above which the selection decision must be confirmed by a higher authority than the minister of finance or planning, such as a delegated subcommittee of ministers or even the council of ministers itself.

Setting thresholds is very much a country-specific decision, and international experience is of little help because conditions and the resulting threshold values vary greatly between countries. In Cyprus, for example, a significant project is defined as having a value of greater than €5.0 million. This threshold compares to the much higher values indicated in box 4.2 for the United Kingdom (between £1 million and £500 million, depending on sectors) or the Republic of Korea (approximately US$50 million),[1] but it is appropriate for a small country with few high-value projects.

When deciding on appropriate thresholds, governments need to consider practical issues such as the capacities and competing workloads of the bodies and decision makers involved. Decisions need to be made regarding a reasonable number of projects for the key players to manage. The size distribution of the ongoing project portfolio and of recently completed projects needs to be examined to determine sensible cutoff values that allow for a manageable workload. If thresholds are set too low, then the level of scrutiny may become superficial; if thresholds are set too high, then too few projects will proceed to the intended deeper scrutiny.

A more sophisticated system of thresholds should be considered only after the simpler system has been shown to work. In this case, government may wish to set lower thresholds for sectors considered to be riskier with regard to the reliability of appraisal findings. It is also important to take account of the combined workload of the key players. In the absence of information on the riskiness of different sectors, thresholds may be lower in sectors where the margin of error of the monetary estimates of benefits is likely to be highest or where benefits are more likely to be assessed in qualitative terms only. This is generally the case in the social and environmental sectors. Lower thresholds may also be set for local government projects, if subject to central government scrutiny, reflecting the likelihood of weaker appraisal capacities at this level.

As in the case of the United Kingdom, it will be helpful for the PIM oversight body to have the authority to override thresholds and to subject lower-value projects to greater scrutiny where there is cause for concern.

Table 4.2 discusses proportionate application of appraisal tools, such as social cost-benefit analysis, which may also involve setting value thresholds, although this is not essential.[2] It would be less confusing if the two sets of thresholds—decision rights and methodological sophistication—were consistent at suitable points of convergence.

It is unwise to define value thresholds in primary legislation (tier 1 in the legal or regulatory hierarchy established in table 3.1), as it will be more difficult to change them when circumstances change or when cost inflation erodes real values. It is more appropriate to use primary legislation to establish the authority to set thresholds and then to define them in tier 2 decisions or regulations. This is the case in Cyprus, where the Fiscal Responsibility and Budget Systems Law authorizes the finance minister to define a significant project; this authority is promulgated through guidelines approved by the Council of Ministers.

DEMARCATION AND COORDINATION WHEN A SEPARATE PLANNING MINISTRY (OR ITS EQUIVALENT) AND FINANCE MINISTRY COEXIST

Where there is a separate state planning agency (ministry or other body), there needs to be a clear demarcation of the roles and responsibilities of the finance ministry versus those of the planning agency. There also needs to be adequate coordination between the two ministries.

Responsibility for preparing the current and capital budgets may be divided between the finance and planning ministries. This divided responsibility is particularly evident where state planning is still practiced, for example, in the Lao People's Democratic Republic and Vietnam. Such a division is not generally recommended (see Asian Development Bank 1999; Tommasi 2010) because of the inefficiencies associated with dual budgeting,[3] including:

- Poor coordination between capital expenditure decisions and their recurrent consequences, usually seen in an underprovision of the operational budget of new facilities
- Failure to consider trade-offs between capital and current expenditures, often to the detriment of current spending and frequently resulting in the suboptimal maintenance of capital stock.

Despite becoming less common, shared responsibility for budgeting exists in many countries,[4] which requires formal coordination to alleviate dual-budgeting problems. Combining responsibilities in the finance ministry does not necessarily resolve these issues if the separation of functions is reproduced within a "united" planning and finance ministry.

A planning agency or ministry may have an important role in coordinating the preparation of strategic guidance for public investment, but this role demands close coordination with the finance ministry to ensure that strategic plans are developed within a realistic macrofiscal framework, within an appropriately long-term horizon (see chapter 6), and with an appropriate level of financial resources. In some Sub-Saharan African countries—for example, Ghana and Tanzania—planning commissions have been created under the office of the president or prime minister to strengthen the strategic thinking behind public investment choices. The impact of this approach has sometimes been disappointing because poor coordination with the finance ministry has resulted in unaffordable strategies and plans, which have limited use in guiding public investment choices.

Some countries with advanced PIM systems have reinvigorated the strategic planning function with a narrower remit covering infrastructure only and involving close coordination with the finance ministry. Infrastructure Australia, "an independent statutory body with a mandate to prioritize and progress nationally significant infrastructure [providing] research and advice to governments," is responsible for coordinating preparation of the Australian infrastructure plan. The United Kingdom's Infrastructure and Projects Authority,[5] a new body reporting jointly to the Cabinet Office and the Treasury, has a similar strategic planning function and has recently issued a national infrastructure delivery plan for 2016–21.

As well as having responsibilities for strategic planning, the planning ministry may also be responsible for overseeing preappraisal, appraisal, and selection; capital budgeting would remain the responsibility of the finance ministry. This separation of responsibilities has previously worked well in Chile, where the Planning Ministry (MIDEPLAN) was responsible for the National Public Investment System (SNI) (see box 4.3) but had no role in capital budgeting, which fell under the Ministry of Finance.[6] Azerbaijan's and Ukraine's economic development ministries follow Chile's example, ensuring that upstream PIM responsibilities remain detached from their finance ministries.

Coordination between the planning and finance ministries is always advisable, even when the latter has the mandate for capital budgeting, because questions of affordability during preappraisal and appraisal can only be addressed with input from the finance ministry. This input may be difficult to obtain, as finance ministries may fear that opinions on affordability will be taken as an

BOX 4.3

Allocation of responsibilities in Chile's national public investment system

Chile's Planning Ministry (MIDEPLAN) managed the country's long-established SNI for many years following its inception. This role continued when MIDEPLAN was transformed into the Ministry of Social Development, with the following responsibilities:

- Regulating the procedures for preparing and appraising projects that apply for public funding
- Developing and managing an information system for all investment initiatives (the so-called Integrated Project Data-Bank)
- Developing project preparation and appraisal methodologies, including the determination of social prices
- Training public officials in project preparation and evaluation.

This role has been strictly segregated from capital budgeting, which rests with the Ministry of Finance.

Source: Gómez-Lobo 2012.

implicit approval of budget funding, which can never be the case. Psychologically, it may be easier for the finance ministry to be asked to give an opinion on the likelihood of a project being unaffordable—rather than affordable—in the medium- to long-term fiscal climate.

In summary, the roles of a planning ministry and a finance ministry should be differentiated and coordinated according to the PIM stage. During the early stages (strategic guidance, preappraisal, and appraisal), the planning ministry will take the lead role, especially for checking the economic viability of projects, and will collaborate with the finance ministry. In later stages, the finance ministry will check budget affordability, still collaborating with the planning ministry. Potentially, the planning ministry could take the lead again in the final stage of ex post review and evaluation.

ESTABLISHING A DEDICATED PIM UNIT

PIM oversight activities are highly specialized, and are perhaps among the most specialized of all activities related to public financial management. Where no planning ministry already performs these functions, having a dedicated central PIM unit would help to bring together the required expertise. If the dedicated PIM unit is established outside the finance ministry, all of the arguments relating to the planning ministry apply. Where the PIM unit is established in the finance ministry, issues will arise concerning its location within the ministry, its responsibilities, and its powers.

If the PIM unit is placed outside the budget department of the finance ministry, its remit needs to be tightly circumscribed in order to avoid coordination issues and intra-agency rivalries; dual-budgeting problems, for example, could emerge if the PIM unit is given significant responsibilities relating to capital budgeting. Limiting the PIM unit's responsibilities to strategic guidance and quality-at-entry activities will help to avoid this problem. In weaker institutional contexts, however, placing the PIM unit outside the budget department could potentially leave it isolated, without influence, and unable to command adequate financial and human resources to establish its reputation (as has been the case in Romania). For many countries, therefore, placing the PIM unit within the budget department or having it report to the budget director may ensure sufficient authority and adequate resourcing.

Table 4.2 summarizes the organizational arrangements and responsibilities of public investment units in five countries that are generally recognized as having good PIM practices. The first thing to note is the diversity of organizational arrangements, which range from New Zealand's unit, located under the budget director in the Finance Ministry, to Korea's Public and Private Infrastructure Investment Management Center (PIMAC), an independent think-tank with important PIM responsibilities. In spite of this diversity of location and reporting lines, the units have similar responsibilities with respect to public investment management, none of which include direct involvement in capital budgeting. These responsibilities include undertaking or coordinating independent reviews of major projects and acting as a center of excellence for the development and dissemination of best-practice assessment methodologies. Units in France, New Zealand, and the United Kingdom also have broader portfolio-monitoring roles for major projects. Their roles are all advisory; decision-making power lies elsewhere.

Even in countries with advanced PIM systems, the creation of a dedicated public investment unit is a relatively recent phenomenon, which can be explained by the following:

- Renewed focus on closing infrastructure deficits, perceived as inhibiting economic growth

TABLE 4.2 Public investment units in some countries with advanced PIM frameworks

INDICATOR	FRANCE	IRELAND	NEW ZEALAND	KOREA, REP.	UNITED KINGDOM
Name of PIM unit	General Commission for Investment (Commissariat Général à l'Investissement)	Central Expenditure Evaluation Unit	National Infrastructure Unit	Public and Private Infrastructure Investment Management Center (PIMAC)	Infrastructure and Projects Authority
Date of creation	2010	2006, but preceded by an independent central evaluation unit created in 1996	2009	2005, but preceded by the Public Investment Management Center, which had no responsibilities for public-private partnerships (PPPs)	2016 (from a merger between Infrastructure UK and the Major Projects Authority)
Location or reporting lines	The commissioner general reports to the prime minister	Situated in the Finance Ministry; acted independently until 2011, when it was integrated into the new Ministry for Public Expenditure and Reform	Finance Ministry reports to the director of budget and public investment	PIMAC—an independent organization under the government's think-tank, Korea Development Institute (KDI)—responds to direction and requests from the Ministry of Economy and Finance	Reports jointly to the Economics and Finance Ministry and the Cabinet Office

continued

TABLE 4.2, *continued*

INDICATOR	FRANCE	IRELAND	NEW ZEALAND	KOREA, REP.	UNITED KINGDOM
Summary of PIM responsibilities	Prepares government decisions for contracts between the state and agencies responsible for managing funds under the special program "Investments for the Future" Coordinates the preparation of specifications that accompany the call for projects and checks that they are consistent with the government's action in terms of future investment and the reform of public policy Coordinates the processing of investment projects, including the independent review process, and provides advice on proposals Oversees the evaluation, a priori and a posteriori, of investments, including cost-effectiveness Provides an annual review of the implementation of the public investment program	*As a central evaluation unit,* Offers advice on and sets standards for cost-benefit analysis (Working Rules on Cost-Benefit Analysis 1999 and Capital Appraisal Guidelines 2005) Offers advice on wider evaluation issues—for example, ex post evaluations *As a central expenditure evaluation unit with a wider remit,* Verifies application of the Capital Appraisal Guidelines Promotes value for money across the system, resulting in publication of the online Public Spending Code in 2013	Formulates and monitors progress on a 20-year national infrastructure plan Establishes robust and reliable cross-government frameworks for infrastructure project appraisal and capital asset management; monitors the implementation and use of those frameworks Provides support to, and acts as a secretariat for, the National Infrastructure Advisory Board, representing stakeholders	*Under the direction and supervision of Ministry of Economy and Finance,* Conducts the preliminary feasibility study (PFS) for major projects, according to general and sector-specific guidelines Develops and revises PFS methodologies and manages the PFS database Conducts a reassessment study of feasibility (RSF) for off-track projects Supports the government in developing policies and plans on PPPs and their implementation Conducts value-for-money tests for PPP projects Carries out ex post evaluation of government programs	Develops the government's major projects portfolio, in collaboration with ministries, and reports regularly to ministers Initiates and oversees integrated [quality] assurance and approval planning process for all major projects or programs, in coordination with the Finance Ministry Initiates and oversees mandatory assurance reviews (formerly gateway reviews) for all new projects and programs Escalates concerns to ministers and accounting officers Provides additional assurance and direct involvement where projects are causing concern Works with ministries to build capability in projects and program management Publishes an annual report on major government projects

- Heightened focus on efficiency and effectiveness in response to tighter fiscal constraints following the global financial crisis
- Emergence of a stronger portfolio approach to public investment management, particularly with respect to major projects and public-private partnership projects
- General dissatisfaction with a more decentralized approach, in terms of choice of projects and efficiency of delivery.

OTHER SPECIFIC ISSUES IN ALLOCATION OF ROLES AND RESPONSIBILITIES

Sector or line ministries

Modern public administration is increasingly emphasizing the policy role of line ministries while delegating implementation to arm's-length bodies. These new arrangements may create potential advantages for performance, but it is important to retain minimum capacities within line ministries to review projects that have been proposed, prepared, and appraised by subordinated implementing agencies. Line ministers should see themselves as the "first line of defense" against any lack of strategic focus, weak project rationale, and optimism bias; they should not simply be conduits for channeling unvalidated projects to the central financial and planning authorities. This process will require an adequate planning and investment unit within a line ministry, mirroring the functions of the national public investment unit at the sector level. This unit should also have a monitoring role in the downstream phase. In fact, the line ministry needs to allocate roles and responsibilities internally for the sectors they manage, similar to those in table 4.1.

Worldwide trends toward performance-oriented management and budgeting have tended to shift expenditure decision making to line ministries within firm fiscal constraints. This decentralization is increasing accountability for outcomes, rather than inputs; in relation to capital budgeting, this shift has often meant a decline in project prioritization and decision making at the center of government. As a result, line ministries have to make decisions within aggregate expenditure envelopes, whereby they trade off current and capital expenditures in pursuit of higher-level performance objectives. There has been some dissatisfaction with this approach recently with regard to capital budgeting, especially with major or megaprojects. This dissatisfaction has resulted in the emergence of a stronger role for the center of government in coordinating and prioritizing capital expenditure decisions in some countries with advanced systems, including France, Ireland, Korea, and the United Kingdom.[7] These changes are intended to accomplish the following:

- Ensure greater consistency between national and sector capital expenditure priorities
- Ensure intertemporal consistency of capital expenditure decisions
- Better manage the macrofiscal consequences of major projects or megaprojects and ensure efficient implementation
- Address intersectoral capital expenditure trade-offs at the government level
- Target resources more effectively toward infrastructure bottlenecks
- Improve deliverability and risk management of the overall portfolio of major government projects.

While the broader arguments and approaches for performance-based management and budgeting remain strong, governments need to make note of the risk of tensions between line ministries and the center of government when it comes to capital budgeting for major projects or megaprojects. These tensions can be addressed when designing PIM roles and responsibilities, but this effort should be done sensitively, without undermining the broader performance framework. Capital budgeting is discussed further in chapters 6 and 7.

Coordination with subnational governments

Spending by subnational governments (SNGs) also uses public financial resources, but the extent to which such spending comes under the national PIM system will depend on country-specific constitutional arrangements. Almost by definition, SNGs have a substantial degree of autonomy in decision making and in the decision-making process. However, where central government is funding local government investment using conditional capital grants or cofunding using matching grants, it has leverage to impose good PIM practices. This leverage is much more limited when SNGs benefit from unconditional transfers determined by a formula.

In Georgia, the central government has no power over the expenditure decisions of local assemblies within their constitutional mandates. Nevertheless, the Budget Code does allow the Ministry of Finance to regulate the budget process at any level of the budget system.[8] Specifically, the Ministry of Finance is authorized to issue a capital budgeting methodology.[9] Local governments have autonomy to allocate roles and responsibilities for implementing PIM, guided by advice from the central government, but it is difficult for the central government to control the process.

In contrast to Georgia, Chile requires projects from all levels of government[10] to use the SNI, overseen by the Planning Ministry.[11] In Korea, all major SNG projects are also subject to the national PIM system when they request funding from the central government beyond a certain threshold.

Council of ministers or delegated committee of ministers

The council of ministers or cabinet will be involved in the capital budgeting process. The council, or a delegated committee of ministers, may be involved in selection and prioritization, especially for projects of national significance. It is important that the selection decision does not become the subject of political horse trading, especially in the budgeting process, as an overly politicized project selection process can lead to distorted choices (rubber stamping), whereby the project's actual quality does not figure in the decision-making process. One way to avoid this distortion is to require a positive decision from the finance or planning minister before a project can go to a higher-level body. Another solution is for the finance or planning minister to act as chair and to have the deciding vote. Whatever the case, higher-level decision-making bodies need usable, robust analysis to assist their decisions.

Development partners

Development partners often have their own project appraisal systems, but governments should not cede too many core roles and responsibilities to organizations operating outside the national system.

National players should perform the roles and responsibilities for preappraisal, even if development partners have equivalent systems. This arrangement is important for national ownership and strategic relevance.

At appraisal and selection, development partners are also likely to be involved in managing and funding appraisal activities, which they will use to decide on the social profitability of a project. They are not immune to optimism bias and, where possible, national authorities need to ensure that they subject donor project appraisals to rigorous independent review; national authorities should also be involved in steering the appraisal process because they need to make the final selection decision, without which no project should proceed. To ensure consistency, government- and donor-funded projects should use the same tracks for decision making.

Capital budgeting should be the preserve of national authorities, and development-partner projects should not be allowed to proceed without prior approval from the budget process—even if a project does not intend to use the national financial management system. The established roles and responsibilities for capital budgeting should apply equally to all projects, regardless of funding source.

Use of consultants

Contracting out analytical tasks is an important way to obtain expertise that the public sector typically lacks. Consultants are frequently used to prepare projects and fulfill the "appraiser" role in countries at all levels of PIM system development. When this is the case, governments need to ensure that the public sector has adequate capacity to (a) prepare adequate terms of reference; (b) fulfill a proactive client role toward consultants; (c) maintain active engagement with internal and external stakeholders; and (d) be able to interpret and communicate appraisal results to reviewers and decision makers. Weaknesses in these areas tend to result in weak project preparation and assessment and poorly informed decision making.

The proposer needs to maintain ownership of a project to ensure the following:

- The rationale is robust and consistently applied.
- The project design is in line with the original concept.
- All sensible options for addressing the identified need have been considered.

Too often, clients do not give consultants enough direction, resulting in suboptimal project design, supported by appraisal documentation that serves more as justification of a decision already made than as an aid to decision making. Irrespective of the source of funding, proposers need to be active rather than passive clients, and this recommendation applies to both donor- and government-funded projects.

Proposers can build and retain ownership by taking control of the preappraisal stage, acting as both proposer and appraiser. If they need to bring in external expertise at this stage, such expertise should be integrated into the proposer's preappraisal team, rather than being contracted out entirely. At the appraisal stage, the proposer should retain responsibility for preparing summary documentation and recommendations for decision makers and not contract out these tasks. This issue may seem minor, but preparation of such documentation helps to foster stronger engagement.

Consultants can also be used to support or carry out the reviewer role. In Norway, consultants employed through framework contracts are used to assist the Ministry of Finance in its reviewer role as part of the country's two-step quality-at-entry process for major projects.[12] In France, the General Commission for Investment (table 4.2) is able to contract individual private sector experts to create teams to conduct independent reviews of major projects.

Where a public investment unit performs the role of reviewer, it needs to have an adequate budget for ad hoc external support in specialist areas where it cannot be expected to retain permanent in-house experts.

Too much reliance on consultants can be problematic, leading to the stalled development or hollowing out of government capacities. In the United Kingdom, excessive reliance on external consultants in key project management roles led to a dearth of project leadership expertise in the public sector. This lack of expertise is being rectified, following establishment of the Major Projects Leadership Academy.

NOTES

1. In Korea, the threshold for major projects is legislated explicitly in the National Finance Act.
2. Some countries choose to apply the same methods to all projects, but vary the degree of effort involved according to project value or novelty.
3. The "dual-budgeting" problem is one of process, not presentation: there are good reasons for clearly separating recurrent and capital expenditures in the budget presentation, provided expenditures are classified properly. However, presentation of a separate development budget covering donor-funded expenditures in aid-dependent countries is problematic, as it often includes a mixture of current and capital expenditures and may use a different classification from the current budget (which may include domestically funded capital expenditures).
4. A recent survey of a sample of 25 low-income countries found that in 44 percent of cases budget formulation was a shared responsibility, compared with 0 percent in 32 Organisation for Economic Co-operation and Development (OECD) countries (see Allen et al. 2015).
5. The new body was created on January 1, 2016, merging Infrastructure UK with the Major Projects Authority.
6. Recently, following an organizational reform, the superior administration of the SNI now corresponds to the Ministry of Social Development and the Ministry of Finance, through the Budget Directorate. Both institutions are responsible for the system and fulfill specific roles, competencies, and responsibilities regarding public investment.
7. New national infrastructure plans are one indication.
8. Article 7 of Georgia's Budget Code, 2009: "The Minister of Finance of Georgia shall issue relevant legislative acts for the purpose of maintaining integrity of the budgetary process and ensuring compliance with the present Code at any level of the budgetary system of Georgia."
9. Article 9 of Georgia's Budget Code, 2009.
10. Central, provincial, local, and major municipalities.
11. For public investment projects of local municipalities in which they contribute more than 50 percent of the investment amount, however, a technical economic analysis is not necessarily conducted.
12. The two-step process entails (a) quality assurance of the choice of concept, prior to a cabinet decision to proceed to more detailed project preparation; and (b) quality assurance of the management base and cost estimate, prior to a decision by parliament to fund the project.

REFERENCES

Allen, R., Y. Hurcan, P. Murphy, M. Queyranne, and S. Yläoutinen. 2015. "Evolving Functions and Organization of Finance Ministries." IMF Working Paper WP/15/232, International Monetary Fund, Washington, DC.

Asian Development Bank. 1999. *Managing Government Expenditure*. Manila: Asian Development Bank.

Gómez-Lobo. A. 2012. "Institutional Safeguards for Cost Benefit Analysis: Lessons from the Chilean National Investment System." *Journal of Benefit-Cost Analysis* 3 (1): 1–30.

Tommasi, D. 2010. *Gestion des dépenses publiques dans les pays en développement.* Paris: Agence Française de Développement.

World Bank. 2014. "Study on Cross-Country Comparison: Technical Assistance for Public Investment Project Appraisal and Selection System Development in Ukraine." World Bank, Washington, DC.

5

Designing the Project Appraisal and Selection System

QUALITY-AT-ENTRY PROCESSES

OVERVIEW

Within the upstream part of the public investment management (PIM) system, quality-at-entry processes ensure that projects proceeding to an implementation decision have been properly vetted as a socially profitable use of public financial resources and that there is no better way to use the financial resources involved.

Quality-at-entry processes combine rigorous analysis with sequenced, disciplined review and decision making. Although the definitions used vary between countries, four distinct processes are involved:

- Preappraisal
- Appraisal
- Independent review
- Project selection.

These processes act together as a filtering system, with projects passing through finer and finer sieves to arrive at those that are eligible to be considered for funding.

PREAPPRAISAL

Why carry out a preappraisal?

By the time a project reaches appraisal (involving a preliminary design and feasibility study), planning will already have gathered momentum, and it may be difficult to stop the project from being implemented. Preappraisal provides an opportunity to address weak concepts before they advance too far in the planning process or before they have gained too much political commitment.[1] Preappraisal is especially important for politically driven "white elephant" projects, which should be culled as early as possible. At preappraisal, projects undergo preliminary screening; those assessed worthy of further study are allowed to proceed to appraisal.

Preappraisal introduces gradualism into the assessment process as a whole, creating space for reflection on the declared merits of a project, its internal logic, and its coherence with government and sector strategic policy priorities. It also provides an opportunity to consider alternative solutions to the reference project. The aim should be to reduce a long list of alternatives to a short list of several alternatives for further analysis alongside the reference project.

Appraisal is costly and a waste of public resources if a project is conspicuously likely to be stopped at this stage anyway; preappraisal presents an opportunity to make the system for selecting PIM projects more efficient.

What does a preappraisal involve?

Preappraisal usually begins with drawing up a project concept note (or equivalent), which forms the basis for the preappraisal decision. This process encourages project promoters to give substance to their proposal and to verify that it satisfies minimum criteria before committing resources to preparation. The components of the concept note and the related preappraisal criteria may differ from country to country, but verification of strategic relevance must be at the core of preappraisal. A comprehensive preappraisal process may involve the following steps.

Checking the project rationale

The project needs to address the identified problem or emerging demand; the logic behind the assumed cause-effect relations needs to make sense. Projects that are tangential to the problem at hand should be dropped and alternatives identified.

Verifying strategic relevance

Good project ideas may not necessarily be consistent with government or sector strategic priorities, and it is not worth taking strategically irrelevant projects beyond the concept stage (the strategic allocation of resources, as described in table 2.1). Determining strategic relevance depends on well-specified, realistic, and authoritative strategic guidance—the first of the eight key features of a good PIM system (see figure 2.2 and chapter 6).

Making an order-of-magnitude assessment of costs and benefits

Preappraisal is not expected to include a quantified cost-benefit analysis, which usually forms part of an appraisal, but it is possible to make rough estimates of costs and to weigh these costs against the likely benefits and demand. The aim is to identify and stop obvious outliers where experience shows that social profitability is extremely unlikely. An effective PIM system examines evidence from ex post evaluations of similar completed projects.

Ensuring that a full range of alternatives is considered

Good appraisal involves comparing the reference project to a small set of reasonable project alternatives; preappraisal provides an opportunity to verify that a sufficiently wide range of alternatives has been considered (including those not involving capital expenditures) and that the more promising will be taken forward to appraisal.

Slowing down unaffordable project concepts and managing the project pipeline

Preappraisal allows central financial authorities to take a view on affordability and to control the flow of projects under preparation and queuing for available fiscal space.

Checking sustainability issues

However promising the project concept, success will hinge on whether the project can be delivered as planned and then operated on a sustainable basis. Preappraisal provides an opportunity to consider the capacities of implementing and operating entities and to examine the adequacy of funding for future operation and maintenance. Clear evidence of insurmountable problems would be a cause for not proceeding, but it is more likely that preappraisal will identify sustainability issues and ensure that appropriate strengthening measures form part of later project design and preparation.

Identifying potential risks and constraints

Preappraisal does not require a full-scale risk analysis; however, early identification of potential risks allows for proper assessment and planning for risk management during the next stage. Insurmountable constraints, such as environmental restrictions or international obligations, must be identified before resources are dedicated to appraisal.

Flagging potential for adopting public-private partnerships

Preappraisal is too early to decide on the procurement-financing modality, but any projects with characteristics that make them conducive to public-private partnerships (PPPs) can be identified, and additional assessments can be planned for the appraisal stage.[2]

Planning for appraisal

The process of preparing a concept note is essential groundwork for appraisal. The issues raised, especially concerning sustainability and risk, should guide the preparation of terms of reference for the feasibility study, which should follow a positive preappraisal decision.

Preappraisal is generally a lighter and technically less demanding form of assessment than a prefeasibility study. If a prefeasibility study is required, it should follow the preappraisal and involve deeper analysis. In many countries, prefeasibility studies are optional—depending on project size, risk, or novelty—whereas preappraisal should be obligatory. Prefeasibility studies are discussed below in the context of appraisal.

Issues to be considered in designing a preappraisal process

The comprehensive preappraisal process just described is the "full-scope" model. It is similar to that of the United Kingdom, where the preappraisal equivalent is known as the strategic outline case (SOC). This discussion emphasizes the strategic case, but economic, commercial, financial, and management cases are also considered. The U.K. case is examined in more detail in chapter 6. Formats for project concept notes in Colombia and the Republic of Korea, which have narrower coverage than the United Kingdom, are illustrated in box 5.1.

BOX 5.1

Examples of formats for project concept notes

Although the detail varies between countries, information requirements for project concept notes are generally similar, covering the nature of the problem to be addressed, the urgency of the need, the rationale for the proposed solution, and the links with national and sector strategies. Colombia and Korea provide examples of two formats for project concept notes, with the former representing the minimum requirement.

Colombia: identification stage

- Identification of the current situation and the expected future situation
- Diagnosis of the problem or the need to be addressed, including identification of the target population and their social and economic characteristics
- Rationale for the project solution and its objectives
- Identification of alternative solutions.

Korea: written request for preliminary feasibility study

- Draft project plan, including
  - Project purpose
  - Related developments and scale of the project
  - Estimated total project costs
  - Implementation system
  - Financing method
  - Anticipated benefits.
- Need for project implementation
- Adequacy of likely central government subsidy (affordability)
- Amount and financing method of necessary resources
- Potential contribution to balanced regional development ("need for technological development" in the case of a research-and-development project)
- Risks associated with project implementation and mitigation measures.

The importance of defining roles and responsibilities is discussed in chapter 4 (see table 4.2). Responsibility for the preappraisal decision needs to be assigned carefully, and the decision needs to be documented properly. Who makes the decision may have implications for project coding in the national public investment database, where one exists. If the central financial authorities are responsible for the preappraisal decision (at least for major projects), preappraisal is the time to issue a unique project code. This code could also serve budget management and accounting purposes for future project preparation work. Coding at this stage is less obvious if the preappraisal decision is made at the level of line ministries or agencies.

Flagging potential PPP projects is an advantage of a preappraisal but should not be seen as a point of departure for creating a separate track for PPP project assessments. As already indicated (see chapter 2), PPP projects should be subject to the same upstream processes as traditionally procured projects, up to and including an appraisal.

Given the extended preparation time for major projects and the lack of direct synchronization between preappraisal and budgeting, it is difficult to reach a definitive conclusion on affordability at the preappraisal stage; however, taking account of broad fiscal trends, the number of high-value projects that can be funded over the medium to long terms should be reasonably evident, particularly for megaprojects, where delivery capacity should also be taken into consideration. The conclusions may require putting some strategically relevant and potentially economically viable projects in a "holding position" rather than moving straight to appraisal.[3] Affordability issues are dealt with in more depth in chapter 6.

A balance needs to be struck between a country's procedural guidelines and methodological guidance when it comes to preappraisal. Procedural guidelines should provide the broad outline of the process and assign roles and responsibilities; methodological guidance should detail the technical methods and provide templates as annexes.

APPRAISAL

Why carry out an appraisal?

Appraisal activities create the analytical basis for making an informed decision on whether a project is viable from a societal perspective—that is, whether it is the most "socially profitable" use of the public financial resources required. Social profitability is not enough for a project to proceed if the sustainable delivery of benefits is in question; an appraisal therefore also provides the basis for assessing the long-term sustainability of the project from financial, budgetary, environmental, social, and managerial perspectives.

What does an appraisal involve?

An appraisal involves preparing a feasibility study or the equivalent. A feasibility study should have both technical and economic dimensions and be supported by a preliminary technical or engineering design for the project, including cost estimates and detailed forecasts of demand for the services provided by the asset to be created or improved. The economic feasibility study examines the social profitability of the project, analyzing market effects and nonmarket social and environmental effects.[4]

The economic feasibility study needs to compare whole-life cost and benefit streams for the reference project with a short list of technically feasible alternatives, including the status quo, to determine which project will provide the highest net benefits to society.[5] Alternatives may include technical variants of the reference project as well as alternative technical solutions. For major projects, a prefeasibility study will help decision makers to decide which of the possible technical solutions to take forward into a feasibility study.[6]

Preparation of an economic feasibility study involves the application of different methodological tools, in isolation or in combination, depending on the nature of the project and its societal costs and benefits. The main tools are social cost-benefit analysis, cost-effectiveness analysis, and multicriteria analysis. The feasibility study should be seen as an input into the appraisal process, resulting in a decision on the social worth and sustainability of a project. An appraisal should be structured around a series of sequential steps.

Social cost-benefit analysis

Social cost-benefit analysis (SCBA), also known as economic cost-benefit analysis, is the default tool for determining the social profitability of a project. SCBA looks at the project from the perspective of the welfare of society as a whole and includes costs and benefits that do not involve market transactions (for example, positive or negative externalities or public goods). Financial cost-benefit analysis, in contrast, looks at the project from the narrower perspective of the operating entity. This difference is often poorly understood by project planners, decision

TABLE 5.1 **Differences between financial and social cost-benefit analysis**

INDICATOR	FINANCIAL ANALYSIS	SOCIAL ANALYSIS
Perspective	Agency, organization, firm	Economy, society
Objective	Analyze the net financial impact of the proposal on the agency	Maximize the social returns to the economy's resources
Pricing	Market prices	Shadow prices to correct for distortions and opportunity costs
Transfer payments (taxes and subsidies)	Included	Usually excluded
Equity and distributional effects	Excluded	Can be included, but usually treated qualitatively
Externalities and values of public goods	Excluded	Included
Depreciation	Excluded (from discounted cash-flow analysis, but included in financial statements)	Excluded

Source: Adapted from Commonwealth of Australia 2006.

makers, and the public,[7] but it is very important, since public policy is concerned with aggregate social welfare, not just narrow profitability. The main differences between the two are summarized in table 5.1. SCBA is central to appraisal, but financial analysis is also required to assess the financial sustainability and profitability of revenue-generating public investment projects. A country's methodological guidelines should cover both types of analysis.

If all costs and benefits, including those for which there are no direct market transactions, can be readily estimated in monetary terms, the results of a social cost-benefit analysis will be sufficient to determine social profitability. Depending on the sector, some significant costs and benefits may not be feasible to value in monetary terms; they will need to be taken into account when reaching a final decision on social profitability. In these cases, a qualitative assessment of the relative importance of these nonmonetized costs and benefits will be required. In some instances, nonmonetized effects may be judged important enough to overturn the findings of the SCBA. Ideally, risk should be quantified and reflected in monetary terms in the SCBA findings, which would then be expressed as expected values.[8] Such quantification may not always be possible; in such cases, the relative scale of risk of each alternative will have to be assessed qualitatively when determining economic feasibility.

Multicriteria analysis

Multicriteria analysis (MCA) can help to structure the qualitative assessment of the nonmonetized costs and benefits of project alternatives, particularly when the array of effects to be considered is complicated. Care is required when providing methodological guidance, as MCA does not provide an absolute measure of costs or benefits, just a ranking of alternatives according to predetermined criteria; therefore, combining it with the results of SCBA to form a single indicator should generally be avoided. However scientific its design might appear and whatever guidance is given on limiting subjectivity, MCA is also based on subjective assessments against specified criteria. It should be seen as providing an additional piece of information to be used alongside SCBA when deciding on the overall worth of a project.

Cost-effectiveness analysis

Where none of a project's benefits can be easily valued and where project alternatives produce the same or very similar outputs (that is, public services), cost-effectiveness analysis (CEA) can be used to compare alternatives and choose the least costly option.[9] CEA can also be used to determine the least-cost solution for meeting a legally mandated public service obligation, when measuring benefits becomes irrelevant because not providing the mandated service is not an alternative.[10] The problem with CEA is that, unlike SCBA, it does not give an absolute measure of a project's social worth; a qualitative assessment must be made as to whether the posited benefits exceed the costs (of the most cost-effective option). In many areas of the public sector, particularly in the social sectors, CEA may turn out to be the most suitable tool. MCA may be used alongside CEA to examine benefits, but the results should not be combined in a single indicator, as with the results of SCBA.

Testing the rationale for PPP: Value-for-money assessment

A project not flagged as a potential PPP during the preappraisal stage may be flagged as such at the appraisal stage if assessment of the project's costs and benefits finds significant PPP potential. A further step in the appraisal process should examine the rationale for flagging a project as a potential PPP. It is performed for those projects with PPP potential, whether this potential is identified at preappraisal or appraisal. It is only performed for projects with PPP potential that have been positively assessed at earlier steps.

Projects for which the rationale for PPP is assessed to be solid will proceed to a more in-depth, value-for-money assessment. When a project is initially flagged as a potential PPP, the following factors should be considered: (a) value for money of the potential PPP, (b) institutional capacity for procuring and managing PPP contracts, and (c) institutional justification for long-term constraints on possible changes to public policy. Further discussions regarding the corresponding check points for guiding the choice of PPP structure as part of a unified PIM framework are provided separately in chapter 10.

Stepwise appraisal analytics

The appraisal process is usually conceptualized as a series of steps. While there are variations, good-practice countries tend to envisage a similarly sequenced process.[11] The following is an amalgamation of this experience:

- *Step 1.* Define project objectives and scope
- *Step 2.* Identify and choose project alternatives for appraisal
- *Step 3.* Demonstrate demand for the services of the project
- *Step 4.* Perform financial analysis
- *Step 5.* Perform economic analysis
- *Step 6.* Analyze risks and risk management
- *Step 7.* Assess environmental and social sustainability of the project
- *Step 8.* Assess implementation and handover arrangement
- *Step 9.* Identify the preferred project alternative and make recommendations to decision makers.

The sequencing in this process is helpful, but it should not be so rigid as to exclude some iteration as the analysis develops. It may, for example, be necessary to go back and develop more accurate estimates of the costs and benefits of a more promising project alternative revealed at step 5. Guidelines should allow for, and indeed encourage, some flexibility in this respect.

The nine steps cover the sequenced analytical work to inform a decision on the social worth of a capital investment project and its long-term sustainability. Balanced and consistent decision making depends on systematic application of these steps during project appraisal; the main technical instrument is the feasibility study. While the detailed content and any supporting studies may be project or sector specific, the overall analytical framework for a feasibility study should reflect these steps.

Step 1. Define project objectives and scope

Step 1 is a review and confirmation of the project concept note (or equivalent), as introduced in the discussion of the preappraisal stage. It includes a review of the project's rationale and strategic case and a description of the project's goal (higher-level objective), purpose (central objective), results or outputs (deliverables), and activities (actions to deliver outputs).

The strategic relevance of the project is central to the project concept note and a core criterion for the preappraisal decision. The continued strategic relevance of the project will need to be verified to take account of any changes in policy direction that may have occurred at the government or ministry level; in the event of such changes, the strategic case for the project should be reviewed.

Once the problem and rationale for government intervention are justified, it is important to have a clear statement of the objectives of the project so that appropriate alternatives for achieving them can be considered.

For appraisal, the scope described in the project concept note must be reviewed and given more detail. This process involves setting out all of the project outputs—that is, what will be delivered by the project upon completion and what are the main activities required to accomplish these outputs.

Step 2. Identify and choose project alternatives for appraisal

Project appraisal involves comparing the life-cycle costs and benefits of the reference project with feasible project alternatives. Project planners should refine the alternatives that have been short-listed in the preappraisal stage and should be open to introducing new alternatives that may have been ignored at preappraisal. These options will then undergo further analysis in the feasibility study.

An analysis period must be determined and should correspond to the useful life of the fixed asset created. Table 5.2 presents reference analysis periods by sector, as recommended by the European Commission. Longer periods may be considered for long-lived assets or for projects with long-term effects, especially environmental effects.

Step 3. Demonstrate the demand for the services of the project

Rigorous demand analysis is at the heart of a good project appraisal; it is essential for designing appropriately sized capital assets, with the necessary capacity for current and future users, and for making reliable cost and benefit estimates for the project.

As part of project appraisal, promoters must develop a quantified forecast of the expected demand for project services, including the expected growth in demand over the lifetime of the project. Depending on the nature of the project,

TABLE 5.2 **Reference analysis periods for a project, by sector**

SECTOR	NUMBER OF YEARS
Railways	30
Roads	25–30
Ports and airport	25
Urban transport	25–30
Water supply and sanitation	30
Waste management	25–30
Energy	15–25
Broadband	15–20
Business infrastructure	10–15
Other sectors	10–15

Source: European Commission 2014.

these forecasts may cover such aspects as school enrollment, hospital caseloads, road traffic, water consumption, and solid waste production.

The level of detail in demand forecasts may vary according to the scale of the project and the extent to which it is innovative. Excessively optimistic demand forecasts are a worldwide cause of poor public investment decisions. This systematic phenomenon, referred to as optimism bias, should be avoided wherever possible, and it is advisable to subject demand forecasts to independent external scrutiny, especially for major projects.

Step 4. Perform financial analysis

A financial analysis should be performed to estimate profitability and financial sustainability. Project promoters should verify that projects are financially affordable and sustainable, both during implementation and during operation. For projects carried out by profit-oriented public enterprises, investments should also be shown to be profitable compared to other alternative investments. Profit maximization may not be an objective for publicly owned enterprises with wider public policy objectives, but their investments generally should be shown to be financially sustainable; if they are not, the budget subsidies required to make them so should be determined. Budgetary analysis is often performed to examine fiscal impact and affordability as well.

Financial analysis to determine project profitability and sustainability. Financial analysis is applicable to revenue-earning projects—for example, investments by energy and water utilities or by public transport operators. Meaningful financial analysis may not be feasible for nonrevenue-earning projects—for example, in health, education, or justice—but financial issues, such as adequacy of recurrent financing and financial management capacities, should be investigated for nonrevenue projects. These projects are generally the focus of a separate budgetary analysis (see below).

Analysis of the project's financial performance will determine whether the project will make a positive contribution to the financial objectives of the operating entity and whether it is sustainable over the longer term.

Analysis to assess financial sustainability of the operating entity. Financial analysis of the operating entity looks at its overall financial strength and its capacity to deal with any negative cash-flow requirements of the project. It also examines the need for subsidies from the state budget.

Usually, a capital investment project will be carried out by an existing entity, which will be performing other ongoing operations. In these cases, the financial analysis of the entity as a whole will be relevant to assessing financial sustainability; a profitable project undertaken by a financially weak entity is unlikely to be sustainable. Sometimes a project is carried out in isolation and a new entity is created to operate it: in these cases, the two dimensions of financial analysis—project level and entity level—effectively merge into one.

Budgetary analysis as an input to assessing budget affordability. Budgetary analysis is required for all projects to determine the net impact on the national budget during implementation and operation and to help to determine whether an investment is fiscally affordable. It assesses affordability in relation to projections of expenditure ceilings and available fiscal space during budget preparation.

The minimum requirements for demonstrating budgetary impact are shown in table 5.3, which identifies total budgetary costs, projected revenues (if any), and net impact. Costs for budgetary impact analysis must be in current prices—that is, adjusted for expected inflation. Economic entities promoting projects should use forward estimates of inflation specified by the finance ministry to ensure consistency. If annual operating and maintenance costs are expected to be similar year on year, the postimplementation analysis period can be truncated, and estimated annual averages may be presented post–year 7.

Full budgetary analysis can be used to estimate the total budgetary impact in present value terms, to learn if it is positive overall. This analysis is wider in its perspective than financial analysis (but not as wide as economic analysis), as it takes account of all direct and indirect financial flows that affect public finances—not just those that affect the project's operating entity. A full budgetary impact analysis should only be prepared for major projects with significant direct revenue-earning potential or substantial tax effects.

Step 5. Perform economic analysis

Economic analysis is the core element of project appraisal, providing the means to assess the economic viability of a project and to rank project alternatives on the basis of net economic benefit so as to facilitate the efficient allocation of resources. It involves assessing the costs and benefits of investment projects in economic terms—that is, looking beyond the narrower effects on the

TABLE 5.3 **Template for summary budgetary analysis**

COSTS	YEAR 1	YEAR 2	YEAR...	YEAR 7	POST-YEAR 7
Budgetary costs					
Capital costs					
Net recurrent costs[a]					
Operations					
Maintenance					
Total costs					
Projected direct budgetary revenues (if any)[a]					
Net budgetary impact					

a. Allowing for any cost savings related to the investment.

financial position of the operating entity to include costs and benefits to society as a whole, including those for which there are no directly observable market prices. As discussed, the two techniques mainly used for economic analysis are social cost-benefit analysis[12] and cost-effectiveness analysis.

Economic analysis has three stages:

- Identify relevant costs and benefits
- Estimate the value of relevant costs and benefits
- Calculate net present values (or net present costs).

Identify relevant costs and benefits. The main types of relevant costs and benefits should be identified, including those that are difficult to value. Evaluations should be based on the additional cost to the state of undertaking the particular project; costs that would have been incurred anyway should be excluded. The stream of costs should cover the life of the proposed investment item.

The degree of accuracy in identifying costs will vary with the significance of the project and the availability of data. Assumptions underlying all capital and recurrent cost estimates should be made explicit in the evaluation, including assumptions regarding real labor costs, real energy costs, demand growth, or real charges and rates.

Costs and benefits estimates need to be undertaken on a consistent basis to enable meaningful comparisons to be made between competing projects.

A distinction should be made between identification and analysis of the environmental and social costs and benefits and assessment of the differential impacts of these costs and benefits. Environmental and social costs and benefits should be identified, valued, and included in the calculation of costs and benefits as part of the economic analysis, wherever possible. If this calculation is not possible, every effort should be made to quantify costs and benefits in terms of their scale and the number of people affected, even if it is not feasible to monetize them.

Estimate the value of relevant costs and benefits. The values of all relevant costs and benefits should be estimated in real terms. Where feasible, costs and benefits, including social effects or environmental externalities, should be given monetary values. They should also be accounted for when monetary values cannot be estimated.

The following are some basic principles for valuing costs and benefits:

- *Proportionality.* Depending on the nature of the project, valuing costs and benefits can be resource intensive, requiring surveys and in-depth analytical work. It is not generally expected, therefore, that the same depth of research and analysis will be carried out for a project costing.
- *Incremental costs and benefits.* Costs and benefits should be estimated incrementally compared to the status quo alternative: relevant costs are those above what would be spent without the project, and relevant benefits are those received above what would be delivered without the project.
- *Use of market prices.* While adjustments may have to be made, the default assumption is that market prices are the best starting point for valuing costs and benefits. They are expected to be a good reflection of opportunity costs such as labor and land, unless there is a clear market failure or distortion.

- *Use of real prices.* Costs and benefits should be expressed in real terms (that is, excluding the effects of general inflation) and valued in the prices of a common base year, declared in advance to all analysts and decision makers. The base year is usually the current year.
- *Adjustment for taxes, subsidies, and transfers that are likely to affect the choice of the preferred alternative in a material way.* Indirect taxes, subsidies, and social transfers do not equate to the consumption or creation of economic resources; they represent the redistribution of resources from one part of society to another (from households to government and from government to households). As such, they should be excluded from the valuation of costs and benefits.

Calculate net present value (or net present costs). Net present value (NPV) is the difference between the streams of costs and benefits of a project, discounted to their present value. The use of net present value facilitates comparison between project alternatives with different profiles of costs and benefits. For a cost-effective analysis, the present value should be provided for costs alone.

Discounting takes account of the fact that initial investment costs are borne up front, while benefits and operating costs may extend far into the future; it reflects the concept of social time preference of money, which is relevant even in the absence of inflation. The use of real interest rates—that is, with the effect of inflation removed—reflects this time preference. The calculation of present value requires the use of a discount rate. All ministries, departments, and agencies in the government sector should use a centrally defined social discount rate for this purpose. Estimation of the social discount rate is considered below and in appendix B.

In a social cost-benefit analysis, NPV is the preferred decision criterion. Complementary decision criteria such as the economic internal rate of return and benefit-cost ratio can also assist in decision making. A project is viable if the NPV is greater than zero—that is, the total discounted value of benefits is greater than the total discounted costs. For cost-effectiveness analysis, net present cost (NPC) is the key decision criterion used to rank projects and to show the lowest-cost alternative.

In step 5, cost-benefit analysis looks at the dimensions of a project that can be expressed in monetary terms. Significant costs or disbenefits and benefits that cannot be monetized should be identified and taken into account in the recommendations.

Step 6. Analyze risks and risk management

The results of project appraisal are subject to various types of risks; the extent of the analysis of these risks should be commensurate with the nature of the issues involved. NPV (and NPC) calculations are performed as if the underlying values of costs and benefits are certain; but in the real world, these values will be uncertain as a result of unavoidable errors and perfectly reasonable assumptions that do not turn out as anticipated. Quantified economic analysis is therefore not complete without a systematic analysis of a project's risks and an assessment of their likelihood and impact.

A risk is an uncertain event or condition that, if it occurs, has a positive or negative effect on a project. Risks exist as a consequence of uncertainty concerning key parameters of a project (for example, cost, implementation time, demand).

Risk analysis and risk management represent a structured approach to identifying, assessing, and controlling risks that could emerge during a project's life cycle. Risks can be categorized according to the following list:

- *Construction risk.* The asset is not completed on time, to budget, or to specification.
- *Demand risk.* Demand for services does not meet forecasts.
- *Design risk.* Design cannot deliver services at the required performance or quality.
- *Economic risk.* Project costs or benefits are affected by economic events, such as inflation or exchange rate movements.
- *Environmental risk.* Environmental impacts may have a negative effect on air, water, or land quality and may give rise to public objection.
- *Funding risk.* Availability of funding delays the project or changes its scope.
- *Legislative risk.* Changes in legislation increase costs—for example, a tightening of environmental standards.
- *Operation and maintenance risk.* Costs of operating and maintaining a new facility deviate from the planned budget.
- *Procurement risk.* There is a shortfall in contractor capacities, or contractual disputes arise.
- *Technological risk.* Services provided use less-than-optimal technology because of rapid technological change.

Risk analysis will begin at the preappraisal stage when the project concept note is drawn up and will be extended to quantitative risk analysis as part of project appraisal. At a minimum, quantitative risk analysis should involve sensitivity analysis or the calculation of switching values.[13] More advanced quantitative analysis should be employed for major projects or highly innovative projects that are likely to be replicated. This analysis involves measuring the uncertainty attaching to critical parameters—such as cost, time, and demand estimates—and the stochastic combination of individual uncertainties to arrive at an expected outcome for the project.[14] Getting the right balance in risk analysis is discussed further below and in appendix B.

Risk management involves formulating management responses to the main risks. The immediate response is to alter the project plan so that the identified risks are mitigated or removed. The contingency response is to make provision in the project plan for actions to be implemented only if any of the identified negative risks materialize.

Step 7. Assess environmental and social sustainability of the project

The notion of sustainability extends beyond financial and budgetary sustainability. Project appraisal should verify that projects are environmentally sustainable and that they do not have unduly unbalanced impacts on different groups in society that could jeopardize their social sustainability. Decision makers will need to receive adequate evidence on the environmental and social sustainability of a project and be made aware of any significant risks that could threaten sustainability.

Infrastructure projects frequently have significant environmental and social impacts arising from construction and operation. Depending on the scale and nature of the project and the likely importance of these effects, a formal environmental or social impact assessment may be necessary. In certain cases, an environmental impact assessment will be required by law.

Preliminary environmental and social impact assessments will need to be conducted early in the appraisal stage, prior to completion of the feasibility study, so that findings can be incorporated in the economic analysis and broader feasibility assessment.[15] Significant environmental and social costs and benefits should be accounted for in monetary terms in the economic analysis at step 5, where feasible. Failing this, they should be identified in quantitative or qualitative terms, and their relative importance should be compared to monetized benefits and costs, as assessed at step 5.

It is not usual to provide comprehensive guidance on how to conduct environmental and social impact assessments as part of the main procedural and methodological guidance for appraisal. These specialized areas are typically governed by their own specific methodologies and are usually performed by specialized practitioners; box 5.2 summarizes approaches to environmental and social impact assessments.

Step 8. Assess implementation and handover arrangements

Efficient project implementation is enabled by a capable organization, with adequate internal arrangements. Appraisal requires an assessment of the adequacy and sustainability of the proposed implementation and operational arrangements. It should include an assessment of the capacities of the organization(s) responsible for implementing and operating the project, indicating any strengthening measures that will be required before construction or operations commence. An assessment of the following elements is therefore necessary:

- The capabilities of the organization(s) responsible for implementing or operating the project, especially determining the adequacy of human resources to meet estimated needs during implementation and operation, identifying any constraints, and proposing capacity-building measures, where required

- The outline plan and timetable for implementing the project, indicating key milestones in detailed planning, approval, and construction and outlining the steps from a positive appraisal decision to commencement of construction—that is, detailed design, preparation of tender documents, procurement arrangements, environmental and spatial planning approvals, and land acquisition

- Planning for the project management arrangements, including the organizational arrangements and the allocation of responsibilities between the parties involved, indicating whether any part of project management is to be handled externally to the organization promoting the project

- Outline of organizational arrangements and the allocation of responsibilities for operating and maintaining the project once completed, including an assessment of the capabilities of the responsible organization and identification of any requirements for strengthening measures.

BOX 5.2

Performing environmental and social impact assessments

An *environmental impact assessment (EIA)* is a formal planning tool used to assess the potential negative and positive consequences of a project on the human and natural environment and to identify possible mitigation measures or project design improvements to reduce negative impacts. A preliminary EIA should be carried out toward the beginning of project preparation to ensure that potential problems are foreseen and addressed at an early stage of the project's planning and design. The EIA looks at the impact in the project area and in associated areas, such as downstream, groundwater, and ambient air. It examines effects on environmental resources, such as biodiversity, land-use changes, and pollutants, among others. The assessment may need to be supported by a mitigation plan and an environmental monitoring plan.

The following are the main steps in performing an EIA:

- Screening to determine if a project requires an environmental impact assessment
- Scoping to identify potential impacts and legal requirements, identify alternative solutions, and prepare terms of reference
- Assessment and evaluation of impacts and development of alternatives
- Design of monitoring, compliance, enforcement, and auditing arrangements
- Report on the environmental impact statement, including a nontechnical summary for a general audience
- Review of the environmental impact statement, including public consultation
- Decisions on issuing authorizations concerning the acceptability of the environmental impacts.

The following are the minimum reporting requirements for the coverage of an EIA:

- Description of the activity and the potentially affected environment
- Description of alternatives
- Assessment of likely or potential impacts of the activity and alternatives (direct, indirect, cumulative, short-term, and long-term effects)
- Identification and assessment of mitigation measures
- Identification of gaps in knowledge and uncertainties
- Nontechnical summary for decision makers
- Public consultation.

A *social impact assessment (SIA)* is an assessment of a project's potential social consequences. It focuses more on where costs and benefits fall and less on the identification and valuation of these impacts, which are the subject of economic analysis. An SIA will therefore focus on the impacts on income distribution—both between income levels and between geographic areas—on poverty, on unemployment, on gender equality, and on minorities.

An SIA looks at impacts on the communities affected by the project. These impacts could include requirements for resettlement and the associated impact on quality of life and livelihoods. There could also be social impacts related to environmental alteration, such as effects on health and livelihoods. The distributional effects of the project are also examined to see how direct and indirect costs and benefits arising from the project will be distributed among different income groups or social categories. Social impact assessments usually involve affected stakeholders in consultations and in the design of mitigation measures.

Step 9. Identify the preferred project alternative and make recommendations to decision makers

The final step is to identify the preferred alternative based on a comprehensive appraisal of all factors and to arrive at a conclusion on whether to proceed with a project proposal. This decision must be based on a balanced evaluation of the findings of the analyses noted above.

In addition to quantitative economic analysis, the determination of the economic viability of a project should consider intangible benefits and costs that cannot be monetized. The environmental and social impacts of the project need to be considered. Different perspectives of project sustainability during implementation and operation also need to be confirmed.

Project planners should use quantitative economic analysis to decide whether the reference project is preferred over the alternatives considered, including retaining the status quo. The robustness of the quantitative economic analysis needs to be taken into account.

A two-stage appraisal judgment process is recommended for projects, for which NPV has been calculated:

- *Stage 1.* Take a position on the economic viability of the project, according to quantified economic analysis, at step 5
- *Stage 2.* Adjust this position according to the sustainability factors addressed—financial, fiscal, environmental, and social—and taking into account the importance of costs and benefits that may not have been captured in monetary terms but have been analyzed qualitatively at other steps.

Findings from and recommendations of this analysis should be presented in a project appraisal summary table, which is an aid to making an informed judgment and an important tool for presenting the basis for recommendations to decision makers.

Recommendations should be based on findings with respect to economic viability and include findings on risk, affordability, sustainability, and nonmonetized effects. When the findings from the economic analysis (stage 1) and analyses of affordability, sustainability, and other intangibles (stage 2) point in the same direction, the recommendation can be considered to be reliable. If the factors considered at stage 2 point in a different direction from the economic analysis, care must be taken with the final recommendation; a full explanation of the reasoning and the relative importance assigned to different factors must be given.

In the case of projects subject to cost-effectiveness analysis, the decision should be based on which project alternative is likely to be the most efficient—that is, is likely to deliver a unit of output at the lowest expected cost. In reaching a final conclusion on whether to proceed with the preferred alternative, an informed position on the scale of benefits relative to costs must be taken, either implicitly in the case of a predetermined and legally binding policy decision to meet a minimum service standard or explicitly when a view is reached on the relative importance of the qualitatively assessed nonmonetized benefits. This step is important when deciding whether the least-cost option represents a better use of public finances than the status quo.

Feasibility study report

A typical feasibility study report might be organized as follows, being mindful that the exact content will depend on the nature and sector of the project:

1. Executive summary
2. Analysis of the existing context for the project
3. Examination of project alternatives
4. Market assessment and demand analysis

5. Summary of technical studies and project costs
6. Spatial planning dimensions of the project
7. Financial analysis
8. Economic analysis
9. Risk analysis and management
10. Environmental and social impacts assessment
11. Implementation and operational arrangements
12. Conclusions on project feasibility.

Making a distinction between the appraisal process and the preparation of a feasibility study may seem artificial, but it is important. The feasibility study is a piece of analytical work that may be, and often is, contracted out; the appraisal process must be managed by the public sector, so that the resulting appraisal decision is "owned" by the responsible public sector body. In this respect, public sector officers' preparation of a formal "appraisal report," which uses input from the feasibility study, should be seen as an important conclusion to the appraisal process.

Key issues in designing an appraisal process

Prescribing the range of project alternatives, including "do nothing" or "do the minimum"

Project proposers and appraisers need guidance on identifying project alternatives. Some countries suggest the number of alternatives that should be examined. The United Kingdom's guidelines suggest about a dozen options for the long list considered at preappraisal and three to four options for the short list considered at appraisal (HM Treasury 2013). These guidelines may be overly prescriptive; for simpler investment ideas, it may be difficult to generate so many alternatives for the long list. Failure to examine alternatives is frequent when appraising infrastructure projects, which often are highly specified, engineering-led solutions.[16]

The business-as-usual alternative should generally be equated with doing nothing (the "do-nothing" alternative), but a "do-the-minimum" alternative may also be defined. The latter represents the minimum level of expenditures required to maintain the status quo or to avoid an unacceptable deterioration in public services over the life cycle of the proposed project. An overly specified "do-the-minimum" solution could make gold-plated solutions look more attractive;[17] and it is therefore advisable to require consultation with the PIM coordinating authority when defining a do-the-minimum alternative for major projects.

There are two types of project alternatives: (1) alternative technical solutions for the identified problem and (2) technical variants of a given solution. A technical variant may involve a change in the specification or phasing of different components so that capacity increases more closely to match growth in demand. For example, different possible horizontal alignments for a road project should be considered as alternative technical solutions (as should alternative solutions such as improvements in traffic management, instead of investment in new infrastructure), whereas choices concerning the vertical alignment or strength of the road pavement should be considered as technical variants.[18]

Proportionate appraisal considering the threshold

An appraisal is intensive in its use of financial resources and skills; the effort dedicated to it should be proportionate to the scale of the project. There are different ways of dealing with this issue: either recommend the same methods for all projects, with reduced effort for smaller projects, as in the Netherlands (Ministry of Finance, the Netherlands 2013) and United Kingdom (HM Treasury n.d.), or require more sophisticated methods only for major projects, as in Ireland (see table 5.4). In practice, the second solution may be preferable in low-capacity environments, although careful consideration of the threshold for applying SCBA will be required. Ireland's threshold is high by international standards,[19] and the requirement for SCBA usually kicks in at a lower project cost. The threshold will be country specific, and the decision on where to place it should be based on an analysis of the size distribution of projects by sector and on an assessment of available analytical capacities.[20]

Publication of national methodological guidance

While international organizations have published many excellent textbooks on appraisal and methodologies, it is important to have a recognized national methodology for appraisal to explain how procedural guidelines and the techniques mentioned therein are put into practice. A national methodology is unlikely to differ substantially from international guidance, but it serves to notify stakeholders, at all levels in the system, of the common standards to be applied in the country. It is especially important when consultancy firms are employed to carry out the feasibility studies that underpin project appraisal.

Methodological guidance should be published and made widely available. Box 5.3 lists the content of Ireland's methodological guidance for appraisal as an example of typical guidance in good-practice countries. The guidance is available online as part of the country's Public Spending Code.[21]

As discussed in box 5.4, a general methodological manual is usually supported by sector-specific methodologies. Box 5.4 details Chile's rich set of sector-specific methodologies, supporting the application of its general methodological guidelines.[22] The Republic of Korea has developed a standard guideline and more than 10 sector-specific guidelines. Most good-practice countries do not have such an extensive range of sector-specific methodologies, but it is common practice to have guidelines for key sectors.

Appendix A to this *PIM Reference Guide* provides some useful references for general methodological and sector-specific methodological guidance assembled from international agency and national government sources that governments

TABLE 5.4 Proportionality in the application of assessment tools in Ireland

PROJECT VALUE	(MINIMUM) TYPE OF ASSESSMENT
< €0.5 million	*Simple assessment* for minor projects, such as those involving minor refurbishment works, fit-outs
> €0.5 million < €50 million	*Single appraisal* (combining elements of preliminary appraisal and detailed appraisal)
> €5.0 million < €20.0 million	*Multicriteria analysis* of options
> €20.0 million	*Cost-benefit analysis* or cost-effectiveness analysis (depending on the extent to which monetary values can be estimated for benefits)

BOX 5.3

Content of Ireland's guide to economic appraisal: Carrying out a cost-benefit analysis

- Introduction
- Principles of cost-benefit analysis (CBA)
  - Effectiveness of the public sector
  - Defining the project
  - Defining the benchmark
  - Rationale for a CBA
  - Steps in carrying out a CBA
  - When to carry out a CBA
  - Limitations of a CBA
- Identifying and valuing costs and benefits
  - Identifying costs and benefits
  - Valuing costs (including opportunity cost and shadow pricing)
  - Valuing benefits (including demand analysis and valuing time and lives)
  - Other technical considerations (including treatment of externalities and taxes or transfers)
- Present value and discounting
  - Basics of discounting
  - Selection of discount rate
  - Inflation and interest rates
- Analyzing the options
  - Net present value
  - Benefit-cost ratio
  - Internal rate of return
- Risk and uncertainty
  - Assessing risk and uncertainty
  - Sensitivity analysis
  - Switching values
  - Optimism bias
  - Scenario analysis
  - Monte Carlo analysis
- Presentation and reporting
- Further reading and resources.

Source: Ireland's Public Spending Code, Central Expenditure Evaluation Unit, Department of Public Expenditure and Reform.

can use to develop methodological guidance on SCBA. Governments may still need to make country-specific decisions on certain key issues.

Optional or obligatory prefeasibility study

Methodologically, a prefeasibility study is the same as a feasibility study, but it is based on a more rudimentary project design and generally uses available secondary data, rather than primary data, to test technical and economic feasibility.[23] If primary data are needed, collection will occur on a very limited scale. Cases of both optional and obligatory prefeasibility studies can be found. A prefeasibility study should be a requirement for the most costly and complex projects (megaprojects). Whether it should be a requirement for all major projects may depend on how "major" is defined: if the value threshold is relatively low, an optional prefeasibility study may be advisable. In Korea, an independent agency, the Public and Private Infrastructure Investment Management Center (PIMAC), performs a prefeasibility study (known as the "preliminary feasibility study") for major projects (those more than US$50 million).[24] This study forms part of Korea's successful independent review process, which has more depth than those of many other countries.

Setting the boundaries of the analysis

Projects are analyzed mostly from a national perspective, accounting for benefits and costs to residents of the country. Sometimes, a wider international perspective may be appropriate. In the case of a cross-border cooperation

BOX 5.4

Chile's guidelines on analytical methods

Chile's general methodology for the presentation and appraisal of projects is supported by more than 30 subsector-specific guidelines. As indicated in table B5.4.1, 12 of these guidelines concern the application of social cost-benefit analysis to projects in the subsector, 12 concern the application of cost-effectiveness analysis, and 2 offer the option of SCBA or CEA.

TABLE B5.4.1 **Guidelines**

PRESCRIBED METHODOLOGICAL APPROACH	TYPE OF PROJECT COVERED BY GUIDELINE
Social cost-benefit analysis (SCBA)	1. Airports
	2. Fishing ports
	3. Low standard roads
	4. Fluvial defenses
	5. Public buildings
	6. Multipurpose dams (reference only, not obligatory)
	7. Ancillary investments related to roads
	8. Small airfields
	9. Equipment replacement
	10. Interurban transport
	11. Intermediate roads
	12. Urban roads
Cost-effectiveness analysis (CEA)	1. Drinking water
	2. Replacement of street lighting
	3. Primary health care
	4. Sports facilities
	5. Educational projects
	6. Juvenile housing and detention centers
	7. Police infrastructure and equipment
	8. Jails
	9. Sustainable reconstruction plans
	10. Information technology
	11. Police surveillance
	12. Rural electrification
SCBA or CEA	1. Rainwater drainage
	2. Residential waste management

Sources: Based on Gómez-Lobo 2012, improved and updated on the basis of comments provided by the Ministry of Social Development.

project benefiting two (or more) neighboring countries, it would be appropriate to take into account the benefits and costs accruing to residents of both (all) countries. A government may also wish to take account of global environmental externalities—carbon dioxide emissions, for example—which is a legitimate reason for widening the scope of the analysis.

In the context of a country's regional development policy, projects need to be analyzed carefully. In principle, it is possible to analyze a project from the perspective of a specific (lagging) region within a country; however, benefits to residents of the region in question might actually be losses to residents of another region, making the project less compelling from a national perspective. If it is important to demonstrate the impact of a project on the welfare of a region, this analysis should include the national perspective; national and subnational analytical perspectives should be presented to decision makers so that they can decide on the importance to give to regional effects.

Allowing for the limitations of quantitative economic analysis

SCBA is an attractively "scientific" tool, but its limitations should be recognized and allowed for in the appraisal process. The quantified results of SCBA can give a false sense of accuracy and may ignore or underplay important factors that cannot be monetized. The appraisal process should be designed to leave room for qualitative assessments of important nonmonetized effects. At the same time, qualitative assessments need to carry more weight in an appraisal if they have a quantitative basis; for example, estimates of the number of people or households affected by an environmental nuisance and the level of the nuisance should be given, rather than vague statements about the severity of environmental externalities. Notwithstanding the need to take account of nonmonetized effects, there is greater potential for manipulation of appraisal findings when they rely heavily on qualitative assessments. In such cases it is a good idea to build in heightened independent scrutiny,[25] which can be done by lowering the value threshold for independent review in sectors where such manipulation is likely to happen, as is done in the United Kingdom.[26]

Considering distributional impacts and environmental sustainability

As well as allowing for qualitative assessment of social costs and benefits that are difficult to monetize, the appraisal process also needs to take into account distributional impact: who loses and who gains? This issue is important for assessing social sustainability and consistency with government equity objectives. Box 5.5 presents the Australian government's guidance on the treatment of distributional impacts. The distribution of environmental impacts across society is also important, as is their scale.[27] There may also be negative environmental impacts that do not necessarily affect humans but are particularly sensitive and thus represent potential "no-go" areas or require mitigation measures.[28] These impacts too should be presented separately to decision makers at appraisal.

Key issues in developing an economic appraisal methodology

Appendix B goes into more depth on some technical aspects related to developing an economic appraisal methodology. Key issues are as follows.

Setting national parameter values and considering conversion factors

Governments should ensure that nationally applicable values for key parameters, especially nonmarket effects, are updated regularly and are available for feasibility study preparation. Having updated values will ensure consistent valuation of costs and benefits across projects, rather than having values estimated and reestimated on a case-by-case basis; it also will improve comparability and deliver savings in analytical effort.

Even where there is a market for project inputs and outputs, market prices may not always represent the best basis for estimating a project's economic costs and benefits. Adjustments may need to be made to financial values in

BOX 5.5

The Australian government's advice on the treatment of the equity and distributional implications of a project

"There may also be broader social justice considerations where a project involves a significant redistribution of income, regardless of the net economic gains to the community. For example, a limitation may arise if the costs fall on low-income earners and the benefits accrue to higher-income earners. Cost-benefit analysts should provide program managers and policy makers with an indication of the income distributional effects of a proposal. This information may be useful where distributional impacts rather than economic efficiency are the objective.

"Benefits are typically measured in terms of estimated willingness to pay prices for a good. However, willingness to pay is generally constrained by income and wealth, which are not distributed equally in the community. In these circumstances, the project's NPV may be considered an inadequate measure of its worth to society, and decision makers would need additional information on the distributional consequences of the project to determine its overall merit.

"Due to the potential redistributive impact of a proposal, determining the 'winners' and 'losers' (along with the size of their wins and losses) is important. However, this is an equity consideration. CBAs aggregate costs and benefits across individuals, without regard to the distribution of those costs and benefits between individuals. To illustrate, a CBA of a new highway that bypasses a country town will compare, primarily, the costs of constructing the new road with the benefits in terms of travel time savings and reduced accidents (involving both travelers and local residents). However, building the road is likely to have distributional consequences: for example, retailers in the town may be adversely affected, while new retailing opportunities—such as service stations, restaurants, and motels—may open up along the new highway. These distributional consequences are not captured by the CBA."

Source: Commonwealth of Australia 2006.
Note: CBA = cost-benefit analysis.

order to yield economic values ("social opportunity costs" or "shadow prices") as a result of distortions in the economy. Such distortions can arise from taxes on trade, production subsidies, or inefficient labor markets. Early guidance on cost-benefit analysis often recommended that the planning authorities use an elaborate set of national conversion factors, covering the major sectors of the economy, to transform market prices to economic values for use in SCBA. This guidance was developed for economies where markets or prices were more distorted than they are today. Authorities rarely followed the guidance; if they did, they rarely employed the factors in actual SCBA, as few planners knew of them or understood how to use them.

For practical reasons, and as a result of the generally more efficient markets in many countries now, in many cases it is no longer considered necessary to devote significant planning resources to developing economywide conversion factors. Good practice is to make adjustments for key inputs or outputs on a case-by-case basis, if the adjustment is likely to make a significant difference in the findings of the SCBA.

Many countries with advanced systems do not estimate these standardized factors because their economies tend to be relatively open and undistorted; the required price correction would therefore be negligible. National financial or planning authorities need to decide whether it is worth making the implied adjustment, taking account of the relative openness of their country's economy.

One final area where a national parameter value may be specified is the deadweight cost of taxation. A generalized loss of social welfare occurs when distortionary tax instruments are used to finance projects. In effect, a part of general taxation is taken from consumers and transferred to no one; this is known as the deadweight economic cost from general taxation or the marginal cost of public funds (see appendix B). Practice with advanced PIM systems is not consistent across countries in the sense that only some countries specify a factor to be applied to the project costs funded out of taxation.

Approach to the social discount rate

The social discount rate may be the most important national parameter value. It is needed to estimate the present value of costs and benefits and thus the net present value of a project and its alternatives. How to set the social discount rate when developing appraisal methodology is an important issue for national governments. There are two different approaches with distinct methodologies:

- *Social rate of time preference.* The SRTP captures the way society values consumption at different points in time. This perspective relies on interpreting the discount rate as the minimum economic compensation per dollar invested required for a representative consumer to be willing to forgo present consumption in return for higher consumption one period later.
- *Social opportunity cost of capital.* The SOC reflects the rate of return on investment and derives from returns in financial markets. This perspective interprets the discount rate as a market-determined opportunity cost, which represents the additional consumption that would have been achieved one period later by investing a dollar in a financial instrument of equivalent risk to the project instead of consuming it now.

Both perspectives are valid and have positive and negative dimensions. The SOC may be difficult to apply in underdeveloped capital markets because it involves strict assumptions about the workings of these markets. The SRTP is frequently applied in countries with advanced PIM systems and is probably easier to estimate, particularly as some simplifying assumptions may be made in applying the Ramsey formula. Neither approach is purely technical, and each involves value judgments by governments (see appendix B).

Approach to valuing labor

When labor markets work efficiently and there is no structural unemployment, the market wage rate is the best measure of the social opportunity cost of labor for SCBA purposes—that is, the marginal value to society of a unit of labor in its next best alternative use. Imperfections in the way labor markets are working, policy-induced rigidities—such as minimum wage legislation—or macroeconomic imbalances may result in the opportunity cost of labor being less than the market rate. In these cases, an adjustment factor can be applied to estimate a shadow wage rate. A method for estimating a shadow wage rate is outlined in appendix B.

Governments need to decide on their approach to the social opportunity cost of labor, keeping in mind that calculation of a shadow wage rate will be technically demanding and may be costly. It is only worth considering if the resulting adjustment is likely to have a significant bearing on investment decisions.

Approaches to estimating nonmarket costs and benefits

Taking account of nonmarket effects is a critical part of SCBA, but their valuation is conceptually difficult for noneconomists to understand. Without in-house experts, governments will need to use external experts if more sophisticated valuation techniques are employed. However, they will still need to be able to specify the work and interpret the results. Good guidance is therefore essential.

When designing appraisal methodologies, governments need to consider the depth and direction of guidance that they provide on valuation techniques, balancing the desire for quantitative estimates of a project's social worth against the availability of skills. The importance of the decision compared with the cost of the research will also have to be weighed.

As much as possible, valuation of project costs and benefits should be based on real or estimated market prices for the costs incurred or services produced by the project. Many public services are free of charge, either because it is difficult or impossible to charge for public goods or because a policy choice is driven by generally accepted equity or social concerns.[29] Health, educational success, family and community stability, and environmental amenity are intangible effects that fall into the category of benefits that have no directly observable market value. By definition, positive and negative externalities have no market value.

Where no markets exist and there are no market prices for valuation purposes, alternative, market-based means of estimating values for costs and benefits can be used. These approaches hinge on estimating potential users' willingness to pay (WTP) for the project's benefits or willingness to accept (WTA) negative consequences. WTP is the maximum payment that a beneficiary would be willing to make to receive a public service;[30] it is therefore a measure of the "utility" that a consumer expects to obtain.[31] WTA is the minimum compensation that an affected party would require to be willing to tolerate a negative economic outcome—increased noise or pollution, for example.

Balanced risk analysis

Identification, analysis, and management of risks are critical components of any project appraisal; however, risk analysis can rapidly become complex and place huge demands on scarce research and analytical capacities. Governments need to decide on the degree of sophistication that they require in national appraisal methodologies. Below is a stepped approach to risk analysis developed by the European Commission:

- *Sensitivity analysis* aims to identify those variables that, when they vary, have the largest impact on the project's social profitability (as measured by the economic NPV)
- *Qualitative risk analysis* involves identifying critical risks and assessing their importance. It also requires assessing the extent to which these risks might be mitigated and the significance of the residual risk remaining after mitigation
- *Quantitative risk analysis* establishes a probability distribution for each of the critical variables identified in the sensitivity analysis in order to estimate the expected value of the NPV.

A more complex quantitative risk analysis, the final step, is only required in certain circumstances—that is, when the residual risk exposure remains significant following qualitative analysis. Governments may wish to consider adopting a similar approach (see also appendix B).

Drawing attention to potential pitfalls in appraisal methodology

When designing an appraisal methodology involving the application of SCBA, it is important to warn against mistakes that are frequently made when identifying and valuing economic costs and benefits. The following are some common mistakes:

- *Double counting benefits.* Sometimes there are two ways of looking at the same effect, and including both views as benefits would lead to double-counting. The benefits of an irrigation project can, for example, be measured either as the present value of the increased future income of farmers or as an increase in the value of farming land, but not both, as land values are a reflection of future income-earning potential. Similarly, it would be wrong to add revenues from user charges and user benefits based on WTP estimates for a water supply or sanitation project, since a user charge is just the financial manifestation of (part of) a consumer's willingness to pay.
- *Counting "job creation" as a benefit.* Wages paid are a project cost, not a benefit. Frequently, job creation and wages generated are mistakenly seen as benefits. If there are reasons to believe that the market price of labor overstates the opportunity cost, either nationally or in a particular locality, and that this situation is likely to persist indefinitely, then the overstatement can be reflected in a suitable downward adjustment of the wage rate to arrive at what is known as a shadow wage. The social benefits of employment are then reflected as a lower monetary value for the cost of labor. Alternatively, the impact of the project on the local labor market can be considered part of a social impact assessment to be taken into account when a decision is based on a comprehensive appraisal. In this case, project planners must be careful not to declare labor costs as benefits (and to take account of displacement effects; see the next point).
- *Ignoring displacement effects.* Additional economic activity generated around a project—for example, along a new road or at new transport hubs—is sometimes counted as a secondary benefit of a project, ignoring the fact that economic activity will often have been displaced from elsewhere. Only the net additional economic activity can be assigned to the project and, even then, any additional investment costs associated with new activities should be taken into account.
- *Counting multiplier effects.* The inclusion of multiplier effects from income and spending generated by a project can only be justified under two strict (and rarely achieved) conditions: (a) the affected resources would otherwise not have been employed and (b) the activities displaced by the project would not have used the idle resources. At the national level, it is usually a mistake to include income generated from multiplier or "second-round" effects as a benefit because alternative uses for the same financial resources could generate similar effects. Occasionally there may be a case for examining multiplier effects when a project targets a particular economically depressed locality. In such cases, it may be useful to understand the net impact of second-round effects on the local economy, but these effects should not be confused with project benefits from a national perspective.

- *Ignoring the opportunity costs of public assets.* A common mistake when valuing project costs is to ignore the opportunity cost of assets already owned by the public sector, particularly land, and to treat these costs incorrectly as sunk costs. Publicly owned assets as inputs to a project should be valued using market valuations, even if there is no actual financial transaction. Publicly owned land should be valued at the best price that it would fetch on the open market (adjusted for any important distortions) and must not be assumed to have zero cost. The next best use of public land that has been identified for new government offices might, for example, be for private sector residential development, and it should be valued at the market rate for residential land. Similarly, any publicly owned equipment or buildings that will be used in the project should be valued at what they would fetch on the open market.

INDEPENDENT REVIEW

Rationale for independent review

The main rationale for independent review derives from the problem of systematic "optimism bias," which has been shown to beset all major projects, across time, across countries, and across sectors (the "iron law of megaprojects"). Optimism bias consists of the statistically demonstrated tendency of project planners to underestimate costs and to overestimate benefits, thus making the ex ante case for the project more convincing than it turns out to be. Box 5.6 summarizes some of the evidence for optimism bias. Box 2.4 in chapter 2 has already given reasons why optimism bias should arise, concluding, "Misinformation about costs, schedules, benefits, and risks is the norm throughout project development and the decision-making process. The result is cost overruns, delays, and

BOX 5.6

The problem of optimism bias in projects

Optimism bias is the systematic tendency for project costs to be underestimated and for project benefits to be overestimated. A research group on large infrastructure at Aalborg University in Denmark tried to quantify the extent of the problem and offer explanations, working from a large sample of major transport projects. This research (summarized in Flyvbjerg 2005) finds significant cost overruns across a sample of 258 major transportation projects, irrespective of country, continent, or transport mode, with no tendency to diminish. Nine out of 10 projects had a cost overrun, and the average (real) cost overrun was 45 percent for rail, 34 percent for bridges and tunnels, and 20 percent for roads. From a sample of 208 rail and road projects, 9 out of 10 rail projects had overestimated traffic, with actual passenger traffic 51 percent lower, on average, than forecast.

Research on large dams found that three out of every four large dams suffered a cost overrun in constant local currency terms and that actual costs were on average 96 percent higher than estimated costs. The research also found that systematic cost overruns were experienced in every region of the world.

Because errors are systematically biased in one direction, poor techniques cannot be the explanation, as they would result in an equal likelihood of underestimation as overestimation. The plausible explanation is that, to obtain funding approval, project promoters and planners systematically make projects look better than they are.

Sources: Ansar et al. 2014; Flyvbjerg 2005.

TABLE 5.5 **The United Kingdom's coefficients for correcting optimism bias**

PROJECT TYPE	HISTORICAL AVERAGE % INCREASE AT OUTLINE BUSINESS CASE	
	CAPITAL EXPENDITURES	WORKS DURATION
Standard buildings	24	4
Nonstandard buildings	51	39
Standard civil engineering works	44	20
Nonstandard civil engineering works	66	25

Source: Presentation on HM Treasury 2003.

benefit shortfalls that undermine project viability during project implementation and operations" (Flyvbjerg 2014). Possible organizational arrangements for dealing with optimism bias are discussed earlier in this chapter. This section deals with the more practical issues of designing an independent review process.

There are other responses to optimism bias, apart from independent review, including the obligatory use of escalation coefficients to uplift cost estimates to reflect demonstrated differences between appraisal estimates and outturns for previous projects of a similar type. The United Kingdom uses this approach, alongside an independent review process for major projects. Table 5.5 indicates the coefficients used at appraisal (outline business case) to uplift capital expenditures and works duration. Estimating such coefficients requires a good ex post review process and strong research capacities, which countries at the beginning of a PIM reform process may not have. Another disadvantage is that planners may "game" such a system and deliberately underestimate costs, knowing that the uplift factor will be applied afterward.

Key issues in designing an independent review function

Meaning of "independence"

Independence does not mean external to the government. The independent reviewer function should be performed by an objective body with nothing to gain from the project going ahead. Ideally, this body should be external to the proposer or appraiser, but still within the public sector. The public sector body charged with independent review may use private sector consultants or experts from elsewhere within the public sector.

Coverage of independent review

Appraisals for all projects should be subject to some form of objective review. Capacity constraints mean that it may not be practical for the nominated organization to carry out this review as a result of specialization for major and riskier projects. However, the appraisal for lower-value projects should at least be reviewed by a part of the proposing or appraising organization with no interest in the project's going ahead.

Depth of review

Independent review varies according to the depth of the analysis performed:

- In the United Kingdom, the Treasury only reviews major projects. A checklist approach is used to ensure that the fundamentals of the appraisal methodology have been followed and to question critically the appraisal findings and underlying assumptions.[32] For all projects, the gateway review system,

BOX 5.7

Questions for independent reviewers in France

The second opinion in France should answer the following questions:

- Does the project documentation respond to the documentary requirements of a socioeconomic evaluation?
- Have the methodological guidelines and ministerial instructions been followed properly?
- Have the prescribed parameter values for appraisal been respected?
- How have the nonmonetized effects of the project been taken into account where these are critical for evaluation of the project?
- Is the scope of the evaluation appropriate to the project?
- What method has been used, and how does this method compare to recognized practices in other comparable sectors and in other countries?
- Are the input parameters realistic and coherent?

Source: PLF 2015.

internal to the agency sponsoring the project, must be reviewed by external peer reviewers elsewhere in the public sector.

- In Chile, all projects are subject to review. All interested institutions do the appraisal, but the review is carried out by the Ministry of Social Development, which rejects projects that do not conform to methodological guidance. The ministry requests corrections until the appraisal is satisfactory. The review is less a "second opinion" and more quality control to ensure that the detailed methodologies (box 5.4) have been applied properly.[33]
- In France, the General Commission for Investment organizes a second opinion on appraisals of major projects (more than €20 million) that critically examines the methodological approach,[34] the calculation of parameters used in the appraisal, and appraisal findings. Box 5.7 provides a list of the overarching questions that reviewers are expected to address.
- In Korea, an independent review precedes appraisal and draws up a preliminary feasibility study for major projects (those more than US$50 million) as a basis for deciding whether to proceed to appraisal. This unusual, but highly effective, approach involves much deeper analysis by the independent reviewer, PIMAC, than in other countries; but, combined with a system for controlling cost escalation, it has proved remarkably effective.[35]

Outcome of independent review

It should be difficult for a project to proceed with a negative independent review. Completing an independent review is not necessarily a decision point (see the section on project selection), as the independent reviewer may often only advise the final decision maker:

- Chile's system is recognized as being rather strict, but even here some projects proceed without positive reviews from the planning ministry.[36]
- In France, the General Commission for Investment prepares an opinion for the prime minister, which also goes to the minister proposing the project and to parliament.[37]

- In Ireland, the review by the Central Expenditure Evaluation Unit is purely advisory for the minister proposing the project.
- In the Netherlands, independent review findings need to be taken into account in making the final decision, but there is no requirement for these findings to determine the final decision.
- In the United Kingdom, independent review is closely tied to a decision point (known as the Treasury approval point); projects will not proceed if they receive a negative review.
- In Korea, the National Finance Law requires PIMAC to conduct an independent review of major projects (those more than US$50 million) for the Ministry of Economy and Finance; in practice, the ministry's decision is closely tied to the result of the independent review.

Timing of independent review

An independent review can take place at any time and should not be driven by the budget preparation calendar. The time needed for an independent review varies between countries and reflects the depth of the analysis performed. In the United Kingdom, the turnaround for a decision at a Treasury approval point is 28 days. France allows one to four months for a second opinion to be prepared after project documentation has been received. Korea's much more elaborate preliminary feasibility study takes around four months and may be extended if the study indicates that the project concept has been altered.

PROJECT SELECTION

Status of project selection

Project selection is a key decision point and the culmination of the quality-at-entry processes. The decision is made based on appraisal findings and recommendations, which are usually presented to decision makers in a summary appraisal report together with the supporting documentation.[38] Selection ends with a formal decision on a project's social viability and sustainability and confirmation of its eligibility to be proposed for budget funding. Selection does not mean that funding is guaranteed; funding can only be guaranteed through the budgetary process, when a project's merits are considered alongside competing claims on budget allocations.

Key issues in designing a project selection process

Status of a selection decision

Selection is a decision in principle to proceed with a project. It is neither a funding commitment nor a final decision to go ahead. Funding commitments are made through the capital budgeting process (see chapters 6 and 7). The final decision to implement a project should only be made following completion of the detailed design and evaluation of bids, when a more accurate estimate of costs is available. Although it is often very difficult to stop a project once a selection decision has been made—hence the significance of this decision point—PIM systems should still review the decision before an irreversible contractual commitment is made.

BOX 5.8

The United Kingdom's full business case

"[The full business case (FBC)] is the procurement phase for the spending proposal, following detailed negotiations with potential service providers/suppliers prior to the formal signing of contracts and the procurement of goods and services.

"The purpose of the FBC is to revisit and where required rework the OBC [outline business case = appraisal/selection] analysis and assumptions building in and recording the findings of the formal procurement. This case at its conclusions recommends the 'most economically advantageous offer,' documents the contractual arrangements, confirms funding and affordability, and sets out the detailed management arrangements and plans for successful delivery and post evaluation.

"... If the OBC has been prepared in accordance with the guidance set out earlier and the procurement run in accordance with accepted and established best practice, much of the work involved in developing the FBC will simply focus on updating the OBC and documenting the outcomes of the procurement rather than starting from scratch."

Source: HM Treasury 2013.

In the United Kingdom, the full business case for a project is reviewed, and a final decision to proceed is made prior to contract signature. The review process need not be elaborate, as box 5.8 indicates. In Ireland, approval to proceed to tender is a decision point, following detailed planning and design, and a verification that the project remains the same as the one approved in principle. A further review precedes contract signature. In Korea, once a selection decision is made, almost all projects are funded.

Organizational arrangements for a selection decision

Selection should be largely a technical decision; achieving the right balance between technical and political inputs to decision making is nevertheless important. Placing the selection decision for major projects in the hands of the finance or planning minister (or equivalent) may be the best option, if politically feasible. Where there is reluctance to place such power in the hands of these ministers, recourse is sometimes made to a broadly representative political body or an interministerial committee of senior officials. The danger with such arrangements is that selection can often become part of a political bargaining process,[39] rather than a decision on the quality of individual projects. One option in such circumstances is to give the finance or planning ministries veto power on a broader decision-making body or to have them chair the body (and thus set the agenda).

In some systems, a minister is "sovereign" in his or her ministry, and the final selection decision remains with the minister who has ultimate responsibility for the project.[40] This approach is the case in Ireland, where the emphasis is on developing and promoting good practices so that ministers and their officials have the tools to make sound decisions. Performance evaluation is used to incentivize the use of these tools (World Bank 2014).

Prioritization and selection

Selection is a form of prioritization to the extent that it involves reducing the set of projects under consideration to those that have been shown to be a potentially good use of public funds; as such, it is one of the filters in the upstream PIM process. Although the capital budgeting process should be the ultimate prioritization mechanism, there may be some merit in attaching priorities to projects that are selected, as not all projects selected are affordable. Priorities will need to be made using the strategic planning process (see chapter 6). Priorities determined outside the budget process can never be binding, as the budget process remains sovereign.

Limiting the size of the pool of selected projects

As well as, or instead of, prioritizing selected projects, there may be advantages to constraining the pool of selected projects more closely to reflect the likely fiscal constraints; thus, the selection decision may include an affordability element. The most sensible way of including an affordability element is to place an expiration date on a selection decision, so that if the project has not been prepared in detail and proposed for funding after a certain length of time, it needs to go back to the beginning of the quality-at-entry system. This requirement makes sense because costs and demand forecasts are likely to become outdated after several years.

In the absence of fiscally constrained, long-term strategic planning (see chapter 6), another approach might be to set financial limits on the total value of a ministry's portfolio of selected projects. If these limits are reached, projects should be "de-selected" to accommodate newly selected projects. There will be a degree of arbitrariness to fixing such limits, but limits need to be tight enough to restrict the potential growth of a "feasibility study industry"—that is, the development of projects with little chance of being implemented, while being generous enough to allow for a sufficient margin of "shovel-ready" projects.

A better way of restricting the pool of selected projects is through a medium-term budget framework, whereby funding for feasibility studies for major projects is programmed in line with the availability of financial resources for implementation (see chapter 6).

Tracking selected projects

If projects were not given a unique code and entered into a database at preappraisal, this task should be done when the selection decision is made.[41] The database should be kept up-to-date, and projects for which approval has lapsed should be suitably categorized.[42] Information systems are important for PIM, but there may be a misconception that they can be used to "automate" the appraisal, selection, and prioritization process. Countries with advanced PIM systems do not use information systems in this way (see chapter 12 on PIM information systems).

NOTES

1. As well as the strategic outline case, discussed below, the United Kingdom also has what is effectively a pre-preappraisal step: the starting gate review, which must be completed at an early stage of planning, before any public commitment has been made.
2. For further discussion on adopting PPP projects, see chapter 10.
3. Best practice is to manage the pipeline for major infrastructure sectors (for example, transport or energy) through a fiscally constrained, rolling long-term infrastructure plan. See chapter 6.
4. The economic tools used in project appraisal are a practical application of welfare economics, a branch of economics that examines how public policy interventions can be used

to maximize aggregate social welfare, a broader concept than is captured in the income, expenditure, and output measures of the economy. The term "economic," when used here and elsewhere in the guidelines, therefore has a wider meaning than just the financial flows captured in the national income accounts, consistent with international practice.

5. Net benefits are benefits minus costs, adjusted so that costs and benefits at different points in time are comparable.
6. See the discussion above concerning the difference between preappraisal and prefeasibility.
7. To avoid some of this confusion, the term "social cost-benefit analysis" is used in this guide, instead of economic cost-benefit analysis, although the two are interchangeable.
8. "Expected" in a statistical sense.
9. The option with the lowest present value of costs per unit of output.
10. The exception is where legislation is passed without attention to the fiscal consequences, which can result in unfunded mandates. In order to avoid this situation, the required minimum is an obligatory fiscal impact assessment of all legislative proposals.
11. See https://www.finance-ni.gov.uk/topics/finance/step-by-step-economic-appraisal-guidance.
12. Sometimes referred to as cost-benefit analysis, but social cost-benefit analysis better conveys the wider perspective of the analysis.
13. A switching value is the required change in a critical parameter that would cause the NPV to turn negative.
14. The statistical definition.
15. Assessments need to be finalized when the detailed project design is completed following a positive appraisal decision.
16. A tendency sometimes referred to as "gold-plating."
17. The incremental costs of the gold-plated solution compared to doing the minimum are considerably lower than the incremental costs compared to doing nothing; the benefits remain similar.
18. Technical variants usually are not analyzed at preappraisal, as cost estimates will almost certainly not be accurate enough, but potential variants can be highlighted for evaluation at appraisal.
19. The threshold was higher, but it has been lowered as capacities have developed.
20. See also chapter 4, which explains different approaches according to project size, sector, and level of government.
21. See http://publicspendingcode.per.gov.ie/d-standard-analytical-techniques/.
22. Box 5.4 also indicates when SCBA is required and when CEA is acceptable.
23. As discussed in the section on preappraisal, a prefeasibility study is different from preappraisal. Preappraisal is generally a lighter and technically less demanding form of assessment than a prefeasibility study.
24. For research and development investment projects in Korea, prefeasibility studies are performed by the Korea Institute of Science and Technology Evaluation and Planning.
25. Reviewers should be suspicious when quantified SCBA points to very low social profitability, but has a positive overall appraisal when qualitative assessments of nonmonetized benefits are taken into account.
26. The threshold at which the U.K. Treasury delegates authority over expenditure decisions is lower in the social sectors than in the transport sector, for example.
27. For valuation purposes, environmental costs and benefits (negative and positive "externalities") are subsumed within social costs and benefits and are captured within the scope of social cost-benefit analysis.
28. Often these areas will be legally prescribed through official designations for protection of species, ecosystems, or areas of outstanding natural beauty.
29. A pure public good (or service) is one where it is not possible to exclude users from consuming the good (service) and where consumption by one consumer does not diminish the amount of the good (service) available for others. These characteristics mean that there is no incentive for the private sector to supply the good (service) because it is impossible to earn revenues and make a profit.
30. WTA is a closely related alternative measure used to value negative impacts. See appendix B.
31. "Utility" is a concept used in welfare economics meaning the satisfaction or change in welfare that a person gets from consumption of a good or service.

32. A similar model is used in Australia and New Zealand.
33. This characteristic explains the range and detail of the sector-specific methodological guidance in Chile.
34. To ensure conformity with guidelines.
35. Of 707 projects subject to a preliminary feasibility study over the period 1999–2018, 253 projects (35.8 percent) were found to be not worth progressing to full feasibility. See PIMAC (2019).
36. Gómez-Lobo (2012) quotes a figure of 11 percent.
37. A summary assessment of the key issues, strengths, weaknesses, or risks attached to the project and either a favorable opinion, with qualifications if necessary, or an unfavorable opinion concerning continuation of the project.
38. Part of the role of the independent reviewer is to assure that the summary appraisal report accurately represents the feasibility study, preliminary design work, and supporting impact studies.
39. Trade-offs at the political level will need to be made, but not at this point in the PIM process. They should be made as part of capital budgeting.
40. In reality, the responsible minister will always need to make a selection decision (or delegate it to one of his or her officials). In some countries, this decision will be referred to a higher authority.
41. The tracking code in selected projects is sometimes inconsistent with the one in budgeted capital projects because some selected projects are not funded in the budgeting process. See chapter 12.
42. It is important to retain information on these projects in case they reappear.

REFERENCES

Ansar, A., B. Flyvbjerg, A. Budzier, and D. Lunn. 2014. "Should We Build More Large Dams? The Actual Costs of Hydropower Megaproject Development." *Energy Policy* 69 (June): 43–56.

Commonwealth of Australia. 2006. "Introduction to Cost-Benefit Analysis and Alternative Evaluation Methodologies." Commonwealth of Australia, Camberra.

European Commission. 2014. *Guide to Cost-Benefit Analysis of Investment Projects: Economic Appraisal Tool for Cohesion Policy 2014–2020.* Brussels: Directorate General for Regional and Urban Policy.

Flyvbjerg. B. 2005. "Policy and Planning for Large Infrastructure Projects: Problems, Causes, and Cures." Policy Research Working Paper 3781, World Bank, Washington, DC.

———. 2014. "What You Should Know about Megaprojects and Why: An Overview." *Project Management Journal* 45 (2): 6–19.

Gómez-Lobo, A. 2012. "Institutional Safeguards for Cost-Benefit Analysis: Lessons from the Chilean National Investment System." *Journal of Benefit-Cost Analysis* 3 (1): 1–30.

HM Treasury. 2003. *The Green Book: Appraisal and Evaluation in Central Government.* Amended in 2011. London: HM Treasury.

———. 2013. *Public Sector Business Cases: Using the Five Case Model.* London: HM Treasury.

———. n.d. "Assessing Business Cases: A Short Plain-English Guide." HM Treasury, London.

Ministry of Finance, the Netherlands. 2013. *Kabinetsbrief bij de algemene MKBA Leidraad.* The Hague: Ministry of Finance.

PIMAC (Public Infrastructure Investment Management Center). 2019. *KDI PIMAC Annual Report 2018* [in Korean]. Seoul: Korea Development Institute.

PLF (Projet de Loi de Finances). 2015. *Évaluation des grands projets d'investissements publics.* Paris: Government of France.

World Bank. 2014. "Study on Cross-Country Comparison: Technical Assistance for Public Investment Project Appraisal and Selection System Development in Ukraine." World Bank, Washington, DC.

6

Integrating the Strategic Planning, Project, and Budgeting Cycles

OVERVIEW

Upstream public investment management (PIM) processes consist of more than quality at entry. A well-designed and functioning upstream subsystem should ensure that (a) strategic planning, (b) project appraisal and quality at entry, and (c) capital budgeting are closely integrated so that the right infrastructure is provided at the right price and at the right time. This process is not straightforward because the strategic planning cycle, the project cycle, and the budgeting cycle are not concurrent and have different planning and implementation horizons. A functioning PIM system must ensure that the three cycles coincide at key points, as illustrated in figure 6.1.

The following are the main direct points of coincidence between the three cycles, as identified in figure 6.1:

- When project concepts are identified on the basis of strategic planning guidance
- When project concepts, confirmed as eligible at preappraisal, have budget funding approved for preparation
- When prepared projects, confirmed as eligible, have budget funding approved for implementation
- When monitoring information confirms the continued eligibility or requirements of ongoing projects for budget funding and availability of resources for new projects is determined and allocated
- When evaluation results of completed projects feed into the revision and update of strategic plans.

The governance structure and methodological manuals for PIM should be designed with a view to strengthening integration of the three upstream stages, while taking account of differences in their timing and scope.

FIGURE 6.1
Intersection of the project cycle with the strategic planning and budgeting cycles

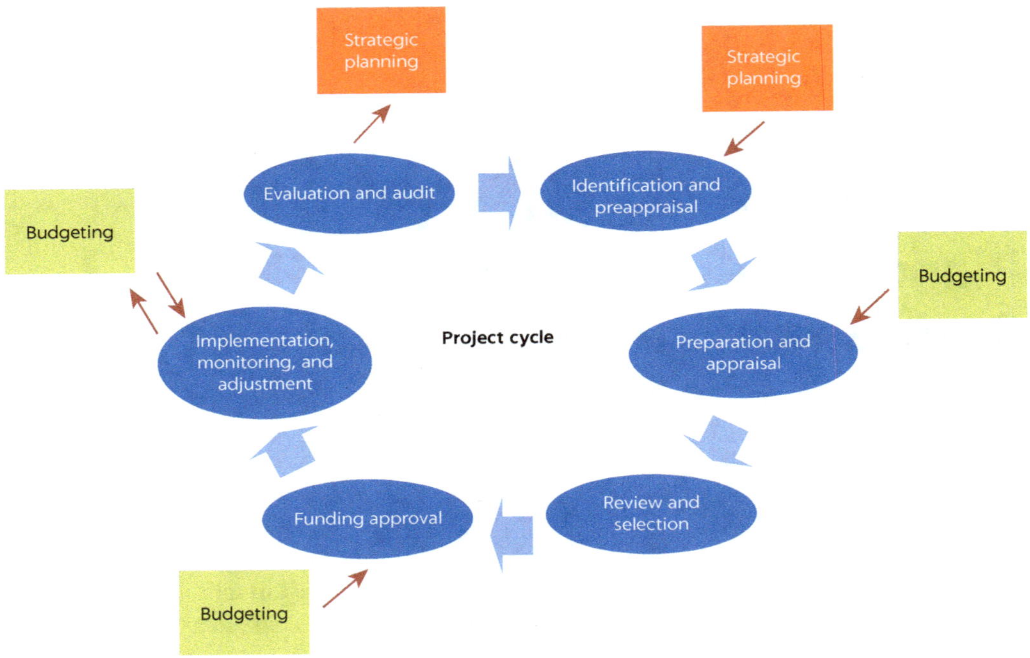

ENSURING INTEGRATION AT THE STRATEGIC PLANNING STAGE

Realistic, operational, and authoritative strategic guidance is essential for identifying projects, prioritizing the budget, and ensuring intertemporal consistency in expenditure decisions. Strategic plans need to be fiscally sustainable and consistent at the different levels of national strategy, sector strategies, sector or subsector investment plans, and subsector master plans. High-level, long-term visions are useful for setting the scene (see box 6.1), but they are most helpful for PIM when supplemented by more operational strategies. Bottom-up lists of investment needs ("wish lists") are not helpful for strategic guidance, unless they can be developed further and prioritized within a realistic expenditure framework. Close coordination between sector ministries, the finance ministry, and the planning ministry (where one exists) is often inadequate and is required to achieve fiscal realism. Creating the right conditions for this coordination is essential for strong PIM.

Strategic investment planning needs to take account of information on existing assets provided by comprehensive and up-to-date asset management systems. Strategic plans should also allow for renewal of assets at the end of their life, maintenance of the existing stock of fixed capital assets, and planning for the creation of new assets. This step is often missing from strategic guidance, which tends to focus on new increments to the capital stock rather than on the contribution of the entire capital stock to the government's service delivery objectives. Asset management systems are often not advanced enough to drive this kind of systematic life-cycle planning, which may only be a long-term aim for many countries; however, strategic planning should aim to encompass maintenance and renewal of existing assets, not just creation of new assets (see chapter 9 for more on asset management).

BOX 6.1

The OECD's definition of a long-term national strategic vision

According to the Organisation for Economic Co-operation and Development (OECD),

> "A *long-term national strategic vision* is a politically sanctioned document that demands concrete action in terms of infrastructure services to society over the long term. This might go beyond a normal political mandate period. The design of the vision requires a process that distils complex and multifaceted infrastructure issues, cutting across a multiplicity of actors, sectors, and interests, into a coherent set of decisions with long-term impact, including projects and processes. Such a process should be anchored in central agencies and have substantial input from policy departments, subnational governments, civil society, and business stakeholders."

Source: OECD 2017.

Strategic guidance is almost always available for planners; in fact, there may be too many incompatible and unconstrained strategic plans, with few, if any, linkages to asset management systems. The case of Moldova described in box 6.2 illustrates the general problems of strategic guidance commonly found in other countries—that is, lack of realism, vague objectives, weak coordination, and limited information on the condition of existing assets.[1] Compared with Moldova, Ireland developed a more cohesive national planning process in the context of significant external funding for investment, as described in box 6.3.

In the absence of coherent strategic guidance, planners must still plan new project ideas; stakeholder consultation and the use of tools, such as the logical framework approach (discussed below), to test the rationale for a project become more important in such cases.

Good practice indicates that linking strategic planning and capital budgeting is best achieved through a rolling, medium-term budgetary framework. The medium-term perspective (usually three to four years) allows resource allocation decisions to be made in line with strategic plans. The rolling dynamic allows plans to adapt to emerging macrofiscal conditions and enables the implementation progress of current projects to be taken into account when deciding on new projects and programming their expenditures. Some coordination difficulties may arise when the strategic planning framework is static and has a relatively short horizon—for example, fixed five-year planning periods, which are often still used in countries that retain the vestiges of central planning such as Belarus and Vietnam. The problems with coordinating a rolling budgetary perspective and a static plan become most apparent toward the end of one planning period, before the new planning period is initiated, when there is no strategic basis for the outer years of the budgetary framework.

From conception to completion, planning and implementation of major infrastructure projects generally take longer than the three- to four-year horizon for medium-term strategic budgeting and the traditional five-year planning perspective. One option is to provide extra time for planning in infrastructure sectors, although this approach may mean that implementation plans may bridge two or more political mandates. Stakeholder consultations and cross-party consensus building should be part of the planning process to avoid abrupt changes

BOX 6.2

Strategic guidance in Moldova

Strategic investment guidance has improved considerably in recent years. . . . However, weaknesses remain in the way strategies are developed. Not all strategies realistically assess resource availability for funding priorities, and identified investment needs often exceed feasible financing capacities. Lack of realism arises because strategies have often been prepared in isolation, with no aggregate resource framework and weak coordination with the Ministry of Finance. Absence of specificity in defining investment priorities is a problem, allowing too much room for maneuver in the choice of projects to pursue. And because monitoring is not strong and updating is irregular, strategies become out of step with the changing fiscal realities.

"Strategic investment guidance is not yet built upon a solid assessment of the condition of assets, trends in service demand, emerging infrastructure gaps, and funding possibilities. The sector strategies for land transport and for water supply and sanitation represent moves in the right direction. . . . Future strategy development would be enhanced by more systematic assessment of asset condition in these and other sectors, requiring regularly updated asset registers and linked asset management systems."

Source: World Bank 2013.

BOX 6.3

Ireland's successful national development planning process

Ireland has successfully used a series of national development plans (NDPs) to guide the identification and prioritization of projects. Ireland's strategic planning process evolved while it was more reliant on European Union funding, but the NDP was retained as a centerpiece of government policy making. Preparation and implementation of the 2000–06 NDP incorporates many features of good process, including extensive public consultation, independent review, and evaluation of progress. It is generally recognized as having been highly successful.

The 2000–06 NDP was made operational through six cross-cutting operational programs, of which the Economic and Social Infrastructure Operational Programme was the largest. This NDP took an integrated approach to planning, incorporating strategies that required both recurrent and capital expenditures, as well as institutional measures. In the case of infrastructure investment, the sectors identified as relevant for public investment were housing, transport, environmental, social, and recreational infrastructure. For each of these sectors, more detailed investment strategies were prepared by the relevant sector ministries and framed within an indicative capital spending envelope agreed to with the Department of Finance.

The NDP was implemented much as planned because it was prepared within realistic estimates of the resources available for implementation, and operational programs were fully costed. This discipline was assisted by the fact that the Finance Ministry led the planning process.

The 2000–06 NDP was succeeded by the 2007–13 NDP, confirming the Irish government's commitment to the planning process. However, the financial crisis that engulfed the country and severely damaged the public finances made this later plan unachievable as originally conceived. In its place, a new strategy for infrastructure was developed, Infrastructure Investment Priorities 2010–2016: A Financial Framework, which was more in line with the new fiscal realities.

Source: World Bank 2014.

of direction with the electoral cycle, although such consensus building may be difficult in many political contexts. Some countries with advanced systems have sought to ensure continuity from one government to the next by creating independent advisory bodies; Infrastructure Australia and the United Kingdom's National Infrastructure Commission are two examples. National planning commissions in some African countries—such as Ethiopia, Ghana, and Tanzania—may fulfill a similar function.

Some countries with advanced systems lack a tradition of national development planning but have been using long-term infrastructure plans to address perceived infrastructure deficits. Their plans are within realistic resource frameworks. Financing is indicative, however, and firm funding is delivered through the usual budgeting process, which is framed within a medium-term perspective. These long-term infrastructure plans are often rolling plans, which allows adjustments to be made in line with progress and shifting macrofiscal constraints and priorities to be updated.

Long-term, rolling infrastructure plans address the issue of a sensible time horizon for strategic planning of major investments and the potential difficulties associated with integrating static planning with dynamic budgeting. The concept has been practiced for some years in Norway, where the first plan was for the period 2006–15, and in Sweden, as described in box 6.4, but it has now been adopted elsewhere (see box 6.5). Cross-party consensus building and stakeholder consultations are an important component of the planning process and are expected to ensure the durability of these plans when governments change; the rolling nature of these plans also allows for priorities to be adjusted over time.

BOX 6.4

Rolling sector investment plans in Norway and Sweden

Norway has a 10-year transport infrastructure plan that is rolled forward every four years. To date, plans have covered 2006–15, 2010–19, and 2014–23. They identify specific major projects and their estimated costs and are developed around four fiscal scenarios: a base case, −20 percent financing, +20 percent financing, and +45 percent financing. Projects are prioritized within each scenario by transport mode.

The procedure to develop the plan begins when the government informs the Public Roads Administration about its policy objectives immediately after publishing the previous plan. The regional offices of the Public Roads Administration then provide a list of projects in their regions that can help to support the defined policy objectives. Based on priorities of the regional offices and in cooperation with the Norwegian National Rail Administration, the Norwegian Coastal Administration, and the owner of the Norwegian public airports, Avinor AS, the regional offices assemble a proposal for the next national transport plan and submit it to the government. After receiving and reviewing stakeholders' comments, the government assembles the plan and sends it to parliament for ratification.

Sweden's first national transport plan covered the period 2010–21. It has subsequently been rolled forward to cover 2014–25. The plan is approved by the government after public consultation. In addition to describing the economic and fiscal framework for development, operation, and maintenance of the national road and rail network, the plan contains several defined projects to be started during the period. Preliminary social cost-benefit analysis is used to prioritize projects within the plan, but political factors and regional distribution also influence the projects that are eventually included.

Source: Forsgren and Westin 2014.

BOX 6.5

Australian infrastructure plan, 2016–31

Infrastructure Australia, an independent statutory body, is tasked with preparing a rolling, long-term national infrastructure plan. The infrastructure plan for 2016–31 was developed through a collaborative 18-month process of research and consultation. To underpin the planning process, two infrastructure audits were performed, the Northern Australia audit and the Australian infrastructure audit. The latter represents the nation's first comprehensive examination of infrastructure across the energy, telecommunications, water, and transport sectors. Together, the two audits provide the primary evidence for the plan. They set out the case for substantially enhancing the quality, capacity, and efficiency of infrastructure and overhauling the way infrastructure is planned, funded, constructed, operated, and maintained.

Following release of these audits, Infrastructure Australia received more than 100 formal submissions from jurisdictions, a wide range of industry associations, public interest groups, local government bodies, and individuals. More than 500 stakeholders were consulted in every state and territory and worked closely with representatives from all levels of government, as well as businesses, industry, peak bodies, and the wider community.

The plan lays out a comprehensive package of reforms focused on improving the way Australia invests in, delivers, and uses its infrastructure. The aim is to extract the greatest value from existing infrastructure, while sustainably funding new investments to deliver better services. The plan identifies focal areas for investment, rather than a list of projects, which is done through a separate infrastructure priority list.

The plan seeks to achieve the following main goals:

- Improved productivity of cities and regions through optimal infrastructure provision
- Efficient markets for supply of infrastructure services
- Sustainable infrastructure with equitable access
- Better decision making and delivery of infrastructure.

The plan has a 15-year horizon but will be reviewed and rolled forward every five years, beginning in 2021.

Source: Infrastructure Australia 2016; http://infrastructureaustralia.gov.au/.

ENSURING INTEGRATION AT THE QUALITY-AT-ENTRY STAGE

Strategic fit and affordability

Chapter 5 summarizes quality-at-entry processes and discusses issues related to system design in some depth. Preappraisal, when the strategic relevance of the project is center stage, represents a critical linkage with strategic planning. Preappraisal also involves a broad-based assessment of affordability (or unaffordability), making the link with capital budgeting. In certain cases, where approval of a distinct budget is required for project preparation and appraisal, as may be the case for a major project or megaproject, a formal preappraisal decision should be a prerequisite for including such activities in a capital budget request and will strengthen the linkage.

At appraisal, the strategic relevance of a project is reviewed again (as summarized in chapter 5). At this point, the continued coherence of the project with higher-level strategic guidance should be confirmed; project objectives need to be framed to make a clear link with the relevant strategic plans. Applying the logical framework approach at appraisal can assist with the strategic orientation of a project.[2] The approach establishes a hierarchy of objectives related to the cause-effect logic, often referred to as the "results chain," that drives the project rationale: the highest level of objectives is expected to be derived from or to be consistent with the strategic planning guidance. Table 6.1 presents an example of a logical framework taken from European Commission guidance. The logical framework includes identification of indicators and means of verification for each level of objectives, so that it also forms a basis for monitoring and evaluation during the downstream stage of PIM (Gasper 1999).[3] The World Bank's results framework is another tool that performs a similar function.

One step in the appraisal process described in chapter 5 involves examining the financial sustainability of the project from the perspective of the operating entity and from a budgetary perspective. As indicated above, the project cycle and the budgetary cycle are not necessarily concurrent, which means that a definitive statement cannot be made regarding the affordability of a project from the perspective of the budget; such a statement can only be made through the budget process when trade-offs are made with other new projects and new spending initiatives. Nevertheless, appraisal should estimate the impact on

TABLE 6.1 **An example of a logical framework**

PROJECT DESCRIPTION	INDICATORS	MEANS OF VERIFICATION	ASSUMPTIONS
Overall objective. Improved family health, particularly for children under five, and improve the general health of the riverine ecosystem	Incidence of water-borne diseases, skin infections, and blood disorders caused by heavy metals is reduced by 50% by 2008, specifically among low-income families living along the river	Municipal hospital and clinic records, including maternal and child health records collected by mobile maternal and child health teams Results summarized in an Annual State of the Environment report by the Environmental Protection Agency	
Purpose. Improved quality of river water	Concentration of heavy-metal compounds (lead, cadmium, mercury) and untreated sewage is reduced by 25% (compared to 2003), and established national health and pollution control standards are met by end of 2007	Weekly water quality surveys, conducted jointly by the Department of Environment and River Authority and reported monthly to the local government minister for the environment (chair of Project Steering Committee)	Public awareness campaign conducted by local government has a positive impact on families, sanitation, and hygiene practices Fishing cooperatives are effective in limiting their members' exploitation of fish "nursery" areas
Result 1. Reduced volume of wastewater discharged directly into the river system by households and factories	70% of wastewater produced by factories and 80% of wastewater produced by households are treated in plants by 2006	Annual sample survey of households and factories conducted by municipalities between 2003 and 2006	River flows are maintained above X megaliters per second for at least eight months of the year Upstream water quality remains stable
Result 2. Wastewater treatment standards established and enforced effectively	Wastewater from four existing treatment plants meets Environmental Protection Agency quality standards (heavy metals and sewerage content) by 2005	Environmental Protection Agency audits (using revised standards and improved audit methods) conducted quarterly and reported to Project Steering Committee	Environmental Protection Agency is successful in reducing solid waste disposal levels by factories from X to X tons per year

Source: Adapted from European Commission 2004.

public finances on a whole-life basis—that is, including recurrent costs—and should identify and assess the realism of intended funding sources, including foreign loans, grants, and nonbudgetary sources.

Linking quality at entry with strategic planning and capital budgeting in the United Kingdom

The integration of appraisal with strategic planning and capital budgeting is best illustrated through a concrete, good-practice example, in this case, the United Kingdom's "business case" model.[4]

Quality at entry in the United Kingdom consists of three sequential assessments and associated decision points:[5] (1) the strategic outline case (SOC), (2) the outline business case (OBC), and (3) the full business case (FBC). At each point, five thematic cases are examined. Box 6.6 summarizes these five

BOX 6.6

The United Kingdom's three business cases and five thematic cases

The U.K. business case model consists of three sequential business cases prepared during the planning phase for a project or program:

1. *Strategic outline business case.* A preliminary screening of a project proposal, on the basis of a detailed outline of the project concept, to confirm its rationale and strategic "fit"
2. *Outline business case.* Equivalent to full-scale ex ante evaluation, based on the preparation of a socioeconomic feasibility study using the mandated methodology for social cost-benefit analysis or cost-effectiveness analysis and including risk analysis
3. *Full business case.* A rerunning of the economic analysis and confirmation of deliverability during the procurement phase of the project, prior to the formal signing of contracts and before the procurement of goods and services takes place; may lead to project adjustment.

Five thematic cases must be examined at each of the three stages forming the phase of the project cycle preceding implementation. The five thematic cases examine different dimensions of a project:

1. *Strategic case.* Sets out the rationale for the proposed investment, making the case at the strategic level and setting out the objective to be achieved, in specific and measurable terms, the fit with wider public policy objectives, and the previous experience of similar projects
2. *Economic case.* Assesses the economic costs and benefits of the proposal to society as a whole over the life span of the project. Must include a sufficiently wide consideration of alternative options for achieving the desired objective, establish the rationale for choosing the preferred option, and include a plan for monitoring the project's effects and evaluating its success
3. *Commercial case.* Examines procurement requirements, assesses their importance for project delivery, develops a procurement strategy, and explores traditional procurement versus possible public-private partnership (PPP) arrangements
4. *Financial case.* Deals with the impact on the budget and is concerned with issues of affordability and sources of budget funding over the life span of the project. Assesses any contingent liabilities, particularly in relation to PPP proposals
5. *Management case.* Is concerned with deliverability of the proposal. Sets out the project management responsibilities and the governance and reporting arrangements. Must include a delivery plan with clear milestones.

Source: HM Treasury 2013.

thematic cases as well as the three sequential business cases. The strategic and financial cases ensure integration of the quality-at-entry subsystem with strategic planning and capital budgeting. Table 6.2 indicates the varying degrees of emphasis placed on each thematic case when developing the business cases. The strategic case is the focus of attention at SOC, while the financial case is the focus at OBC; both of these thematic cases are considered in each of the three business cases.

The strategic context for the project, established as part of the SOC[6] (and reviewed at OBC), has two components:

- *Organizational overview.* Provides a brief profile of the organization, including a statement of its aims and the nature and level of resources currently at its disposal (HM Treasury 2013)
- *Existing business strategies.* Explains how the proposed project supports, promotes, and fits within the agreed-on strategy and work program, of which the project forms an integral part. It explains how the proposed project helps to achieve the organization's business goals, strategic aims, and plans. All relevant strategies should be referenced, including those at national, regional, and local levels. These strategies highlight the high-level policy aims (strategic aims) and business goals of the organization, from which the objectives for the spending will flow (HM Treasury 2013).

The financial case, introduced at SOC, is examined in depth at OBC to ascertain the affordability and funding requirements of the preferred project option in relation to the other short-listed options.[7] This examination estimates the following:

- The capital and current implications of the preferred option and associated deal (in the case of PPPs)
- The impact on the income and expenditure account and the organization's charges for services (if applicable)

TABLE 6.2 **Matrix of thematic and business cases: United Kingdom**

THEMATIC CASE	STRATEGIC OUTLINE CASE (SOC)	OUTLINE BUSINESS CASE (OBC)	FULL BUSINESS CASE (FBC)
Strategic case	Is completed in full but may be revised later	Is revisited	Is revisited and revised if required
Economic case	Is completed as far as the review of a long list of options, recommended way forward, and an initial short list for OBC stage	Is completed according to methodological guidance on appraisal and evaluation in central government (the *Green Book*)	Includes and records the findings of procurement in the economic analysis; reassesses the economic case
Commercial case	Addresses the fundamentals of any potential procurement or "deal"—for example, initial identification of potential public-private partnership (PPP) options[a]	Outlines envisaged "deal" structure(s) and any contractual clauses and payment mechanisms	Writes up the recommended "deal"
Financial case	Discusses likely affordability of the proposed project	Conducts detailed analysis of affordability and any funding gaps	Resolves affordability and funding issues
Management case	Outlines how the project will be set up and managed	Develops how the project will be delivered in more detail, with an outline of the proposed project management plan	Records detailed plans for delivery and arrangements for realization of benefits, management of risk, and ex post evaluation

Source: HM Treasury 2013.
a. Public-private partnerships have been pursued vigorously in the United Kingdom, one of the highest PPP users in the world.

- The impact on the budget, other sources of available funding, and any shortfalls
- The impact on the operating organization's balance sheet.

The design principles applied in the U.K. model—that is, attention to strategic and affordability issues during quality-at-entry processes—should be seen as a broad guide to designing country-specific procedures and methods elsewhere; it is not suggested that the business case model be adopted as a rigid template.

ENSURING INTEGRATION AT THE CAPITAL BUDGETING STAGE

Gatekeeping

Capital budgeting must respect the quality-at-entry processes by preventing projects from being "parachuted" into the budget without first having been appraised and selected as "budget eligible." The absence of a strong gatekeeping function to enforce quality-at-entry decisions is a frequent problem with weak PIM systems. Gatekeeping is an administrative check on projects presented in budget requests to ensure compliance. It is not the same as independent review, which is more of a "challenge function" that should precede budgeting. Gatekeeping is usually performed by the budget department in the finance ministry and relies on the finance ministry having sufficient power to turn away noncompliant projects.

There will be pressures to exempt certain projects from the PIM system, usually because of their supposed "urgency." International experience shows that, if such a fast track exists, it is likely to be overexploited, particularly in relation to politically driven projects, unless adequate safeguards are in place. Such safeguards include being very specific about the circumstances when a project may be fast tracked and establishing a clear set of procedures for determining eligibility. Exemptions must apply only to unforeseeable events and should consider events such as natural disasters, humanitarian emergencies, and national security threats. The final decision on eligibility is best made outside the political arena to avoid political "horse trading." Even for exempt projects, a minimum analysis needs to be performed and documentation prepared to ensure an adequate and proportionate response to the new problem.

Medium-term perspective for expenditure planning

A medium-term perspective for fiscal and expenditure planning is helpful for PIM for the following reasons:

- Project implementation usually lasts longer than one budget cycle.
- Projects have consequences for future expenditures after construction.
- Strategic investment planning, prioritization, and decision making require a longer-term view of resource availability than is provided by the annual budget.

A medium-term budgetary perspective has advantages for PIM as it:

- Allows expenditure planning for the efficient implementation of ongoing multiyear projects (see chapter 7 for a capital expenditure "baseline")

- Assists in estimating the sustainable level of public financing for new spending initiatives, including for new projects (see chapter 7 for estimation of "fiscal space")
- Allows for multiyear expenditure programming, consistent with planning horizons adopted in strategic planning guidance
- Provides a realistic and supportive framework for determining strategic resource allocations, including resource allocation for capital investment expenditures
- Creates a conducive environment for prioritizing new projects in line with strategic planning guidance
- Favors forward planning for the current expenditure requirements of capital investment projects upon completion (chapter 7 looks more closely at the integration of capital and recurrent budgeting).

Despite the advantages of a medium-term expenditure planning perspective, a medium-term perspective (generally three to four years) is often too short to encompass the planning, implementation, and commencement of major projects. As indicated above, supplementary, longer-term strategic expenditure plans may be required for the important infrastructure sectors.

In broad terms, a medium-term expenditure framework (MTEF) is usually seen as the appropriate instrument for implementing a medium-term budgetary perspective. An MTEF can be one of three types: fiscal, budgetary, or performance, corresponding to the stages of development of the instrument. A typology along these lines is described in box 6.7.

A medium-term fiscal framework is a prerequisite for any minimally functional budgetary system and therefore for PIM. The medium-term budget framework is the next stage of development and aims to support a more strategic allocation of budgetary resources (level II in the hierarchy of

BOX 6.7

MTEF typologies

A *medium-term fiscal framework (MTFF)* determines the availability of aggregate resources as an input into budget formulation and sets expenditure ceilings for spending agencies as a basis for budget implementation. The MTFF is top-down in nature, focuses on allocating resources to purchase inputs, and holds spending agencies accountable for the use of inputs.

A *medium-term budgetary framework (MTBF)* specifies spending agency and program expenditure ceilings based on a compromise between the availability of top-down resources determined using an MTFF and the need for bottom-up resources to finance sector spending plans. MTBFs are primarily input based, in that expenditure allocations may be determined by reference to outputs or outcomes, but spending agencies are still held accountable for the use of inputs.

A *medium-term performance framework (MTPF)*[a]—the highest form of MTEF—shifts the focus of attention away from spending agency or program inputs and toward agency or program outputs and outcomes, holding spending agencies responsible for their performance and linking funding to results.

Source: World Bank 2012.

a. MTPF is a term created by the World Bank. The International Monetary Fund (IMF) uses a different term, referring to the advanced stage as a medium-term expenditure framework. MTEF is not used generically in IMF typology. See IMF 2007.

public financial management objectives shown in table 2.1). A functioning MTBF is essential for a fully effective PIM system, where medium-term capital budgeting allocations need to be linked to strategic plans.

The more advanced form of MTEF, the medium-term performance framework, is a desirable objective, but may not be feasible for many countries because it places heavy demands on limited technical, administrative, and political capacities. It is possible to have a fully functional PIM system without having the equivalent of an MTPF, but PIM could be enhanced further by introducing a stronger performance orientation over time.

Box 6.8 provides a short guide to MTEF good practices according to each stage of development. The MTPF will be out of reach for most countries, and many will even struggle to achieve a functioning MTBF, to the detriment of PIM system performance. Nevertheless, it is important to understand how PIM can be supported by best practice in budgeting to be able to visualize and lay the foundations for longer-term reform goals.

While the broad principles and methods will be similar, the exact form and pace of development of an MTEF will vary from country to country according to

BOX 6.8

Guide to MTEF good practices

Medium-term fiscal framework

- Debt and deficit targets are established using model-based debt sustainability analysis, taking into account constraints imposed by policy rules.
- Revenue forecasts are based on revenue department or other tax and nontax receipt models.
- Independent macroeconomic forecasts are used, and fiscal forecasts are subject to scrutiny by an audit office, fiscal council, or similar consultative body.
- Aid commitments are covered by debt sustainability analysis and revenue forecasts.
- The ministry of finance issues a background paper on macrofiscal objectives to inform budget decision making and form part of the budget documentation.

Medium-term budgetary framework

- The ministry of finance issues a budget strategy paper describing the macrofiscal framework with a broad indication of national development and budgetary priorities for the medium term.
- A budget circular is sent to spending agencies outlining the basis on which they should prepare their medium-term budget requests. This circular indicates the availability of budget resources, usually in the form of provisional agency or program expenditure ceilings, and the aggregate cost assumptions to be used, including changes in inflation and public sector pay.
- The budget requests of spending agencies reflect strategic objectives, the costs of current and new activities, expected cost recovery, and other relevant factors.
- Final expenditure ceilings are reflected in the annual budget submitted to the legislature for consideration.
- Spending agency budgets are finalized, and sector strategies are revised to reflect budget realities.
- Spending agency budgets and sector strategies are published.

Medium-term performance framework

- Sector strategies discuss program outputs, outcomes, and performance.
- Agency output, outcome, and performance indicators are used to establish budget targets.
- Spending agencies report on results relative to targets. Comprehensive spending reviews are conducted periodically.

Source: World Bank 2012.

administrative, budgetary, and political traditions. For example, the approach to MTBF expenditure ceilings is highly variable: ceilings by sector versus ceilings by organization or aggregate ceilings versus separate capital and current ceilings. There is greater room for variation when an MTPF has been achieved, depending on the form and degree of sophistication of the performance management system. It is therefore not possible to be as prescriptive when it comes to design issues, unlike the quality-at-entry part of upstream PIM processes. Box 6.9 sets out an integrated MTBF[8] and budgeting process, adapted to include more depth on capital budgeting. Variations on this model should be expected, depending on a country's institutional framework for public financial management and political contexts.

BOX 6.9

An integrated MTBF and budget preparation process

Phase 1: 9–12 months before the new fiscal year

- Cabinet and spending agencies set out national and sector strategic priorities consistent with national and sector plans.
- The ministry of finance, in consultation with other economic agencies, develops the macrofiscal framework and determines the MTEF resource envelope, based on the previous year's MTEF and high-level fiscal targets and rules.
- Spending agencies cost existing expenditure policies and new initiatives, including major projects.
- The ministry of finance prepares a medium-term budget strategy paper and budget-MTEF guidelines that include provisional expenditure ceilings. There may or may not be separate ceilings for capital and current expenditures, depending on whether the government wishes to control these aggregates.

Phase 2: 6–9 months before the new fiscal year

- The cabinet reviews and endorses the medium-term budget strategy paper and provisional ceilings.
- The budget strategy paper is submitted to parliament for information.
- Budget and MTEF guidelines are circulated to spending agencies. (The nature of the guidelines will depend on whether the MTEF is a medium-term budget with hard multiyear ceilings or an annual budget combined with forward estimates, hard budget-year ceilings, and indicative out-year ceilings.)
- Spending agencies prepare their budget and MTEF submissions, taking into account sector strategies, costings for existing expenditure policies, and new initiatives, including capital costs of new major projects, their future recurrent costs, and proposed ceilings.

Phase 3: 3–6 months before the new fiscal year

- The ministry of finance reviews the submissions of spending agencies, and hearings are held with spending agencies to resolve technical differences, including with respect to new major projects.
- The cabinet is consulted about policy differences, including with respect to new major projects, and other issues that could require significant reallocation of budget resources across spending agencies or expenditure programs.
- The ministry of finance updates the macrofiscal framework.
- The ministry of finance prepares the final budget and MTEF, incorporating revised expenditure ceilings.

Phase 4: 0–3 months before the new fiscal year

- The cabinet reviews the final budget or MTEF, endorses ceilings, and submits the budget to parliament for approval.
- Spending agencies revise sector expenditure strategies and prepare business plans, including for the acquisition and improvement of fixed capital assets, consistent with their ceilings.

Source: World Bank 2012, extended by authors to cover capital expenditure dimensions of medium-term budgetary framework (MTBF).

In the absence of a functioning MTBF, the minimum requirement, in addition to an MTFF, is to prepare forward estimates as an input into the budgetary process and then to revise them when the budget is agreed to. Forward estimates capture the implications of ongoing public investment projects for future expenditures.[9] Their value is in presenting budget officials and decision makers with a full picture (by year) of the forward funding requirements for the efficient implementation of the portfolio of ongoing projects. Forward estimates should be presented by year for at least three years—but preferably longer—with a balance to complete after three years. While it may not be practical to present project-specific forward estimates for all ongoing projects as part of budget documentation, consolidated forward estimates should be built up from information on individual projects and should include detailed information on the most important projects in the national investment portfolio. Forward estimates should also be produced for new projects included in the budget, but these forward estimates should be kept separate from those of ongoing projects. With these two pieces of information—(a) forward estimates for ongoing projects and (b) forward estimates for new projects—budget officials and decision makers will have a necessary minimum amount of information to ensure adequate financing for projects to be realized as planned and to balance strategic priorities against the fiscal realities in the case of new projects.

Where PIM systems are still weak, it may not be possible to produce forward estimates for all spending ministries at first. In these cases, the first step is to produce estimates for the major investing ministries.

After the budget is agreed to, it is important to update the forward estimates to take account of the latest decisions. Updated forward estimates will then form the starting point for the following year's budget preparation.

When integrated into a two-step decision-making process, agreed-on forward estimates will form the basis for the capital baselines described more fully in chapter 7. A format for presenting forward estimates is given in table 7.1.

Ireland provides an interesting example of how the adoption of a medium-term expenditure planning perspective has supported PIM and how the approach has developed over time (see box 6.10).

Managing the project pipeline

A medium-term budget framework can be a useful instrument for managing the pipeline of major projects and avoiding the situation where too many projects have been selected and are waiting for budget funding. The latter can put pressure on finance ministries and governments to begin more projects than are affordable over the medium term, resulting in inefficient "drip funding" and delayed completion (see chapter 7 for more on this situation and how to deal with it).

Managing budgetary allocations for conducting feasibility studies for major projects within an MTBF may control the flow of "budget-eligible" projects coming forward. To be effective, such a system would require imposing subceilings for feasibility study funding, forcing spending agencies to prioritize those projects they wish to move from preappraisal to appraisal. It would also require early coding of projects (see chapter 5), so that expenditures on individual feasibility studies can be allocated and accounted for in the budget system. This approach may require a higher degree of management by the center of government than some countries are prepared to countenance and

BOX 6.10

Capital budgeting in a medium-term perspective in Ireland

Ireland's 2004 budget introduced rolling multiannual envelopes for capital expenditures. An envelope is a binding aggregate expenditure allocation—that is, it is not defined by project—that is valid for an extended period of time and cannot be exceeded. This envelope provides a stable and predictable financial framework within which multiyear projects can be planned, programmed, and implemented.

The envelopes are set for five years and are rolled forward annually by one year. The aggregate capital allocation is broken down by ministry ("department") or other relevant higher-order spending agency. The envelope is allocated by year over the five-year period, but unused allocations can be carried over, subject to certain restrictions. Spending ministries must plan and implement their capital expenditures within the limits set by the envelopes.

In the case of capital investment in transport infrastructure, the Irish government decided in November 2005 to go further and to provide for a 10-year multiannual envelope—Transport 21—to take account of the longer time scale for planning and implementing major transport infrastructure projects and to tackle the transport infrastructure deficit. Transport 21 was not, however, a rolling framework; it covered the fixed period 2006–15. It was subsequently pushed off track when the global financial crisis engulfed the country.

An unallocated reserve providing additional amounts is available for allocation each year (except the first year) to support new government priorities for capital investment. This reserve represented around 7 percent of the total within the aggregate allocation for capital expenditures for 2004–08. The unallocated reserve is not for meeting price and physical contingencies arising from planned and ongoing projects: ministries must plan for such contingencies within their allocated capital envelopes.

As part of the Comprehensive Review of Expenditure 2012–14, Ireland introduced an MTEF with binding medium-term financial constraints for most current and all capital expenditures for a three-year period. The ceilings for current expenditures do not apply to demand-driven expenditures (unemployment benefits, for example), which are still planned and managed on an annual basis. This approach is similar to the U.K. model.

The aggregate expenditure ceilings for the MTEF are set by the government upon the recommendation of the minister of finance, who consults with the minister for public expenditure and reform. The allocations between ministries ("ministerial ceilings") are set by the government upon the recommendation of the minister for public expenditure and reform. Having regard to fiscal and economic conditions, the minister of finance makes a recommendation to the minister for public expenditure and reform on the proportions of total expenditures that should go to capital and current expenditures.

Source: World Bank 2014.

may be seen to contradict the philosophy of delegated decision making, which is inherent in performance-oriented budgeting systems. In practice, countries with advanced systems such as the Netherlands and the United Kingdom restrict central management of the project pipeline to major projects only. In Latin America, countries such as Chile and Colombia enforce more discipline from the center.

Project prioritization and capital budgeting decisions

When the quality-at-entry system and gatekeeping function are working effectively, only projects that have been confirmed as a good use of public funds ought to be presented for budget funding. As a result, the appraisal findings will generally have less relevance than other factors at the capital budgeting stage, except to the extent that they will have been instrumental in determining a project's eligibility to be presented for budgeting. This does not mean that appraisal findings are irrelevant to budget decisions. When all other factors are equal, it makes sense to focus public financing on projects that bring a higher social return; however, other factors are usually not equal when it comes to these budgetary decisions.

Some countries, such as Australia and the United Kingdom, have been trying to give more weight to the results of social cost-benefit analysis in budgetary decision making, but the practical impact has tended to be restricted. In the 2010 spending review,[10] the United Kingdom introduced a capital-ranking exercise based on the benefit-cost ratio estimated from social cost-benefit analysis. In Australia, Infrastructure Australia is required to draw up an infrastructure priority list, using benefit-cost ratio and strategic fit as criteria for prioritizing budgetary decisions; however, the government does not necessarily follow the advice.

The complexity of budgetary decisions is illustrated by the U.K. National Audit Office's summing up of expenditure decisions made in the 2010 spending review (U.K. National Audit Office 2012):

> Final prioritisation also reflected other factors [apart from ranking based on benefit-cost ratio], including the government's political and strategic priorities, deliverability, commitments, and regional distribution.

Bearing in mind the political dimension of budgeting, broad technical criteria should generally guide capital budgeting decisions, including

- Strategic importance of the project and the sector based on government policy as expressed in strategic planning documentation and the budget strategy paper (or equivalent)
- Indications, following positive appraisal decisions,[11] that the project will deliver better value for public money than competing, comparable projects
- Significance and sustainability of future budgetary consequences on completion (operation and maintenance costs and "availability" payments for some types of PPPs)
- Compatibility with other proposals for new projects and noncapital expenditures
- Readiness to proceed in the forthcoming budget year, including deliverability of plans for detailed design and procurement and status of land acquisition, compensation, and resettlement arrangements
- Compatibility with the spending ministry's portfolio of ongoing projects in terms of implementation capacity (based on monitoring reports)
- Impact on the overall balance and risk profile of the national public investment program.

Integrating capital budgeting and program-based budgeting

Capital budgeting as part of a developed PIM system should be fully compatible with program-based budgeting;[12] however, care needs to be taken when relating projects to the program structure. It is a mistake to situate projects at the same level as budgetary programs or subprograms; projects should be seen as activities, or components of activities, that are carried out within subprograms.

Projects should contribute to the achievement of subprogram and therefore program objectives.

When fully implemented, program-based budgeting should have implications for decision rights in the budget process. Line ministries are typically responsible for expenditure decisions, including capital investment projects, within their program expenditure allocations. They are then held accountable for achieving subprogram and program objectives. Governments may wish to consider the extent to which they delegate decision making for major projects because they may want to have a stronger say in the strategic orientation, deliverability, and riskiness of their national investment program.

KEY ISSUES IN RELATION TO LINKAGES BETWEEN STRATEGIC PLANNING, QUALITY AT ENTRY, AND BUDGETING

The following issues need to be considered to integrate strategic planning, project, and budgeting cycles:

- At the *strategic planning stage,* the national strategy, sector plans, and subsector master plans, among others, need to be compatible and feasible, to the greatest extent possible. Three linkages are important to consider:
  - Strategic planning is the basis for identifying projects for preparation and appraisal.
  - Strategic plans should be an important reference point for prioritization during capital budgeting.
  - Strategic plans need to be fiscally constrained to improve consistency with future capital budgets.
- During the *quality-at-entry stage,* project compliance with the relevant strategic documents should be a critical assessment criterion. Two linkages are important to consider:
  - Strategic relevance is assessed at preappraisal, as a basis for a decision to proceed to appraisal, and is reviewed again at appraisal.
  - To the extent possible, affordability and fiscal sustainability needs are taken into account at preappraisal and appraisal, making the link with capital budgeting.
- At the *capital budgeting stage,* strategic guidance is reflected in resource allocation decisions and prioritization of new projects, and quality-at-entry decisions are respected. Three linkages are important to consider:
  - Effective gatekeeping is needed to ensure that projects entering the capital budgeting process have been positively appraised and selected beforehand.
  - A medium-term budget framework, possibly supplemented by a longer-term strategic expenditure framework for infrastructure sectors, provides a conducive environment for linking strategic plans, appraisal, and capital budgets.
  - Emphasis is placed on strategic prioritization in capital budget decisions.

Box 6.11 captures how strategic planning, project appraisal, and budgeting are integrated in the Netherlands.

BOX 6.11

Linking strategic planning, project appraisal, and budgeting in the Netherlands

In the Netherlands, the National Policy Strategy for Infrastructure and Spatial Planning (SVIR), a comprehensive vision for the country to 2040 with goals to 2028, is implemented through the Multi-Year Plan for Infrastructure, Spatial Planning, and Transport (MIRT).

MIRT is both a medium-term investment plan (the "MIRT Project Book") and a set of rules (the "MIRT Rules") for project development and implementation. The MIRT Project Book is the medium-term investment program of the government, which is rolled over annually. It brings together national investment and local or regional investment.

The MIRT Project Book is annexed to the annual budget and presents projects to be funded in line with priorities set out in the SVIR and the government program. The Project Book, recently renamed the MIRT Overview and available online, explains the basis for selection, referring to the focal areas for central government action identified in the SVIR.

Source: World Bank 2014.

NOTES

1. Since adoption of the government's PIM resolution in 2013, however, strategic orientation and monitoring have improved in Moldova.
2. The logical framework approach is well described. See Asian Development Bank (2007).
3. The logical framework methodology can and should be used as early as possible in the project cycle (before appraisal) to assist in identifying alternatives and testing their rationale. The methodology is often described as a project cycle management tool because it relates to the whole project cycle. This approach has some drawbacks and should never be used to replace a rigorous quality-at-entry system.
4. A similar model is used in Australia and New Zealand. See http://www.finance.gov.au/property/property/two-stage/ and http://www.treasury.govt.nz/statesector/investmentmanagement/plan/bbc/.
5. These decision points are dealt with in other chapters.
6. See cell 1 in table 6.2.
7. See cell 11 in table 6.2.
8. The process described in box 6.9 is for the MTBF stage of development. The same process is required for an MTPF, with more emphasis on using information on performance to guide expenditure allocation decisions.
9. Forward baseline estimates are estimates of expenditures that are required if policies remain unchanged—that is, there are no new spending initiatives. Forward baseline estimates for both capital and recurrent expenditures are essential for a medium-term budgeting system.
10. The spending review is conducted when multiyear budgets are prepared for expenditures that are not managed annually.
11. Only projects that have been positively appraised and selected should be allowed to request budget funding (see chapter 5). Gatekeeping should control this.
12. Program-based budgeting is the most common approach used to introduce a stronger strategic focus and performance orientation into budgeting.

REFERENCES

Asian Development Bank. 2007. "Project Performance Management System: Guidelines for Preparing a Design and Monitoring Framework." Asian Development Bank, Manila.

European Commission. 2004. *Project Cycle Management (PCM) Handbook*. Brussels: European Commission.

Forsgren, A., and J. Westin. 2014. *Infrastructure Planning: A Challenge for Cross-Border Cooperation*. CERUM Report 41/2014. Umea, Sweden: Umea University, Centrum för Regionalvetenskap.

Gasper, D. 1999. "Problems in the Logical Framework Approach and Challenges for Project Cycle Management." *ACP-EU Courier* 173 (January–February): 75–77.

HM Treasury. 2013. *Public Sector Business Cases: Using the Five Case Model*. London: HM Treasury.

IMF (International Monetary Fund). 2007. *Manual on Fiscal Transparency*. Washington, DC: IMF.

Infrastructure Australia. 2016. *Australian Infrastructure Plan: Priorities and Reforms for Our Nation's Future Report*. Canberra: Infrastructure Australia.

OECD (Organisation for Economic Co-operation and Development). 2017. *Getting Infrastructure Right: A Framework for Better Governance*. Paris: OECD Publishing.

U.K. National Audit Office. 2012. *Managing Budgeting in Government*. London: National Audit Office.

World Bank. 2012. *Beyond the Annual Budget: Global Experience with Medium-Term Expenditure Frameworks*. Washington, DC: World Bank.

———. 2013. "Making Public Investment Work for Competitiveness and Inclusive Growth in Moldova." Public Expenditure Review, World Bank, Washington, DC.

———. 2014. "Study on Cross-Country Comparison: Technical Assistance for Public Investment Project Appraisal and Selection System Development in Ukraine." World Bank, Washington, DC.

7

Upgrading Capital Budgeting Practices

SOME COMMON PROBLEMS

In weaker public investment management (PIM) systems, where budgeting practices are not well developed, ongoing projects typically compete for available fiscal space directly with proposed new projects and frequently lose out, resulting in their either being "drip funded" or stalled. Starving ongoing projects of funds for efficient implementation often leads to higher overall costs and delayed realization of benefits, eroding their social viability.

Another problem in many PIM systems is the failure to plan for the operation and maintenance costs of newly completed projects. A medium-term budgetary perspective can help to avoid this problem, which is often caused by poorly integrated capital and recurrent budgeting.

This chapter looks at approaches to ensuring continuity of funding for the implementation of ongoing projects. These approaches include estimating and agreeing on a capital baseline, allowing for carryover between budget years, and introducing multiannual commitment appropriations. The chapter also examines approaches to better budget integration.

For many countries, the reforms discussed in this chapter will be longer term, and more basic reforms should perhaps be given higher priority. Estimating and agreeing on a capital baseline as part of a medium-term budgetary framework (MTBF)–budget process is a relatively complex reform, requiring a reliable medium-term fiscal framework (MTFF) as well as an accurate and timely monitoring system (see chapter 8). Introducing a system of multiannual commitment appropriations has many advantages, but this reform is even more advanced and should follow successful implementation of a process for estimating and agreeing on a capital baseline.

ESTIMATING A CAPITAL BASELINE

Ceiling setting as part of a medium-term budgetary perspective

As discussed in chapter 6, budgeting is best performed within a medium-term perspective, especially capital budgeting, because of the multiyear nature of expenditures for major capital investment projects. Box 6.9 shows how the medium-term budgetary perspective needs to establish a sustainable medium-term macrofiscal framework (the MTFF) and, subject to this constraint, create firm, strategic expenditure ceilings for the annual budget plus several years. Establishing ceilings involves an arbitration process in which competing "bottom-up" claims on budget allocations by line ministries are reconciled with (fixed) "top-down" constraints on aggregate expenditures. Ceilings are usually established early in the MTEF-budget process. Unlike open-ended bidding, fixed ceilings provide strong incentives for line ministries to prioritize expenditures. Box 6.9 presents a stylized model, within which choices need to be made concerning the following:

- *The "firmness" of ceilings.* The ceiling for the annual budget must be binding, but the outer years of the medium-term perspective may be indicative only. Firm outer-year ceilings are ideal, with technical adjustments made only when the MTEF is rolled over; however, the reliability of forecasts, potential macroeconomic instability, and political resistance may make the use of firm outer-year ceilings difficult in some country contexts.
- *The level of disaggregation of ceilings.* Line ministry expenditure ceilings may be either aggregate ceilings or ceilings disaggregated by current and capital expenditures.[1] Disaggregated ceilings are the preferred approach where a government wishes to ensure minimum expenditures on capital investment (perhaps where such spending has been neglected in the past) and is in line with a commitment to a robust PIM system. On the negative side, separate capital ceilings also diminish the ability of line ministries to make internal trade-offs between current and capital spending in pursuit of their strategic objectives and may be harder to reconcile with a stronger orientation toward performance.[2]

Advantages of a two-step capital budgeting process

In addition to these important choices regarding the scope of ceilings, the approach to setting ceilings and prioritizing expenditures needs to be designed carefully to avoid problems associated with inadequate provision for ongoing projects.

Introducing a two-step ceiling-setting process helps to guard against these problems and to preserve the intertemporal consistency of decision making. This process involves projecting the expenditures needed to continue existing expenditure policies before allocating discretionary fiscal space to new spending initiatives. As far as capital expenditures are is concerned, this process means establishing expenditure requirements for efficient completion of ongoing or committed projects (the "capital baseline") before making decisions on budgetary allocations for new projects. It serves four purposes:

- Establishes minimum expenditure requirements for ongoing projects, setting a lower boundary for ceilings[3]
- Reduces the potential for competition over available financing between ongoing and new projects by directing budgetary discussions toward the allocation of genuinely discretionary fiscal space for new capital projects
- Provides information on how ceilings may have to be adjusted between line

ministries to accommodate major new projects considered as priorities,[4] while ensuring efficient funding for ongoing projects
- Helps to program the efficient implementation of new projects over the medium term to avoid funding shortfalls.

The advantages of the two-step approach apply if there is an aggregate ceiling or are separate capital and recurrent ceilings. In either case, capital and recurrent baselines need to be created as a starting point; the difference comes in the direct trade-offs between new current spending initiatives and new capital projects that will be required when establishing aggregate ceilings.

Figure 7.1 illustrates these concepts. The fiscal space for new projects is shown as the difference between the total resources available for public investment, minus a contingency, and the capital baseline. As illustrated, available fiscal space for capital spending can be expected to increase over time as ongoing projects are completed and financial resources are freed up for new projects; as a result, it becomes easier to allocate funding to new projects toward the end of the medium-term horizon.

Line ministries also should adopt a two-step process internally when deciding how to allocate their designated capital expenditure ceilings. Resources should first be allocated for capital baselines before proposing new projects, while remaining within ceilings.

Figure 7.1 should be interpreted as being applied at the aggregate level, with the resource envelope for public investment derived from the MTFF and reflecting government preferences for capital over recurrent spending.

Figure 7.1 would be similar in the case of aggregate expenditure ceilings: the resource envelope would be for all spending, the baseline would combine the capital and recurrent baselines, and the discretionary fiscal space would be available for new recurrent initiatives and new projects. The difference would lie in the ability to realize efficiency savings on the current baseline[5] and open up further fiscal space for new initiatives or projects.

At the beginning of the first phase of the MTEF-budget process (see box 6.9), line ministries should be required to prepare baseline estimates for capital expenditures,[6] showing the forward funding implications of ongoing and already

FIGURE 7.1

Capital baseline and fiscal space for public investment projects

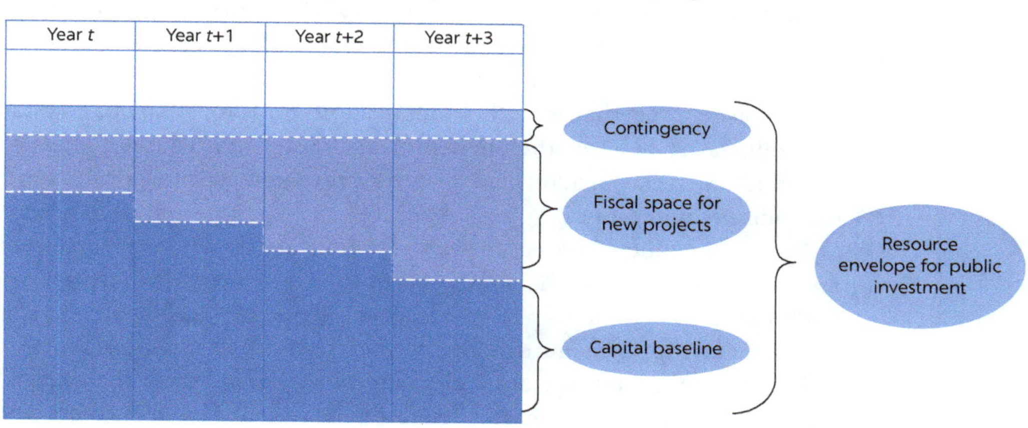

committed projects, based on the latest monitoring information, procurement plans, and financial plans for projects, updated as necessary.

The finance ministry should independently verify the coherence and practicality of the line ministries' forward financing estimates for ongoing and already committed capital investment projects. These estimates should be agreed to with the respective ministries before discussing new projects. The finance ministry should then consolidate the agreed-on estimates to arrive at aggregate forward capital estimates, which are important inputs into determining the aggregate discretionary fiscal space available for capital spending, and should then set provisional capital expenditure ceilings for individual ministries.[7]

The provisional capital ceilings for line ministries should account for the overall resource limits as determined in the MTFF, the ministry capital baselines that have been agreed to, the previous year's ceilings for the relevant years, and the pipeline of major projects under development.

Although estimation of the capital baseline and its incorporation in the ceiling-setting process are good practices, they may not always be feasible. Estimating the forward financing needs of capital projects is information intensive and requires monitoring systems that can track progress and provide a basis for forward projections. Two-step ceiling setting requires strong administrative capacities as well as a tightly disciplined MTEF-budget preparation calendar. These conditions may not exist in low-capacity environments, where an MTEF process is still in the early stages of development and capacity strengthening may be required as a first step.

Budget documentation

The budget documentation should be fully transparent regarding the forward expenditure implications of ongoing and new projects, so that legislators and the public are aware of the commitments entered into through previous and current expenditure decisions. Table 7.1 presents a stylized template for such a presentation, which would normally come as an annex to the budget. The first part of this table builds directly from information on the capital baselines presented by and agreed to with line ministries.

Including information on all projects would be unwieldy, and the focus should be on major projects, with aggregate figures for smaller projects.

The forward estimates provided with the budget provide a starting point for estimating the capital baseline in the next year's exercise and a benchmark for validating line ministry submissions. The information provided on new projects will depend on whether MTEF ceilings are binding or indicative. If indicative, then it is wiser to present only new projects agreed to in the annual budget, together with their implications for future expenditures. If the ceilings are binding, then new projects to begin in the outer years of the medium-term horizon may also be presented, with their forward expenditure implications.

In the Republic of Korea, forward expenditure estimates for projects must be presented to parliament as part of the budgetary documentation. For "continuing expenditures,"[8] the budget bill must be accompanied by "a statement on the payments or estimated payments up to the end of the preceding year, predetermined payments to be disbursed after the current year, an overall activity plan, and details on the status of progress thereof."[9]

TABLE 7.1 **Forward capital expenditure estimates**

PROJECT TITLE	TOTAL ESTIMATED COST	START DATE	CUMULATIVE EXPENDITURES TO END YEAR *T*−2	PLANNED CAPITAL EXPENDITURES[a]						
				YEAR *T*−1	YEAR *T*	YEAR *T*+1	YEAR *T*+2	YEAR *T*+3	YEAR *T*+4	YEAR *T*+I[b]
a. Expenditures on ongoing projects										
Total										
a. Expenditures on new projects within ceilings										
Total										
Grand total										
Expenditure ceiling										

a. Where *t* is the budget year under preparation and years *t*+1 and *t*+2 are the medium horizon for fiscal planning.
b. Expenditure projections required to the end of the implementation period for all projects.

Moldova has instituted a similar requirement as part of its budgetary reforms.

PROVIDING FOR CARRYOVER OF UNUSED BUDGET APPROPRIATIONS FOR CAPITAL PROJECTS

Slower-than-planned implementation as a result of unforeseen factors may cause discontinuities in project funding between years, unless handled carefully. One method of dealing with this problem is to allow carryover of unused expenditure appropriations from one year to the next, as this practice can help to prevent inefficient bunching of expenditures at year end. Slower-moving projects will also not have to compete for funding against new priorities in the new budget year. Where this practice is allowed for multiyear projects, a limit is usually placed on the extent of carryover, typically up to 5 percent of annual appropriations (Lienert and Ljungman 2009).

Box 7.1 summarizes the carryover provisions in Ireland, where the approach is relatively flexible and allows carryover of up to 10 percent of the voted capital allocation. Too liberal a policy can lead to problems, however, as the United Kingdom found when the extent of carryover that had built up over time threatened to jeopardize fiscal sustainability rules. In this case, no limits were placed on the amount of carryover for capital projects, and

BOX 7.1

Carryover provisions in Ireland

As part of the capital envelope system (see box 6.10), ministries are allowed to carry over from one budget year to the next an amount of unspent capital not exceeding 10 percent of the voted capital allocation for the first year. This practice is referred to as "deferred surrender" since the default rule is that all unused budgetary allocations should be given up at the end of the budget year.

Carryover is subject to approval by the minister of public expenditure and reform, and each request is assessed on its own merits. Ministries are no longer required to spend the carryover on projects where there has been underspending; they are allowed to redirect it to other priorities. A case must be made for carryover and for any reallocation to other priorities, and this case is assessed by the Ministry of Public Expenditure and Reform.

The amount of the carryover is identified separately in the law granting ministries the right to spend (the Appropriations Act); if the amount is not spent by the end of the second year, it must be given up definitively (hence the term "deferred surrender").

The carryover provisions give ministries some flexibility in cases where implementation of one or more projects is proceeding more slowly than expected. There is also an incentive to realize savings, since these amounts can be retained and redirected to other priorities in the subsequent year. Any deliberate slowdown in implementation in order to free up resources to start new projects at the expense of ongoing projects is prevented by the requirement for approval by the minister of public expenditure and reform.

Source: World Bank 2014.

carryover could be accumulated over several years. In response, the United Kingdom tightened up its rules and reactivated an annual control on carryover (Lienert and Ljungman 2009).

The International Monetary Fund (IMF) has provided some practical guidance on carryover of budget authority (Lienert and Ljungman 2009). Several preconditions determine whether provision for carryover should be considered:

- Accurate estimation of appropriations so that carryover can be confidently assumed to be a result of efficiency savings or unforeseen delays rather than overbudgeting
- Well-developed accounting and reporting systems to be able to determine the amount by which the budget has been underspent at the end of the year
- Access to finance, so that a government can finance payments when requested and there is no cash rationing
- Well-functioning internal and external audits to prevent wasteful or misdirected expenditures
- Devolved budget management powers that enable adequate managerial authority over the use of carryover funds.

Where the preconditions are not met, carryover should not be allowed or should only be allowed on a restricted basis, as indicated in box 7.2. This situation is likely to be more prevalent in countries with less-developed public financial management systems.

BOX 7.2

Potential for carryover provisions by public financial management status

High-income countries

A generalized system of carryover for both capital and operating expenditures could be introduced once the preconditions are met. Multiyear projects can be granted large carryover, subject to a case-by-case evaluation. For most types of spending, however, carryover should be subject to a quantitative limit of say 3–5 percent of the appropriation. If budget regulations do not make it feasible to single out appropriations for entitlements, grants, interest payments, and other exogenously determined expenditures, the carryover limit for these types of expenditures should be set at zero. To ensure that aggregate fiscal management is not threatened, the government will need to have the ability to limit both the right to carry over unused appropriations and the right to spend accumulated carryovers in individual years.

Emerging-market countries

When emerging-market countries have low levels of investments as a percentage of spending and gross domestic product, carryover of investments could be introduced without creating problems for aggregate fiscal management or cash management. However, a more cautious approach is needed for the general carryover provisions for operational expenditures, as many of the preconditions are not met.

Low-income countries

Most low-income countries do not meet the criteria necessary to introduce generalized carryover. Where multiyear controls on capital projects are in place and work reasonably well, selected carryovers could be considered to avoid having to reappropriate funds in the event that there is a delay in project implementation. Carryovers could also be allowed for donor-financed projects to reduce the administrative burden when expenditures are shifted from one year to the next.

Source: Lienert and Ljungman 2009.

INTRODUCING MULTIANNUAL COMMITMENT APPROPRIATIONS

Overview

To combat the buildup of an excessive stock of ongoing projects, the budget preparation process needs to impose constraints on funding approval for new projects to ensure that the amount approved is not greater than the amount the budget can finance for timely and efficient project completion.

Beginning the budget process by estimating and agreeing on the capital baseline, as discussed above, is one part of the solution. Restricting the approval of new projects within the available fiscal space is the other part. Such restrictions can be approached through less formal, administrative means or through the establishment of more formal, legal restrictions, known as multiannual commitment appropriations, which are approved as part of the legislative process for budgeting. Although the solution will be influenced by administrative and legal traditions, the introduction of multiannual commitment appropriations has much to recommend it.

The adoption of multiannual commitment appropriations for investment projects could assist in resolving the problem of having an excessive number of drip-funded projects. Under this system, an initial multiannual commitment appropriation equal to the approved total project cost is made for each investment project. This appropriation will be drawn on each time a legal contract is entered into in relation to project implementation. The unused balance of the multiannual appropriation is carried forward to subsequent years and remains available to be used as further contracts are signed. The multiannual commitment appropriation for an investment project is reserved specifically for that project and may not be used for other projects. The total amount of multiannual commitment appropriations for investment projects across the whole of government is limited in line with the resource envelope available to government for capital expenditures. The advantage of such a system is that it makes transparent the amount required to complete all projects that are already under way, avoiding the illusion that, by splitting available payment appropriations between more projects, additional fiscal space is being created.

Multiannual commitment appropriations within a system of dual cash and commitment appropriations

Multiannual appropriations fit into a system of dual cash and commitment appropriations, as exemplified by the French system of budget appropriations. Multiannual commitment appropriations for investment projects were introduced in France through the 2001 Organic Budget Law (see box 7.3).

Under a system of dual cash and commitment appropriations, each line ministry receives two types of appropriation (budget allocation) per year in the annual budget. The first is an appropriation for payments, and the second is an appropriation for commitments. The total cost of each investment project is included within the commitment appropriation of the spending ministry concerned and is reserved exclusively for that project.[10] This amount is reserved irrespective of whether contracts equivalent to the total project cost are anticipated to be assigned immediately or whether contracts are expected to be signed at several stages during the multiyear construction period. For each investment project, at any point in time there is a reserved (blocked) commitment appropriation that is equal to the portion of the total approved project cost for which contracts have not yet been signed, but which will be signed during the remainder of the construction period. This system requires the ability to carry over unused commitment appropriations for investment projects during the construction period of the project.

How multiannual appropriations prevent drip funding

Multiannual appropriations for investment projects, if properly implemented, make it impossible to fund new investment projects by "drip funding" current projects or by placing them on the inactive list. The proper implementation of a system similar to that of France is based on two principles: (a) the multiannual appropriation for a specific project must be reserved for that project and may not be diverted to another project,[11] and (b) the government must control the total value of multiannual appropriations for investment project purposes to keep the stock of approved investment projects at an affordable level. When a limit is placed on the value of multiannual appropriations for investment projects and specific multiannual appropriations are reserved for specific projects, it is no longer possible to make room for new projects by cutting funding for current projects. New projects may not be adopted unless the government

BOX 7.3

Multiannual commitment appropriations in France

France has an advanced system that uses commitment authorizations (appropriations) voted by parliament to enhance control over multiannual contractual commitments (*engagements juridiques*) and to ensure the sustainability of the budget. The 2001 Organic Budget Law (*Loi Organique Relative aux Lois de Finances*, the LOLF) established the annually approved commitment authorizations (*autorisations d'engagements*), which extend over several years for investment projects. This authorization creates an upper limit on the total value of new commitments, not just their value for the budget year in question, for which a spending authority can legally contract in a budget year. Payments against these contractual commitments can only be made if there is an accompanying annual payment appropriation: a *crédit de paiement*, or annual limit on the issuing of payment orders, voted by parliament. The commitment authorizations for spending other than investment lapse at the end of the budget year, as do payment authorizations for all spending.

Since a commitment appropriation does not represent authority to pay, payment appropriations for the years beyond the budget year in question must be voted on by parliament in subsequent budgets. Parliament thus exercises a double control, first over contractual commitments entered into and then over payments against these commitments. The intention is to ensure that there can be no unchecked buildup of multiyear commitments that might potentially undermine medium- to long-term fiscal sustainability or the efficient implementation of the portfolio of ongoing projects. The approach increases transparency and strengthens the hand of the legislature over the executive (a key motivation behind France's LOLF).

Notably, France's Constitutional Council did not judge the introduction of multiannual commitment appropriations to be in contradiction to the constitutional requirement for annuality of the budget. The relevant article of the LOLF reads as follows:

> "Article 8
>
> The appropriations made comprise commitment authorizations and cash-limit appropriations. The commitment authorizations set the upper limit on the expenditure that may be committed.
>
> In the case of an investment transaction, the commitment authorization covers a consistent whole able to be implemented or executed without any additions.
>
> The cash-limit appropriations set the upper limit for the expenditure that may be authorized for payment or paid during the year to cover commitments contracted under commitment authorizations.
>
> The sum of commitment authorizations made for personnel expenditure is equal to the sum of cash-limit appropriations made.
>
> Multiannuality of commitment authorization is captured by the requirement for an investment transaction to be a 'consistent whole.'"

Source: The official translation of the 2001 LOLF is from Ministry of Economy and Finance, France 2001.

provides an additional multiannual appropriation equal to the total project cost. Figure 7.2 illustrates how multiannual commitments would work for a notional project of US$500 million carried out over five years through a series of contracts.

Multiannual investment project appropriations also give line ministries an incentive to complete the construction of existing projects in a timely manner. As long as an existing project remains incomplete, the total project cost remaining, up to the point of completion, is reserved as a multiannual appropriation for that project. Only by completing the project can the amount of the ministry's commitment appropriation be reduced and space freed up for new projects. When the total multiannual appropriation for current projects is reduced, it becomes easier for the ministry to request approval of new projects.

FIGURE 7.2

Example of a US$500 million multiannual appropriation carried over five years

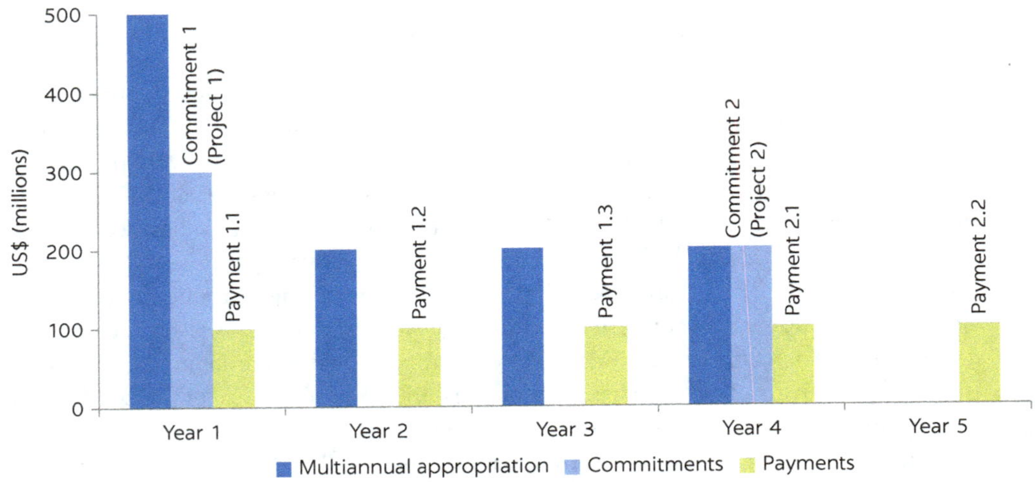

Source: World Bank 2016.
Note: After making an initial multiannual appropriation of US$500 million for the total cost of the project in year 1, a first contract is entered into in year 1, involving a commitment of US$300 million and leading to three separate payments to the contractor of US$100 million in each of years 1, 2, and 3. No further contracts are signed in years 2 and 3, so commitments for those years are zero. In year 4, the remaining US$200 million is committed in the form of a second contract. This process results in two separate payments of US$100 million in each of years 4 and 5. Nothing remains of the initial multiannual project appropriation in year 5, as the total of US$500 million had been contracted for by year 4.

Design issues for implementing a system of multiannual commitment appropriations

Some key design issues must be addressed when implementing a system of multiannual appropriations:

- A prerequisite for adopting a system of multiannual commitment appropriations is the introduction of a credible, rolling multiannual fiscal and expenditure framework within which aggregate expenditure limits and ceilings on line ministries' expenditures are defined (see chapter 6). Without such a framework, it is difficult to place realistic limits on the total value of multiannual commitment appropriations and their allocation across credit holders.
- The positive effects of reserving multiannual appropriations for the remaining total cost of each investment project depend entirely on constraining the total value of such commitment appropriations in line with affordability across the whole of government. To achieve this balance, the total value of multiannual appropriations across the government as a whole must be made a function of the aggregate resource envelope that is available for capital expenditures, as derived in the MTFF prepared for the budget strategy paper or its equivalent.
- An essential prerequisite for introducing the new project appropriation system is rationalization of any excessive stock of existing investment projects (active or inactive) in line with affordability. If the estimated cost of completing the existing portfolio is already many times more than what the government can afford, then a system of multiannual appropriations cannot begin to function. This system can only work if the stock is sufficiently

rationalized, resulting in projects being definitively canceled, mothballed for possible subsequent completion, or prioritized for swift completion.

- Institutional and technical reforms to improve the reliability of cost estimates are essential. The system depends on reliable estimates of total project costs.
- Operating a system of commitment appropriations requires the ability to monitor and control the value of the contractual commitments into which line ministries enter. This ability requires the development of a satisfactory commitment control system, an essential component of a functioning public financial management system.[12] Operating the dual system of commitment and payment appropriations will only be feasible when this system is in place. So, for prioritizing reforms, countries need to focus on building stronger commitment controls before introducing multiannual commitment controls.
- The system needs to be able to carry over unused commitment appropriations during the construction period of the project concerned.
- Aggregate fiscal discipline is needed to ensure that the government retains firm control over annual aggregate cash expenditures. Under any system of dual commitment and cash appropriations, individual ministries and the government as a whole need to manage the interaction between multiannual commitments and cash expenditures. Each time a line ministry signs a contract requiring payments that extend over several years, it commits the government to cash expenditures beyond the current fiscal year. It is essential that the volume of these future cash expenditures is monitored and managed carefully to ensure that it is not excessive.
- Clear rules about the treatment of donor-funded projects are needed within this framework. Donor-funded projects are also limited by the availability of fiscal space in the national budget because they often require national cofinancing. In these cases, the national cofinancing component of the total project cost[13]—not the total project cost—needs to be reserved through commitment appropriations.

INTEGRATING CAPITAL AND RECURRENT BUDGETING

Introduction

Provision for the sustainable operations of newly created assets has been identified as one of the eight key components of a minimally functional PIM system (see chapter 2, figure 2.2). Sustainable operation requires planning and budgeting for adequate funds to cover the costs of operation and maintenance over the planned economic life of a new facility.[14]

Poor integration of capital and recurrent expenditure planning and budgeting are frequently cited as weaknesses of public financial management systems. Poor integration often leads to the planned benefits of investment not being realized in full because a shortage of funding for operating expenses or maintenance prematurely ends an asset's planned operating life. This shortage may be particularly problematic where a large share of public investment is planned and financed by donors and inadequate attention is paid to the financing of operation and maintenance through domestic financial resources.

The importance of these failings is illustrated by the public expenditure and financial accountability (PEFA) assessment framework, where the rationale for dimension 11.3 of PI-11, "Public investment management," is described as follows (PEFA Secretariat 2016):[15]

> Dimension 11.3 evaluates whether budget documentation includes medium-term projections of investment projects on a full-cost basis and whether the budget process for capital and recurrent spending is fully integrated. Sound budget management requires preparation of comprehensive and forward-looking project budget plans for capital and recurrent costs over the life of the investment. Projections of recurrent cost implications from projects are needed to plan and incorporate costs into budgets. Solid budget and cash-flow management, as well as cost-benefit analysis, depend on comprehensive financial analysis of investment projects.

Under this dimension, the highest score is reserved for those systems where "projections of the total life-cycle cost of major investment projects, including both capital and recurrent costs together with a year-by-year breakdown of the costs for at least the next three years, are included in the budget documents."

The ideal model is one where information on the total life-cycle costs of major projects[16] is presented to decision makers at budget time and includes an annual breakdown of expenditures over the medium term. At the technical level, this information needs to be supported by cost estimates for the entire life of a project, which are developed during preparation of a feasibility study and updated after detailed design, before a project is selected for budget funding.

Country public financial management systems with a high degree of integration between capital and recurrent expenditure planning usually have the following key features (Webber 2007):

- A single (combined) annual budget law and appropriation process
- Clear and unified responsibilities for budgetary preparation and implementation within the relevant public sector institutions
- A unified budget presentation, with supporting classification and accounting systems
- Budget planning and management techniques within individual spending agencies that encourage and enable the effective use of financial resources.

Budget integration encompasses more than sustainable financing of individual investment projects, once operational; it also covers the wider issue of achieving an optimal balance between recurrent and capital spending in pursuit of government and sector policy objectives. A program-based approach to budgeting, set within a medium-term perspective, is often seen as a suitable way to achieve this balance, whereby capital and recurrent expenditures are planned jointly to achieve desired budgetary outcomes.

Reasons for poor integration

Poor integration of capital and recurrent budgeting can arise for various reasons, which may apply in combination or separately:

- *Dual budgets.* Two separate budgets are prepared and approved, one for recurrent expenditures and one for capital or "development" expenditures.[17]
- *Dual budgeting.* Dual budgets themselves need not cause problems, provided preparation is coordinated adequately; institutional constraints may impede this coordination, however.
- *Institutionalized dual budgeting.* Where there are separate budgets, responsibilities for their preparation may be allocated to two different organizations, the finance ministry for the recurrent budget and the planning ministry (or equivalent) for the development budget. Such an allocation of

responsibilities can impede integrated budget planning, unless strong coordination mechanisms are in place.

- *Internalized dual budgeting.* Even where one organization is responsible for preparing both budgets, separate departments may be responsible for each. Inadequate internal coordination may then prevent integrated budget planning. This problem often arises where finance and planning ministries have been merged in the interests of, among other things, better budget integration, for example. It may even occur in the context of an apparently unified budget.
- *Dual budgeting at the line ministry level.* Even where the central financial and planning authorities are organized for integrated budgeting, dualism can continue to exist at the line ministry level, with responsibilities separated between the finance department (recurrent) and planning department (capital and recurrent). This impediment may also accompany and intensify weak coordination at the center. Even if there appears to be integration at the center, this integration is illusory if spending agencies maintain a dichotomy between capital and recurrent expenditures.
- *Absence of medium-term budgetary perspective.* Integrated budgeting has limited meaning when the budgetary planning horizon is annual. Major projects take more than a year to complete, and the consequences of recurrent expenditures will only be felt on completion. Operation and maintenance expenditure requirements for new projects can only be considered within a medium- to long-term planning perspective.

A comprehensive solution to budget integration

World Bank guidance on the integration of recurrent and capital "development" budgets (Sarraf 2005) identifies four necessary elements to achieving fully integrated budgeting:[18]

- *Organizational and staffing integration within a single ministry.* Good-practice experience suggests that responsibility for coordinating budget preparation should reside with a single ministry. This ministry may be a strengthened finance ministry with upgraded analytical capabilities for budgeting capital or development expenditures, or it may be a unified finance and planning ministry, bringing together the budgetary and planning expertise of two previously separate ministries.
- *Integrated budget preparation.* Organizational integration is not sufficient by itself and generally needs to be accompanied by bringing budget preparation staff together in a single department with a single manager. The same staff also needs to be responsible for both capital and recurrent spending in any sector or subsector. The same arrangements should be mirrored at the line ministry level.
- *Unified budget documentation and presentation.* A budget presentation that brings together capital and recurrent spending in a single place, using a common classification, is an important foundation for integrated budgeting,[19] although it is not enough to ensure the integration of underlying processes. The use of different budget classifications for recurrent and development budgets is a frequent concern and allows for the emergence of a hybrid development budget containing both capital and recurrent expenditures. This issue frequently arises where the development budget is heavily donor financed.
- *Unified execution, accounting, and reporting systems.* Integrated budgeting needs to be supported by integrated flows of financial information. The lack

of integrated financial information can be a particular weakness where donor projects make up a significant share of investment and where donors do not systematically use national financial management systems. In these cases, integrated budgeting becomes very difficult because of irregular and inaccurate information on projects and their progress.

While reforms of this nature are desirable goals, it may be difficult to achieve them in the near term. The presumption in favor of a single budgeting entity, driven by the simplicity of the arrangement, among other things,[20] may need to be tempered according to the country context, as the following extract from World Bank guidance on budgeting (Dorotinsky 2004) explains,

> When the current and investment budget processes are separate, whether or not they should be unified depends on the institutional characteristics of the country. In countries where the agency responsible for the investment budget is weak, and the ministry of finance is not deeply involved in ex ante line-item control and day-to-day management, transferring responsibilities for the investment budget to the ministry of finance would tend to improve budget preparation as a whole. (Whether this option is preferable to the alternative of strengthening the agency responsible for the investment budget can be decided only on a country-specific basis.) In other countries, one should first study carefully the existing processes and administrative capacities. For example, when the budgetary system is strongly oriented toward ex ante controls, the capacity of the ministry of finance to prepare and manage a development budget may be inadequate. A unified budget process would in this case risk dismantling the existing network of civil servants who prepare the investment budget, without adequate replacement. Also, as noted, coordination problems may be as severe between separate departments of a single ministry as between separate ministries.

Governance issues may also make it preferable to sequence reforms—for example, ensure that robust quality assurance arrangements are in place for public investment projects—before unifying responsibilities for capital and recurrent budgeting under a single ministry (Dorotinsky 2004).

In the interim, before major reforms can be implemented, operational solutions to the budget integration question are needed, with an emphasis on the narrower issue of providing for the sustainable operation of new projects on completion.

NOTES

1. Within current expenditures, governments may also wish to put a ceiling on the wage bill while allowing wage bill savings to be spent on other goods and services.
2. Where line ministries are held accountable for budgetary outputs and outcomes rather than inputs.
3. When the system is stable and has been functioning well. If this is not the case, it may not be possible to fund the capital baseline; a rationalization of the national portfolio of public investment projects will be required before attention to the capital baseline will yield results. See chapter 11 for a further discussion on the rationalization.
4. Because of the scale and indivisibility of major capital projects, step-changes in ceilings will generally be required to accommodate new projects. Generally, such step-changes can be accommodated more readily in the final year of the MTEF horizon, which will not have been included in the previous year's MTEF.
5. Savings in the capital baseline would not normally be expected. Attention is focused on delivering well-designed projects on time and within budget. The exception might be if a failing project is canceled.

6. Line ministries should also provide baseline estimates for current expenditures.
7. Or aggregate ceilings, taking into account estimates of the current baseline and any potential savings if this is the preferred approach.
8. In Korea, "continuing expenditure" is defined as "expenditure on the projects for construction works, manufacturing, [and] research and development, which take several years for completion."
9. Article 34 of the National Finance Act, 2006 as amended.
10. Since the 2001 passage of the LOLF in France, the nature of commitment appropriations in respect of investment projects was changed to require reservation (blocking) of the full amount of project costs within the total amount of each ministry's commitment appropriation. Article 9 states that commitment appropriation is required to cover the costs of a project that is complete and of a nature that can be put into service without the addition of further components.
11. Other than in redefined circumstances, such as cancellation of an existing project.
12. PEFA Secretariat (2016). See dimension 2, "Effectiveness of expenditure commitment controls."
13. More generally, when developing a system that requires appropriations for investment projects to be committed up front, the anticipated cost to the national budget should be reserved. If there is other nongovernment funding (for example, private), this funding should be disregarded in reserving funding from the commitment appropriation. As in France, rules will need to be developed for commitments associated with the use of innovative funding mechanisms, such as public-private partnerships.
14. User charges may be a source of financing for operation and maintenance, but careful planning is needed.
15. This preoccupation is not new. The previous version of the PEFA assessment framework included dimension IV of PI–12, "Linkages between investment budgets and forward expenditure estimates." A "D" score was applied in cases where "budgeting for investment and recurrent expenditure are separate processes with no recurrent cost estimates being shared."
16. The appropriate way to present this information is in present value terms—discounting future costs to the budget year in question using the applicable public sector discount rate. In the United Kingdom, when the government reports on the size and composition of its government major projects portfolio (GMPP), it addresses the whole-life cost of projects, not just their initial capital cost: "The total whole-life cost of those projects on the GMPP reporting cost data this year is £489bn [billion]" (Major Projects Authority 2015).
17. A further complication is that development budgets often include expenditures that are recurrent in nature. This situation often occurs where the development budget is funded mainly by donors and the recurrent budget is funded through domestic resource mobilization.
18. Other commentators have set out similar requirements for an integrated approach that emphasizes legislative, institutional, presentational, and management dimensions of reform (see Webber 2007).
19. Different types of expenditures should be distinguishable from one another. A separate presentation of capital and recurrent funding within a unified budget, using a common economic classification, is essential.
20. According to Caiden and Wildavsky (1974), "Where coherence is at a premium, where any consistent policy may be better than several that cancel each other out, where layers of bureaucracy already frustrate each other, and where a single budget hardly works, choosing two budgets and two sets of officials over one seems strange. The keynote in poor countries should be simplicity. Designs for decisions should be as simple as anyone knows how to make them. The more complicated they are, the less likely they are to work. On this basis, there seems little reason to have several organizations dealing with the same expenditure policies. One good organization would represent an enormous advance. Moreover, choosing the finance ministry puts the burden of reform where it should be—in the budgetary sphere."

REFERENCES

Caiden, N., and A. Wildavsky. 1974. *Planning and Budgeting in Poor Countries.* Piscataway, NJ: Transaction Publishers.

Dorotinsky, W. 2004. "The Budget Preparation Process." In *PFM Training Course*, ch. 4. Washington, DC: World Bank.

Lienert, I., and G. Ljungman. 2009. "Carry-Over of Budget Authority." Public Financial Management Technical Guidance Note, Fiscal Affairs Department, International Monetary Fund, Washington, DC.

Major Projects Authority. 2015. *Major Projects Authority Annual Report 2014–15*. London: Cabinet Office.

Ministry of Economy and Finance, France. 2001. *Loi organique relative aux lois de finances*. Ministry of Economy and Finance, Paris.

PEFA Secretariat. 2016. "Effectiveness of Expenditure Commitment Controls of PI–25." In *Framework for Assessing Public Financial Management*. Washington, DC: PEFA Secretariat.

Sarraf, F. 2005. "Integration of Recurrent and Capital 'Development' Budgets: Issues, Problems, Country Experiences, and the Way Forward." Public Expenditure Working Group Implementation Note, World Bank, Washington, DC.

Webber, D. 2007. "Integrating Current and Capital Budgets: A Four-Dimensional Process." *OECD Journal of Budgeting* 7 (2): 93–107.

World Bank. 2014. "Study on Cross-Country Comparison: Technical Assistance for Public Investment Project Appraisal and Selection System Development in Ukraine." World Bank, Washington, DC.

———. 2016. "Romania: Advisory Services Agreement on Support to Strengthening Public Investment Management. Output 2: Draft Report Identifying Potential Improvements to Information System for Monitoring the Public Investment Portfolio." World Bank, Washington, DC.

8

Project Implementation, Monitoring, and Adjustment

OVERVIEW

The previous chapters have mainly dealt with upstream public investment management (PIM) processes and their treatment in the regulatory framework. The downstream stages of the project cycle and broader PIM system also need to be addressed in the PIM framework. Procedural guidelines will be required, supported by detailed methodological guidance, with the aim to establish a system that ensures the following:

- Works and services are procured economically and contracts are managed properly.
- Projects are delivered on time, to budget, and in accordance with design specification.
- Implementation progress is monitored against plans, any deviation or emerging problems are identified early and transparently, and suitable solutions are put in place in a timely fashion.
- Where necessary, projects are adjusted to reflect changes in cost, scheduling, and demand conditions, including termination if this solution is the most economically efficient.

Where aspects of downstream processes are already defined in existing legal and regulatory instruments—for example, public procurement or budget execution—they do not need to be repeated in the regulatory framework for PIM, which may risk setting up unintended contradictions. Instead, PIM guidelines should refer users to the relevant parts of existing laws and regulations.

The rest of this chapter looks at management, monitoring, and adjustment of project implementation. Procurement and contract management are specialist subjects and are not yet dealt with in this guide.[1]

PROJECT IMPLEMENTATION ARRANGEMENTS

Organizational arrangements and responsibilities for managing project implementation

The PIM procedural guide (tier 2 in the hierarchy described in chapter 3) must establish organizational arrangements for project implementation. Their sophistication may vary based on project size, but accountabilities and responsibilities need to be assigned clearly and should indicate the following:

- Who is accountable at the senior management level of the project's sponsor or owner (hereafter referred to simply as the sponsor) for achieving project objectives and making critical implementation decisions
- Who is responsible for managing project delivery according to the plan agreed on with senior management
- What decisions are delegated to the project manager, what deviations from plan can be decided at this level, and what must be escalated to senior management
- What are the reporting obligations from the lower to the senior management levels.

Using the U.K. model, the following hierarchy of roles and responsibilities represents a good basis for managing and controlling the implementation of major projects, irrespective of the level of development of a country:

- *Senior responsible owner* (also known as project executive or director in other systems). The senior responsible owner (SRO) chairs the project board and has executive responsibility for decisions relating to the project. The SRO ensures that the project remains focused on achieving its objectives and delivers the anticipated benefits.
- *Project board* (also known as project steering committee in other systems). The project board comprises representatives with authority to make decisions and commit resources, including from the user and supplier sides. Chaired by the SRO, it has overall accountability for successful project delivery. It should include one person, the senior user, who represents senior managers with an interest in the project and whose activities will be affected by it. This person should also represent end users to promote their concerns and interests. The senior supplier represents those units that are designing, developing, facilitating, procuring, and implementing the project and is responsible for the quality of project outputs. Additional expert opinions may be sought to help the SRO and project board in decision making. Membership of the board should be kept to a minimum to facilitate effective decisions and provide clear leadership and direction.
- *Project manager*. The project manager is responsible for managing project development and delivery on behalf of the project sponsor or delegated agency. The project manager leads and manages the project team and has the authority and responsibility to run the project on a day-to-day basis, within the remit provided by the project sponsor and agreed-on constraints or delegations provided by the SRO or project board.
- *Project team* (also known as the project implementation unit in other systems). The project team assembles the necessary professional technical or specialist skills and reports to the project manager. It is responsible for

activities defined by the project manager within the time, cost, and quality constraints set by the project board. The size and makeup of the team will depend on the nature of the work and may be supplemented by specialists at key points in the project. It may also include staff from different organizations working together as a team.

Although the titles may vary, this management structure is useful for countries that are implementing major projects. For less sophisticated projects, it may not be necessary to nominate a project board (or equivalent); for the simplest projects, a full-time project team may not be required. Figure 8.1 summarizes project manager and SRO responsibilities.

Figure 8.2 shows how arrangements similar to those in the United Kingdom have been applied in Ghana for complex health sector projects. In this case, the user panel is a country-specific addition.

The SRO, project board, project manager, and project team come from the project sponsor or the subordinate government agency where project implementation has been delegated. If services or works are contracted out, the contractors will have their own arrangements, which will interface with those of the project sponsor. The contractor should appoint a project director as the senior point of contact with the project sponsor.

FIGURE 8.1

Responsibilities of the project manager and senior responsible owner (SRO) in the United Kingdom

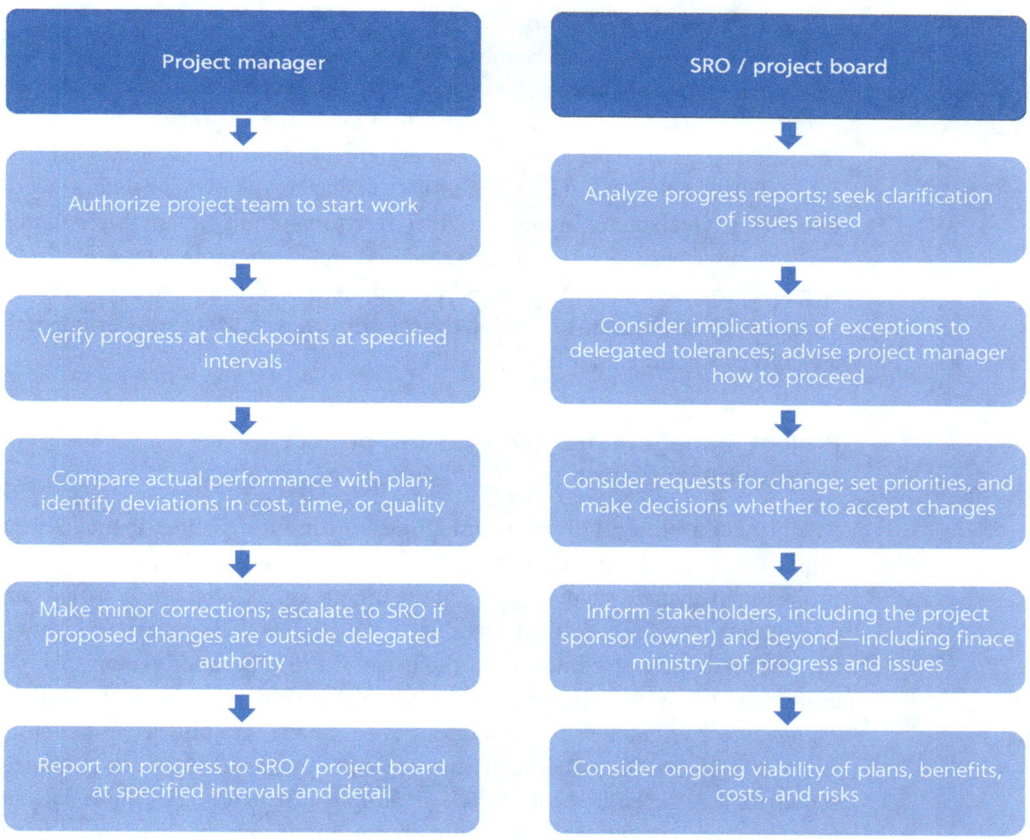

Source: Adapted from U.K. Department for Business, Innovation, and Skills 2010.

FIGURE 8.2

Project management arrangements for complex health projects in Ghana

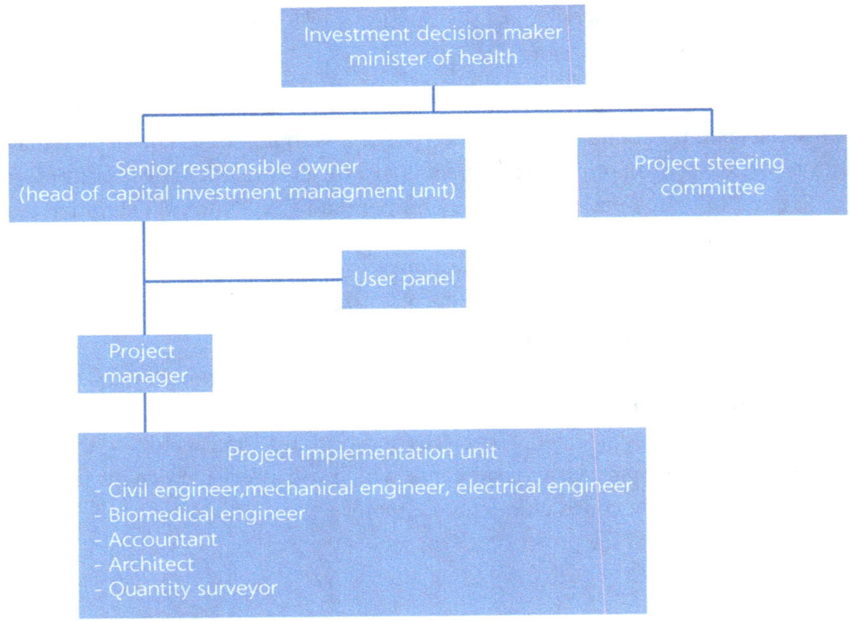

Source: Ministry of Health, Ghana.

If the project sponsor lacks the capacity to perform some of the roles in full, additional human resources may be contracted for; but these resources must be integrated into the organization for the duration of the project, and the SRO, or equivalent, must be a permanent member of the organization. A common error is to rely too much on outsourcing project management, even at senior levels, resulting in inadequate internal control over project implementation. Senior managers may also lack the necessary skills to perform their roles effectively. Negative experiences in these areas have led the United Kingdom to embark on a major training program to develop the capacities needed within government to lead projects at the senior level.[2]

Project management guidance and project management planning

PIM procedural regulations or guidelines outline the project management requirements, and more detailed guidance should be issued in the form of a project management manual (tier 3 in the hierarchy; see chapter 3), which can be general or sector specific. Individual agencies may then prepare their own project management guidance on the basis of the general or sector-specific guidance. The U.S. Federal Transit Administration's *Construction Project Management Handbook* is an example of relatively straightforward sector-specific guidance (U.S. Federal Transit Administration 2012). Such guidance usually covers the entire project cycle, including upstream stages, but it does so from the management perspective, not the methodological perspective covered in the project appraisal manuals considered in chapter 5. Following on the example of the U.S. Federal Transit Administration, box 8.1 summarizes the

BOX 8.1

Example from the United States: Table of contents of the Metrolink project management manual

1. Introduction
   - 1.1. Purpose and structure of the manual
   - 1.2. Metrolink's service territory
   - 1.3. Typical Metrolink projects
   - 1.4. Safe working
   - 1.5. Nonconstruction projects
2. Metrolink project structure
   - 2.1. General
   - 2.2. Strategy and capital planning group
   - 2.3. Project executive group
   - 2.4. Project sponsor
   - 2.5. Program manager
   - 2.6. Project manager
3. Project life cycle
   - 3.1. Strategic phase
   - 3.2. Initiation phase
   - 3.3. Planning phase
   - 3.4. Design phase
   - 3.5. Bid award phase
   - 3.6. Construction phase
   - 3.7. Closeout phase
4. Procurement or contract delivery
   - 4.1. Teaming with technical groups
   - 4.2. Contract management
   - 4.3. Coordination with the program management office
5. Project manager role and responsibilities
   - 5.1. Qualifications and training
   - 5.2. How project managers are assigned
   - 5.3. Project manager work loads
   - 5.4. Project manager duties
6. Program management office

Source: Southern California Regional Rail Authority 2011.

project management manual of the Metrolink commuter rail system for Southern California in the United States.

Based on project management guidance, it is good practice for the project manager to prepare a project management plan, setting out how the project will be managed, executed, monitored, controlled, and closed. The plan should lay out the project delivery strategy, organization and management structure, assignment of responsibilities between the project owner and contractors, and delegation of management and financial authority within the project team. Box 8.2 indicates a possible structure for a project management plan.

Planning implementation activities

Implementation of a construction project, once it has been agreed to in principle on the basis of an appraisal, has four main components:

1. Implementation planning and land acquisition
2. Detailed design
3. Construction supervision
4. Construction.

BOX 8.2

Example from the United States: Federal Transit Administration project management plan outline

1. Project overview
   - Background (authorization)
   - Stakeholders
   - Scope, budget, schedule
   - Delivery strategy
2. Organization and staffing
   - Position within owner organization
   - Project organization
   - Key personnel job functions
3. Project management and controls
   - Scope control and configuration management
   - Budget and cost control
   - Schedule control
   - Project accounting
   - Project reporting
   - Records management
4. Planning and conceptual design phase management
   - Sustainability goals
   - Planning studies
   - Site investigations
   - Permitting
   - Environmental clearance
   - Real property acquisition
5. Final design phase management
   - Design management
   - Design standards
   - Design reviews
   - Value engineering
   - Constructability reviews
6. Construction phase management
   - Construction management
   - Field inspection
   - Third-party construction
   - Change management
   - Construction safety
   - Design support
7. Closeout phase management
   - Test and start-up
   - Operator training
   - Contract closeout
   - Administrative closeout
8. Quality management
   - Design quality assurance and control
   - Construction quality assurance and control
   - Final acceptance and approval
9. Risk management
   - Risk identification and analysis
   - Risk monitoring and response
10. Procurement and contract administration
    - Procurement plan
    - Contract administration
      - Professional services
      - Construction
      - Equipment supply and install
    - Third-party agreements
11. Communications
    - Project team
    - Community
    - Media
    - Government

Source: U.S. Federal Transit Administration 2012.

PIM guidelines should emphasize that activities under each component must be carefully planned,[3] sequenced, and managed by the project manager within the constraints set by senior management within the project sponsor. As much of the work will be outsourced, contract management will be an important part of the project management team's responsibilities. Separate and sequential funding allocations should be planned for each component during budgeting, linked to the achievement of important project milestones. Appropriate sequencing of procurement and contracting activities and of related budget allocations is important. Premature selection and contracting can lead to penalty payments if, for example, land acquisition, resettlement, and permitting issues have not already been resolved. Failure to plan properly for preconstruction activities is a frequent problem in many countries. Budgeting for project implementation when these issues have not been resolved runs the risk of underexecuting the budget and tying up funding that could be better used elsewhere.

The project management team should begin implementation by updating and deepening the project implementation plan, an outline of which should have been prepared at appraisal. Typical activities under the main components of project implementation could be sequenced as follows for a standard construction project:

1. Planning and land acquisition:
   - Selection of site and administration
     - Select site, align road; decide on location of facilities and route for power lines
     - Obtain licenses and approvals
   - Resettlement action plan
     - Conduct resettlement study
     - Draw up a resettlement plan
     - Fix the cost for resettlement and request funding for this action
   - Compensation for crops, land, and infrastructure
     - Determine crops, land, and infrastructure that could be influenced by the project
     - Complete detailed survey of land required and submit it to relevant authority
     - Estimate cost for crop compensation
     - Estimate cost for infrastructure compensation
     - Estimate cost for land compensation
     - Consolidate cost and request funding
     - Initiate consultative and legal steps for land acquisition and resettlement
     - Make compensation payments
     - Source funding for procurement of design consultants
     - Obtain approval of funding for procurement of design consultants

2. Procurement of consultants and detailed design
     - Compile terms of reference for design consultants
     - Start the bidding process
     - Evaluate bids submitted
     - Receive the approval and award of the tender committee
     - Sign the contract
     - Set timelines for completion of design, agree, and sign-off
     - Provide consultants with land acquisition detail
     - Make progress payments for consultants
     - Have consultants issue preliminary designs for comments or approval
     - Have consultants compile detailed designs, specifications, and bill of quantities, as well as draft tender documentation
     - Have consultants issue works contract estimate
     - Apply for funding to appoint construction supervision consultants

- Receive approval for funding for appointment of construction supervision consultants
- Apply for funding based on the approved and agreed-on works contract estimates
- Receive funding approval from the finance ministry for execution of works contract

3. Procurement of construction supervision consultants
   - Compile terms of reference for supervision consultants
   - Start the bidding process
   - Evaluate bids submitted
   - Receive approval and award from the tender committee
   - Sign contracts

4. Works contract procurement, implementation, and completion
   - Start the bidding process
   - Evaluate bids submitted
   - Have the tender committee issue approvals and awards
   - Sign agreement
   - Hand over the site
   - Mobilize the contractor
   - Have the contractor issue a baseline program shortly after signing the contract
   - Have the contractor issue a detailed program cash flow shortly after signing contract
   - Have the contractor issue legally required documentation
   - Have the contractor issue a health and safety plan
   - Have the contractor issue an environmental management plan
   - Have the supervision consultants conduct monthly progress meetings and complete monthly progress reports
   - Have the contractor update program and cash flow on a monthly basis
   - Have the contractor hire an engineer to certify interim payment certificates for contractor on a monthly basis
   - Complete the works contract
   - Have a practical completion certificate issued
   - Have the engineer submit as-built drawings
   - Begin the defects liability period
   - Conduct a final inspection at the end of the defects liability period
   - Have the engineer issue a final completion certificate
   - Have the engineer issue a final contract certificate for payment
   - Complete the contract
   - Conduct a contract review.

MONITORING

Introduction

In a well-functioning PIM system, financial and physical progress is monitored closely during project implementation. Monitoring should provide early warning of any implementation problems and be accompanied by formal procedures to ensure that such warnings are followed up. More sophisticated, performance monitoring after implementation ensures that projects are delivering the expected results with the intended outcomes—that is, services are delivered to target beneficiaries with the anticipated positive effects on their welfare. Performance monitoring provides the raw material in terms of information for midterm and ex post evaluation exercises.

The World Bank (2008) offers one definition of monitoring:

> The continuous assessment of project implementation in relation to agreed schedules and of the use of inputs, infrastructure, and services by project beneficiaries. It is an integral part of good management by a project implementing agency. Its main objectives are to provide continuous feedback on implementation and to identify actual or potential successes and problems as early as possible to facilitate timely adjustments to project operation.

This is a good general definition, but it does not capture the variations in frequency or detail of monitoring activities. Monitoring differs in intensity because information requirements vary according to the roles and responsibilities of organizations at different levels of public investment management and delivery. Organizations at the center of government, such as the finance or planning ministries,[4] will have different information needs from the project manager, who has direct responsibility for delivering an investment project on time and within budget, and from the spending agency that is financially accountable for the project. Finance ministries should be more concerned with the aggregate picture and less concerned with day-to-day progress on individual projects, except in the case of major projects with significant fiscal consequences or where inadequate implementation might threaten value for money.

A good monitoring system is built on reliable information flows within the public investment management and delivery system. Basic summary information on individual projects needs to be available to persons at the top of the system to be able to (a) identify potential problems early on, (b) request more information, and, if necessary, (c) solicit remedial action. The extent to which the finance ministry itself requires direct access to information on *all* individual projects will depend on the nature of the public financial management system—for example, how much expenditure decision making has been decentralized to spending agencies and what is the degree of performance orientation.

In general, finance ministries in Organisation for Economic Co-operation and Development (OECD) countries with more advanced public financial management systems and stronger performance are less likely to be concerned with individual projects and more likely to focus on the overall performance of a budget program to which a project is contributing—that is, whether service delivery targets and wider policy objectives are being achieved. Major projects are the exception, and some finance ministries, as in New Zealand and the United Kingdom, are increasingly undertaking formalized monitoring of their major project portfolios.

Countries that are still building robust public financial management systems or are in the early stages of performance-oriented or program budgeting may need to adopt a different approach. Public investment management capacities in spending agencies may also be weak, such that the finance ministry needs to remain involved in monitoring and supporting a more distinct role in monitoring at the project level. The finance ministry should not be swamped by having too much detail or too many small projects in the system; only the most pertinent information should reach the finance ministry, and there should be fewer projects that are more strategic in scope—that is, programmatic projects. A middle ground between intensive monitoring at the center and the "light touch" approach might help the finance ministry to assure the quality of line ministry monitoring systems, rather than follow individual projects, and to carry out spot checks to ensure that these systems are working. Monitoring of individual projects at the center could then focus on the major project portfolio.

At whatever level in the system it takes place, monitoring should ideally:

> "Test that the defined control limits for each project, and for the portfolio of government projects, are appropriate and highlight whether they have exceeded or are in danger of exceeding:
> - *Time.* Variance against milestones
> - *Cost.* Variance against planned budget
> - *Quality.* Degrees off the quality target
> - *Scope.* Variance agreed to against what will be delivered
> - *Risk.* Limits on identified risks as a percentage of the overall budget
> - *Benefit.* Variance against level of benefit identified as part of the business justification." (U.K. National Audit Office 2010)

Box 8.3 presents a typical example of project reporting requirements that may be used to inform PIM guidelines. A minimum reporting standard,

BOX 8.3

Example of project reporting requirements

"Although all projects differ, a minimum reporting standard should be established which is general and flexible to allow for specific project reporting needs, while providing concrete guidelines and requirements for all projects.

As a minimum requirement, capital project reporting should incorporate the following concepts:

1. *Cost.* Project cost in constant and current dollars
2. *Time.* Target dates, impact of missing target dates on the project and on departmental operations, and all target dates missed and revised
3. *Performance.* Expected quantity and characteristics of outputs resulting from the project.

In all cases, a permissible variance should be established for each project and, if necessary, for each factor being measured. This information will enable management to review and analyze pertinent variances only and will allow for the timely recognition of what constitutes a material variance.

More specifically, to be effective, progress reports and reporting requirements should incorporate the following minimum standards:

- Comparison of actual costs to budgets, with explanations for variances above the established threshold
- Corrective action to be taken on the variances identified
- Progress of design against schedule, reason for delays, and remedial action taken
- Details of changes in scope and related costs
- A narrative including:
  - Accomplishments for the period
  - A simple statement indicating project is on, ahead, or behind schedule
  - A listing of any changes to project objectives or scope
  - A listing of any factors or changes that have affected the business climate
  - Any unanticipated problems that are currently being faced
  - Any changes required due to such problems
  - A listing of persons whose approval is required to implement these changes
  - Any additional anticipated problems
  - All action steps that are being taken or planned
  - All potential constraints should be identified, analyzed, and reported
  - Additional relevant comments."

Source: Deloitte Consulting 2000.

which is general and flexible, should be established to allow for specific project-reporting needs, while providing concrete guidelines and requirements for all projects.

A basic monitoring system for budgeting and financial control

Project implementation plans

Monitoring needs to reflect a predetermined implementation plan. Timely preparation and updating of project implementation plans, particularly with respect to the budget preparation cycle, can be problematic, but without these plans the feasibility and usefulness of a monitoring system is compromised. PIM guidelines need to specify the content and timetable for updating implementation plans.

Investment project monitoring systems need project financial plans to be prepared and updated as an integral part of the medium-term budgetary framework (MTBF)–budget preparation process to fulfill their function in supplying information for budgeting; this step cannot wait until capital budgets are agreed to. The finance ministry needs to be able to establish capital baseline spending—that is, the expenditures required to meet forward commitments to ongoing projects—early in the MTBF–budget preparation process so that it can then determine the fiscal space for new capital spending and its allocation between sectors and first-line spending agencies (see chapter 7). The responsible spending agencies therefore need to provide updated expenditure plans for ongoing projects. These plans must take account of actual expenditures since the last update and include any approved adjustments to the total estimated cost of projects, which should then receive final approval through the budget process.

Realistic implementation plans need to support requests for new project funding. These plans are an essential component of sound budgeting as well as an important signal that the project is ready for implementation in the next budget year. In the more disciplined PIM systems, where central agencies retain a strong role, spending agencies need to submit detailed implementation plans, including disbursement and procurement plans, before budget preparation is completed if proposals are to be considered for funding in the following year's budget. All too frequently in countries with weaker systems, planning for project implementation begins once the budget has been approved and often after the budget year has begun, making poor execution almost an inevitability.

Information requirements

At its most basic level, an effective centralized monitoring system must provide the finance ministry with the essential information it needs to have financial control over capital spending and to perform designated tasks when budgeting public investment. These latter tasks include setting realistic expenditure ceilings for spending agencies that conform to aggregate fiscal constraints and take adequate account of forward funding commitments to implement ongoing projects efficiently. The required information must be complete and timely in relation to the budget cycle. Often, finance ministries with less advanced systems lack the necessary information because of the absence of a systematic monitoring process for nationally funded capital projects based around a modern information system. In these contexts, monitoring can be ad hoc, irregular, and incomplete. PIM guidelines should be designed to address these weaknesses.

In its simplest form, monitoring requires a register of public investment projects to be created and updated regularly by the finance ministry. This register should track financial progress at the aggregate, sector, organization, program, and individual project levels. Such a database can technically be handled in spreadsheet format, but this format is cumbersome, and appropriate off-the-shelf database software is preferred when the number of projects is significant. The following are the minimum reporting requirements of such a monitoring system:

- A short description of each project that summarizes the objectives and nature of the investment. It should also give the location and name the implementation body.
- The total estimated cost of the project as approved by the budget process, which is a key financial management control figure. The sum of actual and forecast expenditures must not exceed the total estimated cost without the necessary approvals (supplementary funding request).
- Details of actual expenditures to date, budgeted expenditures for the coming fiscal year, and the forecast expenditures for each subsequent year of the project until completion. The information on actual expenditures should come from regular accounting reports generated by a computerized financial management information system.[5] Expenditure forecasts must come from spending agencies with overall responsibility for project implementation, generated by individual project managers. These forecasts should be updated annually through the MTBF–annual budget preparation process.

In-year monitoring should involve updating actual expenditures on the basis of budget execution data and comparisons to planned expenditures. Such monitoring can be done monthly if data flows are automated but should be done at least quarterly. Comparing actual to plan can be done on the crude assumption of an even disbursement profile but will be radically improved if spending agencies make realistic monthly or quarterly disbursement plans in advance of the commencement of the financial year; these comparisons will also be important for broader cash management planning. Regular monitoring reports should be produced that cover different levels of aggregation (total, sector, organization, and program), depending on the audience, and should address individual projects only in the case of major problems.

On the basis of monitoring reports, reallocations from slow- to fast-moving projects may be needed to maximize the effectiveness of the annual capital budget. Spending agencies are normally expected to take the lead with such reallocations (within legislated virement limits), but the finance ministry must have the minimum information to understand the issue and agree on any reallocations. If capacity in spending agencies is weak, the finance ministry should be ready to identify this fact and instigate action. Such reallocations represent in-year adjustments to implementation plans and must be authorized and reflected in the monitoring system.

The finance ministry must also be in a position to assess whether transfers to "faster-moving projects" do not, in fact, represent unauthorized increases in the total estimated cost of a project. The basic monitoring framework described above should allow this. Frequent major reallocations (for example, in excess of virement limits and requiring parliamentary approval through a supplementary budget) may have short-term advantages, but do not create an environment conducive to improving implementation planning; they may also allow poorly prepared, politicized projects to slip into the budget. Reallocations should therefore be limited and longer-term improvements in implementation planning should be instigated.

Spending agencies with capital investment programs should have their own systems that mirror and feed the central system, but also contain more detail than is required by the finance ministry. Project managers will probably require more detailed and more frequent information.

Financial management information system

A well-designed and automated financial management information system (FMIS) should be able to provide timely and comprehensive information on the financial implementation of capital projects. Using such a system to generate information on actual expenditures by project requires the design and use of a project-level expenditure coding structure, without which it is impossible to record expenditures systematically against individual projects. To exercise tighter financial control from the center, Kenya and Uganda have recently introduced project codes to the budget classification for individual projects.

Linked to the issue of project-level codes, there also needs to be an agreed-on final list of projects (new and ongoing) to be funded through the capital budget approved through the budget preparation process. This list does not need to be part of the budget law itself, although it could form an annex to it; it should, however, be prepared before budget approval and made available to approval bodies in the executive and the legislature.

Monitoring physical progress

As well as monitoring financial progress, the computerized monitoring system should be extended to monitoring physical progress. It needs to assess the actual physical implementation of the project compared to the plan and to examine any gaps between financial and physical progress.

The implementation plans described above need to be extended to include projections of physical progress. Projections of financial and physical progress should be broadly similar for a project that is expected to be on track. Variations would normally only occur if advance payments are needed or if payment schedules are lumpy. Where projections of physical progress for multiyear projects lag projections of financial progress, such lags could indicate the buildup of potential cost overruns that have not yet been reflected in an adjustment of the approved total estimated cost. Such overruns would be a cause for concern for the finance ministry during budget preparation.

While a centralized financial management information system is the obvious source of information on financial execution, information on physical execution must come from responsible first-line spending agencies and should originate with the project management team for individual projects. The finance ministry would not usually be expected to make direct observations of the physical progress of projects, although this inspection function still exists in some current and former centrally planned economies. Nevertheless, the finance ministry should have the right to demand such information as a matter of course and to insist on the creation of adequate systems to collect it where these do not already exist. Rights and responsibilities can be vague in weaker systems and should be embodied in primary legislation at the framework level, to be expounded in detailed procedural guidelines.

Defining project milestones

Monitoring physical progress is best done using project implementation "milestones," rather than percentage completion, which is difficult to gauge and subject to manipulation. Monitoring based on the final project deliverables—for example, 120 kilometers of national standard road or a 200-bed general hospital constructed[6]—is also not desirable, as it gives no idea of progress toward achieving the deliverables.

A milestone is the achievement of a significant step in the project, usually the completion or acceptance of an important component of the final deliverable. Milestones are generally indicative of the project having reached a status that is readily recognizable. This recognition may be based on starting or completing a key project management stage or making significant progress with construction work. A milestone should be clearly indicated in the project plan, even though it is not technically an item of work.

Examples of milestones include the following:

- Detailed design completed
- Tender launched
- Land acquisition completed
- Foundation for new building completed
- Buildings watertight
- New equipment received and ready for use
- Handover of completed facility
- Facility operational and delivering services.

The number of milestones depends on project complexity and duration. A relatively straightforward project with a short implementation period will have few milestones; a complex project with a multiyear construction period could have many milestones, perhaps organized in a hierarchy. For example, the following construction milestones were adopted in London's extremely complex Crossrail project, implemented over 10 years:

- Tunneling completed
- Station construction and civil engineering works completed
- Network rail works finalized
- Railway systems in place
- Trains and railway depot delivered
- Public space and development around stations completed
- Introduction of services—in five phases.

Underlying these high-level milestones are intermediate milestones—for example, completion of each of the five tunneled sections.

The following is key information when monitoring against project milestones:

- Name of the milestone
- Planned completion date
- Expected completion date
- Deviation from plan
- Explanation for deviation
- Remedial actions where deviation exceeds agreed-on tolerances.[7]

Organizational arrangements in the finance ministry

Efficiency considerations indicate that the central monitoring function should be as close as possible to the directorate of the finance ministry with direct responsibility for capital budgeting and budgetary performance. Information flows should be organized so that monitoring data go directly from spending agencies and the treasury to this directorate; otherwise the monitoring process is likely to suffer from coordination difficulties.

Risk-based monitoring

A responsive monitoring system should focus attention on problem projects so that necessary adjustments can be made. Some countries—for example, New Zealand and the United Kingdom—practice risk-based monitoring at the central level using a red-amber-green (RAG) traffic light system to identify projects according to the risk of delivery failure. Box 8.4 summarizes the basis for the RAG ratings in the United Kingdom. The results can help to focus high-level managerial attention on projects with red or red-amber ratings. Movements between higher- and lower-risk projects are used to assess trends in the overall delivery risk of the portfolio.

In the United Kingdom, RAG ratings are derived from delivery confidence assessments (DCA). DCAs are a component of the project assessment review (PAR) carried out as part of the assurance processes set up and overseen by the Infrastructure and Projects Authority,[8] the body responsible for monitoring the government major project portfolio (GMPP). PARs are carried out on a planned basis during project implementation but may also be triggered by any new circumstances likely to influence project deliverability.[9] The RAG ratings are published in the annual report on the implementation of the GMPP by the Infrastructure and Projects Authority.

Performance monitoring

After strengthening the basic system of monitoring financial and physical progress, the next step is to extend the system to include more performance information, especially that related to performance after implementation. This step could be initially confined to high-value projects and to basic information on budgetary outputs and outcomes to supplement financial control information. The system could then be expanded to cover lower-value projects and to include more sophisticated information on performance. Some projects may be completed in stages and may start delivering benefits before the entire project is completed. In these cases, performance monitoring can begin earlier and may even inform the development of subsequent stages.

As with physical monitoring, the finance ministry should not be collecting the performance information itself; it should ensure that spending agencies have adequate systems in place to ensure that this information is being generated and verified at the appropriate level in the system. Project managers are responsible for carrying out project activities and delivering project outputs and should be expected to report on these matters; they should not be expected to report on outcomes, which is a policy analysis responsibility. Procedures also need to be in place to ensure that performance information is transmitted to the finance ministry.

BOX 8.4

The United Kingdom's delivery confidence assessment

Each project in the government major project portfolio is subject to a delivery confidence assessment (DCA); overall progress in delivering the portfolio is examined in terms of aggregate movements in the ratings from the DCAs.

Delivery confidence is defined as the confidence in a project's ability to deliver its aims and objectives:

- Within the time scales
- Within the budget
- To the quality requirements, including delivery of benefits, both financial and nonfinancial.
- The DCA reflects the following objective and subjective factors:
- Specific issues that threaten delivery on time, to cost, and to quality and jeopardize the delivery of benefits
- The review team's professional judgment of the likelihood that the project will succeed, even when there may be no definitively clear evidence either way
- The resilience of the project to overcome identified shortcomings or threats.

Delivery confidence is reported using a traffic light system, the red-amber-green (RAG) rating. Projects rated green are those most likely to succeed; those rated red are facing serious delivery problems. The definitions of the RAG ratings are given in table B8.4.1:

TABLE B8.4.1 **Delivery confidence assessment: Red-amber-green (RAG) ratings and criteria**

DELIVERY CONFIDENCE RAG RATING	CRITERIA FOR RAG RATING
Green	Successful delivery of the project on time, budget, and quality appears highly likely, and there are no major outstanding issues that at this stage appear to threaten delivery significantly.
Amber-green	Successful delivery appears probable; however, constant attention will be needed to ensure that risks do not materialize into major issues threatening delivery.
Amber	Successful delivery appears feasible but significant issues already exist, requiring management attention. These appear resolvable at this stage and, if addressed promptly, should not present a cost-schedule overrun.
Amber-red	Successful delivery of the project is in doubt, with major risks or issues apparent in a number of key areas. Urgent action is needed to ensure that these issues are addressed and to determine if resolution is feasible.
Red	Successful delivery of the project appears unachievable. There are major issues with project definition, schedule, budget, quality, and/or benefit delivery, which at this stage do not appear to be manageable or resolvable. The project may need rescoping and/or to have its viability reassessed.

Source: Major Projects Authority 2015.

The logical framework is a planning and monitoring tool based around preparing and updating a matrix that describes project objectives and measures of achievement. This tool is therefore particularly useful in providing a basis for performance monitoring.

Initiated at project conception and detailed and refined during project preparation and appraisal, the logical framework sets out a hierarchical description of a project's objectives based on cause and effect (the internal project logic). A project is described in terms of its:

- *Overall goal.* The general policy objective to which the project will contribute along with other interventions, which are usually only achievable in the longer term

- *Project purpose.* The project's central objective expressed in terms of the achievement of sustainable benefits for the target group
- *Outputs.* The direct results of the project required to achieve the project purpose—that is, services or facilities delivered; project management can be held accountable for their delivery
- *Activities.* The actions required to produce the project outputs.

Measurable indicators of achievement and the means of verification are identified in the logical framework matrix for each level; they form the basis for subsequent monitoring. Baseline values must be established for indicators of the goal and purpose before the project begins, so that project effects can be determined.

PROJECT ADJUSTMENT

When monitoring reports indicate that projects are going off track—exceeding agreed-on tolerances with respect to budget, schedule, or specification—action must be taken. Where these deviations risk threatening the overall viability of the project, there should be scope within the PIM system for making fundamental adjustments to improve the chances of success. If projects are so badly off track that successful achievement of the objectives within reasonable budgetary and time constraints is no longer feasible, the possibility of terminating the project should exist. Box 8.5 describes Ireland's guidance on project adjustment as set out in the country's Public Spending Code.

BOX 8.5

Ireland's guidelines on project adjustment

Adverse developments or changes in circumstances

"Regular management reports should be prepared by the Sponsoring Agency covering all significant developments relating to the project and its costs. If adverse developments occur, including unforeseen cost increases, which call into question the desirability or viability of the project, the Sponsoring Agency should submit a report at the earliest possible moment to the Sanctioning Authority, detailing the necessary measures proposed to rectify the situation.

Where, despite these measures, increased costs above those already approved are likely to arise, the approval of the Sanctioning Authority for the extra expenditure should be obtained before any commitment is made to accept cost increases. Any application for such approval should outline the reasons for the excess, along with a detailed explanation of why it was not possible to take appropriate measures to offset the increased cost. The viability of the project, given the changed circumstances, should also be reported on.

If a project is going badly wrong, there should be a willingness to terminate it before completion. Action of this kind can be justified if the cost of the project escalates above earlier estimates or if the benefits expected from it are not likely to be realised. An attitude that, once work on a project commences, it must be completed regardless of changed circumstances, is to be avoided. Before making a final decision to terminate a project that is not going according to plan, the costs of termination (for example, payments that might have to be paid by way of compensation to contractors, etc.) should be ascertained and made known to the appropriate authorities."

Source: Ireland's Public Spending Code (http://publicspendingcode.per.gov.ie/).

The legal framework and supporting guidelines should incorporate formal procedures for project adjustment and a mechanism for officially terminating a project.[10] Without this framework, a failing project will continue to be a drain on the budget. For major projects, organizations that are external to the project sponsor (or owner) should be involved in the closure decision so as to counter vested interests in continuing a poor project.

The Republic of Korea has a particularly effective system for project adjustment, described in detail in box 8.6. A starting point is the country's total project cost management (TPCM) system, a centralized monitoring system focused on controlling the total costs of the country's largest multiyear projects. The TPCM is based on strict principles that limit the justifications for cost increases and the authority to agree to them. If real cost increases, as captured through the TPCM, exceed a defined threshold, then a reassessment of project feasibility is required. If the cost increases are then shown to undermine the project's viability, an adjustment is needed, such as cutting costs by changing the project's scope or closing down the project entirely. As box 8.6 indicates, the decision to end failing projects has resulted in considerable savings. The TPCM and the reassessment and adjustment processes are detailed in a specific regulation (Ministry of Economy and Finance, Korea 2009). This regulation defines general and specific guidance on procedures for adjusting different project components.

The principles of the Korean model should be replicable, provided there is adequate monitoring of total project costs. Triggers for activating a fundamental review may vary according to country preferences.

Any reassessment of feasibility must use costs that are net of sunk costs. Sunk costs are resources that have already been used up in project implementation

BOX 8.6

Reassessment study of feasibility and project adjustment in Korea

In Korea, a reassessment study of feasibility (RSF), was introduced in 1999 and strengthened in 2006. An RSF can be triggered by significant changes in project conditions that risk undermining the forecast economic returns from the investment.

According to Articles 50 and 50-(2) of the National Finance Act, an RSF is performed for projects in the total project cost management (TCPM) if the following occurs:

- The total cost for a project increases by more than 20 percent in real terms (excluding land acquisition) compared to the previously approved cost.
- The demand forecast for a project falls by 30 percent or more (on the basis of the reassessment of demand forecast).
- The prefeasibility study (PFS) has not been conducted, even though the project falls under the PFS coverage.
- The Board of Audit and Inspection formally requests the RSF.
- The National Assembly formally requests the RSF.

On the basis of the results of the new RSF, a decision is made on whether to continue, rescope, or stop the project. Rescoping involves looking for ways to reduce the size and cost of the project to achieve continued viability and avoid cancellation.

More than 20 out of 172 projects subject to RSF were stopped between 2003 and 2013. Total savings of 11.4 percent of project costs were estimated for this period (compared to the requested increase) on projects that continued.

Source: Kim 2015.

and can no longer be used for any other purpose—that is, their opportunity costs are zero. For example, if a bridge project has been partially constructed (in physical terms), the costs associated with the completed works should not be counted in the new economic feasibility study.

NOTES

1. See chapter 1 on limits to the reference guide and challenges for further discussion on procurement and contract management.
2. Between 2012 and 2016, 120 senior civil servants completed training at the newly created Major Projects Leadership Academy.
3. Provisional plans should already have been prepared as part of the feasibility study.
4. The rest of this section refers to the finance ministry, which should be taken to include the planning ministry where such a ministry exists and has a designated role in monitoring.
5. See further details in chapter 12.
6. Some output-based budgeting systems monitor performance in this way.
7. As indicated, project managers should be allowed to make decisions within pre-agreed-on deviations from plans; these are the agreed-on "tolerances." Larger than agreed-on deviations must be escalated to higher authorities.
8. Formerly known as the Major Projects Authority.
9. A project assessment review (PAR) is usually initiated by the SRO of a project in the sponsoring ministry, but may be requested by senior officials or ministers with key roles in public investment management. In exceptional circumstances, the Infrastructure and Projects Authority may initiate a PAR. The PAR team reports to the SRO in the sponsoring ministry. At the request of the SRO, the Infrastructure and Projects Authority will assemble a team of independent reviewers from outside the sponsoring ministry for the review. A reviewer from inside the sponsoring ministry, but from a different department, is also part of the review team. DCA findings are given at the end of the PAR and included in the draft report to the SRO.
10. Chapter 11 discusses methods and principles for rationalizing and prioritizing ongoing portfolio projects. Underperforming projects in the pipeline are a priority to recost, reshape, or terminate.

REFERENCES

Deloitte Consulting. 2000. "Capital Management Process Review for the Government of British Columbia." Deloitte, New York.

Kim, J.-H. 2015. "Public Investment Management: Framework, Lessons, and Challenges." Workshop presentation, Bogotá, September.

Major Projects Authority. 2015. *Major Projects Authority Annual Report 2014–15.* London: Cabinet Office.

Ministry of Economy and Finance, Korea. 2009. "Guidelines for Total Project Cost Management [in Korean]." Ministry of Economy and Finance, Seoul.

Southern California Regional Rail Authority. 2011. *Metrolink Project Management Manual, Southern California 2011.* Los Angeles: Southern California Regional Rail Authority.

U.K. Department for Business, Innovation, and Skills. 2010. "Guidelines for Managing Projects: How to Organize, Plan, and Control Projects." U.K. Department for Business, Innovation, and Skills, London.

U.K. National Audit Office. 2010. "Assurance for High Risk Projects." National Audit Office, London.

U.S. Federal Transit Administration. 2012. *Construction Project Management Handbook.* FTA Report 0015. Washington, DC: Federal Transit Administration. https://www.transit.dot.gov/sites/fta.dot.gov/files/docs/FTA_Construction_Project_Management_Handbook_2016.pdf.

World Bank. 2008. "Operational Manual." World Bank, Washington, DC. http://documents.worldbank.org/curated/en/597381468040174626/Operational-Manual.

9

Ex Post Review and Asset Management

OVERVIEW

A minimum requirement for a functioning public investment management (PIM) system is a basic review immediately after project completion. This review should provide some analysis and lessons learned from project implementation. More advanced PIM systems further evaluate project impact and assess whether project objectives have been achieved. An effective PIM system needs to inform the design of policy and the development of similar future projects and to strengthen accountability for project results. Evaluations should also assess the functioning of the overall PIM system, particularly when reforms are ongoing, to ensure that appropriate feedback is reflected in the reform process.

After a project has been completed, custodianship should be established by recording the asset in the country's asset register and management system. This effort requires a procedure to hand over management responsibility for future operation and maintenance, as well as adequate budget funding for service delivery agencies in charge of operating and maintaining the asset. Asset registers need to be updated regularly, and asset values need to be recorded. Countries should require their operating agencies to compile balance sheets, where the value of assets created from new fixed capital expenditures can be recorded alongside existing assets. Active asset management will help assets to serve their purpose throughout their intended life span; for this reason, asset quality needs to be tracked over time.[1] Agencies responsible for service delivery should be held accountable for results to incentivize them to optimize the economic lives of the assets.

EX POST REVIEW

Basic completion review

PIM guidelines should specify requirements for a project completion review, including the timetable and content of the report. A completion review should usually be carried out within six months of the end of the project. The completion review should assess the success in delivering the project on time, within budget,

BOX 9.1

Example of a format for a project completion report in the United States

1. General project information
   - 1.1 Background
   - 1.2 Postimplementation review objectives and scope
   - 1.3 Postimplementation review team members
2. Findings
   - 2.1 Management effectiveness
   - 2.2 Cost
   - 2.3 Schedule
   - 2.4 Unplanned side effects
   - 2.5 Residual risks
3. Administrative closure and accomplishments
   - 3.1 Performance metrics
   - 3.2 Customers' and users' satisfaction
4. Open issues
5. Lessons learned
   - 5.1 Recommendations
6. Contract closure

Source: U.S. Department of Housing and Urban Development 2015.

and to the specified design. Major departures from the planned implementation timetable, budget, or design should be identified and any reasons for departures explained. The extent to which any risks that materialized had been foreseen and whether risk management plans and mitigation measures were adequate should also be considered. Any lessons for improved design or implementation of similar projects in the future need to be identified and recommendations made.

A completion review should also include an assessment of whether the project has started to deliver the expected services to the intended beneficiaries, together with any available evidence on user satisfaction and user demand compared to what was forecast during planning.

The completion review should be performed by the project sponsor or owner (hereafter referred to simply as the sponsor), and the findings and recommendations should be internalized. To ensure objectivity, the review should be carried out by a part of the organization that is not involved in project implementation. Arrangements need to be in place to ensure that lessons learned feed into the planning of new projects.

Completion reports should be submitted to the ministry or agency to which a project sponsor is subordinated. In addition, reports for major projects should be submitted to the finance ministry and, where relevant, the planning ministry. The central ministries should review the quality of the reports and, where necessary, request additional information or analysis. The finance or planning ministry should prepare an annual report summarizing the main findings of project completion reports submitted during the year and containing recommendations for improving project planning and implementation in the future.

Decision makers should take into account failure to finish a completion review or to submit a report on time when assessing proposals for new projects by the same sponsor; this failure may be a reason for questioning these proposals on the grounds of internal institutional weaknesses in existing PIM.

Box 9.1 summarizes the content of a template for a project completion report as used by the U.S. Department of Housing and Urban Development.

Ex post impact evaluation

An ex post impact evaluation[2] is deeper than a basic completion review and requires careful design and more expertise. Like appraisal, detailed methodological guidance is needed to support the procedural arrangements set out in PIM regulations and guidelines.

Ex post evaluation can have two complementary perspectives, the emphasis given to each perspective may vary with the nature of the project. The first is strategic performance, and the second is social welfare. The strategic performance perspective looks at the project in relation to the hierarchy of objectives, including the strategic goals that were set during planning and approval. It also considers the achieved efficiency, effectiveness, impact, and relevance of the project in relation to these objectives. The aim is to evaluate the operational, tactical, and strategic success of the project (as indicated in table 9.1). The social welfare (or socioeconomic profitability) perspective looks at a project's economic performance, as measured by social cost-benefit analysis. This analysis involves estimating the achieved economic performance indicators (net present value, economic internal rate of return, and cost-benefit ratio) and comparing the same indicators from planning and approval.

For projects where a social cost-benefit analysis can be performed and where the scale of the investment justifies the effort of such an evaluation, the social welfare perspective is generally given more weight in the evaluation. For projects where social cost-benefit analysis is difficult to conduct or cannot capture significant costs or benefits, the strategic performance perspective will necessarily carry more weight. In most cases, however, it will be important to incorporate both perspectives to provide a comprehensive assessment of the actual performance of a project compared to what was foreseen during planning and formed the basis for decision making.

PIM guides should establish both perspectives as valid approaches to evaluation and encourage joint application, where feasible. The strategic performance perspective and the social welfare perspective are explored in more detail below. Box 9.2 reproduces Ireland's approach to evaluation, which effectively incorporates a dual perspective.

TABLE 9.1 **Evaluation criteria**

CRITERION	INDICATOR
Strategic performance evaluation[a]	
Efficiency	Measures operational success: to what degree have the outputs achieved derived from efficient use of financial, human, and material resources?
Effectiveness	Measures tactical success: were the stated objectives achieved and to what extent did the project contribute to the achievement of the goal?
Impact	Measures strategic success: has the project had any positive or negative consequences other than those planned?
Relevance	Measures strategic success: has the project been in line with the needs and priorities of the owners, the intended users, and other affected parties?
Sustainability	Measures strategic success: are the positive effects from the project likely to continue after the project has been completed?
Socioeconomic profitability[b]	Has the project delivered a positive net present value?

Source: Welde and Volden 2018.

Note: The Concept Research Program (Norway) develops ways of improving the use of resources and enhancing the effects of major public investments. It is financed by the Ministry of Finance.

a. Referred to as "goal-oriented evaluation criteria" in the original paper.

b. Measures the change in society's aggregate welfare.

BOX 9.2

Ireland's approach to ex post evaluation (postproject review)

All large capital projects and a proportion of other capital projects have to be subjected to a post-project review to see if the predicted benefits of the project were realised. Post-project reviews should be undertaken once sufficient time has elapsed to allow the project to be properly evaluated with sufficient evidence of the flow of benefits/costs from it. There are two separate focuses of review—(i) project outturn and (ii) appraisal and management procedures. The second element can be done after project completion as it involves reviewing administrative and management procedures. The timing of the first element will depend on the nature of the project, i.e., the period required to observe the expected benefits. This period should be no longer than one third of the time frame used in the Appraisal. The detailed appraisal provides the base against which the outturn review is made. The aim of a review of project outturn is to determine whether:

- The basis on which a project was undertaken proved correct
- The expected benefits and outcomes materialised
- The planned outcomes were the appropriate responses to actual public needs
- The appraisal and management procedures adopted were satisfactory
- Conclusions can be drawn which are applicable to other projects, to the ongoing use of the asset, or to associated policies.

Mandatory evaluation/post-project review requirements

- All capital projects costing > €20 million are to be subject of a post-project review
- At least 5% of other capital projects should be reviewed

Additional evaluation/post-project review requirements

Departments and agencies should not restrict themselves to the mandatory evaluation or post-project review requirements. From time to time it may be apparent that while not mandatory, an area of expenditure would benefit from a more in-depth review based on the picture the performance indicators paint or maybe because the performance indicators are not as informative as originally thought.

Communicating lessons learned

As with all parts of the Public Spending Code any significant lessons should be translated into changes in the Sponsoring Agency's practices and communicated within the organization and to the sanctioning authority so that it can apply any general lessons learned to this Code or to supplementary information.

Responsibility for evaluation/review

It is the responsibility of the Sponsoring Agency to carry out the evaluations or post-project reviews. Those conducting reviews and evaluations should not be the same people as conducted the appraisal or managed the implementation.

Source: Reproduced from Ireland's Public Spending Code (http://publicspendingcode.per.gov.ie/c-03-periodic-evaluationpost-project-review/).

Strategic performance perspective

The strategic performance perspective is based on the results chain approach to project design. The results chain is the cause-effect logic that provides the rationale for a project by establishing the relationship between the project inputs and the project's ultimate goal. The results chain approach is used by the World Bank and by many governments. The logic of the results chain is also embodied in the logical framework approach as discussed in chapter 6.

If a project has not been conceptualized and planned with the logic of the results chain or a similar approach to establishing the project rationale, it becomes very difficult to apply the strategic performance perspective (or the social welfare perspective). For this reason, strict consistency is required between the PIM guidelines for upstream processes of project development and appraisal and the PIM guidelines for downstream processes of monitoring and evaluation. The same requirement applies to methodologies for appraisal and evaluation. Without such consistency, a systematic approach to evaluation becomes very difficult. This requirement also influences the sequencing of PIM reforms: there is little point in establishing elaborate performance monitoring and evaluation processes as long as project planning and appraisal processes remain poorly defined.

The conceptual logic of the results chain is set out in figures 9.1 and 9.2 using real examples. The logic of the results chain runs from inputs to impacts, but the project design process should work in reverse, with desired impacts being the starting point for strategically driven project identification and design. This process is illustrated in figure 9.3 for a road project.

FIGURE 9.1

The results chain: Conceptual logic

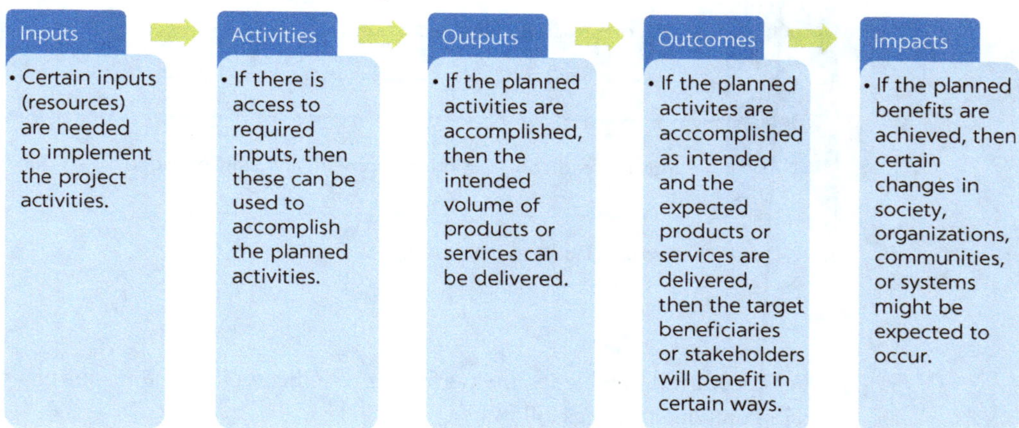

Source: Based on World Bank Independent Evaluation Group 2017.

FIGURE 9.2

The results chain: Illustrations

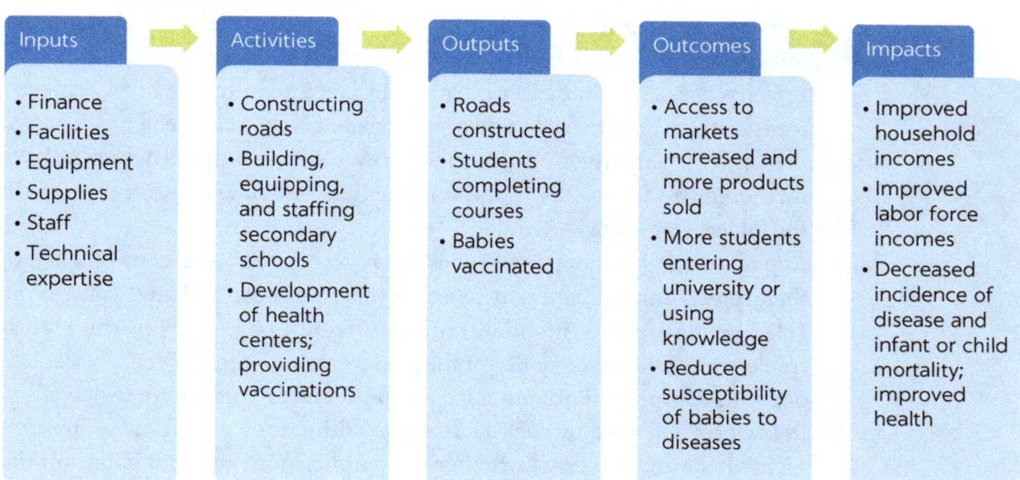

Source: Based on World Bank Independent Evaluation Group 2017.

FIGURE 9.3
Design process for a road project following the results chain

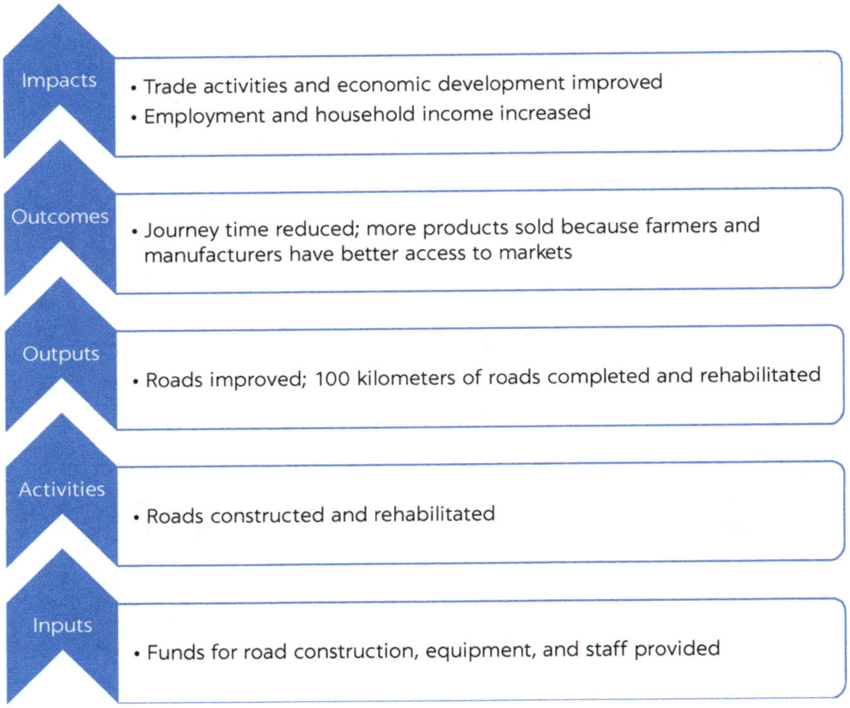

Source: Based on World Bank Independent Evaluation Group 2017.

As introduced in table 9.1, the performance indicators for the results chain and its components are as follows:[3]

- *Efficiency.* Does the quantity and quality of the results of the project justify the quantity and quality of the means used for achieving them? Efficiency concerns the relation between the results and the means—that is, whether the process of transforming means into results has been cost-effective. Efficiency assessments are normally part of the monitoring process and part of a basic completion review. They should also form part of ex post evaluations, especially if evaluation covers management performance.
- *Effectiveness.* To what extent has the immediate outcome been achieved (or is likely to be achieved), and to what extent is the achievement a result of the project? Effectiveness describes how well the outputs achieved have furthered the achievement of the immediate outcome (project purpose in the logical framework).
- *Impact.* What has happened (or is likely to happen) as a consequence of the project? Impact concerns whether there has been a change toward the achievement of the intended impacts (overall objectives in the logical framework) as a consequence of the achievement of the project's immediate outcome (purpose). Both intended and unintended impacts are reviewed.
- *Relevance.* Does the project make sense within the context of its environment? Relevance assesses whether the outputs, outcome, and impact of the project are aligned with the needs and aspirations of the beneficiaries and with the policy environment of the project.

- *Sustainability.* What has happened (or is likely to happen) to the positive effects of the project over the long term, now that construction has been completed? In terms of a single project, sustainability can be described as the degree to which the benefits produced by the project continue after physical implementation has come to an end. This is a central theme in all evaluation work and relates to all elements of the logical framework for a specific project.

Social welfare (or socioeconomic profitability) perspective

In addition to strategic performance, achieving value for public money also matters. A completed project may be evaluated positively according to strategic performance criteria, but performance may be poor with respect to socioeconomic profitability. This situation may occur when actual costs prove higher than estimated, actual demand is lower than forecast, or unexpected disbenefits occur (for example, negative externalities). Net costs or benefits are important in assessing whether a project has turned out to be a worthwhile use of public financial resources. It is also possible to imagine a project that has achieved a positive net present value but has failed to deliver a broader impact or is of questionable relevance. In this case, the resources involved could potentially have been spent on another (economically viable) project with a stronger impact or more directly correlated with stakeholders' needs. An ex post evaluation will be more complete if both the strategic and the socioeconomic perspectives are taken into consideration.

Evaluating socioeconomic profitability involves a rerun of the social cost-benefit analysis that was carried out for appraisal but using actual construction costs and realized demand for services and benefits after the project has been operating for some time. This analysis seems relatively straightforward, more so than appraisal, where costs and benefits are only forecasts, but it is not necessarily so. Difficulties arise from a lack of data, particularly with respect to realized demand, and from problems in determining the net contribution of the project because of significant and unforeseen external changes within the zone of influence that could not be foreseen during appraisal. The problem of attribution—determining what effects can be attributed to the project and what effects are due to factors beyond the project's control—is a fundamental difficulty of ex post evaluation, especially for outcome and impact indicators in the strategic performance perspective. The usual approach to addressing the attribution problem is to develop a "counterfactual" scenario against which to compare with-project effects.

The following practical steps, based on U.K. guidelines,[4] form a good basis for performing an ex post evaluation from the perspective of socioeconomic profitability:

- *Step 1. Establish what is being evaluated and how.* The scope of the evaluation must first be established, and then performance indicators need to be defined and quantified as precisely as possible for use in step 3. Indicators should have been established and reviewed at the preappraisal (project concept note) and appraisal (feasibility study) stages, but these indicators will need to be reconfirmed at evaluation. The availability of data on the identified indicators must be established and, if necessary, additional data should be collected if available monitoring data fall short of what is required.
- *Step 2. Decide on the counterfactual situation against which the completed project will be compared.* The impact of a project may turn out to be different

from the impact forecast in the feasibility study because of significant and unexpected changes in background conditions (unpredictable shifts in demand or unexpected increases in the cost of key construction inputs, for example) or the actions of those responsible for implementing the project, rather than forecasting or design issues. It is therefore important to define a realistic counterfactual situation against which the evaluation will be made, because this situation may be significantly different from what was assumed in the planning of the project. Thus, if underlying background conditions have changed substantially, a scenario representing unchanged conditions needs to be constructed as a comparator. Similarly, if management actions have resulted in the project being implemented differently than planned, an artificial comparator scenario needs to be constructed where management behaves as planned.

- *Step 3. Compare the actual results with targeted results.* Feasibility and evaluation methodologies are similar, but with the difference that the former is based on forecasts and the latter is based on actual data. Both methodologies should aim to identify direct and indirect benefits or disbenefits from a project. An evaluation should include (a) an assessment, preferably quantified, of what happened; (b) a comparison of this information with the targeted project results; and (c) a comparative assessment of the alternative results that might have happened if background conditions and implementation had been as planned and the envisaged situation if the project had not happened—that is, a comparison with the counterfactuals defined at step 2. The last element will not be necessary if everything materializes as planned, but this is rarely the case.
- *Step 4. Present the findings and recommendations.* Findings should cover (a) why the project results differ from those in the feasibility study (if indeed they do); (b) the effectiveness of the project in achieving its specific and wider objectives and an explanation of why; (c) an estimate of the cost-effectiveness of the project; and (d) the implications of the findings for the identification, design, and implementation of future projects and the resulting recommendations.
- *Step 5. Disseminate the findings and recommendations.* It is important to ensure that the findings and recommendations are fed into the decision making of future projects; hence the importance of obtaining the approval of evaluations from senior management within the project sponsor and any ministry or agency to which it is subordinated. Project sponsors should generally aim to publicize evaluation findings and recommendations on their websites and in other media once they have been approved. Summaries and syntheses of evaluation reports are important for wider dissemination and should be prepared.

Sampling for ex post evaluation

Systematic ex post evaluation of all completed projects is rarely performed,[5] probably for good reason, as it is intensive in its use of skilled human resources. Even in good-practice countries, evaluation is usually on a sample basis, with some sectors covered more intensively than others. In Ireland, only major projects—those with a value in excess of €20 million—are systematically evaluated; lower-value projects are evaluated on a sample basis, using a

5 percent sample. The U.K. Highways Agency's post-opening project evaluation (POPE) is one of the relatively few examples of systematic ex post evaluation of transport sector projects (see box 9.3), but almost all of these projects are likely to be large scale, given the agency's responsibilities.

Timing of ex post evaluation

The timing of evaluation varies with the nature of the project, depending on the time before the full extent of the realized benefits is revealed; however, it does seem reasonable to set a limit on the maximum time that can elapse before an evaluation is performed. This limit will ensure that results are not influenced by too much extraneous "noise." In the case of Ireland, the time that passes before evaluation should not exceed one-third of the time frame used in appraisal. In the case of national roads in the United Kingdom, evaluations are performed one year and five years after opening to assess the immediate outcome and the longer-term impact separately.

Responsibilities for ex post evaluation

Evaluation should be performed by the project sponsor and the results shared with higher-level decision-making bodies and more broadly; however, the evaluation should ideally be performed by a part of the organization that is independent of the department that promoted and implemented the project.

On top of their responsibilities for compliance and financial audits, external audit bodies often undertake impact evaluations (or "performance audits") of major projects. These audits are most often performed on a sample basis, frequently focusing on a small number of projects from which important lessons are expected to be learned—usually notable failures or notable successes. Box 9.4 summarizes some of the work of the U.K. National Audit Office in this respect.

BOX 9.3

U.K. Highways Agency's post-opening project evaluation

Comprehensive ex post analyses of transport projects are rare. A noticeable exception is the post-opening project evaluation (POPE) of the U.K. Highways Agency (HA), which are undertaken for all of the HA's major schemes. The key objective of POPE is to identify the extent to which the expected impacts of highway schemes have materialised and to inform thinking on current and future national scheme appraisal methods. POPE also measures whether schemes have offered value for money, i.e., positive net present values, and the level of accuracy associated with estimates of costs and benefits. POPE studies are undertaken for each Major Scheme one year and five years after opening. The latest summary report showed that 94% of schemes achieved their objectives. Most schemes, 72%, offered high value for money and 85% achieved medium or high value for money. Forecasts were accurate—a majority (65%) of the schemes accurately forecasted traffic flows (within +/- 15%), and half of the schemes had costs in the appraisal within +/- 15% of outturn costs.

Source: Reproduced from Welde and Volden 2018.

BOX 9.4

Performance audit of projects by the U.K. National Audit Office

The U.K. National Audit Office is an independent body responsible for auditing central government spending only. It has no judicial or administrative authority reporting to parliament. Its reports are used by the Public Accounts Committee, which holds hearings and then reports to Parliament.

It is legally empowered to carry out performance audits, including for projects. It performs audits on a (small) sample basis with a focus on problem or innovative projects. Recent examples of audits include the following:

- Evaluation of a failed public-private partnership (PPP) project to rehabilitate the London Underground
- Evaluation of a canceled project to improve the efficiency and resilience of fire and rescue services by replacing 46 local control centers with 9 regional centers.

The National Audit Office also produces good-practice guidance based on its audits, for example:

- Delivering successful information technology-enabled business change, including case studies of nine successful projects
- Initiating successful projects, including five examples of good project planning.

The Ghana Audit Service has recently issued a Guide to Performance Audit of Infrastructure Projects, which could serve as a useful reference for other countries. In addition to general guidance, the guide gives specific guidance on implementing audits of road, building, energy, railway, and port projects.

Evaluating the PIM system

In addition to examining the performance of individual projects, ex post evaluation is important for assessing and improving PIM system performance. PIM guides should be supportive of this aim. Norway, which has initiated important PIM reforms aimed at improving front-end quality assurance of public investment projects, provides a notable example. At the same time as the reforms were initiated, the Concept Research Program was set up (see box 9.5 for an overview). Funded by the Ministry of Finance and led by the Norwegian University of Science and Technology, the research program "develops knowledge that will ensure efficient use of resources and enhance the benefits of major public investments." In particular, the Concept Research Program organizes ex post evaluation of completed projects that have been through the new quality assurance process. The lessons learned are seen as being crucial to improving know-how and practices in the front-end phase of projects and in the quality assurance effort itself. The Republic of Korea instituted similar feedback mechanisms as part of its PIM reforms.

ASSET REGISTRATION AND MANAGEMENT

Asset registers

An asset register is a record of the property owned by the state and its institutions. Asset registers should cover all fixed assets that are owned directly by the central government's ministries, departments, and agencies, as

BOX 9.5

Norway's Concept Research Program

The Concept Research Program

Front-end management of major projects

- The Concept Research Program develops knowledge that will ensure efficient use of resources and enhance the benefits of major public investments. Our focus is on project governance, and the projects' long term utility as seen from the financing party's perspective. This calls for interdisciplinary research, where the social sciences merge with project management and engineering.
- We focus on the front-end phase, from the initial idea until the decision to implement is made. This is the period when the most essential decisions are made. There is also an urgency, since the possibility to make major changes decreases as projects enter into their implementation phase.
- One of our main activities is to do formative research on major public investments under the Norwegian Quality Assurance scheme; see text box. Large amounts of information are compiled from the projects as the basis for empirical and theoretical research.
- The Concept program is based at the Norwegian University of Science and Technology (NTNU) and co-operates with several research institutions both in Norway and abroad.

The Norwegian scheme for quality assurance of major public investments

Compulsive for land based public investment projects with an expected budget exceeding NOK 750 mill. (about EUR 100 million).

Front-end analyses and decision document to be prepared by the ministries according to a common format issued by the Ministry of Finance

Documents to be reviewed by external Quality assurers pre-qualified by the Ministry of Finance

Two decision gates, only:

- QA1: Quality assurance of the analyses of alternative conceptual solution. The Government will choose among the alternatives and decide whether or not to proceed to a pre-project phase
- QA2: Quality assurance of the management base and cost estimates. The Parliament makes the final approval whether or not to implement, and sets the budget for the project.

- The program is funded by the Norwegian Ministry of Finance
- Results are openly available and published in a series of scientific reports, in addition to textbooks, working papers, scientific papers in journals and conference proceedings, etc. We have developed several courses at Master and PhD level, and students are directly involved in the program in various ways.
- The first projects that were quality assured under the QA scheme after it was introduced year 2000, have now been completed and are in their operational phase. The Concept Program organizes *ex post* evaluation of these to measure their effects, societal relevance, and sustainability. Lessons learned are crucial to improve know-how and practices in the front-end phase of projects, and the QA scheme itself.
- The Concept International Symposium on Project Governance is held biannually. This is a forum for decision makers, project managers, consultants, and researchers from home and abroad for networking and exchange of experiences and ideas in this field. The Concept Symposium 2016 is entitled *Governing the Front-End of Major Projects.*

Source: See www.ntnu.concept.no.

FIGURE 9.4

Example of an asset register and of asset management in South Africa, by function

Acquisition	Identification	Accountability	Performance	Disposal	Accounting
• Date • Supplier • Reference • Amount	• Descripion • Model • Manufacturer • Serial number • Unique asset number	• Location • Program • Custodian • Convertants or restrictions • Heritage or cultural "identifier"	• Capacity • Condition • Useful life • Residual value • Warranties or guarantees • Measures	• Capacity • Condition • Useful life • Residual value	• Historic cost • Replacement value • Depreciation rate • Accumulated depreciation

Source: Republic of South Africa 2004.

well as assets in which the government has a direct interest, usually meaning through the regular use of the asset. An asset register is the foundation of sound asset management.

PIM regulations need to stipulate when a newly created asset is to be entered in the asset register, the required information to be recorded at each entry, and the obligation to keep the relevant information up-to-date, particularly with respect to variable parameters, such as the current condition, valuation, and depreciation of the asset. As PIM regulations or guidelines may not provide sufficient instruction or detail, an asset management policy framework document may be helpful to support legislation. This is the case in South Africa, where the legal foundations for public asset management are embodied in the Public Financial Management Act (1999) and implementation was achieved through the development of an asset management framework and supporting practical guides (figure 9.4). The act's legal framework has subsequently been strengthened with enactment of the Government Immoveable Asset Management Act (2007).

Benefits of asset registers

An asset register facilitates good asset management practices, with the following main benefits.

First, asset registers enable accountability and audit tracing. In theory, governments acquire assets to assist in the provision of economic and social infrastructure services. Assets should be acquired following a robust appraisal and feasibility process that assesses the need for the asset and its viability against alternative options. This assessment should be followed by an open and competitive procurement process. As assets are funded from public resources, government officials in charge of their custodianship should be held accountable for ensuring that they are properly maintained and used.

Second, asset registers serve as supporting public investment planning and appraisal tools. Effective and regularly updated asset registers can become an essential tool for the medium-term planning of future public investment. Asset registers allow planners to understand the condition of existing public assets and the likely timeline for replacement or capital renovation. A fully functioning asset register can provide information on appraisal options as well—for example, whether new requirements are best met by making new investments or by sharing or repurposing underused existing assets. A good example is government office space, where using existing assets better can be an alternative to building new assets. To facilitate a more comprehensive appraisal, the asset register needs to be updated constantly to ensure that newly completed assets have been added.

Third, asset registers provide national, regional, and sector statistical information. The information in a well-maintained asset register can allow economists and statisticians to monitor key indicators, such as average age and total depreciated value of assets. Such monitoring can highlight underinvestment (for example, for roads) that should be addressed as priorities in strategic investment planning or identify downward trends in public investment that might need to be addressed. Some asset registers can be used to understand the geographic service coverage in important sectors such as health care and education. Such information is relevant to decisions regarding where future public investments should be located to improve coverage of public services. It can also inform policy makers about the required scale of regional development initiatives and any disparities between them.

Fourth, asset registers monitor operating and maintenance costs. A fully functioning asset register can help governments to monitor the maintenance and operating costs of assets. Such monitoring is particularly important to compare costs for similar asset classes. Significant differences in unit expenditures—for example, for roads of a similar class—might identify a need for further investigation and, if necessary, corrective action.

Fifth, asset registers assist the identification of targets for divestment. An asset register can help to identify underused or unwanted assets that can be sold off; any proceeds from divestment could then be reinvested in more productive assets. Such sales can make governments more efficient by transforming unwanted assets into a source of income rather than an expense.

Coverage and scope of asset registers

Clarity of asset ownership is important. Unclear ownership structures run the risk of double counting assets or failing to include them in the asset register. Assets that are assumed to belong to a city or a regional authority may in fact be owned by the state. The reverse may also be true—that is, presumed "state-owned" assets may in fact be owned by regional or local administrations. Furthermore, assets that are *used* by the state may not always be *owned* by the state; PPPs are an example, as the asset being used often belongs to the private partner.[6] Another example is an office building that is leased from a private company.

Governments may opt to specify thresholds for the value of equipment to ensure that the register is not "overwhelmed" by a large number of relatively insignificant entries. There is no best practice for such thresholds, and individual governments should establish relevant thresholds that reflect country context, including the size of the economy, the expected number of assets, and the government's capacity to manage the resulting information. Examples for threshold exclusions may be low-value items such as desks and chairs in schools or hospitals. These items should be recorded locally. Alternatively, groups of items may be bundled into a single line item, for example, "352 chairs," with the average age, condition, and value recorded alongside. Bulk buying and acquiring operational assets at the time of project handover facilitate this kind of bundling. Accounting practices are also likely to differ for fixed assets and short-life, disposable items that are not required to be included in an asset register.

The gathering of information required to create an asset register is a significant undertaking. The scale of information required should be considered carefully and assessed against the capacity needed to undertake the exercise. Only information that is of future value should be collected. Different governments will have different views on what information is appropriate or even possible within given capacity constraints. At a minimum, information should be collected that allows assets to be easily identified, including their age and condition, and that covers financial information on initial acquisition cost and current value. Additional information can be added at a more advanced stage of development.

To facilitate asset register analysis, a coding system is needed. Some countries use a coding system known as a unique asset number. Suggested headings for required data (or "column headings" in Excel or in database terms) related to land assets are shown in table 9.2. A coding system could use the budget code to assist in identifying assets.

Institutional arrangements for developing and operating an asset register

The central agency of government responsible for economic planning or finance may be considered as most likely to house the national asset register, as it may benefit the most from analysis of the data. However, this information may also be of value to other central institutions, such as the prime minister's office or the presidential administration.

The sophistication of the asset register system in place determines which institution is in charge of data entry and updating. Entry-level systems may require line ministries to complete paper or online forms before sending them to the central agency for consolidation. For basic systems, it may only be practical to update data on an annual basis. More sophisticated systems, such as the example from Belarus described in box 9.6, allow line ministries to upload changes "in real time," ensuring that data are current and reducing the burden on the central agency.

Developing a national asset register from scratch requires careful coordination between the responsible central agency and the asset owners, as illustrated in box 9.7 for the case of Northern Ireland.

TABLE 9.2 **Example of suggested data requirements for land assets**

LAND ASSETS										
BUDGET CODE REFERENCE	PHYSICAL DESCRIPTION (INCLUDES DIMENSIONS AND SURFACE AREA)	LOCATION (BY GPS OR SIMILAR COORDINATES)	DATE ACQUIRED	INITIAL INVESTMENT COST (IF ANY)	BOOK VALUE	ESTIMATED MARKET VALUE	ANNUAL COST OF OWNERSHIP	CURRENT PURPOSE OF OWNERSHIP	UTILIZATION %
Average									
Totals									

BOX 9.6

Asset register: Areas of good practice in Belarus

The asset database operates in "real time," and all users are able to access the same information at the same time. The database is open to "authorized users" in central and local government, and data are often updated by authorized users on a daily basis. The real estate section is open-access and uses "categorization codes" for each registered asset; it allows users to identify quickly assets that are not in use (Code 06) or that are used inefficiently (Code 07); those assets are highlighted, and decisions can be made readily regarding their future use.

Source: World Bank 2018.

BOX 9.7

Developing Northern Ireland's national asset register

During 2004, a first attempt at creating a database in Northern Ireland involved a centralized Strategic Investment Board that coordinated teams responsible for data collection. Each team member was assigned between two or three line ministries. Under the guidance of the relevant team member, each line ministry was responsible for collecting the asset data from its own departments and agencies and for reporting them for consolidation by the Strategic Investment Board. Line ministries were asked to nominate a senior official to coordinate the task internally; this step was essential, as central agencies are not always sufficiently informed about the detailed workings of line ministries and their departments and agencies.

Source: Northern Ireland, Strategic Investment Board.

When gathering information for the asset register, the central coordinating agency should validate any information provided. It is essential for the information to be both reliable and trustworthy; if not, the purpose of the asset register will be undermined and benefits will not materialize.

Regardless of which institution is in charge of coordinating or housing the asset register, the line ministries or agencies that own the asset should always be responsible for presenting the required information, for ensuring the accuracy of the information, and for updating the relevant information in the asset register. This process is important for public accountability purposes.

The institution that houses the asset register should adopt a monitoring and oversight role that includes occasional on-the-spot physical compliance checks to verify the existence of listed assets, their claimed physical condition, their actual usage, and any records related to operating and maintenance costs. Checks should also seek to identify unreported assets that are not included in the register.

Subnational and sector asset registers and management

The large scale of public asset ownership often makes central-level monitoring challenging and is the main reason why governments with established asset management practices devolve most of the practical work to entities in lower levels of government. The State of Victoria in Australia, for example, has issued guidance on how its assets should be managed (Auditor General's Office, Victoria 2014).

It is good practice for line ministries, agencies, and state-owned enterprises to maintain their own asset register, which is then used as baseline data for the national register. Keeping a property register at a line ministry or a state-owned enterprise is an essential tool for sector investment planning; it also makes reporting to the central or national asset register less burdensome.

At a practical level, most assets are managed (that is, operated and maintained) by the owner or custodian of the asset, which could be a line ministry, an agency of the line ministry, or a state-owned enterprise. However, some asset classes may best be managed centrally; land and buildings are a good example. The United Kingdom has created the Office of Government Property under the Cabinet Office to maximize the efficiency of its estate on a national scale.[7]

The thresholds for accounting for and reporting on individual pieces of equipment may be much lower at lower levels of government, leading to low-value items such as tables and chairs being "tagged" with asset identification labels, as is the case in Australia, Canada, the United Kingdom, and other countries. More sophisticated electronic tags are now available that would help to prevent the theft or misuse of assets. When line ministries report their asset information to the central agency, only the aggregate numbers and values of these lower-value items are likely to be recorded.

It is important to avoid subnational entities using their own asset registers as an excuse not to report asset information at the national level. Failure to report to the national register reduces the benefits of having a single unified register; it also reduces the oversight and audit capability of the central government agencies.

Operation and maintenance of assets and monitoring their cost of ownership

Assets need to be maintained to ensure continuing ability to function and deliver the public services for which they were created. Governments should understand the need to provide adequate operation and maintenance funding in recurrent budgets; otherwise, the condition of assets will decline more rapidly, leading to calls for new capital investment within shorter-than-expected timelines.

Annual operation and maintenance costs are rarely found in basic asset registers, but their inclusion might be considered in a subsequent development phase. Operating and maintaining assets are a significant cost to government. It is sensible, therefore, to search for ways to monitor these costs with a view to managing them most efficiently.

Information about operation and maintenance costs, potentially obtained through more advanced asset registers and management, will assist budget holders to plan for future demand on resources and help them to compare costs when making difficult spending decisions. It also helps to make "whole-life cost" comparisons when assessing the potential to renovate, upgrade, or replace assets. Estimates of predicted operation and maintenance costs and, in particular, major upgrade or replacement costs help planners to make more informed choices about calls on recurrent and capital budgets in future years.

Records of individual assets and their operation and maintenance costs should be kept by officials of the public body responsible for the asset. The officials collecting and monitoring operation and maintenance costs should be knowledgeable about the specific asset class, understand the expected performance data under different operating conditions, and be able to identify anomalies. Anomalies may occur because of poor maintenance, poor operating practices, poor initial design, the need to replace or renovate an older asset, or, potentially, fraud. Identifying differences in operation and maintenance performance is not only about rectifying poor performance, but also about understanding good performance—that is, why performance might be superior to comparator assets and what lessons can be shared with other operators to improve performance. The regular monitoring of operation and maintenance costs further provides insurance against possible theft and fraud. The scope for potential savings from better maintenance and monitoring of the costs of ownership is indicated in box 9.8 for the case of the United Kingdom.

Disposal of surplus or underused assets

Effective asset management allows the identification of assets that are no longer functional, are no longer required, or have simply outlived their original purpose. Even when an asset has lost its value for the current owner, it may still have value for some other part of the public sector. An asset transfer can benefit both the original and the new owner; the original owner is freed from storage and security costs for a redundant asset, while the new owner can benefit from lower cost and faster procurement times. An asset transfer should occur at the asset's "book value."

BOX 9.8

Extracting value through good asset management practices

The devolved governments of Northern Ireland and Wales have benefited from various asset management initiatives over the past 10 years:

- Northern Ireland's asset register revealed that the operation and maintenance cost of assets was the second-largest individual cost to central government, after staff costs. This fact helped to elevate the importance of the subject, winning political support that led to targeted savings of £33 million to £54 million per year in the costs of government office accommodation.
- Wales has been able to target a 30 percent reduction in government office running costs as a result of availability of better asset data.

Sources: Strategic Investment Board, Northern Ireland; Welsh Assembly Government.

Some assets are of no further use to the government, which opens up the option of divesting to a nongovernment entity that can make the asset economically productive. The rules for divesting should be clear and transparent and preferably enshrined in legislation.

Great attention should be paid to the entire process of divestiture. Establishing whether an asset has monetary value is important for public accountability. Valuations should be undertaken independently from the divesting authority, as collusion in the undervaluation of government assets is a major form of corruption. Independent valuation can be achieved through the use of government valuation offices (central or local statutory bodies) or alternatively through private regulated or licensed valuation services.

If an asset has monetary value, divestiture rules should ensure maximum value from it. An important incentive for encouraging public authorities to divest redundant assets and to ensure maximum value is to allow them to retain the receipts from the asset sale and to reinvest them in new assets. This policy has proven successful in Ireland and the United Kingdom, which even brought to light redundant assets that were previously unknown to central authorities.[8]

In order to ensure maximum value from a divestiture, asset owners should, for the sake of transparency, avoid single bidding. Rules should describe how the asset is offered for sale and the criteria for approving the sale. The divestiture process, the buyers, and the prices offered should be fully transparent. Furthermore, the process should be time-bound, while allowing buyers sufficient time to assess the value of the asset. In the case of divesting immovable assets such as land, state authorities may set a "guide price." If offers are significantly below the expected value, public authorities are advised to review the process and should not be obliged to proceed with a sale until they are satisfied with the authenticity of the procedures.

Since choosing the successful buyer is often influenced by the monetary offer, divesting entities might be tempted simply to choose the highest bid. However, other criteria also need to be considered, such as conditions attached to the bid or warranties requested from the public authority. Unconditional bids (sometimes known as "sold as seen" or "caveat emptor") are preferred but may not always be forthcoming.

Under the right circumstances, offers of value "uplift" may be considered. "Uplifts" are additional payments offered by the buyer to the public authority that are conditional on certain risks being managed appropriately or not materializing. An example would be a site where contamination is suspected but subsequent detailed investigations find that this is not the case.

If an asset has no monetary value or has a negative value, the public authority's concern should be able to dispose of the asset in an environmentally responsible manner.

Assets used in public-private partnerships

Assets used in PPPs are critical to the structure and financing of the transaction. In most cases assets are owned by the private company, and the public authority pays for the services provided through the assets. The management of these assets is therefore entirely the responsibility of the private operator. However, it is important for public authorities to be aware of the exact nature of the contractual arrangements of the PPP.

Under some forms of PPPs—which are common, for example, in the power generation sector and are known as build, own, operate (BOO)—the asset remains the property of the private company even after the contract to supply power has expired. The private company can then decide what to do with the residual assets. Under other forms of PPPs—which are common for highways, airports, and social infrastructure and are known as build, operate, transfer (BOT)—the asset reverts to the public authority at the end of the contract. With BOT contracts, which often last more than 20 years, public authorities run the risk of inheriting time-expired assets with expensive repair and maintenance costs. To protect against such liabilities, public authorities should ensure that PPP contracts contain provisions that oblige the private operator to maintain the asset in good condition (particularly in the final few years of the contract) and to guarantee its functional capability for several years after the contract expires.

NOTES

1. Public sector asset management generally refers to all government-owned assets—that is, financial assets, including assets held as part of the foreign currency reserve, and nonfinancial assets. This chapter refers only to public nonfinancial assets, such as land and buildings, plants, and equipment.
2. Ex post evaluation is sometimes divided into two stages. The first, undertaken after a project has been operating for a few years, examines efficiency and effectiveness; the second, undertaken several years later, examines the contribution of the project to the achievement of higher-level policy goals, usually referred to as "impact." The second stage may be referred to as impact evaluation.
3. See http://formin.finland.fi/public/default.aspx?contentid=69920.
4. Guidance on evaluation in HM Treasury (2003).
5. According to Florio and Vignetti (2013), "Evidence from international practices shows that ex post CBA [cost-benefit analysis] is not as widespread as its potential role in terms of policy learning would recommend."
6. Until the end of the contract term, when ownership often reverts to the state. A few examples of PPPs—such as build, transfer, operate (BTO)—transfer the asset to the contracting entity on completion of the asset.
7. Formerly known as the Government Property Unit.
8. The receipts were only allowed to be reinvested—not to supplement recurrent budgets.

REFERENCES

Auditor General's Office, Victoria. 2014. "Asset Management and Maintenance by Councils." Auditor General's Office, Melbourne.

Florio, M., and S. Vignetti. 2013. "The Use of Ex Post Cost-Benefit Analysis to Assess the Long-Term Effects of Major Infrastructure Projects." Working Paper 2/2013, Centre for Industrial Studies, Milan.

HM Treasury. 2003. *The Green Book: Appraisal and Evaluation in Central Government*. Amended in 2011. London: HM Treasury.

Republic of South Africa. 2004. "Asset Management Framework: Management of Tangible Non-Current Assets in the Public Sector." Cape Town.

U.S. Department of Housing and Urban Development. 2015. "Project Completion Report: PPM Version 2.0." U.S. Department of Housing and Urban Development, Washington, DC. portal.hud.gov/hudportal/documents/huddoc?id=proj_compl.docx.

Welde, M., and G. H. Volden. 2018. "Measuring Efficiency and Effectiveness through Ex Post Evaluation: Case Studies of Norwegian Transport Projects." *Research in Transportation Business and Management* 28 (September): 33–39.

World Bank. 2018. "Belarus: Strengthening Public Investment and Public-Private Partnerships, Assessment Report (P160080)." Governance Global Practice, World Bank, Washington, DC.

World Bank Independent Evaluation Group. 2017. Presentation at the IEG conference on "Harnessing the Power of the Private Sector in Support of Sustainable Development," Washington, DC, October 12, 2017.

10

Integrating PIM and PPP in a Unified Framework

OVERVIEW

The last two decades have seen growing global interest in public investment management (PIM) and public-private partnership (PPP). Public investment projects, implemented through a PPP or through more conventional means, should aim to support the creation of viable economic infrastructure—such as roads, airports, and railways—or to provide social infrastructure and public services, such as hospitals and schools. Both implementation modalities should stem from the same basic government demands or policy objectives. Nonetheless, traditional public investment and PPPs are often managed through distinctly different systems and institutions.

In many countries, most PPPs have been prepared, appraised, selected, budgeted, and monitored separately from traditionally implemented projects (TIPs). This disparity has undermined efficient public financial management and created undue fiscal risks and opacity, leading to concerns about appropriate forms of accounting, reporting, budgeting, and more. For example, a line ministry may seek capital funding from the ministry of finance for a project that it sees as important for its own strategic reasons. The ministry of finance might then reject this application for various reasons, and the proposing authority may then attempt to pass off its project as a PPP project in order to bypass the system that has just rejected the project. PPP projects should always be required to seek final approval from the ministry of finance before entering into contracts or financing agreements. Parallel systems should not be allowed to develop. Intrinsically, there is no such a thing as a PPP project; PPP is a way of implementing a public investment project. A bad project idea will remain a bad project idea, and PPP implementation will not transform it into a good one. It is therefore important to use a unified system of project identification, appraisal, and implementation—which includes projects funded by the budget, by donors, or by the PPP—to ensure consistency in selection choices and throughout the life cycle of the project.

The World Bank has developed a PIM-for-PPP (PIM4PPP) diagnostic tool to help governments to put in place a unified approach to public investment that encompasses traditional project financing and PPPs (Kim, Biletska, and Darcy 2015). This tool provides an analytical framework for assessing the whole investment cycle, from ex ante appraisal to ex post review, under a unified system for effectively managing traditional public investment and PPP. The PIM4PPP diagnostic has been pilot-tested in some countries, including Ukraine (Biletska et al. 2016), and a key lesson from the results is the need for clear guidance to assist the development of country-specific practices, procedures, and roles and responsibilities of the main stakeholders to integrate PIM and PPP effectively into a unified framework. More and more countries are interested in developing an integrated public investment system for PIM and PPP.[1]

This chapter provides guidance on the harmonization and integration of PIM and PPP, presenting the rationale for why PIM and PPP integration matters and discussing "must-have" elements for PIM-PPP integration.

WHY PIM-PPP INTEGRATION MATTERS

Benefits and risks of implementing public investment projects using a PPP methodology

Since it is clear that implementation through PPP is a possibility for many public investment projects, it is of critical importance for public authorities to be aware of both the benefits and risks of using a PPP approach to procure the project. Many country PPP units still take the role of PPP promotion too literally, meaning that they concentrate on benefits rather than risks. This focus on benefits creates a strategic risk for governments, in that it creates a subjective bias toward PPP that increases the probability of making mistakes, leading to poor choices with long-lasting consequences. This section describes both the benefits and risks in order to provide the best information on which to make informed choices and to advise decision makers accordingly.[2]

Benefits

Economically, the main benefit of encouraging a policy of PPP projects is that it promotes intergenerational equity by spreading the budgetary cost of providing a service or infrastructure over the same period of time as the benefits of the projects are realized.

The most commonly cited benefit of PPP implementation is greater efficiency in project delivery, but other important benefits are associated with PPP as well:

- Transferring important risks from governments to private business
- Encouraging better project management and outcomes
- Indicating increasing openness in the economy, thus encouraging further foreign direct investment, when the investment and financing include an element of foreign direct investment
- "Locking in" the cost of maintenance over the contractual period, thus supporting sustainability of the assets, where maintenance budgets are suboptimal or not adequately protected
- Building service delivery quality standards into the project agreement.

Risks

As with all projects, whether they are initiated by governments or by private enterprises, PPP projects entail risks. PPP is often considered more suitable for larger projects, resulting in a higher public profile, which creates a perceived difference in the risks faced. Care needs to be taken to distinguish between the perceived risk from people who are simply opposed to PPP as a policy and the real risks to the successful outcome of the project as actually experienced by officials and their advisers in many countries. Most risks can be avoided, minimized, or managed within a well-designed holistic PIM-PPP framework for strategic-level risks and a carefully implemented risk management program for project-level risks.

There are two principal categories of risks in PPP:[3]

1. *Strategic risks.* Those risks that are not specific to an individual project
2. *Project risks.* Those risks that are project specific.

Strategic risks may have several characteristics:

- Overpromotion and bias toward PPP implementation in the PPP unit
- Weak objectivity among advisers who can earn more in fees from PPP implementation than from TIP implementation, raising the risk of conflicts of interest
- Unrealistic expectations of affordability, schedule, and cost of preparation, all leading to inadequate preparation and putting the outcome at risk
- Incorrect problem identification
- Unchecked, unsolicited proposals from private companies
- Inability to communicate the objectives of the project to bidders
- Inability to express the project requirements in terms of "outputs" and "outcomes"
- Poor project governance and decision-making structure
- Poor coordination between government bodies
- Fiscal risks, which are perhaps the most important strategic risks and therefore are considered separately.

Project risks may include the following:

- Lack of preparation and implementation capacity
- Unwillingness to accept external advice or support
- Inaccurate or overly optimistic demand forecast
- Site risk
- Planning and permitting risks
- Construction risks
- Risk of the authority changing the scope of the project
- Insolvency of the private partner
- Risk of force majeure
- Risk of vandalism
- Miscalculation by the private partner during implementation
- Miscalculation of the responsible public authority's costs during implementation
- Change of law risk (general)
- Discriminatory change of law
- Funding risk
- Risks in use or operation
- Risks of unexpected maintenance, including cost and disruption.

Benefits from the integration of PIM and PPP

A unified framework provides several advantages across the whole investment cycle for both traditional public investment and PPPs.[4] First of all, a unified framework can help to ensure that assessments of and decisions about public investment projects are consistent with maintaining the value-for-money (VFM) objective throughout the project cycle, even though objective decisions cannot always be guaranteed. According to an Organisation for Economic Co-operation and Development (OECD) survey, the VFM objective is often blurred in practice, and the choice between a PPP and traditional procurement is skewed by factors other than VFM; government officials in many countries feel that the rules in place impede attaining the maximum VFM by creating incentives for either traditional procurement or PPPs (OECD 2010).

Second, a unified framework helps to accomplish optimal risk transfer. It is important to note that all service delivery mechanisms—whether they are public, private, or partnership models—are exposed to risks. Failure by the government to mitigate these risks not only may have fiscal consequences for the government but also may affect service delivery. The key advantage with PPPs, if executed properly, is that much of the efficiency or VFM gain is derived from effective identification, pricing, and transfer of risk from the public to the private sector. Good risk management practice allocates risk to the party best able to manage it. If each project (traditional or PPP) is subject to separate appraisal arrangements, the transfer of risk from one project to the other may not be optimal, opening the door to inadequate risk shifting at different steps in the project cycle. A unified framework, therefore, might be considered one of the conditions for achieving optimal risk transfer in both traditional and PPP options.

Third, a unified framework may help to avoid unidentified and unmanaged fiscal risks and improve transparency in the public financial management system. It should lead to the incorporation of all PPP fiscal commitments and risks into the government's routine fiscal screening and monitoring process. As such, it enables the government to assess effectively the real burden of PPP commitments and risks within a medium- to longer-term fiscal framework. A unified framework should discourage parallel budgeting by reporting the known and potential future fiscal costs of PPPs in the traditional budget system, which is considered good practice.

LEGAL AND INSTITUTIONAL FRAMEWORK FOR PIM-PPP INTEGRATION

Relevant legal framework for PIM-PPP integration

"Legal framework" refers to laws, decrees, regulations, by-laws, and policy papers that permit or prevent PPP forms of implementation, as well as creating the conditions that encourage or discourage private sector partners to engage with the government. It should meet the needs of project proposers, investors, and lenders, regardless of the chosen means of implementation. Sector legislation should be considered in addition to national laws.

Common law versus civil law

The best PPP policy document in the world is meaningless without the will to implement it. In countries with little or no previous experience of PPPs, risk-averse officials may resist attempts to implement projects through PPP. Furthermore, policy statements are often considered to be more aspirational than instructional. Many countries require a legal intervention to direct specific actions. There are clear differences between countries that have a "common law" legal tradition and those that have an "administrative civil law" system. Common law countries, such as the United Kingdom, do not necessarily need a PPP law, whereas administrative civil law countries find it nearly impossible to take any action unless there is a specific law allowing them to do so. Therefore, PIM-PPP integration will need to take account of the differences between the different systems; what is considered a necessary part of a legal framework in one country may not be necessary in another.

"Must-have" elements for PPP legislation

The presence or absence of a specific legal framework for PPP does not form the whole picture. There are often sector laws and regulations, some of which may, without sufficient attention to harmonization, even contradict provisions in a PPP law and regulation, so a broader legal picture needs to be established. It is most important to ensure that project proposals being considered for PPP implementation are appraised equally under national legislation within the existing PIM system.

The PPP legal and regulatory framework needs to have the following elements:

- Principles on which PPP projects are initiated and contracts are awarded
- Unambiguous authority to award PPP contracts, including who can award what types of contracts and for how long
- How projects are assessed and appraised for value for money (which should be the same for all public investment projects regardless of funding source)
- Long-term fiscal affordability of financial obligations
- How fiscal risks are assessed, managed, monitored, and reported
- How unsolicited proposals are handled
- Termination provisions, specifically compensation on termination
- Direct agreements
- Forms of permitted government support, if necessary
- Appropriate procurement procedures within the public procurement law
- Dispute resolution procedures, including international arbitration.

Dedicated legislation versus adaptation of existing legislation

In countries where many PPP projects have been initiated and implemented, the must-have legal and regulatory elements for a functional system have been adopted through two different approaches to developing the legal framework (or combinations of the two):

- Developing dedicated PPP legislation to clarify conditions for PPP implementation
- Adapting and strengthening the existing laws and regulations in sectors, procurement, contracting, and public financial management to support PPP implementation.

The first model has been adopted widely in many countries. A country's legal and administrative systems will determine whether a dedicated PPP law or regulation is needed or would be beneficial. A PPP-specific law or regulation can help to demonstrate political commitment to the PPP program and raise its profile, although care is needed to avoid conflict with other laws and above all to avoid an impression of bias. A well-designed PPP law generally sets out principles that may then be supported by more detailed regulations. PPP laws may establish guiding principles for a PPP program, processes, and institutional responsibilities—such as for selecting PPP projects, handling procurement, and dealing with disputes—and for policies, such as public financial management rules governing PPPs. Dedicated PPP legislation is most common in civil law countries,[5] as is the case in many African, Asian, European, and Latin American countries implementing PPPs. These countries do so under a specific PPP-concession law or regulation, or both. Some common law countries have also adopted PPP laws, which are more binding than a statement of PPP policy.[6]

Another less common, but equally successful, model is where no specific PPP law has been adopted. In Germany, for example, the Budget Law establishes guiding principles and appraisal requirements for all public procurement, including PPP projects. In Portugal, which has more PPPs than Germany, there is no PPP law or dedicated PPP legislation.[7] Permitting legal texts include one section on PPPs in the Public Procurement Law and one in the Budgetary Framework Law.

Existing administrative laws or regulations—such as those for sector policies, procurement, or resolution of contractual disputes—may define processes and institutional roles for PIM and PPP. The following existing laws and regulations may be adapted and applied to PPP processes (World Bank 2017d, sec. 2.2):

- *Sector-specific laws and regulations.* PPPs are often implemented in sectors that are already governed by laws and regulations that may constrain the government's ability to contract with the private sector or provide rules for doing so.
- *Procurement law.* The transaction process for a PPP must typically comply with or preferably be integrated with a public procurement law and regulations.
- *Contract law.* Insolvency and contract resolution mechanisms are included.
- *Public financial management law.* Institutional responsibilities, processes, and rules established in public financial management laws and regulations can contribute to the PPP framework, including project approval requirements, fiscal limits, budgeting processes, and reporting requirements.

Country examples for legal integration of PIM and PPP

The PPP legal structure has been developed and strengthened in many countries using dedicated PPP legislation or adapting the existing sector, procurement, contract, or public financial management laws and regulations. Integrating PIM and PPP into the legal framework has been considered only recently in most countries. Separate PPP legislation has encouraged or facilitated fragmented treatment of PPP projects, separate from TIPs, especially when new legislation assigns specific roles to newly formed PPP units that duplicate or supersede those of existing PIM institutions. This fragmentation should be avoided; PIM units should only be given the powers to deal with matters that are specific to PPP implementation and should not be given a mandate to promote PPP as a "preferred" method of implementation.

PIM-PPP legal integration has recently become an important agenda in PIM and PPP management; as such, some countries have made specific efforts to establish an integrated legal framework. Cyprus, for example, enacted the Fiscal Responsibility and Budgetary System Law in 2014, which includes a special chapter for public investment projects, reserved for regulating PIM and PPP projects in an integrated system. The law makes both TIP and PPP projects subject to the same provisions for project preselection, assessment, and selection; there is, however, a supplementary provision for an economic entity considering the PPP procurement option, which requires additional steps in the selection stage in order to assess the desirability of a PPP option (see box 10.1).

In the Republic of Korea, the PPP Law provides legislative support for PPP preparation and management. It is a special law and has precedence over other laws; however, efforts to integrate equal treatment and flexible interchangeability between TIPs and PPPs have been addressed through several pieces of secondary legislation under PPP law. PPP projects need to be reviewed and approved by the PPP Review Committee (PRC), chaired by the finance minister in alignment with TIP projects at three critical stages: (1) project appraisal and selection, (2) contract agreement, and (3)

BOX 10.1

Cyprus's legal framework for integrating PIM and PPP

The 2014 enactment of the Fiscal Responsibility and Budgetary System Law (FRBSL) includes a chapter (chapter 11, on selection and implementation of public investment projects) for public investment projects.

The FRBSL requires all public investment projects—whether TIP or PPP—to follow the same preselection, assessment, and selection processes; if an economic entity is considering the PPP procurement option, further steps need to be taken at the selection stage in order to assess the desirability of a PPP option.

Under the FRBSL, PIM guidelines provide more specific regulation of the decision to select a PPP project in a unified framework with traditional public investment procurement. Only when a project has been preselected, appraised, and selected can economic entities proceed to deciding the most appropriate procurement method for PPP. Public procurement options available to economic entities are defined in the Coordination of Procedures for the Award of Public Works Contracts, Public Supply Contracts, and Public Service Contracts and for Related Matters Law, of 2006 (12(I)/2006).

For the purpose of determining the desirability of a PPP option, economic entities considering this procurement option should undertake a procurement option pretest, select the most appropriate PPP modality, and perform a value-for-money (VFM) analysis to prove the desirability of the PPP option over the traditional public procurement option.

If the results of the procurement option pretest suggest that undertaking a PPP procurement option is worth exploring, the PPP modality (type of PPP contract) should be chosen for further investigation.

As a next step, when the economic entity has decided on the PPP modality, a VFM assessment has to be undertaken. In this assessment, the public sector comparator tool is used to determine whether implementing the project through a PPP would be more cost-effective than implementing it through traditional public investment. The net present value of the PPP (determined by a feasibility study analysis for the PPP project) is compared with the net present value of the preferred option as a TIP. Implementing a project through a PPP yields value for money if it results in a net positive gain to society greater than that which could be achieved by implementing the preferred option as a TIP.

The PPP procurement method will be selected if the VFM assessment is positive and if the project does not exceed the ceilings imposed by the minister of finance on the annual commitments of PPPs in the economic entity's budget; otherwise, the project will be implemented through the traditional public procurement method.

Sources: Government of Cyprus 2014, 2016.

renegotiation or refinancing (see box 10.2).[8] At the appraisal and selection stage, a PPP project should be assessed using VFM analysis and approved by the PRC over a TIP procurement option. At the contract agreement stage, the PRC should review the analysis to ensure that the negotiated PPP contract still provides better value for money. During renegotiation or refinancing, changes to the PPP contract agreement should be reviewed and approved by the PRC to confirm value for money. The legislative framework allows a project to switch modality during preparation and implementation; the PPP Basic Policy regulation states that TIP and PPP project modality may be interchanged to produce better value for money.

According to the National Finance Law, the Korean government's medium-term expenditure framework (MTEF) considers PIM-PPP integration. The MTEF has a PPP section that includes agriculture, defense, education, environment, health, research and development, welfare, and other sectors, where all active PPP projects are systematically considered and formulated with all other TIP infrastructure projects.

BOX 10.2

Korea's PPP law and regulation for PIM and PPP integration

Under the Republic of Korea's PPP Law, the PPP Review Committee (PRC) chaired by the finance minister, is responsible for reviewing and approving every PPP project at critical stages of PPP implementation:

- *Article 10 (2)*. When a master plan for a PPP project meets the requirements specified in the PPP Decree, it shall undergo prior deliberation by the PRC. The same shall apply where modification is required.
- *Article 13 (3)*. The competent authority shall designate a concessionaire by making a concession agreement with the potential concessionaire, including the conditions for project implementation, such as the total project cost and the concession period. Matters regarding the designation of a concessionaire who meets the requirements determined by PPP Decree shall undergo a prior deliberation by the PRC.

According to the regulation of PPP Basic Policy, value-for-money (VFM) analysis is required to ensure a better value for money of the PPP project. The assessment is carried out to compare the value for money of PPP procurement with that of TIP procurement. The analysis consists of three phases:

- *Phase 1 (feasibility assessment)*. Economic feasibility (mainly cost-benefit analysis) is examined and a policy analysis is conducted.
- *Phase 2 (VFM assessment)*. A comparative analysis is conducted between a public sector comparator and the PPP proposal to examine the VFM of the PPP option.
- *Phase 3 (development of an alternative option using the PPP approach)*. Additional financial analysis is conducted to calculate an appropriate level of project cost, user fee, government subsidy, and so forth from a public sector perspective and an alternative option using the PPP approach.

In the PPP Basic Policy, Articles 161–162 regulate how TIP and PPP projects can be interchangeable in the context of achieving a better VFM option. Article 161 regulates how an ongoing TIP project can be transferred to a PPP project, and Article 162 regulates how an ongoing PPP project can be transferred to a TIP project if needed to meet the better VFM requirement.

Sources: Government of Korea, Act on Public Private Partnerships in Infrastructure, Enforcement Decree on the Act on Public Private Partnerships in Infrastructure, and Regulation of Basic Policy Plan on the Act on Public Private Partnerships in Infrastructure.

The World Bank has been working with several countries to develop the relevant legal framework to harmonize and integrate PIM and PPP management.[9] In 2018, the government of Jordan worked with the World Bank to develop a PIM-PPP framework, including provisions for aligning PPP decision making with project appraisal and selection for TIPs (World Bank 2018). The government of Jamaica developed a coordinated and integrated decision-making system in 2015 covering all projects funded by the budget (Capital A), donor funds (Capital B), public corporations' funds, and PPPs.[10] The PIM Committee was established, supported by a secretariat, to screen, review, and prioritize all projects, including TIPs and PPPs, at an early stage (see box 10.3 for Jamaica's PIM system).

BOX 10.3

Jamaica's PIM system for integrating PPP

Jamaica has significantly strengthened its public investment management since 2013. Under the new system, all proposed public investment projects, regardless of funding source, including PPPs, are now screened, approved, and managed through an integrated process. This process extends across all public entities and sectors, includes all types of public sector expenditures (actuals and contingencies), covers all steps and phases that a project has to complete through its productive life, ensures that all projects and the overall portfolio are aligned with a larger development purpose, and ensures that both future capital and recurrent spending associated with investment projects is provided for in budget forecasts.

The World Bank supported the government in two operations throughout the reform process.[a] World Bank technical advisory services helped the government to design the new PIM system and supported cabinet approval of it.

The first operation supported amendment of the Financial Audit and Administration Act in 2014 to establish two new institutions: (a) the PIM Committee, which reviews the feasibility and strategic alignment of all investment proposals, sets investment project priorities, and recommends projects to the cabinet for approval; and (b) the PIM Secretariat, which provides technical support to the PIM Committee, assesses proposals, and undertakes evaluations.

The second operation supported the government in making these institutions operational. The cabinet appointed the PIM Committee in 2016. The executive director was hired in August 2015, and other core staff members of the PIM Secretariat were hired during 2016. In December 2016 the cabinet approved operational guidelines that govern the PIM system from proposal to impact evaluation. Investment project financing is funding investments (including a pre-investment evaluation facility) and additional technical support for the new PIM system.

Important improvements in PIM performance have been achieved: the quality of project proposals has improved, and project costing is now incorporated into the budget. (Projections of the total life-cycle cost of major investment projects, including both capital and recurrent costs together with a year-by-year breakdown of costs for at least the next three years, are included in the budget.) Interinstitutional coordination has improved, minimizing overlapping projects across ministries, departments, and agencies and ensuring that linkages are clear in project proposals. The strategic alignment is better, and the policy focus is sharper.

Source: World Bank 2016b.
a. One was a development policy loan (the first operation) and the other was investment project financing (second operation). The development policy loan helped to move the legislative actions forward, while the investment project financing is financing the underlying investments.

BOX 10.4

Zimbabwe's PIM guidelines, including integrated treatment of PPP projects

The Zimbabwe PIM guidelines define the scope and coverage of public investment projects. The appraisal and approval of all public sector investment projects, including PPPs, should follow these guidelines, which define projects such as those financed through

1. National budget or centrally managed resources
2. Public entities and grant-aided institutions when:
   a. Requesting capital budgetary funding
   b. Imposing recurrent expenditures on the budget
   c. Seeking government guarantees.
3. Public-private partnership projects (joint-venture projects)
4. Development partner projects when:
   a. Cofinanced from the budget
   b. Imposing recurrent costs on the budget.

Source: Ministry of Finance and Economic Development, Zimbabwe 2017.

In 2017, the government of Zimbabwe approved a new regulation establishing PIM guidelines through a Treasury circular, whereby PPP appraisal and selection decisions are incorporated into the PIM decision-making framework (see box 10.4).[11]

Relevant institutional arrangements for PIM-PPP integration

Governments need experience, capacity, and coordination to implement PPPs. While the private party will design, finance, build, and maintain the infrastructure and provide services, the government is responsible for ensuring that public services are provided in accord with expected quality standards in a way that achieves good value for money. Many governments choose to define institutional responsibilities for PPPs in order to select the right project and a competent partner as well as to manage the contract.

Institutional arrangements and the allocation of functions differ depending on the PPP program and player needs.

Two key institutional roles for PPP are often described (Rajaram et al. 2014, ch. 7):

- *A promoter role.* Doing the day-to-day management work for the PPP process, involving identifying potential projects, conducting an appraisal, structuring the project, drafting the contract, handling bidding, and managing the contract after it is signed
- *A gatekeeper role.* Overseeing the PPP process through review and approvals at key stages to ensure that the project represents a good investment decision.

The roles and responsibilities of dedicated PPP units need to be examined carefully to avoid distortions in the overall PIM system. Inherent conflicts of interest should be avoided, which means that the "promoter" should be different from the "gatekeeper," as should be the case in traditionally implemented projects.

Finance ministries play a central gatekeeping role in the overall PIM system in most countries. The avoidance of parallel systems for TIP and PPP implementation is essential; finance ministries (through their role in coordinating other actors) should therefore be at the heart of PPP institutional arrangements. Sector ministries and agencies should generally play the role of promoter in day-to-day implementation of the steps involved in bringing a PPP project to fruition.

It is important to highlight the recent trend toward changing the roles of PPP units as they become more "mainstream" within traditional PIM institutional arrangements.

The United Kingdom has a long-running experience of PPP that serves as a useful case study. Since the mid-1990s, institutional development to support the PPP form of implementation has been adapted to changing perceptions regarding the best role for PIM and PPP units. When the first major wave of PPP projects was being developed alongside important policy measures, HM Treasury appointed external full-time advisers to provide market-oriented guidance on policy making. A further iteration known as Partnership UK, established in 2001, was merged into Infrastructure UK under the umbrella of HM Treasury in 2010 in order to harmonize TIP and PPP implementation and to ensure objective assessment of project proposals, regardless of the means of implementation, and there has not been a separate PPP unit since then.[12] The intention behind these changes was for PPP to be used as the implementation modality only when it provides better value for money than TIP.

Korea also has a long history of a unified PIM-PPP unit, putting PIM-PPP integration into practice (see box 10.5). According to the PPP Law and the National Finance Law, a dedicated unit called the Public and Private Infrastructure Investment Management Center (PIMAC) has been mandated to provide review and oversight services for the decision making of the

BOX 10.5

Korea's PIM and PPP unit responsibilities under the PPP law and national finance law

According to Article 38 of Korea's National Finance Law, in order to formulate a budget for any new large-scale project, including PPPs, defined as a project with a total cost of at least almost US$50 million, the minister of economy and finance shall conduct a preliminary feasibility study. The preliminary feasibility study shall be undertaken by PIMAC, which works as a professional PIM unit.

Article 23 of the PPP Law also articulates the establishment of PIMAC. In order to support and review PPP preparation and implementation comprehensively, the article describes the mandates of the PIMAC. At all stages of a PPP project—preparation, feasibility appraisal, procurement bidding and negotiation, contract agreement and management, implementation, renegotiation, and so on—the PIMAC is responsible for working as the professional PPP unit of the government.

Source: Government of Korea, Act on National Finance and Act on Public Private Partnerships in Infrastructure.

Ministry of Economy and Finance in TIP and PPP project preparation and implementation. The dedicated unit is therefore able to provide consistent quality assurance for both TIP and PPP projects.

INTEGRATED PROJECT SELECTION PRACTICES FOR PIM AND PPP

Consistency in PIM and PPP project identification and initial development

PIM-PPP integration requires cohesive decision making. Project identification and initial concept development require a standard methodology to examine the need for government intervention to address a given situation. How these issues are handled can affect how the government allocates resources and may affect future value for money. Designating projects as "PPPs" at this stage should be avoided, as the potential for PPP implementation is largely irrelevant until the decision has been made about whether there should be any project at all and about what are the objectives, scope, scale, and desired outcomes.

BOX 10.6

Country PPP policy statements

Australia's State of Victoria's policy statement describes the aim of PPPs as being "to deliver improved services and better value for money, primarily through appropriate risk transfer, encouraging innovation, greater asset utilization, and an integrated whole-of-life management, underpinned by private financing."

India's draft National PPP Policy sets several objectives for PPPs:

- Harnessing private sector efficiencies in asset creation, maintenance, and service delivery
- Providing a focus on the life-cycle approach for development of a project, involving asset creation and maintenance over its life cycle
- Creating opportunities to bring in innovation and technological improvements
- Enabling affordable and improved services to the users in a responsible and sustainable manner.

Korea defines a public-private partnership project as a project to build and operate infrastructure such as road, port, railway, school, and environmental facilities, which have traditionally been constructed and run by government funding, with private capital, thus tapping into the creativity and efficiency of the private sector.

South Africa defines a public-private partnership as a commercial transaction between a government institution and a private partner in which the private party either performs an institutional function on behalf of the institution for a specified or indefinite period or acquires the use of state property for its own commercial purposes for a specified or indefinite period. The private party receives a benefit for performing the function or for utilizing state property, either by way of compensation from a revenue fund, collection of charges or fees by the private party from users of a service provided to them, or a combination of compensation and charges or fees.

Source: World Bank 2017d.

A comprehensive system to ensure that PPP is a viable implementing option within PIM needs to start with a PPP policy statement. A policy document should lay out the rationale for PPP implementation within a country's economic and development context. It should explain the benefits of PPP to citizens and reach out to potential partners to fund and operate projects. Australia,[13] India, Korea, South Africa, and Slovakia provide examples of good-practice PPP policy papers (see box 10.6).

Management of the early stages of TIP and PPP project identification and initial development needs to be addressed in official guidance, which should emphasize that management applies to all forms of implementation. PPP legal instruments and policy statements should avoid references to PPP projects as being separately identified or as being somehow outside the normal PIM system. Identifying the need for intervention of any kind, with a clear elucidation of the nature of the problem and various options for resolving it, should precede thoughts on whether a PPP or any other form of implementation makes the most sense.

Integrated preappraisal for PIM and PPP projects

A good PIM system will attempt to keep the number of project proposals to a minimum, as there typically are more projects than resources. The most common way to keep the number of proposals manageable is to use a preappraisal system that identifies and eliminates projects that have little or no chance of being approved later on (as set out in chapter 5). If a project proposal passes the preappraisal stage, this fact gives project proposers enough confidence to devote resources to a feasibility study. The process could also help proposers to improve the project design.

The basic project concept should be introduced in the preappraisal template. The template should include enough information to support an informed decision on whether to prepare the project for a detailed proposal and possible implementation as well as an assessment of the potential for PPP implementation, if the project's characteristics indicate that a PPP could be the best means of implementation. The process also needs to be able to screen out projects that are unsuitable for PPP implementation. A section on suitability for PPP implementation should be included in the preappraisal template and should be completed by relevant government experts.

A manual recently prepared for the government of Cyprus is a good example of a process for screening for PPP potential at preappraisal. According to the World Bank (2016a), the following factors and preconditions favor a PPP solution:

> It will be important to highlight any characteristics that would suggest that PPP may be considered as a procurement option. These would include the potential for proper allocation of risk between public and private partners or for private sector innovation in design solutions or operational practices. There should also be the possibility of formulating a long duration contract of sufficient size to outweigh the significant fixed costs of negotiating a PPP deal. Good candidates for PPP procurement are as long as: (a) outputs and quality can be defined and monitored in a clear way; (b) user needs are stable over time; (c) the project is reasonably robust to policy changes; and (d) fast technological change is not expected to require significant changes in project design.

Integrated appraisal for PIM and PPP projects

PPP is merely an alternative form of project implementation. Recognizing this characteristic, national project appraisal rules should clearly state that they apply to PPP as well as TIP. Projects should be appraised for their economic value, not their means of implementation. Good practice demands a single appraisal manual that explicitly includes PPP implementation.

At the project appraisal stage, all projects should follow the process laid down in the PIM system, regardless of whether they are flagged as potential PPPs at the preappraisal stage. A project not flagged as a potential PPP during the preappraisal stage may still be flagged as such at the appraisal stage.

Separate guidance on matters of technical relevance to PPP implementation is acceptable as long as the guidance operates within the PIM framework.[14] The guidance must warn against potential distortions in appraisal that PPP can bring, including:

- *Describing projects as "PPP projects" before an appraisal has been conducted.* Such descriptions are poor practice and lead to distortions and subjective decision making.
- *Incentivizing PPP over TIP.* Governments sometimes create special funds to promote private sector involvement, which may result in project promoters from public authorities refusing to consider non-PPP options.
- *Fast-tracking PPPs.* In addition to being labeled PPP projects before appraisal, projects are often given preferential treatment, which could easily influence the implementation route. Ministers and officials may expedite their projects, bypassing normal quality assurance systems to avoid the full scrutiny that would normally be required.

If the rationale for PPP is assessed to be solid, projects will proceed to a more in-depth VFM assessment or public sector comparator assessment.

When flagging a project as a potential PPP, the following factors should be considered:

- *VFM proposition for the potential PPP.* Achieving value for money from private capital for building and operating public infrastructure requires efficiency savings that compensate for the additional financing cost of private capital. A public investment project should not be flagged as a potential PPP simply because of the need to leverage public investment with private capital.
- *Institutional capacity for procuring and managing PPP contracts.* Potential for value for money is not enough; the relevant authorities must have the capacity to prepare, procure, monitor, and manage contracts to ensure value for money.
- *Marketability of the proposed project.* Market interest in the project from suitably qualified bidders needs to be sufficient to ensure meaningful competition.
- *Affordability and acceptability of fiscal commitments.* Fiscal commitments include guarantees and contingent liabilities.

VFM proposition

A comparative assessment of the costs of PPP and non-PPP implementation routes has become an essential element in assessing the merits of each implementation option. However, these assessments are riddled with potential distortions through their (necessarily) subjective nature: skilled officials or consultants can manipulate comparative assessment inputs in order to achieve the results they want.

This assessment has two essential components: qualitative assessment and quantitative assessment (World Bank 2013). A key area of concern in quantitative assessment is risk pricing; significant focus is placed on risk pricing in PPP arrangements, but it is often not given the same level of importance in conventional implementation, and possibly none at all. Each identified risk should be priced consistently as part of the comparative assessment.

Officials and their advisers should be able to identify risks to be transferred to the private sector and to assess the cost of those risks. The adjudged values can then be assigned to the benefits column of the PPP option appraisal. Subjectivity enters into the assessment of risk and the valuation of associated costs, leading to the possibility of manipulation. In recent times, this difficulty has led to quantitative assessments being given less importance in the overall VFM assessment. Instead, governments appear to be focusing more on qualitative assessment to guide decision making, although such a focus is also fraught with subjectivity.

There is significant scope for managing an assessment in such a way as to reach a prejudged conclusion ("case making"). In order to ensure consistency across projects and to avoid case making, governments should issue formal written guidance for pricing risks. There is also the legitimate concern that such a comparative assessment should not create an administrative burden by being too complex. Comparative assessments can be slow and involve substantial bureaucracy if not designed well.

Institutional capacity

Assessments of PPP implementation viability should assess whether the awarding authority has the capacity to prepare and implement a successful PPP project. Knowledge and skills for preparing and procuring a PPP project are often scarce in public authorities. It is reckless to attempt to implement a PPP project without the necessary skills; the liabilities connected with a badly executed project could last for decades.

Marketability of the proposed project

PPP implementation needs interest from private sector investors and lending institutions. A "soft market test," an assessment of the competitive environment for the project, should be carried out to establish the potential level of interest from likely bidders. It should also assess their competence to deliver PPP and their ability to bring anything extra to the process.

Affordability and acceptability of likely fiscal commitments

PPP contracts can create fiscal commitments in the form of (a) up-front capital payments, (b) obligations to provide connecting infrastructure or utilities, or (c) obligations to pay for the availability of assets and their associated services. PPP contracts also contain contingent liabilities such as debt guarantees, minimum revenue guarantees, early termination payments, or environmental warranties. All of these liabilities need to be part of the decision-making process so that the government enters into contracts knowing the risks and with a plan to manage and monitor them. Increasingly, international accounting standards[15] require that the value of PPP assets be scored against national debt statistics, thus removing a previously attractive motivation for PPP transactions.

Overall rationale

The rationale for PPP implementation is presented through the identification of possible "drivers" of value for money. Table 10.1 summarizes the possible drivers and the corresponding questions for guiding the choice of PPP structure.

TABLE 10.1 Summary of possible drivers and questions relating to public-private partnership (PPP) implementation

POSSIBLE DRIVER	WHY MIGHT THIS APPLY?	WHEN MIGHT IT APPLY?	PPP STRUCTURE QUESTIONS
More effective management under a PPP delivers the infrastructure asset and associated services more quickly or more cost-efficiently than the alternative.	PPPs may bring in experience and expertise not available in the public sector or may strengthen managerial incentives by linking payments to performance.	May apply to projects where there is: • Current sector underperformance or significant delivery capacity constraints in the public sector that could not readily be overcome internally • Significant scope to improve quality or to lower overall project cost and risk through management improvements	• Can payments be linked to performance? • Can sufficient private capital be placed at risk to ensure the private party faces a strong incentive to perform over the long term? • Can project risks be reasonably defined, identified, and measured, such that the right risks can be transferred to the private party?
A whole-of-life costing approach is expected to lower the lifetime cost of the project.	PPPs integrate up-front design and construction with ongoing operation and maintenance under one company. This integration creates an incentive to carry out each function in a way that minimizes total lifetime project cost.	May apply to projects for which operation and maintenance costs are expected to vary significantly according to design and quality of construction	• Can sufficient private capital be placed at risk to ensure that the private party faces a strong incentive to perform over the long term?
Private management under a PPP is expected to allow for innovation in infrastructure service delivery, resulting in improved reliability, lower cost, or both.	Specifying required outputs rather than inputs in a PPP contract provides scope and incentives for innovation.	May apply to projects with a range of possible delivery technologies	• Can performance be specified in terms of outputs?
PPP may lead to reduced public liabilities and fiscal risk compared to public financing and provision.	By requiring the private company to raise finance for a PPP project and bear substantial risks, a good PPP contract *can* reduce the public liabilities and fiscal risk associated with providing the infrastructure. The extent of the reduction depends on the structure of the PPP project.	May create liabilities that are harder to assess than those associated with traditional infrastructure procurement funded from public debt; the potential risks and benefits should be treated with caution	• Can sufficient private capital be involved?
"User pays" PPPs may increase the overall resources available for funding infrastructure assets and services.	Private operation may be more effective in charging users for services.	May apply when there is substantial scope to reduce commercial losses or when significant revenues can be generated from alternative uses in addition to the core project purpose	• Can revenue risk (demand and payment risk) be transferred to the private sector?

Source: Government of Cyprus 2016.

Independent review of appraisal for PIM and PPP projects

Independent review of project proposals is the main means of applying quality assurance to a PIM system. It is also an important means of screening out unsuitable projects, correcting mistakes and inaccurate assumptions, and avoiding the natural bias that comes with officials or consultants who are concerned with the promotion of a PPP project.

When PPP has been chosen, extra vigilance is required, as authorities often realize that they may be pitching their project to a skeptical private sector and try to overcompensate by painting a particularly rosy picture of potential demand for the project or by minimizing the costs and risks involved (optimism bias). In an attempt to encourage private participation and investment, they may also offer contractual terms that could lead to unacceptable fiscal risks.

Optimism bias can affect the private sector as well; private bidders may be so keen to participate in a project that they overlook faults in the appraisal. Worse still, they may not care, thinking that the government will be the ultimate guarantor of the liabilities involved in failure. This guide therefore strongly promotes independent review.

The rules on providing independent scrutiny should be the same regardless of whether the chosen implementation method is TIP or PPP. Conflicts of interest may emerge when national PPP units have a promotional role for PPP but are also asked to review proposals involving PPP implementation; reviewer independence is therefore essential. A "challenge and review" system is needed to stop unsuitable projects from progressing as well as to identify improvements in design and appraisal for potentially suitable projects that might improve outcomes. Independent review should be more than a simple "stop-go" technique; it should offer a "checklist" for conducting reviews of project proposals and for quality management.

Decisions regarding unsolicited proposals

PPP projects are categorized into solicited and unsolicited proposals, depending on who initiates the project. An unsolicited proposal is initiated by a private partner, in contrast to one submitted in response to a government request. This approach is the opposite of conventional proposals, which are initiated by the government. Most countries give the public sector the sole right to initiate PPP projects; however, some countries also allow unsolicited proposals.

When appropriately adopted, unsolicited proposals can allow governments to benefit from the creativity of a private partner. However, unsolicited proposals also create challenges that may increase the risk of funding mismatches or shifts in government strategic prioritization for infrastructure projects. They also can act as a conduit for corrupt practices. Solicited PPP projects are selected within the scope, sectors, and boundaries established by a national strategy, but unsolicited projects may not be part of a national strategy. Accepting unsolicited proposals may therefore cause distortion within the public investment portfolio, especially if they are prioritized over existing high-priority government projects.

To minimize the risks from unsolicited proposals, specific eligibility criteria should be developed and covered by legislation. These criteria should ensure that an unsolicited proposal is consistent or compatible with the existing national plan or sector strategy to avoid distorting already-agreed-on priorities (Rajaram

BOX 10.7

VFM assessment method for unsolicited proposal projects in Korea: Comparing all options with the same level of scrutiny

According to the regulations of the PPP Basic Policy in Korea, value-for-money (VFM) analysis should be carried out and reviewed by PIMAC to screen and ensure that an unsolicited proposal provides better VFM than other options. The analysis calculates the value for money from all procurement options, covering the unsolicited proposal itself, a comparable solicited project with public initiative, and a traditionally implemented project (TIP) project.

The VFM from the option of "a comparable solicited project with public initiative" and a TIP project are compared to the VFM from the unsolicited proposal, based on the assumption that the comparable solicited project is designed on the same reference package as the unsolicited proposal while the TIP project is not.

This way of comparing VFM has proven effective in encouraging private partners to propose more creative unsolicited projects and in helping the government to expect and reap greater benefits from the creative ideas of the private partner.

Source: PIMAC 2016.

et al. 2014, ch. 7). They should also be creative and efficient enough to deliver extra value to the sector to compensate for the possible costs of distortion.

A recent World Bank study provides guidelines for managing unsolicited proposals, which governments should adapt to fit local contexts (World Bank 2017b). The principles are relevant from initial concept assessment, appraisal, project development, procurement, and implementation, and should be embedded in the same approval and decision-making processes required for solicited proposals.

When unsolicited projects are subject to the same checks as publicly initiated PPPs, stakeholders are less likely to see them as controversial; when projects are seen to be subject to the same level of scrutiny, stakeholders can be assured that project decisions will be equally robust. Harmonizing procedures will have important benefits for government oversight and may reduce public transaction costs as well as the risk of corrupt practices.

Korea provides an example of an advanced approach to keeping the same level of appraisal scrutiny and robustness across the three options: (1) unsolicited PPP, (2) solicited PPP, and (3) TIP (see box 10.7).

INTEGRATED FISCAL MANAGEMENT FOR PIM AND PPP

PPP fiscal risk management

Fiscal risk singles out PPP implementation for special attention. There is increasing scrutiny of this subject, and bodies such as the International Monetary Fund (IMF) have been highly focused on it. This section assesses the latest work on the subject.

The subject of risk is always raised when preparing project proposals in the context of PPP; however, within project teams, risk is always construed to mean project risks,[16] which tend to be issues such as construction, operational, demand, and future regulatory risks. Important as they are, these risks are of principal concern to investors and lenders, although inasmuch as they affect the ultimate price of the project, they should be of concern to the government too.

Additional risks can be and often are transferred in the process of negotiation between public and private entities and subsequently appear in the contract between the parties. Sometimes these are risks that only the government can absorb. Since PPP projects are governed entirely by the project agreement and the associated financing documents, governments can unwittingly expose themselves to significant fiscal risk by agreeing to explicit guarantees and contingent liabilities when entering into PPP contracts. The following are the main types of instruments in project agreements that can create fiscal risks:

- State guarantees on the debt raised against the project
- Guaranteed payments against minimum levels of demand (for example, volume of traffic or megawatts of generated power through "take or pay" agreements)
- Change in the law causing contractual claims
- Material adverse government action, which is a discriminatory step that results in the private company being unable to manage the contract in the way originally intended, potentially leading to claims or early termination
- Environmental warranties
- Viability gap funding
- Early termination provisions that require the state to buy back assets at market or write-down value
- Other "buy back" clauses.

There are several examples of how governments have been exposed to these risks and have suffered the consequences when the risks materialized. There are even cautionary tales from highly regarded PPP systems in countries such as Korea and the United Kingdom as well as in countries with less-developed PPP systems.

Four key challenges arise with respect to fiscal risk in PPP projects:

- Understanding risks and how they are incurred,
- Knowing how to measure these risks,
- Recording the risks in individual projects and cumulatively, and
- Monitoring the likelihood of risks occurring.

The following are essential points to consider:

- Explicit liabilities should be recorded clearly and should be managed within the budget system.
- Contingent liabilities in PPP contracts should be assessed and priced before commitments are made through signed contracts.
- Even when PPP projects are entirely "user-funded" and are not accounted for on the project's balance sheet, the government should still monitor and record their contingent liabilities, as the government is always the funder of last resort.
- Accumulated aggregate fiscal risks related to increasing numbers of PPP commitments should be recorded and monitored, and their impact should be considered in the selection process.
- The Ministry of Finance should sign off on PPP projects before they are approved.

Controlling the aggregate amount of fiscal commitments under PPP contracts

Some governments introduce rules to control the aggregate fiscal commitments to PPP projects. Types of fiscal commitments should be defined, but determining how to aggregate a long-term flow of different fiscal commitments represents a challenge. Whether to apply the rule to direct liabilities only or to include contingent liabilities should be decided, and liabilities should be measured and aggregated. The following are some examples of safeguards introduced to reduce aggregate exposure to risk from PPPs (see some updates from Irwin 2007; World Bank 2017d, 87–90):

- *Brazil.* The Federal PPP Law (2004) initially limited total financial commitments undertaken in PPP contracts to a maximum of 1 percent of annual net revenue.[17] In 2009 this limit was raised to 3 percent, and in 2012 it was raised again to 5 percent in the cases of subnational governments.
- *Cyprus.* The Fiscal Responsibility and Budget Systems Law (2012) determines the total budget ceiling of each economic operator regarding annual commitments toward public-private partnerships.
- *Hungary.* Act 38 (1992) limits the total nominal value of multiyear commitments to PPPs to 3 percent of government revenue.
- *Peru.* Legislative Decree no. 410-2015-EF (2015) states that the present value of the total fiscal commitments to PPPs—excluding government finance entities—shall not exceed 12 percent of gross domestic product. The president may change this limit every three years, with the endorsement of the Ministry of the Economy and Finance, depending on the infrastructure needs of the country.

The Korean government also considered the idea of setting a safeguard ceiling for annual PPP commitments and disbursement. Noting that PPP fiscal commitments were important fiscal burdens, a regulatory fiscal rule was considered that consisted of imposing an upper limit to control annual PPP disbursements. It was proposed that the government should manage its PPP fiscal burden on a medium- to long-term basis by setting an annual safeguard ceiling on government PPP disbursements at 2 percent of the total annual government expenditure budget (Kim et al. 2011).

Given the difficulties of deciding whether a particular PPP commitment is affordable, controlling limits on aggregate fiscal risk exposure can help to ensure that the government's aggregate exposure to PPP costs and risks remains within manageable limits. An alternative is to incorporate limits on PPP commitments within other fiscal targets. For example, some governments introduce targets or limits on public debt. Some types of PPP commitments may be included within measurements of public debt, according to international norms or national rules (Irwin 2007). The IMF–World Bank PPP fiscal risk assessment model (PFRAM) can be used to identify and analyze fiscal risks; it advises the user on how to consider the allocation of risks and how to assess the likelihood of the risks materializing, the fiscal impact if they do materialize, and what should be done to mitigate them (IMF and World Bank 2016).

PPP transparency and accounting treatment

In many countries, significant decisions about the use of PPP as opposed to traditional implementation have been made on the basis of an expectation of "off-balance-sheet" accounting treatment. How different governments register their projects in national accounts can influence the choice of implementation route, perhaps more than considerations of efficiency and risk allocation. Adopting international accounting standards that apply to PPP contracts can help to avoid these distortions. Examples include the International Public Sector Accounting Standards (IPSAS), the IMF's *Government Finance Statistics Manual*, and the Eurostat method used by many European Union countries (see box 10.8). These standards have been developed relatively recently to deal with the increasing popularity of PPP and the tendency for PPP to be used as an off-balance-sheet financing modality. Without such rules, the assets used in a PPP contract may appear on the balance sheet of the service provider, the financial institutions involved in the deal, the government, or none of these.

Transparency is needed in the way PPP contract awards and PPP projects are reported and presented to the media, civil society, and the general public. Finance ministries and national assemblies or parliaments need full information on future liabilities for payments against PPP contracts as part of the budget planning and approval processes.

BOX 10.8

International financial standards for PPP accounting treatment

International financial standards vary in their treatment of PPP fiscal commitments. A few standards specifically address when and how direct liabilities and assets of PPP projects should be recognized by contracting governments:

- International Public Sector Accounting Standard no. 32 (IPSAS-32), introduced in 2011, define when PPP assets and liabilities should be recognized, assuming that a government is following IPSAS accrual accounting standards, meaning that it records revenues and expenses when they are incurred, regardless of when cash is exchanged. Under IPSAS-32, PPP assets and liabilities appear on the government's balance sheet, provided the government controls or regulates the services that the operator must provide with the PPP asset, to whom, and at what price and controls any significant residual interest in the asset at the end of the contract. Under this definition, government-pays PPPs appear on the government's balance sheet; the treatment of user-pays PPPs depends on the details of the contract.
- The IMF's *Government Finance Statistics Manual* (IMF 2014) sets out criteria for classifying PPP assets and liabilities for statistical reporting purposes. Under these criteria, PPP assets and liabilities are accounted for in the government's balance sheet if the government bears most of the project's risks and rewards—for example, taking into consideration the degree to which the government controls the design, quality, size, and maintenance of the asset and bears construction risk—as well as the allocation of demand risk, residual value and obsolescence risk, and availability risk.
- Eurostat guidelines require European governments to recognize PPP liabilities in debt statistics where the government retains construction risk or demand or availability risk. Since PPPs transfer those risks to the private party, under this rule most PPPs tend to remain off the government's balance sheet. Realizing that an excessive focus on off-government-balance-sheet recording can come at the expense of sound project preparation and value for money and may push public authorities to use PPPs where they are not appropriate, Eurostat, with the European PPP Expertise Centre, prepared the *2016 Eurostat Guide to the Statistical Treatment of PPPs* (EPEC 2016).

Source: Based on World Bank 2017d, 91–92.

Integrated budgeting and reporting for PIM and PPP projects

Upfront government payments to PPP projects are similar to those for TIPs. Given that they are typically made within the first few years of a project, they need to be built into annual capital budgets and medium-term expenditures frameworks. Budgeting for long-term direct commitments for PPPs, such as availability payments, is more challenging. Availability payments are not capital payments; rather, they come from the recurrent budget of the responsible public entity. The mismatch between the annual budget appropriation cycle and the multiyear payment commitments to PPP exposes the private party to the risk that payments may not be appropriated in a timely fashion. Many governments do not introduce any particular budgeting approach for direct, long-term PPP commitments, on the assumption that a responsible legislature will approve appropriations to meet the government's legally binding payment commitments. Where appropriations risk is high, mechanisms to minimize this risk may be needed to give potential private partners some confidence.

At the federal level in Brazil, the Fiscal Responsibility Law requires subsidy payments to PPPs to be treated in the same way as debt service payments—that is, they are not discretionary and are automatically appropriated so that as soon as the subsidy is approved, appropriations are not subject to further legislative approval.[18] In addition, since the sixth edition of the *Manual de contabilidade aplicada ao setor público*, inspired by IPSAS-32, the government must consider the assets and the respective liabilities related to PPP contracts as being "on balance sheet," with consequences for debt capacity. Such an approach is intended to provide investors with more certainty.

In Korea, Article 7 (2)–(4) of the PPP Law requires availability payments in build, transfer, lease (BTL) projects to be treated in the same way as debt service payments, but not liabilities and contingent liabilities in build, transfer, operate (BTO) projects.[19] The aggregate amount for BTL availability payments should be subject to advance legislative approval. The government therefore needs to submit the aggregate ceiling for BTL projects to the national assembly at the same time as the details of fiscal disbursements for all BTL projects.

INTEGRATED PROJECT IMPLEMENTATION FOR PIM AND PPP

Effectiveness of PPP project implementation and procurement

The differences in project implementation rules and practices between traditional contracting practices and PPP methodologies need to be understood. PPP is not common in many public authorities, and the degree of involvement in the implementation phase of TIPs and PPPs varies markedly. In a TIP project, the asset under implementation will become the authority's property, and the authority will naturally take a hands-on approach to monitoring progress—albeit often through a supervising agent (consulting engineer, for example) for day-to-day monitoring. When a project is implemented as a PPP, the asset generally belongs to the private consortium,[20] and the consortium is responsible for its correct and timely completion. Failure to do so may result in significant financial consequences.

The authorities naturally have a direct interest in the project, but they should avoid the same hands-on approach of more traditional implementation. Too much interference by the authority might be seen as impairment by the private entity. It may also run the risk of inadvertently transferring risk back from the contractor.

PPP-implemented projects should be subject to the same procurement rules and conditions as any other form of PIM contract. With no special rules or preferences, procurement processes should be transparent and fair and should encourage open competition, while allowing for some flexibility (which may also be advantageous for traditional procurement).[21] The costs of bidding for a PPP-implemented project are significantly higher than those for a typical TIP project, and potential bidders will always look at the bidding risk before committing themselves to the costs.

Award criteria should be objective, fair, and easy to measure. They should be aligned with the project objectives as set by the implementing authority in their project rationale. The number of participants in a bidding competition is indicative of the quality of requests for proposals as well as the country's general PPP framework.

Timeliness of implementation

Information on the timeliness of implementation can provide empirical evidence on the comparative merits of PPP versus TIP implementation. It can also be used for the qualitative and quantitative analysis of the VFM test.

Common reasons for delays in project procurement need to be identified so as to flag those that might be reduced through PPP implementation. These issues include the following:

- Private sector administrative and approval processes
- Negotiations concerning the bid of the preferred bidder
- Delays caused by public sector administrative and approval processes
- Delays caused by planning procedures
- Delays caused by having to adapt to policy changes
- Reiterations of project design that are caused by a poor response from bidders
- Reiterations of design as a result of authority-led scope and specification changes or affordability issues
- Lack of expertise, experience, or resources within public sector procurement teams
- Insufficient development of specifications prior to the project going to the market
- Poor process management
- Unforeseeable events, such as the impact of the terrorist attacks on the United States on September 11, 2001, on insurance markets and the financial collapse of private companies involved in PPP activity in the wake of the 2008 financial crisis.

There are two distinct stages to implementation: (a) project approval through to contract signature and (b) contract signature through to the completed assets being available for service.

Project approval through to contract signature

The implementation stage of a project starts when it has been approved by the government. The first implementation stage covers the period from the point of approval to the point where a contract has been signed and physical work can proceed. Delays in this period are often good indicators of weaknesses in the overall system, such as a legal impediment or the quality of project preparation. They may also suggest weaknesses in the procurement system or lack of interest among bidders, which, in turn, could indicate inadequate preparation and a failure to identify problems in the review and challenge function.

Contract signature through to the completed assets being available for service

The second stage covers activities between the moment when the public authority signs the contract with the private company and the moment when the assets become available for use, the service commencement date. Most of these activities are construction related and may require permits from utility companies or others. Delays may indicate poor preparation, including permit and land acquisition issues, as well as a failure of the review and challenge function to identify such weaknesses. Thorough project preparation and coordination between all public stakeholders is the best way to avoid implementation problems.

The best sources of reliable performance data are audit functions, where these exist. Ideally, this body would be the national external auditing authority, but not all such bodies measure time-based performance. Internal audit functions may also be a source of information, where these are working effectively.

Refinancing practices

The majority of PPP projects using project finance will undergo a refinancing, and this is to be expected during the life of a contract. It makes sense to refinance, as it is usually in the interests of both the public authority and the private contractor, if it is executed correctly. However, the rules under which refinancing takes place are changing constantly. In the early period of PPP development in leading countries, refinancing resulted in some significant financial gains for PPP company shareholders. While it might be argued that these gains were nothing more than a reward for managing the risks of construction and early implementation well, it may also be argued that the gains came partially from factors outside the influence of a PPP company, such as favorable macroeconomic conditions or greater confidence in PPP generally. Large windfall gains made by private companies from the taxpayer may lead to political difficulties and negative media attention, which may lead to pressure to reduce or eliminate PPP as an implementation option. Sharing the financial gains from refinancing between a PPP company and the authorities is often considered more appropriate and has been built into the regulatory framework and contractual agreements in several cases (see box 10.9).

Change management and renegotiation practices

PPP arrangements are long term and can last 25 years or longer, making some form of change to the contract inevitable. It is impossible to predict long-term needs over such time frames, so it is better to accept that change is

BOX 10.9

Refinancing examples

Under the terms of many PPP project agreements, the competent authority may expect to share the refinancing benefits equally with the project company. The refinancing benefit is measured as the increase in the investor's expected internal rate of return in the post-refinancing financial model against the base case financial model. Several governments have already introduced rules for how refinancing benefits will be treated. The public authority and the concessionaire may split the benefit 50/50 or in other ways.

The United Kingdom's HM Treasury introduced into its standard Private Finance Initiative contracts a 50/50 split of any refinancing gain (HM Treasury 2003), but this split was subsequently revised to a 70/30 split in favor of the government in the wake of the global financial crisis of the late 2000s.

Korea also introduced a refinancing rule (the 50/50 rule) in the PPP regulation.

likely and to take great care with contract design to ensure that all eventualities can be accommodated within the framework of clauses. These clauses are often referred to as "change mechanisms." The need to make changes does not necessarily indicate failure; changes are quite common in operational PPP contracts.

The most common type of adjustment is to the prices paid on the basis of inflation. Price escalation formulas must be included in a PPP contract, together with the relevant inflation index and the permitted application of any price increases. Cost escalation formulas can go from the simple, such as those relating to changes in the costs of raw material inputs in power purchase agreements, to more complex public service contracts requiring periodic benchmarking exercises to determine market prices.

Projects that are implemented through PPP should, in principle, bring about fewer adjustments and changes during the implementation period as a result of disciplined preparation and due diligence. When the need to adjust is apparent, the PPP unit, or equivalent, should monitor the changes and the reasons for them in case they indicate other weaknesses in the project, in the capacity of the implementing authority, or in the wider framework itself. Awareness may help to avoid such issues in the future or help to develop guidance on how to resolve them in future projects.

The contract should identify a mechanism to facilitate these changes. Changes during construction that are initiated by the authority are considered poor practice and can be highly costly for the authority. These projects are likely to take longer due to concerns about adjusting the risk profile of the project and often leave private partners with residual concerns. Investors and lenders may also be concerned about the resultant shift in the financial model, as any need to remodel or renegotiate the contract can lead to substantial delay. Better project preparation and planning and improved stakeholder consultation will help to avoid any disruption or inefficient practices. Any changes required after signing the PPP contract will be of concern to investors and lenders, and they should be fully engaged throughout the process. Box 10.10 presents some guidelines for managing change.

BOX 10.10

Guidelines for effective change management and renegotiation

Renegotiation requires agreement among public and private partners along with their financiers. The following principles may help to strengthen renegotiations:

- The rules and procedures for making changes should be included in the contract.
- Renegotiation should take into account the original project rationale and appraisal of the project as well as the project agreement. Many countries (especially European Union countries) have strict rules on adding to the original scope or scale of the project without changing the nature of the original tender process.
- Renegotiation should not negatively affect ex ante value for money.
- The government should consider compensating the private partner only when conditions change because of discretionary public policy actions.
- Careful consideration is needed regarding any shifts in the project risk profile.
- Project financiers will want to be sure that their rewards are not diluted through a renegotiation. Financing documents almost always have strict conditions on seeking the active engagement of and approval from financiers before any change can be agreed to.
- Any renegotiation process should be transparent and subject to the law.

Source: Rajaram et al. 2014, ch. 7.

Dispute resolution procedures

Disagreements do occur between parties in most contractual arrangements, and PPP is no different. However, the motivation to resolve disagreements is stronger for both parties in PPP contracts than in TIPs, as disputes may lead to early termination, which is in no one's interest and should only be a measure of last resort. Litigation costs can be huge in PPP contract disputes, and it is better to deal with problems before they escalate.

Many minor disputes can be resolved through careful negotiations, and most PPP contracts in high-income economies include clauses that require at least two steps before legal proceedings are initiated. The first step is a formal meeting for both sides to discuss the issue. If they cannot reach an agreement, the second step is to move to independent arbitration, usually conducted by an outside expert agreed to by both parties to be independent. Both parties agree to be bound by the recommendations of the arbitration, and legal proceedings may be initiated only if the dispute is still not resolved.

Asset registers

It is good practice for governments to compile registers of existing fixed assets and newly completed fixed assets in TIP (see chapter 9). If projects are implemented as a PPP, they are often not considered public assets because they are owned by the private company. They are, however, assets in public use for the delivery of public services, and they should be considered as such. Also, due to the potential of these projects to incur substantial liabilities, the entire "stock" of PPP projects should be monitored closely. Even though they do not form an integral part of the asset register, PPP projects should still be recorded, preferably as an annex to the asset register of the state.[22] An appropriately designed template should also allow financial obligations and fiscal risks that come with PPP contracts to be monitored.

Ex post review

Conducting ex post reviews of PPP projects, which are fully aligned with the TIP approach, is a key means of understanding how well project preparation and implementation have gone. The following will need to be decided:

- The appropriateness of different public entities to conduct ex post reviews
- What exactly should be reviewed
- How results should be disseminated.

Governments typically carry out a completion review of a traditionally procured project. Templates for completion reviews from other countries are helpful for designing a country-specific template. Completion review is an important and necessary step; however, many officials confuse it with ex post evaluation, which is an assessment of project performance in terms of activities, outputs, and results (see chapter 9).

Many public authorities claim to conduct ex post evaluations, but further discussion reveals that this may be a simple financial compliance check. Most governments are keen to ensure financial compliance during project execution, but performance reviews are not common.

Performance reviews challenge the project at two levels:

- *At the project level.* Assessment of how well the individual PPP project fulfilled its objectives
- *At a strategic level.* Exploration of claims that PPP implementation is more efficient than traditional procurement. Evidence found here can help to determine which option might perform better in future situations and may become key for future option assessments in the VFM analysis. Policy makers are also keen to learn about the challenges and difficulties faced during the project.

Ex post evaluations should not be undertaken to allocate blame for mistakes or to investigate misconduct. In the event of suspicions of wrongdoing, the appropriate authorities should be notified; however, there should be no sanctions for genuine mistakes, particularly mistakes caused by the relative novelty of PPP as an implementation method.

As PPP is relatively new in many countries, it is important to learn whether it is advantageous over conventional implementation. The government needs to seek out data and assess whether the use of a PPP:

- Achieved its objectives in terms of outcomes or intermediate outcomes
- Offered time advantages over more conventional means
- Offered cost-efficiency advantages over more conventional means
- Offered better overall performance of service indicators over more conventional means.

On the basis of strategic performance evaluation, the U.K. National Audit Office (2011) provides the recommendations given in box 10.11.

BOX 10.11

U.K. National Audit Office: Highlighting insufficient data in evaluating Private Finance Initiative projects

The U.K. National Audit Office highlights greater focus on data, including, in particular,

- Government has failed too often to identify, collect, and use the data it needs to help support decision making and secure the best value for money. Greater focus should be given to the types of data that should be gathered to improve decision making, who should collect them, and how much collection should cost.
- The Major Projects Authority, the Treasury, and departments should work collaboratively to agree on the data required to support the preparation, assurance, and scrutiny of major projects in government. Data should be collected where the information adds demonstrable value and supports decisions but only where the benefits clearly outweigh the costs and burden of data collection.
- Those setting the data requirements should consider whether good-quality, up-to-date data are available to challenge whether the best solution to a defined requirement is being pursued and the best commercial terms are being obtained.
- Departments should undertake periodic value-for-money (VFM) reviews of their programs, highlighting any areas where value for money has diminished. These reviews should be high level, with sufficient project data to inform the reviews, but should not revisit all aspects of project business cases. Program reviews should be used to improve performance and to assess how well the procurement method is working.
- As there has not been a government assessment of the value contributed by Private Finance Initiative equity investors, the Treasury should consider how data can be collected to understand better the relationship between investors' returns and the risks they have borne.

Source: U.K. National Audit Office 2011.

NOTES

1. Including Cyprus, Ethiopia, Jamaica, Jordan, Romania, Vietnam, and Zimbabwe.
2. For further discussion on PPP benefits and risks, see World Bank (2017d).
3. Other common risks such as country risk or sector risk are important to investors and financiers; these risks are mentioned only briefly because they are not specific to PPPs.
4. This section draws from Rajaram et al. (2014, ch. 7).
5. Examples include Brazil, Colombia, Indonesia, the Republic of Korea, Mexico, and the Philippines.
6. For example, Zimbabwe.
7. Portugal has a PPP Decree-Law on the work of the PPP unit.
8. South Africa has a similar regulation. To ensure that PIM and PPP projects are treated equally and reviewed, the Treasury must give approval at four stages: (1) after the feasibility study, (2) after preparation of tender documents and a draft contract, (3) for appointment of the preferred bidder, and (4) prior to contract signatures.
9. Including Jamaica, Jordan, and Serbia.
10. Capital A and Capital B have been combined into Capital C (since fiscal year 2019/2020), so there is no longer a distinction.
11. Ethiopia's draft PIM proclamation has similar requirements for incorporating PPPs under the PIM scope of application.
12. In 2016 Infrastructure UK merged with the Major Projects Authority to create the Infrastructure and Projects Authority.
13. In the State of Victoria.
14. For example, market testing, contractual terms, or fiscal risks.

15. Such as the International Public Sector Accounting Standards (IPSAS-32), introduced in 2011. See box 10.8.
16. Risks contained within the project from the perspective of the private sector.
17. Accounting rules for PPPs are being defined, including the valuation of guarantees and their treatment in relation to this limit.
18. Law no. 101 of 2000.
19. The PPP Law in Korea defines two types of PPP modalities: build, transfer, lease (BTL), which involves a service availability type of payment, and build, transfer, operate (BTO), which involves a concession type of payment. Given that measuring the liabilities and contingent liabilities in BTO projects is difficult, BTO payments are not required to obtain legislative approval in advance. However, all BTO payments are reported to the national assembly as incorporated later in the annual budget appropriations.
20. Not always, for example, with a BTO model of implementation.
21. The competitive dialogue used throughout the European Union was created largely to provide flexibility for PPP procurement when the competitive pool is small, but it is not used exclusively for PPPs.
22. Or the relevant public authority.

REFERENCES

Biletska, N., J. H. Kim, M. Darcy, M. P. Dunne, and I. Zapatrina. 2016. *Public-Private Partnerships in the Context of Public Investment Management in Ukraine: An Assessment.* World Bank, Washington, DC. https://openknowledge.worldbank.org/handle/10986/24772.

EPEC (European PPP Expertise Centre). 2016. *2016 Eurostat Guide to the Statistical Treatment of Public-Private Partnerships.* Kirchberg, Luxembourg: European Investment Bank.

Government of Cyprus. 2014. "The Fiscal Responsibility and Budgetary System Law." Government of Cyprus, Nicosia.

———. 2016. "Guidelines for the Selection and Implementation of Public Investment Projects." Government of Cyprus, Nicosia.

HM Treasury. 2003. *The Green Book: Appraisal and Evaluation in Central Government.* Amended in 2011. London: HM Treasury.

IMF (International Monetary Fund). 2014. *Government Finance Statistics Manual 2014.* Washington, DC: IMF.

IMF and World Bank. 2016. *Public-Private Partnership Fiscal Risk Assessment Model (PFRAM) User Guide.* Preliminary version. Washington, DC: IMF and World Bank.

Irwin, T. 2007. *Government Guarantees: Allocating and Valuing Risk in Privately Financed Infrastructure Projects.* Directions in Development—Infrastructure. Washington, DC: World Bank.

Kim, J. H., N. Biletska, and M. Darcy. 2015. "Public Investment Management for Public Private Partnership: Analytical Framework and Assessment Tool." Unpublished paper, World Bank, Washington, DC.

Kim, J. H., J. Kim, S. Shin, and S.-Y. Lee. 2011. *Public-Private Partnership Infrastructure Projects: Case Studies from the Republic of Korea, Volume 1: Institutional Arrangements and Performance.* Manila: Asian Development Bank.

Ministry of Finance and Economic Development, Zimbabwe. 2017. "The Public Investment Management Guidelines." Secretary to the Treasury, Harare.

OECD (Organisation for Economic Co-operation and Development). 2010. "How to Attain Value for Money: Comparing PPP and Traditional Infrastructure Public Procurement." OECD Working Paper, OECD, Paris.

PIMAC (Public and Private Infrastructure Investment Management Center). 2016. "Guidelines for the Value for Money Assessment." PIMAC, Korea Development Institute (KDI), Seoul.

Rajaram, A., T. M. Le, K. Kaiser, J. H. Kim, and J. Frank, eds. 2014. *The Power of Public Investment Management: Transforming Resources into Assets for Growth.* Washington, DC: World Bank.

U.K. National Audit Office. 2011. "Lessons from PFI and Other Projects." Report by the Comptroller and Auditor General, HC 920, session 2010–2012, National Audit Office, London.

World Bank. 2013. "Value for Money Analysis Practices and Challenges: How Governments Choose When to Use PPP to Deliver Public Infrastructure and Services." World Bank, Washington, DC.

———. 2016a. "Cyprus Manual for Pre-Selection and Appraisal of Public Investment Projects: Reimbursable Advisory Service Report." World Bank, Washington, DC.

———. 2016b. "Jamaica: The Second Competitiveness and Fiscal Management Programmatic for Development Policy Financing." World Bank, Washington, DC.

———. 2017a. "Maximizing Finance for Development (MFD): Guidance for Applying an MFD Lens." Unpublished paper, World Bank, Washington, DC.

———. 2017b. "Policy Guidelines for Managing Unsolicited Proposals in Infrastructure Projects." World Bank, Washington, DC.

———. 2017c. "Public Investment Management Systems: Summary Note on PIM Systems." Note delivered to the Financial Management Information Systems Community of Practice, World Bank, Washington, DC.

———. 2017d. *Public-Private Partnerships: Reference Guide Version 3.* Washington, DC: World Bank.

———. 2018. "Jordan 2018 Public Investment Management: Public-Private Partnership Governance Framework." World Bank, Washington, DC.

11

Rationalizing a Nonperforming PIM Portfolio

OVERVIEW

Many countries face issues with an overcommitted portfolio of public investment projects. A portfolio is overcommitted when the financing requirements to deliver projects according to the originally envisaged implementation schedules significantly exceed the funding available.

Faced with a shortage of funds and too many projects, decision makers often feel compelled to spread funds across the public investment portfolio (PIP). This "drip funding" may lead to the need to revise project schedules to fit the reduced funding and to stop-go implementation of projects. Box 11.1 presents an example from Romania of an overcommitted PIP: the cost of completing the portfolio was found to be seven times the amount allocated in the 2015 budget; in an adequately funded program, it would have been no more than three to four times the allocated amount.[1] Box 11.2 presents another example from Ukraine.

An overcommitted portfolio is a legacy of inadequate quality-at-entry processes for public investment projects. Projects have been selected for financing despite planned allocations exceeding the fiscal limits set for the fiscal year and for the medium term. Overcommitment is a symptom of an ineffective gatekeeping mechanism by which a central finance agency should be checking that all requirements have been met, especially with respect to project affordability in the context of the wider portfolio. Inadequate gatekeeping may lead to admitting "too many" projects as well as admitting projects that have not been subject to the usual scrutiny and quality steps essential for good international practice.

The problem with an overcommitted portfolio can be exacerbated by inadequacies in project implementation—for example, delays in procurement or appointment of project managers and teams, delays in the release or approval of funding, and delays caused by limited capacity for project management. Delays in project implementation mean that a project remains in the portfolio longer than necessary and blocks scarce resources that could be used for new projects.

BOX 11.1

Underresourcing of the PIP in Romania

A World Bank reimbursable advisory services (RAS) project reviewed Romania's public investment portfolio (PIP) and concluded that it was substantially underresourced. When adequately funded, PIP completion costs should be less than three to four times the 2015 budget allocation; the cost to complete this underresourced PIP was seven times the allocation.

Funding levels were particularly inadequate for domestically funded projects, where completion costs were 13 times the 2015 budget allocations. The equivalent figure for externally funded projects was a more reasonable six times (see figure B11.1.1).

Inadequate funding leads to substantial delays in completion. More than 11 percent of all projects in Romania's PIP had been under implementation for more than 10 years; 11 projects had been in the investment program for more than 20 years. The RAS project concluded that a major rationalization of the PIP was required to address the underfunding and improve PIP implementation performance.

FIGURE B11.1.1

Cost of completion of the 2015 project portfolio in Romania

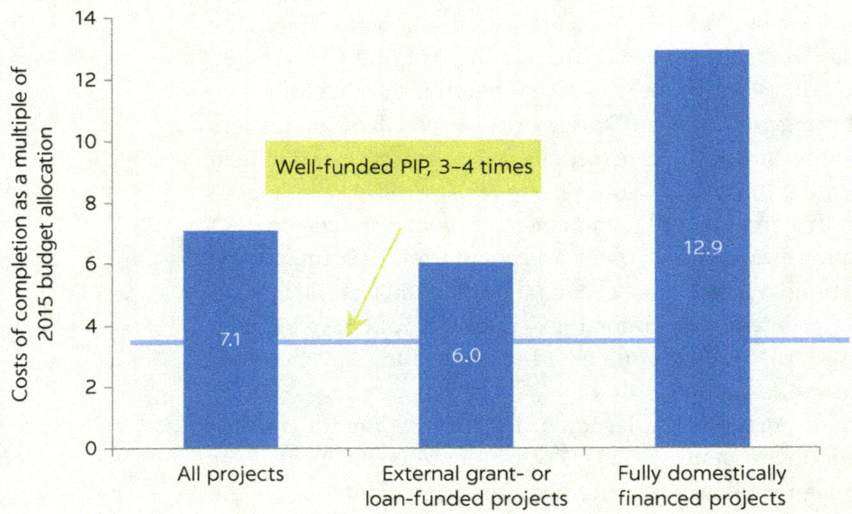

Note: PIP = public investment portfolio.

Source: World Bank 2015.

An excessive number of ongoing projects, some with little prospect of social profitability, may have a negative impact on overall PIM system performance, including:

- *Delays in achieving benefits from public investment projects.* Since the completion of ongoing projects is delayed, the time at which project benefits should start accruing is also delayed, negatively affecting social profitability. Long delays may also mean that a project loses its strategic relevance.

BOX 11.2

Fundamental quality issues affecting PIM performance in Ukraine

Historical weaknesses in Ukraine's public investment management (PIM) procedures have exacerbated an overcommitted and poorly performing state-level public investment portfolio. A 2013 survey of construction projects in Ukraine identified 1,653 uncompleted state-level projects, of which 1,005 were currently suspended, with no implementation taking place.

The existence of two overlapping categories of public investment providing alternative financing windows, coupled with weak or absent appraisal procedures, resulted in a portfolio in which more than 90 percent of public capital investment projects had avoided any significant economic analysis. Additional quality issues included the following:

- Most projects avoided scrutiny due to loopholes in classification (lack of definition of a public investment project).
- The PIM system did not seem to block new projects from entering the budget, but it did allow ministries to delay ongoing ones and to squeeze in new ones.
- Lack of strategic guidance on how to prioritize projects complicated project selection.

The poorly performing PIM portfolio led to the adoption of some reforms to PIM procedures for the 2016 budget. A methodology for rationalizing the PIM portfolio, drafted by the World Bank in 2016, led to improvements.

Sources: World Bank 2013, 2016.

- *Increases in overall project costs.* Significant delays in implementation tend to drive up the costs of project implementation, as staff and other resources have to be deployed for a longer time and contractors have to remobilize after suspending or reducing activity.
- *Lack of fiscal space for new projects irrespective of their merits.* An excessive number of poorly prepared ongoing projects could mean that fiscal space for capital projects is fully used and funding is not available for new projects, even if they show better prospects of achieving stronger development outcomes.
- *Undermining of reforms to improve quality-at-entry processes.* A poorly performing project portfolio might prevent other public investment management (PIM) and public financial management reforms from being implemented. As an example, many countries aspire to strengthen their multiyear budget planning through medium-term budgetary frameworks (MTBFs); however, a prerequisite for a well-designed MTBF is the establishment of a credible capital expenditure baseline that realistically budgets for capital projects. Creating an expenditure baseline in the case of an underresourced PIP will result in either a baseline that is not affordable or a baseline that is disconnected from underlying project implementation schedules and therefore lacks credibility.

Problems with an overcommitted PIP may be resolved in the long run by successfully implementing reforms to strengthen quality-at-entry processes, as long as affordability issues and time constraints are addressed early on. As ongoing projects are completed and fiscal space for new projects gradually builds, successfully implemented reforms of quality-at-entry processes should prevent poor project proposals and unaffordable project commitments from proceeding. Reforms that address typical implementation bottlenecks and raise the capacity

BOX 11.3

Implementation of public investment portfolio rationalization in Turkey

The Turkish government undertook a major PIP rationalization in 2001–02 that led to a leaner, better prioritized, and better financed portfolio. It involved the following steps:

- *Reassessment of sectoral investment portfolios taking into consideration sectoral, regional, and project-specific priorities.* The process was used to identify projects that were no longer considered to reflect public investment priorities.
- *Screening of the portfolio.* This screening identified 1,602 projects that were no longer considered a priority, were not economically feasible, or could not be implemented due to insufficient funding.
- *Elimination of 1,702 projects and subprojects from the portfolio.* These projects represented a total investment of US$30 billion.

The initial exercise to screen for and remove poorly performing projects was complemented by a series of follow-up measures to improve the performance of the public investment portfolio:

- A moratorium on introducing new multiyear projects until the current portfolio was adequately funded
- Further reprioritization of existing projects to identify those at an early stage of implementation, previously not considered urgent, or considered to be low priority, which enabled funding to be redirected to projects that were a higher priority or closer to completion
- Rescheduling of some multiyear projects to align their spending more closely with available resources
- Halting of implementation on several major projects to allow their feasibility to be reassessed prior to deciding whether they should receive further funding.

Source: Former Ministry of Development, Republic of Turkey.

of project managers and project teams can also reduce time and cost overruns. However, such reforms are complex and demanding, and their full effect may only materialize in the medium to long term. In the meantime, an underresourced PIP can cause significant damage to PIM outcomes.

A short- to medium-term option is to initiate portfolio rationalization; this process involves reviewing the portfolio, identifying poorly performing projects, and creating a resolution procedure to restructure, curtail, or terminate projects.

There are no international standards for rationalization, and the literature on the subject is limited. Box 11.3 describes a successfully implemented portfolio rationalization in Turkey. Previous World Bank diagnostics and technical assistance projects have supported attempts to review or rationalize project portfolios in several countries, including Belarus, Mongolia, Romania, and Ukraine.

MAIN FEATURES OF PORTFOLIO RATIONALIZATION

The overall objectives of portfolio rationalization are twofold: (a) to ensure that projects remaining in the PIP are adequately financed to avoid delays and that benefits from finalized projects accrue as soon as possible and (b) to free up fiscal space to finance new high-priority projects instead of drip feeding ongoing projects that are of poor quality or are strategically irrelevant.

Within these objectives, a portfolio rationalization exercise consists of three core steps: (a) use systemic features of nonperformance to identify projects that are candidates for rationalization, (b) immediately suspend and remove from the public investment portfolio projects that are identified and confirmed as nonperforming, and (c) enter a project removed from the public investment portfolio into a procedure that assesses options for resolving its status and identifies a preferred resolution.

Identifying nonperforming projects and removing them from the public investment portfolio makes explicit those prioritization decisions that have occurred implicitly by denying projects sufficient funding. Portfolio rationalization often builds heavily on information about the level of funding made available to projects, as funding is used as a proxy for information about priorities. Where a project has been halted or is receiving only token levels of funding over longer periods of time, it reveals that, implicitly, the relevant authority does not consider it to be a high priority.

PIP rationalization is usually planned and conducted as a one-off, discrete exercise. Rationalization is politically sensitive and resource demanding, and should be reserved for significant portfolio issues. In general, PIP rationalization should not be seen as a substitute for addressing reform issues, but as a complementary way to achieve results in the short term and to prepare for successful implementation of more thorough reforms. In an ideal situation, fixing weaknesses in PIM procedures should happen before or at the same time as PIP rationalization, so as to avoid a recurrence of problems associated with an underfunded public investment portfolio. Box 11.4 provides an example of how unreformed procedures caused previous attempts at a much-needed rationalization to fail in Bangladesh.

Rationalization should be conducted in an integrated manner covering all ongoing projects irrespective of financing source and implementation modality, as this would be in line with the general recommendation to harmonize procedures and create a level playing field for all public investment projects. However, the scope and design of a rationalization exercise will need to begin in the local context, where the PIP is often divided by financing source or implementation modality and different parts are subject to different procedures.

Differences in financing sources also affect the relevance of various criteria for determining project and portfolio nonperformance. Nonperformance criteria for budget-financed projects will to some extent build on the availability of annual budget allocations, while criteria for loan-financed projects will rely on information about disbursements within the financial plan agreed on for the projects. These differences in criteria give rise to differences in interpretation. For example, the availability of budget allocations reflects shifts in current political priorities, while the level of disbursements reflects the extent of various other constraints on implementation. These differences also mean that the timing of fiscal effects of rationalization decisions will vary depending on the financing source.[2]

Despite similarities and overlaps, donor-led portfolio reviews differ from country-driven rationalizations in their scope, frequency, and objectives. Donor-led portfolio reviews are commonly practiced; they are typically done for each donor portfolio individually, although joint reviews of the loan-financed portfolio may occur. Portfolio reviews are generally confined to loan- and grant-financed portfolios, while reviews of budget-financed projects and combined country-project portfolio reviews are rare. The objectives are also

BOX 11.4

Unreformed procedures for approval and selection impede portfolio rationalization in Bangladesh

The Annual Development Program (ADP) is the key instrument for public investment in Bangladesh. The ADP document consists of several differently colored sections listing public investment projects based on various combinations of approval status (approved by the National Economic Council, the planning minister, or the line ministry; or not approved), funding status (funded or unfunded), and mode of financing. Given that the ADP comprises projects in very different stages of funding and approval, it constitutes a mix of a traditional development budget (approved projects with funding), project pipelines, and even "pre-project pipelines" (the "Green Pages").

The standard practice of adding more new projects to the ADP at the beginning of the fiscal year and during the midyear revision than have actually been completed since the start of the year has stretched scarce resources. The sheer number of approved and unapproved projects within the system strains project implementation resources and is a reason for the overload of the key bodies involved in project design, appraisal, and approval. As a result, time and cost overruns and low returns on investment have historically been associated with management of the ADP. The practice of including projects in the ADP documentation that have not been approved has created expectations among project proponents and potential beneficiaries that these projects will eventually be approved and selected.

Past attempts to rationalize the ADP portfolio had only a limited effect. In fiscal year 2011, a rationalization exercise took place with the aim of reducing the number of unapproved projects included in the Green Pages. At the beginning of fiscal year 2011, the number of unapproved projects in the ADP was considerably lower than in previous fiscal years. However, after the midyear revision of the ADP, the effect of this rationalization was almost neutralized, as many new unapproved projects were added. At the same time, the portfolio of approved projects with funding continued to rise (see figure B11.4.1).

FIGURE B11.4.1

Number of approved and unapproved projects in the Annual Development Program (ADP) and revised ADP

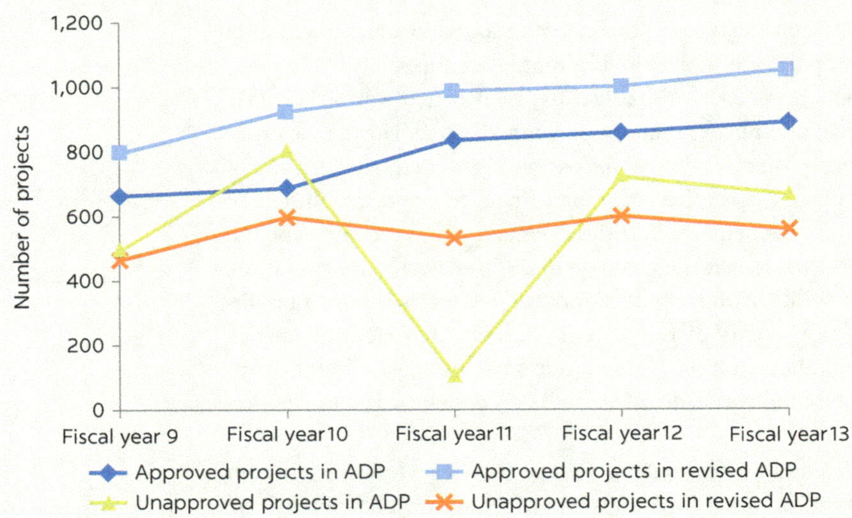

Source: World Bank 2014.

BOX 11.5

World Bank portfolio reviews

The World Bank conducts regular reviews of its portfolio of loan-financed projects with a view to monitoring project progress and addressing implementation issues.

Portfolio reviews are based on information from the Bank's operations portal, including:

- Disbursement rates as a percentage of total project cost and compared to the original disbursement plan
- Ratings of implementation progress and recommendations from regular (typically semiannual) implementation support missions conducted by World Bank task teams
- Results of midterm reviews of projects.

Poorly performing projects are identified through their designation as "problem projects." A problem project is a project with a performance rating of "moderately unsatisfactory" or below. This rating is given based on the likelihood that the project will achieve its objectives at project closure. Very low disbursement rates may also be used to single out projects for further review.

Systemic issues affecting project implementation are identified and discussed with government counterparts in order to find solutions.

Among the prerequisites for World Bank portfolio reviews are the formulation of a comprehensive results framework at project initiation and the ability to track and actively monitor project information throughout a project's lifetime.

Source: Based on World Bank 2017.

different: a rationalization aims to curtail, restructure, or terminate projects in order to prioritize and save on fiscal space, while donor reviews have more modest aims: they focus on monitoring and unblocking the implementation of individual projects. If problems persist, project cancellation may be considered. Portfolio reviews are somewhat regular, occurring annually or semiannually, while portfolio rationalizations occur only when significant portfolio issues arise. There are still opportunities to apply some knowledge gained from the donor-driven reviews of loan-financed portfolios to broader-based portfolio rationalizations. Box 11.5 summarizes features and experience from the World Bank's portfolio reviews.

STEPS IN PREPARING AND CONDUCTING PORTFOLIO RATIONALIZATION

While practices naturally vary with country context, portfolio rationalization involves conducting several procedural steps (see figure 11.1).

Step 1. Identification and verification of nonperforming projects to be moved to the rationalization program

Projects primarily enter the rationalization program by being identified as nonperforming according to specific criteria, as detailed below. This process typically focuses on identifying (a) projects that have been in the PIP for a long time, (b) projects that have received inadequate levels of funding over several

FIGURE 11.1
Diagrammatic representation of the main steps in public investment portfolio (PIP) rationalization

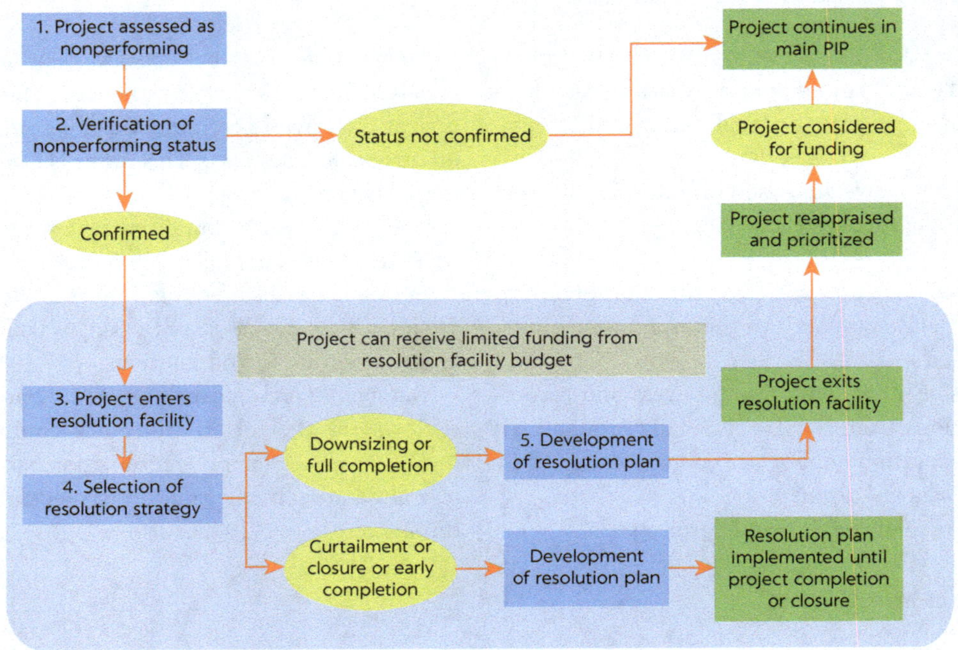

Source: World Bank 2015.

years and are unlikely to be completed in the near future, and (c) projects that have been suspended and have received no recent financing. Establishing objective criteria will help to avoid accusations of bias in the process and to ensure that only the least necessary or worst-performing projects are identified as candidates for rationalization.

Projects also enter the rationalization process in other ways, including:

- *Projects identified as poorly performing in periodic sectoral reviews, program reviews, and evaluations.* Such government reviews provide a broad assessment to determine the likelihood that the project or program will achieve its objectives and represent value for money.
- *Projects requested to be brought to early closure.* These requests may be based on findings from ministries' own internal monitoring and review processes or from external audits.

Internal prioritization by line ministries can be a useful "preliminary step" for identifying nonperforming projects. If there are conflicts of interest, line ministries are usually well placed to understand the specific needs of the sector and can bring an important perspective to decisions about their public investment portfolio. Line ministries and agencies could be requested to prioritize and rank their projects in order of priority; this ranking could make it easier to remove less important projects from the PIP. This preliminary step should also help to relieve political pressure on the central finance agency, which is an inevitable consequence of a PIP rationalization.

Verification of nonperformance is a critical component of portfolio rationalization, as it typically relies on a limited number of indicators. Verification should be done quickly and decisively to facilitate decision making, as nonperforming projects would otherwise be allowed to remain in the portfolio by default. Failure to make a decision has occurred with PIP rationalization exercises in some countries, leading to relatively few projects leaving the portfolio and resulting in an underfunded and poorly performing PIP.

Step 2. Transfer of nonperforming projects to a resolution facility

A resolution facility consists of projects identified and verified as nonperforming and awaiting a resolution on their future status. It should be allocated funds within the budget to cover unavoidable expenses such as settling outstanding payments or protecting a partially completed physical asset. Such funding is best provided through a separate (and rather small) budget allocation for portfolio rationalization; spending related to the resolution procedure may be ring-fenced and managed separately from PIP project funding.

Step 3. Determination of a resolution strategy for the project

This process would involve an initial assessment of options, including (a) full completion, (b) downscaling to enable early completion, and (c) closure. The assessment should take into account the likelihood that the project or its components will be able to achieve the original objectives. Projects identified for full completion and downscaling would then require reappraisal and reprioritization. The share of total costs that nonperforming projects have incurred will be important in influencing the resolution strategy. A least-cost option for project resolution should be developed in each case and considered alongside the preferred option.

Step 4. Development and implementation of a resolution plan for the project

The final step should be to formulate a resolution plan and set out the proposed phases and costs of implementing the chosen option for each project. The plan should include the following key elements:

- A technical assessment
- A legal assessment
- A social and environmental impact assessment
- A cost assessment
- Actions required to implement the chosen option for the project and the responsibilities and arrangements for managing its realization
- A timetable for the required actions
- Potential causes of delay to the timetable, risks associated with delays and cost overruns, and how these risks are to be managed and minimized.

To ensure that timely decisions are made on the implementation and conclusion of the resolution plan, a time limit should be introduced after which the project would automatically be closed down. Such a "sunset clause" for conclusion of the resolution plan could provide a time limit of, say, three years, with a possible extension to five years in exceptional cases endorsed by the central finance agency and approved by the relevant cabinet committee.

CRITERIA AND BENCHMARKS TO IDENTIFY NONPERFORMING PROJECTS

A set of screening criteria for identifying nonperformance would help to identify projects for inclusion in a rationalization program. An example of an analytical framework to identify projects for a rationalization program is set out below, based on experience from Mongolia, Romania, and Ukraine.[3] The criteria and benchmarks may also help to analyze portfolio performance, even if no decision has been made to proceed with a rationalization, and to serve as regular indicators for portfolio monitoring. The analytical framework comprises three criteria for measuring historic performance and financing adequacy. Benchmarks may be developed for each of these criteria to define thresholds that would lead to a project being transferred to the rationalization program. Benchmarks can also be used to highlight the extent of nonperformance across the portfolio. The analytical framework includes two criteria to indicate the feasibility and impact of including a project within the rationalization program.

Historic performance and adequacy of financing

Period under implementation

This criterion is a simple measure of historical performance and is defined as the number of years that a project has been under implementation. *Nonperformance at the project level* is considered to be an issue if the project has been under implementation for more than five years. If the project has been under implementation for 10 years or more, then historic nonperformance would be assessed as critical; unless it is now being financed adequately, the project should be included in the rationalization program. *Portfolio performance* is assessed by the average number of years that projects in the portfolio have been under implementation. If this figure exceeds five years, then nonperformance could be considered an historic and entrenched issue across the investment portfolio.

Time to complete at current levels of funding

This criterion measures financial credibility and sustainability of the investment project or portfolio. It is defined in terms of the number of years that it would take to complete projects at the level of budget allocation for the current fiscal year. Projects started in the current or previous year may be excluded from the assessment, as start-up funding tends to be a low proportion of total cost and its inclusion would distort the picture.

Nonperformance at the *project level* could be an issue if it were to take more than four years to complete the project at the current fiscal year level of budget allocation. If this figure exceeds 8–10 years, then the project could be considered to be significantly underfinanced and should be considered for automatic inclusion in the rationalization program. *Portfolio performance* is measured by the number of years that it would take to complete the current portfolio of projects at the current level of budget allocation. If this figure exceeds three to four years, then the current level of financing could be considered inadequate and the investment project portfolio is underfinanced.

Dormancy

The idea behind this criterion is to identify inactive or dormant projects with consistently low levels of funding. The extent of dormancy is measured by the size of the budget in each of the last three years as a percentage of the balance to complete the project at the end of the prior budget year.

At the *project level,* dormancy could be said to exist when budget allocations in two of the last three years have fallen below 10 percent of total project costs (in one of the last three years for projects started in the previous budget year). A project that has been allocated less than 10 percent of its total project cost in each of the last three years could be considered a severe case of dormancy and an automatic candidate for inclusion in the rationalization program. Nonperformance at the *portfolio level* is assessed by (a) the proportion of projects classified as dormant and (b) the proportion of expenditures required to complete all ongoing dormant projects.

Feasibility and impact

Implementation stage

This criterion divides projects into implementation stages based on the percentage of total costs incurred. Nonperforming projects that are at an early stage of implementation are likely to be easier and less costly to close down than projects that have already incurred substantial expenditures. At the same time, closing large projects at an early stage of implementation can result in a significant reduction in forward financing demands on the PIP.

Projects in the middle stages of implementation (for example, 30–70 percent of total project costs incurred) are more problematic because significant costs have already been incurred. Where forward financing demands are significant, projects should be subjected to reappraisal, on a sunk-cost basis, to determine the most appropriate option. Significant resources are likely to be required to update feasibility studies and to assess different options for resolving these projects.

By contrast, closing down projects at an advanced stage of implementation (for example, with more than 70 percent of total costs incurred) would have only a limited impact on reducing forward financing demands.[4] Most of these projects should be completed, and the scope for possible cost savings should be identified.

Project-level indicators are the total expenditures incurred for the project to date as a percentage of the total project cost. *Portfolio-level* indicators are the number of projects at each stage of implementation and the proportion of the forward investment program funding required for each stage of implementation.

Relative size of forward spending requirements

This criterion assesses the funding required to complete the current investment portfolio. It helps to identify those sectors, ministry budgets, and projects that have the greatest potential for reducing forward financing demands on the PIP.

At the *project level,* it assesses the significance of forward spending requirements on a project within the ministry's overall forward investment program. At the *portfolio level,* it measures the relative size of each ministry-level budget within the current PIP.

Table 11.1 summarizes an example of criteria, indicators, and project-level benchmarks that may be used to identify nonperforming projects. It illustrates the possible use of traffic lights to classify projects for inclusion in the rationalization program in order of nonperformance: a red light signifies serious nonperformance and a yellow light means that nonperformance is likely. Projects with two red lights or one red light for dormancy could be transferred to the rationalization program. Box 11.6 applies the framework to Romania.

TABLE 11.1 **Summary of possible project-level criteria, indicators, and performance benchmarks for identifying nonperforming projects**

CRITERIA	INDICATOR	WHAT IT SHOWS?	NONPERFORMANCE BENCHMARKS
A.1 Period under implementation	Number of years since project commenced implementation	Extent of delay in implementation; whether project is likely to require reappraisal or an updated feasibility study	🔴 > 10 years since project commenced implementation 🟡 > 5 years since project commenced implementation
A.2 Time to complete ongoing project(s) at current level of budgeted funding	Total project cost less expenditures to the end of the current fiscal year budget allocation divided by fiscal year budget allocation	Project credibility or sustainability: extent to which project is underfunded	🔴 > 10 years to complete project at current budget year's level of funding (projects started in budget year 0 and budget year 1 are not included) 🟡 > 4 years to complete project at current budget year's level of funding (> 5 years for projects started in budget year 2; projects started in budget years 0 and 1 are not included)
A.3 Evidence and extent of dormancy	Budget in each of last three years as % of the balance to complete project at end of prior budget year	Whether project has been significantly underfunded for an extended period	🔴 Budget in each of last 3 years < 10% of balance of expenditures to complete project at start of the current budget year 🟡 Budget in 2 of last 3 years < 10% of balance of expenditures to complete project at start of current budget year (in 1 of last 3 years for projects starting in budget year 1, projects starting in year 0 and projects > 90% spent are not considered)
B.1 Implementation stage	Total expenditures on project to end prior budget year / Total project cost	Financial progress as a measure of the implementation stage of project	Not applicable
B.2 Relative size of forward spending requirements	Funding required to complete project (at beginning of current budget year) as % of total required for all projects of a particular ministry or sector	Relative significance of project in ministry or sector program	Not applicable

Source: Based on development of criteria for a suggested rationalization procedure in Romania (World Bank 2015).

BOX 11.6

Application of the analytical framework to three ministry PIPs in Romania

The rationalization criteria were tested on three major ministries (transport, environment, and regional development), which together represented 66 percent of the 2015 investment budget (see figure B11.6.1). Of 157 projects in the three ministries, 46 had two red lights and were recommended for automatic removal from the public investment portfolio. A further 11 projects had a single red light for dormancy and were also recommended for removal from the public investment portfolio on the grounds that implicit prioritization decisions had been made by not providing them with adequate funding. Thus, 57 projects were considered "severely underresourced."

While the initial identification of nonperforming projects focused on the red-light assessments, the yellow-light scorings identified projects that were of concern and might need to be looked at in more detail.

It was calculated that the removal of projects identified as nonperforming from the public investment portfolio would reduce forward funding requirements by US$12 billion, or five times the total portfolio budget allocation for 2015. Their removal would result in a significantly more affordable PIP, in which existing and new projects could be financed more adequately.

FIGURE B11.6.1

Analysis of public investment projects in three ministries in Romania

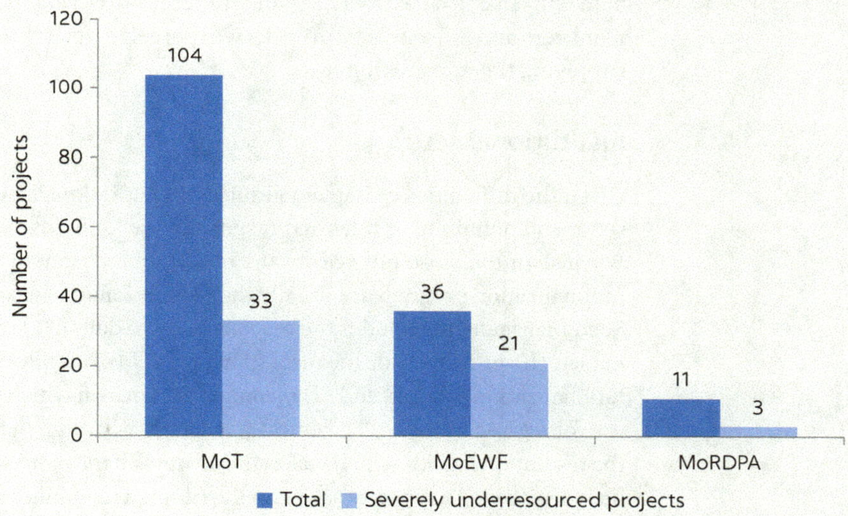

Note: MoEWF = Ministry of Environment, Water, and Forestry. MoRDPA = Ministry of Regional Development and Public Administration. MoT = Ministry of Transport.

Source: World Bank 2015.

MANAGING THE PORTFOLIO RATIONALIZATION PROGRAM

The relatively few examples of successful rationalization programs speak to their political sensitivity and difficulty of implementation. To navigate the issues associated with implementing a rationalization program, the responsible authorities need to identify and manage carefully potential impediments to successful implementation by taking into account data issues, allocation of roles and responsibilities, resistance and sensitivities of the implementing agency, legal issues associated with curtailment or closure of contracts, and the need to ensure sustainability of the results of the program.

Data issues

A rationalization program based on clear criteria for nonperformance requires data to be available for several dimensions of project status and progress. Consistent data over at least a three- to five-year period are needed on total project cost (project value), annual budget allocations and other financing, annual expenditures and disbursements, project start dates, and original and revised end dates. Projects should be identifiable by year, sector, ministry, and, possibly, function; it is important to track information about a given project from at least three to five years ago. A good monitoring system collects this information; without it, rationalization is more difficult. If information is missing, rationalization could be a catalyst for establishing such a system.

An integrated project database is useful for ensuring that credible information is available on which to formulate indicators of nonperformance and for project-portfolio monitoring in general (see chapter 12). Without such information, it may be necessary to conduct a survey specifically for the purpose of project rationalization; however, data collection may be difficult, partly because data will have to be extracted from different sources and partly because project managers and line ministry officials will perceive that there is little to gain from supplying the information.

Institutional setup

Given the difficulties of implementing a project rationalization, the institutional setup and definition of roles and responsibilities should be considered carefully. Because of the close linkages to the budget, management and oversight of the rationalization program are usually the responsibility of a central finance agency. Such management includes the responsibility to define (a) criteria for nonperformance, (b) guidelines for the resolution process, (c) monitoring of progress in the rationalization process, and (d) recommendations on which resolution options to use for a given project. The central finance agency often manages the budget for the resolution facility, which makes the process all the more sensitive. Clear guidelines are needed to ensure clarity on the (limited) eligibility of funding within the resolution budget. The central finance agency normally retains responsibility for approving resolution plans, but development and execution of the plans are the responsibility of the respective line ministries. Decisions on initiating a rationalization program, as well as decisions on choosing concrete options for resolving individual projects, are normally subject to a high-level cabinet decision.

Legal issues

Concerns about possible financial and legal repercussions may create a reluctance to close down poorly performing and inadequately financed projects. While potential legal impediments to rationalization are strongly tied to local legal, auditing, and contracting traditions and practices, specific concerns may arise regarding the following:

- Provisions in contracts covering project changes, curtailment, and closure
- Legal status of assets already created by the project and what to do with them

- Provision for costs and related accounting arrangements associated with change, curtailment, or cancellation
- Possibility of audit-driven claims against the decision makers who authorized the projects, particularly in countries where officials can be held personally liable for their decisions and where separation of powers is weakly defined
- Potential size of settlements accepted by the courts for contractor claims.

Government liabilities may arise from a unilateral decision to close a contract. Some countries may use standard contracts that allow for unilateral closure of a project. This entitlement to unilateral termination may protect the government from liabilities associated with compensating the contractor for the loss of profit. In the absence of such clauses, unilateral termination could expose the government to the payment of damages to the contractor.

Alternative solutions to avoid legal repercussions from rationalization include negotiation and consultation with contracting partners and associations. If a project has been inactive for a considerable time, a potential solution would be to terminate the contract by mutual agreement. Governments could also consult with contractors' associations on the need for and implications of the closure of nonperforming projects to develop a common understanding of the issues involved. This dialogue should emphasize that the rationalization program is a short-term measure and a step toward establishing a realistic and fully funded PIP. Ensuring that such situations are addressed in public works contracts would facilitate curtailment and closure and help to make the likely costs transparent. Standardizing and improving the procedures for handling disputes are also important.

Additional considerations in conducting rationalization

Project rationalization may offer a good opportunity to conduct a quick reassessment of the strategic relevance of a given project. A typical issue faced by many governments is that projects may have outlived their original objectives or may no longer be relevant. This issue can arise as a result of delays in implementation or changes in the policy landscape; it can be especially important if the screening of projects for strategic relevance and quality is known to have been weak when projects were originally selected.

Project rationalization may also be used to dispose of spending items that do not fit commonly agreed-on definitions of a public investment project. Having an unclear definition of what consitutes a public investment project may allow noncapital spending items to be included in the PIP in order to circumvent restrictions on recurrent spending. However, removing recurrent spending items from the PIP will not necessarily alleviate the overall spending squeeze, as recurrent items may still have to be funded outside of the PIP.

Projects that are "frozen" or put on hold could automatically be considered for rationalization. Many countries have used the practice of "freezing" projects or putting them on hold, which normally entails suspending their funding for a given period of time. This practice has typically been used to cut capital spending during periods of fiscal consolidation or to make room for new priority projects. A lack of transparency is often evident in the criteria for the freeze as well as in the timing and conditions for reentry into the PIP. Where a list of frozen projects already exists, these projects should automatically be considered for the rationalization program, as the decision to freeze them indicates a low level of priority.

Ensuring the sustainability of rationalization results

Consideration should be given to avoiding a recurrence of the problems that trigger a portfolio rationalization. By far the best way to prevent the PIP from becoming oversubscribed is to engage in a comprehensive reform of current public investment planning and management practices, particularly selection and budgeting. A successfully operating PIM system should render obsolete the need to rationalize the PIP in future years. In the absence of a well-designed and perfectly implemented PIM reform, prevention to ensure sustainability could include the following measures:

- *Actively monitor the portfolio, including implementation of just-in-time measures to resolve implementation issues.* Active monitoring would require a comprehensive database with data similar to the requirements for a project rationalization.
- *Streamline the rationalization criteria into the relevant regulation.* Streamlining would ensure that projects under implementation are checked against criteria for nonperformance on an ongoing basis.
- *Introduce multiyear budget commitment ceilings or commitment appropriations.* If properly implemented and managed, such a system would guard against overcommitting the PIP in the future.

NOTES

1. The envisaged implementation period for public investment projects rarely exceeds five years. A snapshot at any point in time will reveal projects at different stages of implementation. Three to four years is therefore a reasonable estimate for the time it takes to complete a well-funded portfolio.
2. Portfolio rationalization should also apply to public-private partnerships (PPPs), although relatively few PPPs are under implementation in most countries. The criteria for nonperformance should be adjusted to reflect the external financing of project costs and the effects on public debt, state guarantees, and the budget in the longer term.
3. The example is based on analysis of budget-financed projects, but can be adjusted to include other parts of the portfolio.
4. The classification of implementation stages could vary with the country context. For example, it could include the following six stages: (1) start-up, less than 10 percent of total project costs incurred; (2) stage 1, 10–29 percent of costs incurred; (3) stage 2, 30–49 percent of costs incurred; (4) stage 3, 50–69 percent of costs incurred; (5) stage 4, 70–89 percent of costs incurred; and (6) completion, more than 90 percent of project costs incurred.

REFERENCES

World Bank. 2013. "Ukraine Public Investment Management Performance Assessment 2012." World Bank, Washington, DC.

———. 2014. "A Public Investment Management Review and Reform Roadmap for Bangladesh." World Bank, Washington, DC.

———. 2015. "Romania: Advisory Services on Strengthening Public Investment Management—Output 10: Rationalization of the Existing Public Investment Portfolio." World Bank, Washington, DC.

———. 2016. "Methodology for Public Investment Portfolio Cleaning." World Bank, Washington, DC.

———. 2017. "Bank Guidance: Investment Project Financing: Implementation Support." World Bank, Washington, DC.

12

PIM Information Systems

REQUIREMENTS, OPTIONS, AND ISSUES

OVERVIEW

An effective public investment management (PIM) system needs to manage complex information as it intersects with numerous public expenditure management processes, including planning, budget formulation, budget execution, and ex post evaluation. Comprehensive data handling supports monitoring and timely decision making, which require large amounts of data and documents that need to be collected, stored, and processed into easily digestible formats and made available to decision makers and project participants in a timely manner.

A well-designed PIM information system can be very supportive of management. However, levels of automation of PIM processes vary by country and may reflect the degree to which decision making is centralized. Many countries with advanced systems—including Denmark, Ireland, and the United Kingdom—do not implement PIM information systems at the central level because decision making for public investment projects is largely decentralized to line ministries and agencies. And although central finance agencies need to monitor the preparation and implementation of capital projects, the scope is limited: automation is generally confined to supporting budget formulation and execution functions as part of a larger budget and financial management information system (FMIS). Some countries with centralized PIM systems do not even have a simple database to provide decision makers with an overview of the portfolio of projects under implementation. In other countries, database information is fragmented or incomplete; it may only cover projects from one financing source or may allow project information to be tracked only through part of the cycle or just in the current fiscal year. Relevant project data may be scattered across different systems or data sources, which means that information requests regarding the status of the portfolio will require ad hoc data surveys and inefficient manual data processing.

A PIM information system may provide the following potential benefits:

- Serve as the one place of record for all public investment projects from conception to fruition and, as such, encapsulate the project pipeline

BOX 12.1

Guiding principles for developing and implementing a PIM information system

- A clear business case for developing the system should be presented, including the chosen scope and system development strategy. The business case should demonstrate that the system will deliver economic benefits that outweigh the costs.
- System development should be based on reforms of underlying business processes and formalization of procedures through appropriate regulation. Simply automating existing practices is not likely to yield significant benefits.
- A clear and logical sequence is needed for formulating system requirements; functional (business) requirements should be prioritized so that they can drive the choice of technological solutions, not the other way around.
- System design should consider issues that are known to have a negative impact on system adoption and to reduce benefits. These impacts include lack of incentives for timely provision of data and inconsistency of data between different systems.
- The choice of system architecture should balance the pros and cons of establishing a stand-alone PIM system that may need to interface with other systems versus a system that is integrated with existing platforms.
- Planning for system implementation should factor in the need for change management and solid governance arrangements to ensure communication and effective decision-making procedures throughout the project.

- Provide information for a consolidated overview and analysis of project and portfolio performance
- Achieve efficiency gains through automation of PIM work flows and processes—for example, performance monitoring and reporting
- Improve data quality and transparency.

This chapter provides an overview of requirements and options needed to develop and implement PIM information systems and seeks to inspire the country-level formulation of system development strategies and implementation plans. Box 12.1 summarizes some guiding principles for the development and implementation of PIM information systems based on country experiences and previous World Bank support of system requirements.

CONCEPTUAL DESCRIPTION OF PIM INFORMATION SYSTEMS

Objective

The overall objectives of a PIM information system are to increase efficiency, transparency, and accountability in public investment management. Different countries may emphasize different aspects of these objectives. A PIM information system would improve *efficiency* as it becomes the primary mechanism for administering and managing PIM and could automate information flows for many processes associated with the life-cycle stages of public investment projects. It would potentially serve as the single place of record for all public investment projects. It would improve *accountability* by providing the tools to control, monitor, and evaluate process operations as well as the performance of individual projects and the full project portfolio. Finally, it would improve *transparency* by building in the ability to disclose information on the project portfolio to the public, even allowing the public to interrogate the information system.

Stakeholders

There is a potentially large and diverse group of stakeholders for PIM information systems. Based on figure 12.1, the following is a general description of the possible roles and responsibilities of information system stakeholders.

Key decision-making and financing bodies

These bodies include the legislature, the president or prime minister's office, central finance agencies, and international financing agencies and donors. All of these stakeholders have overall decision-making or financing powers for the PIM system. Their direct use of the system may vary, but each is important for the efficiency, accountability, and transparency of the system.

Civil society organizations and the general public

As voters, taxpayers, and users of public services, the general public is interested in the proper use of public funds and should be able to provide social oversight of the public investment portfolio (PIP). Their direct use of the system will

FIGURE 12.1

Stakeholder map for a PIM information system

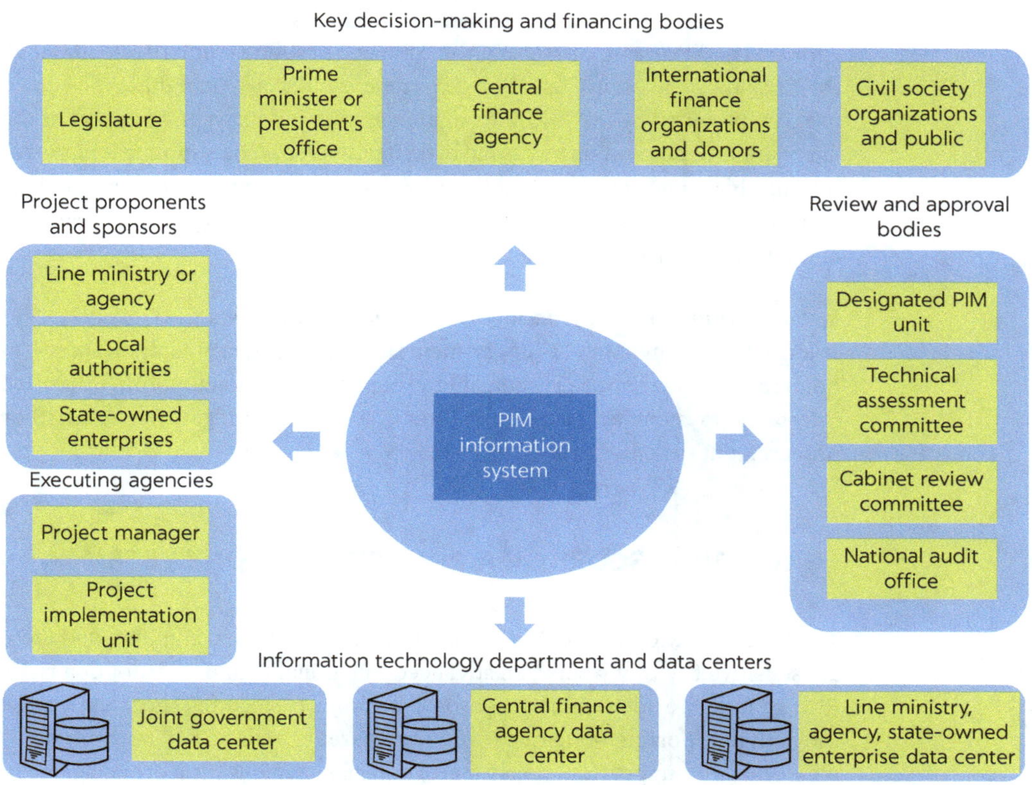

Sources: Adapted from World Bank 2016a, 2016b.

depend on the availability of data and information in an open and transparent manner, following the international trend toward increasing the transparency of budget-related processes, including "open data."

Project proponents and sponsors

Line ministries or their agencies, local authorities, or state-owned enterprises formulate and propose investment projects. They commit their capital investment budget to particular projects and are ultimately responsible for project monitoring and results. They use the PIM information system to support budget planning, monitoring, and reporting of public investment projects under their purview.

Executing agencies

Executing agencies are the organizational entities whose key staff within a line ministry, local authority, or state-owned enterprise are responsible for project implementation. Executing agencies can be designated project implementation units or, in some cases, technical departments of the relevant ministry or agency. Executing agencies designate the project manager for day-to-day management of the investment project (see chapter 8). The executing agencies and their key staff use the project-level capabilities of the PIM information system.

Approval and oversight bodies

Approval and oversight bodies include such bodies both within and external to the government. Within government, they may include a designated PIM oversight unit or the relevant departments of central finance agencies if the oversight and coordination functions have been streamlined into their work programs. They may also include any technical committees established to review the appraisal of project proposals and the cabinet or cabinet committees that issue the final approval of projects. The government internal oversight bodies could use data provided by the PIM information system for analysis in support of the oversight function. Among external oversight bodies is the supreme audit institution, which may examine compliance with procurement and other regulations and, in some cases, assess the broader analysis of the efficiency and effectiveness of public investment.

Information technology departments and data centers

Information technology (IT) departments and data centers are important stakeholders because they are responsible for operating and maintaining the PIM information system itself or related systems, such as the budget system, FMIS, or procurement system.

FUNCTIONAL SCOPE OF A PIM INFORMATION SYSTEM

The functional scope of a PIM system is potentially large and complex, and there are sensitive trade-offs between advanced functionality and nonadoption risks. PIM systems are inherently burdensome for project-executing agencies because they entail reporting obligations and transparency risks. They may provide a whole range of support functions for program management, project management, and public information. Overreaching in one category may discourage adoption and compliance in another. Clearly, a system designed to facilitate top-down monitoring by program managers will not generate much enthusiasm among project managers who are responsible for supplying the required information; a system that adds value for project managers may be more successful.

Even within the same category of functionality, there may be significant trade-offs. A system that indicates delays in a majority of projects in a ministry is less useful than one that also enables users to analyze the reasons for the delays. In addition to its more complex calculations, the more comprehensive system may have higher adoption risk because it requires more periodic data entries to function correctly. In addition, advanced PIM systems with rich functionality for all categories of users are very complex and difficult to build in one go. Some countries have taken a decade or longer to build them and make them work reliably. The definition of the functional scope and coverage of a PIM information system should start with addressing the following key points.

Database or work flow management

A comprehensive database is at the heart of any PIM information system, and an essential question is whether to confine the system to providing database functionality or whether to automate the work flows around proposals, reviews, and approvals of project documentation. The extent to which work flow functionality is covered varies by country. Whether automating work flows constitutes a good investment depends on the number of new projects under preparation and the existence of clear, formalized procedures on which to base the work flow functionality.

If a government decides that the PIM information system should cover work flow management, its reach—the number stakeholders it affects and the level of detail of the tasks it performs—will have to be defined based on careful consultations with affected stakeholders. The required mapping of reformed PIM processes will provide the basic input for this decision. Two key trade-offs are involved in this decision:

- Increased project management capacity afforded by precise and timely data collection versus the higher level of standardization and increased oversight acceptable to stakeholders
- Increased speed, precision, and quality of PIM work processes versus the increased complexity and risk in system specification, testing, and deployment.

These trade-offs sometimes lead to the system being implemented in phases—for example, automation of higher-level work flows in a first phase and system design and change management strategy in a more detailed second phase.

Project cycle coverage

Knowing which parts of the project cycle would be covered by the system will also guide the functional requirements. Figure 12.2 summarizes three main options.

Project implementation focus

The minimum scope for a PIM information system is to collect, store, and report data relating only to project implementation. Thus a project would enter the system after a budget has been allocated and work begins, and it would exit upon completion of the works and handover to the operational facility. This scope would allow managers to focus support on reporting, monitoring, and

FIGURE 12.2

Options for defining the functional scope of a PIM information system

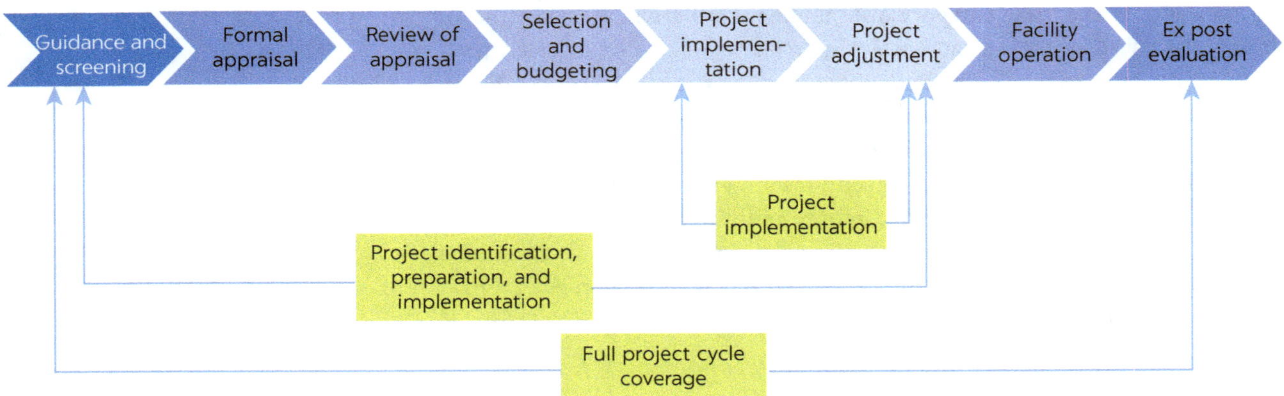

adjustments during implementation, which is the stage with the greatest need for frequent and active monitoring. Unfortunately, many implementation issues are rooted in poor planning and preparation of projects, which is why it is highly preferable for the system to extend to planning and preparation.

Project identification, preparation, and implementation focus

This scope would allow the system to collect, store, and report information from the initiation stage in order to cover first-level screening and appraisal of projects. A project would enter the system after the relevant authority has approved the project idea, and it would exit the system once implementation is completed. This scope would allow all stages of project identification, preparation, and implementation to be supported—including processes related to appraisal, review of appraisal—as well as prioritization and selection for financing. The system would be able to store relevant project documentation and maintain a pipeline of ready-to-go projects. Centralized procedures to approve project proposals at the project idea or concept note stage need to be in place for this option to be viable. Many countries decentralize these approvals to line ministries or other project proponent entities; in this case, a broad scope for the PIM information system may not be appropriate.

Coverage of the full project cycle

A wider scope would cover the full project cycle, including functionality to support operations and ex post evaluation. Under this option, the project would enter the system at project identification, and the system would track the project through to ex post evaluation. However, this wider scope raises some issues: supporting simple project completion reports is relatively easy, but including functionality in support of service delivery monitoring or impact evaluations of completed projects is less clear-cut. These aspects of PIM are typically among the least developed and often do not have clear, formalized procedures; these cases will not benefit from automation. Even if ex post evaluations are performed, they typically cover only a sample of projects. A related technical challenge for automating these PIM stages is that the unit of analysis changes once a project has been finalized and becomes a facility for service delivery.

Management levels

While portfolio-level management functionality is an essential feature of most PIM information systems, the inclusion of functionality in support of project-level management is more disputed. Two project-level management functions—contract management and procurement management—are important.

Contract management

Adding a contract management module is a major decision in designing a PIM information system. Many PIM systems in Latin America (Argentina, Chile, Colombia, Guatemala, and Nicaragua) have such modules; other countries and jurisdictions (Western Australia) have developed contract management modules as part of the electronic procurement system. Contract management is at the heart of project management, but if it is implemented as part of a PIM information system, this system will be skewed toward project-level rather than program-level management. This skewing occurs because contract management underpins other crucial project management functions, especially budgeting and financial planning.

Procurement management

Procurement management is a crucial, specialized aspect of project management. It involves monitoring all plans, steps, approvals, and results for all contract procurement under the project. The lowest level of capability of a PIM information system would be to keep track of bid submission and contract award dates for each procurement process in order to calculate each project's procurement performance ranking in the public investment portfolio.

Public investment portfolio management versus program management

PIP management is a different concept from program management as associated with program budgeting. PIP management refers to management of a set of projects within the same line ministry or across the whole government portfolio; program management refers to management of public sector activities that have been structured into programs in order to better align the management of activities with the government's policies and priorities. Program management also increases the transparency of planned and achieved results. If a methodology for program budgeting has been implemented, the budget formulation system is usually expected to include functionality to support program budgeting and to store information on the nonfinancial performance of government programs. The systems of several countries in Latin America combine PIM with program management, although this approach has made the systems more complex. Boxes 12.2 and 12.3 present examples of comprehensive PIM information systems from Chile and Colombia, respectively.

General capabilities

Under the greater of the three options for functional scope (see figure 12.2), the general capabilities of a comprehensive PIM information system can be described as follows:

- Maintain a comprehensive, official record of all data associated with investment projects throughout their life cycle, from prescreening of the initial

BOX 12.2

The Integrated Bank of Projects in Chile

The Banco Integrado de Proyectos is a comprehensive PIM information system covering the full public investment project cycle (see figure B12.2.1). The system has the following main features:

- Comprehensive coverage of all sectors and project stages, with more than 200,000 entries
- Shared responsibility between the Ministry of Social Development and the Ministry of Finance within an integrated architecture
- Advanced functionality to support the medium-term budgetary framework (MTBF), including scenario building based on capital baseline and "above baseline" spending
- Monitoring of financial and nonfinancial performance
- Focus on ex post evaluation.

The system consists of four subsystems and corresponding relational databases:

- *Subsystem for technical-economic analysis.* The database tracks projects in various phases of preparation—that is, project ideas, profiles, prefeasibility studies, feasibility studies, design, and execution. The Integrated Bank of Projects includes information stretching back some 25 years.
- *Subsystem for budget formulation.* This subsystem tracks preparation of the next annual budget for selected capital projects for internal government discussion and for negotiations with congress. It models and simulates different scenarios for a three- to five-year period and accounts for dual budgeting (separates capital budgeting from the recurrent budget), and it separates baseline budgets from new-initiative budgets.
- *Subsystem for budget execution.* This subsystem monitors the cash flow of every line item and project implemented within the current budget. It detects any cost overruns or underruns early on as well as any deviations from schedule, allowing for timely corrective action. It also supports progress on nonfinancial indicators.
- *Subsystem for ex post evaluation.* This subsystem supports ex post evaluation by documenting lessons learned for future projects. It supports the Ministry of Social Development in performing staff evaluations and conducting project performance reviews, among others, of formally completed projects.

FIGURE B12.2.1

Diagrammatic representation of the Integrated Bank of Projects in Chile

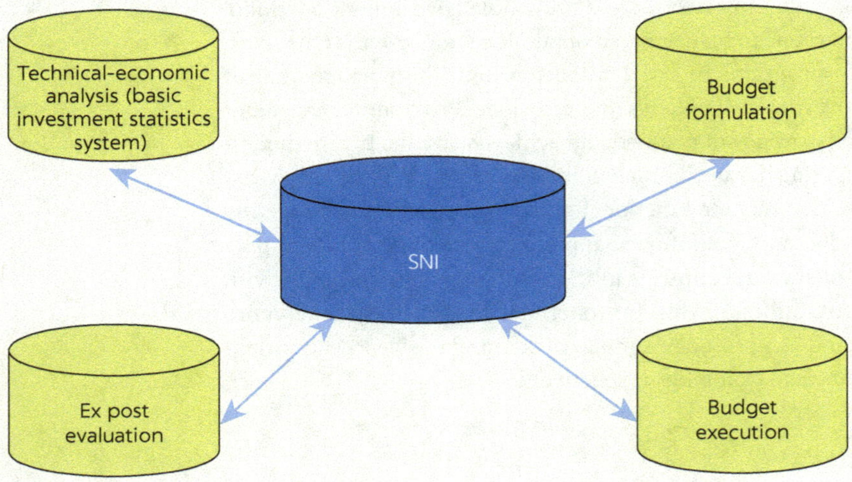

Note: SNI = National Public Investment System.

Sources: USAID 2015, updated in response to comments by the Ministry of Social Development.

BOX 12.3

An integrated database of public investment projects in Colombia

The Unified System for Public Finance and Investments (SUIFP) in Colombia captures information on public investment projects throughout a project's life cycle, from inception to completion and ex post evaluation. The system is made up of different modules designed to address specific project cycle issues. These modules have been developed for more than 20 years and are integrated under a single platform. The SUIFP includes a database of projects with information on all public investments, a module used for budget programming, an FMIS used for execution of the annual budget, and a monitoring platform used during project execution and after project completion.

The database of investment projects, Banco Nacional de Programas y Proyectos, is a key component of the system. It stores information on an investment project from the moment that the sponsoring entity starts the approval process for the use of public funds through to project execution and evaluation. A project template must be completed and updated regularly, including different sets of information, including name, code, start and end dates, responsible entity, geographic impact, links to the country's development strategy, and value chain, as well as cost, financing, and beneficiaries.

Before a project is formally approved, rigorous quality checks are conducted by the planning offices at all levels of government. Once project execution starts, the sponsoring agency updates the template to reflect progress in the project's execution, especially how objectives and intermediate targets are being met and whether any changes to the original plan are required.

During the execution phase, the use of public funds is updated automatically from the FMIS module, as are any adjustments to the resources allocated in any given year. The release of funds from the national budget can be put on hold if the project template is not up-to-date. Moreover, the National Planning Department can reject a request for budget reallocations if a line ministry has not provided the required information.

The information in the database is also available for use by different stakeholders, including the general public, who can search online for information on specific initiatives. Planning authorities can use information in the database to decide which projects receive funding. For smaller projects, the stakeholders may only include the sponsoring agency, the National Planning Department, and the Ministry of Finance. For larger initiatives, especially those requiring multiyear funding, the final approval falls on the Consejo Nacional de Política Económica y Social, which is headed by the president.

The information in this database is also used at the project monitoring stage to track project execution. In particular, the National Planning Department closely monitors activities and products proposed during the project design stage to ensure that they are being executed within the specified time frames and are delivering the expected outcomes and outputs. The monitoring information is available to the general public on the National Planning Department's website and is also used as an input for the budget reviews headed by the president during cabinet meetings.

Source: IMF 2011.

project idea or concepts by the relevant authority until the information is no longer relevant for public financial management purposes

- Permit online and offline data entry
- Enforce rigorous control over the entry and modification of data, ensuring that changes can be traced to authorized individual users of the system; alert the project manager, project sponsor, program coordinator, and portfolio administrator when important, authorized changes are made to project profile (fiche) data; lock down data that should not be changed past a certain stage; and keep a record of authorized changes for audit and historical analysis

- Provide specialized, online interfaces (portals) authorizing primary stakeholders to perform their functional responsibilities with respect to the PIP. Portals should be logically distinct online interfaces, accessible only on a properly authenticated, need-to-know basis, providing only the information and functions authorized for each primary stakeholder
- Provide stakeholder-oriented monitoring dashboards with PIP performance aggregates, indicators, and highlights by relevant classifications; provide access to data analysis, graphic representation (tables, charts, maps), and data drill-down tools for use in connection with these dashboards; and allow production of data feeds for customized analysis using external applications (for example, Excel)
- Allow online queries to scrutinize the PIP by any combination of variables (sector, funding source, project status, executing agency, geographic location, policy objective, value)
- Generate reports on project progress, budget execution, or performance monitoring and evaluation using a configurable report-building facility
- Interoperate with the FMIS, budget system, and other relevant public financial management systems and provide a standard application programming interface (API) with other systems
- Provide interfaces to project management software to allow project managers to upload work planning and performance data required by the PIM information system database
- Automate the PIM work flow across all primary stakeholders
- Store, link to, and track key files and documents associated with the functional work flows of the PIM information system. For all other documents associated with portfolio and project management, provide reference numbers that can be traced to the physical paper files kept at source.

Appendix C provides a list of possible functional support capabilities that the PIM information system should provide at the project and program levels. While project managers, project reviewers (project sponsors, auditors), and members of project oversight committees are expected to be the primary users of project-level capabilities, users may also include portfolio managers and sector managers for drill-down examinations associated with their program-monitoring responsibilities. Aggregate database elements are also required to provide project-level capabilities for PIP management purposes.

SYSTEM DESIGN ISSUES AND OPTIONS

Once the high-level functional scope of the PIM information system has been defined, detailed requirements for key design issues need to be addressed. These measures include requirements for the identification and coding of projects, data collection, database and dashboard design, and project financial accounting and reporting.

Identification and coding of projects

A critical requirement of a PIM system is the ability to identify a project with the same number for the duration of the project. Therefore, the PIM information system should generate a unique project identifier when a project is first entered into the database and put that identifier on all financial and nonfinancial transactions that determine the performance of the project. If identifiers already exist for old projects, these projects may have to be given new numbers and the linkage between new and old numbers has to be preserved.

Data collection

Collection of timely and correct information on investment project progress is the Achilles' heel of PIM systems. Lower-level managers have few incentives to be exposed to open scrutiny on the progress of work and accomplishments, particularly when such scrutiny may lead to inquiries and sanctions instead of solutions and rewards. This problem could trigger a vicious circle of no transparency, delayed corrective action, poor performance, and economic losses in the PIP.

The solutions to this problem could involve some of the following:

- *Collecting data only when fully justified by their value for decision making.* This approach requires a careful analysis of the burdens and potential benefits of collecting particular data elements.
- *Balancing the needs and interests of suppliers and consumers of information at all levels of the institutional hierarchy.* This approach is accomplished mainly by regulating the timing and diffusion of data by the PIM information system—for example, by restricting the access of line ministries or other project sponsors to individual financial transactions or allowing access only for financial aggregates. Collecting data only when justified is a system design decision—for example, financial aggregates are calculated only at particular intervals, as dictated by the budget calendar. Such measures give project managers effective confidentiality in day-to-day work and expose them to top-down monitoring only at preagreed intervals and in preagreed formats, as determined by regulation. Similar arrangements could operate at higher levels—for example, by restricting real-time drill-down access by top-level sector managers to detailed project transaction data. These controversial measures require careful discussion, as their purpose is to ensure that top-down visibility does not discourage bottom-up data collection. The need of top-level managers or auditors to look at detailed data can be met through system features such as ad hoc reporting under proper authentication.
- *Designing incentives for timely, reliable data collection.* PIM information system design may embed positive and negative incentives for data collection. The following are the most common incentives:

    - Rewiring the FMIS to stop accepting and processing financial transactions of projects when it receives a command to this effect from the PIM information system
    - Submitting budget appropriation proposals for new projects only upon verification of quality-of-planning elements (financial plan, work plan, performance plan, and procurement plan) in the PIM information system database
    - Locking baseline plans to incentivize timely updating of actual plans. For example, the system may trigger a delayed performance status when the date associated with a baseline progress indicator has elapsed and the actual completion date for that indicator has not been entered.

Database requirements

The PIM information system database should capture data and information related to the entire project life cycle in the format and to the extent necessary to provide the functional capabilities of the system. Appendix D shows the possible content of a database organized according to the project life-cycle stage when the data elements are first created or used. The specific system design will need to harmonize database content with system functionality and specify all data elements in detail.

Data warehouse and dashboards

Dashboards are real-time, graphic visualizations of the status, dimensions, and performance of the PIP, filtered by various criteria and key performance indicators. They typically build on so-called data warehouse and business intelligence solutions that can extract and transform data from different data sources to produce powerful tools for rapid reporting, decision making, and analysis of management information. Such data warehouse and business intelligence solutions are disruptive technologies, which can significantly move the boundaries on how information on capital spending and public investment projects can be presented and analyzed. Their capabilities are usually configured for the specific interests of each category of authorized user (portfolio administrator, program coordinators, project manager, the public).

PIM information system dashboards should allow the following types of data operations:

- *Filtering.* Restricting the visualization to data that meet the chosen filter values—for example, ministry, sector, subsector, location
- *Drill down.* Moving from aggregate to discrete data (bearing in mind the provisos mentioned previously)
- *Mapping.* Visualizing data according to geographic location
- *Analysis.* Using analytical tools, such as tables and charts
- *Data extraction, transformation, and loading.* Extracting, transforming, and loading data into customized formats (pivot tables) or spreadsheet files.

While these and other operations make dashboards powerful presentational tools, their value depends fundamentally on the data available. It is better to target limited yet high-value data and apply powerful positive and negative incentives to secure timely collection. As a first approximation, a PIM information system could involve the collection of high-level data from four project planning or project management instruments—namely, the financial plan, the work plan, the performance plan, and the procurement plan. As these plans are updated, they leave a history of project performance during the implementation stage. The system locks the baseline version of these plans when the project becomes effective and keeps track of the annual budget allocation for the project. Using these plans and other basic project data such as start time and project cost, the PIM information system can periodically calculate various status indicators and performance rankings for each project, as shown in table 12.1. Dashboard users can use the indicators and performance rankings for any combination of filtered analyses over the whole—or sections of the—PIP portfolio, according to their access rights.

TABLE 12.1 Examples of status indicators and performance rankings available for dashboard operations

STATUS INDICATORS	PERFORMANCE RANKINGS
• Project stage • Implementation status: active, delayed, dormant • Project risk: low, medium, high	• Budgeting performance • Funding performance • Implementation performance • Disbursement performance • Procurement performance

Project financial accounting and reporting

Investment projects are complex managerial endeavors requiring special organizational arrangements, budgets, and financial accounts. Their financial transactions need to be differentiated by project component and subcomponent, in addition to all other segments of the budget classification structure and chart of accounts. Project financial accounting involves monitoring commitments, invoices, and disbursements for each source of financing and for each project component and subcomponent.

A key design principle of public financial management systems is to have only one "source of truth" for budget execution. Project accounts ideally should be fully differentiated in the FMIS ledger by project component and subcomponent, such that project financial reports can be obtained directly from the FMIS. However, if project and project component codes do not exist in the budget classification structure, project financial reporting becomes an ad hoc problem within the FMIS and not amenable to the standard aggregation logic of all other general ledger accounts.

Enhancing the budget classification structure is administratively and technically difficult and would be justified only in connection with more comprehensive FMIS redesign. One alternative is to maintain the budget classification structure unchanged but to ensure that project-related transactions can be distinguished from all others in the FMIS. If a program segment exists in the budget classification structure, it can contain a unique project code that can be distinguished automatically from a program code, allowing for project-level accounting in the FMIS.[1]

SYSTEM ARCHITECTURE

A key consideration when designing a PIM information system is the system architecture, including whether to integrate it with other systems or to build or acquire it as a stand-alone system. An integrated model typically means developing or adding the PIM information system as a module in a larger system using the same database or the same technological platform. Two of the most common integration models are to develop the PIM information system either as a module of the budget system or an integrated FMIS (if it exists) or as a module or enhancement of existing aid management platforms. A stand-alone system means developing the system separately, with its own database and technology, and relying purely on technical interfaces for exchanging data with other systems. In practice, the difference between "integration" and "stand-alone" is not clear-cut: the nature of system integration is a continuum, with interfaces between separate systems at the "low" end and a fully integrated database at the "high" end.

Integration with budget system or FMIS

Some countries have chosen integration with existing budget or FMIS systems due to the high volume and frequency of exchanges on budgetary and financial aspects of public investment, especially for projects that are fully or partially funded by the budget. A PIM information system could provide information on budget requests and estimates for the out years of an MTBF to the budget system, while receiving information about budget appropriations from the budget or FMIS system. Likewise, during the budget execution stage, there would be several data exchanges on financial transactions, reports, and budget virements. Some suppliers of commercial off-the-shelf budget solutions have developed capital budgeting modules that can provide some of the sought-after PIM capabilities.

Some of the disadvantages of integration with the budget system or FMIS revolve around differences in logic and specifications. The specifications of an already-developed budget system or FMIS may fall short of the requirements of a PIM information system, or there may be little common logic between the two systems: the database for the PIM information system may require unique content that has little overlap with that of the budget system database. If the architecture of the budget system or FMIS is not designed to integrate PIM information system requirements from the start, this integration might become a second-best technical solution and effectively result in two different, unrelated systems running under the same name and technical environment (see box 12.4 for the case of Romania).

BOX 12.4

Integration of a PIM module in the Romanian budget planning system

The Romanian PIP database is an example of a PIM database system developed as a module of the budget system that has proven inadequate to provide the functionality of a reformed PIM system. The functionality of the PIP database was built with the purpose of supporting the annual budget process, but it does not help to establish a link between strategic objectives and investment proposals or to track the financial, procurement, physical, or managerial performance of projects over time. Its limited information is available only to insiders and usually only with the help of IT experts. Neither senior government officials nor the public can use the database for PIP monitoring. The PIP database lacks critical data elements necessary for central PIP oversight by the Romanian Ministry of Public Finance. In addition, the assignment of unique project identifiers only at the stage of selection for financing excludes project proposals from the database, and the lack of detailed historical performance data reduces the opportunities for analysis.

Source: World Bank 2016b.

Integration with aid management platforms

Many countries that receive large amounts of foreign aid operate aid management platforms to support coordination and monitoring of aid programs and initiatives. These platforms are typically designed as integrated database systems that support collection, storing, and reporting of information on aid initiatives. They often include interfaces for data input as well as dashboards and graphical options to represent aid effectiveness in various dimensions.

For countries that rely heavily on donor assistance to finance their PIPs, the overlap with the requirements of a potential PIM information system may be large. It is therefore relevant to explore the extent to which such a system, with proper adjustments, could serve the purposes of a PIM information system. Such systems generally have limited or no work flow management capabilities and may be the best fit in situations where the focus is mainly on monitoring and management during the project implementation stage. The limitations include (a) inadequate procedures for the timely input of data, which can depend heavily on the goodwill of donors where there are no requirements to use national systems; and (b) the typical lack of automated interfaces with the budget or FMIS system. In order to cover the PIP comprehensively, aid management platforms should be customized to include not only foreign-financed investment but also domestically financed investments. Finally, the platform needs to be able to distinguish between capital investment and technical assistance and other types of activities. Some countries have created PIM systems by customizing off-the-shelf aid management platforms (see box 12.5).

BOX 12.5

PIM systems based on aid management platforms in Iraq and Mauritania

Iraq and Mauritania use platforms originally developed for aid management that have been enhanced by the provider to cover public investment projects irrespective of financing sources. The Iraq Development Management System was launched in April 2016 and manages the entire cycle of government and donor-funded development projects. The system is fully aligned with the National Development Plan and empowers the government of Iraq to select, plan, and implement investment projects. It includes all of the internal work flow and business processes that a project goes through from its initial request through the review and approval process involving the ministry of planning, line ministries, the council of ministers, and parliament.

PIM implementation in Mauritania was launched quite recently. The system supports the management aspects of programming (thanks to World Bank development policy financing) and consists of modules (projects, agreements, disbursements, organizations) that have their own separate work flows. It is a governmentwide system.

Source: World Bank 2017a.

Stand-alone PIM information systems

A stand-alone PIM information system can be considered in cases where requirements exceed what can be delivered by integrating with existing systems (see figure 12.3). An advantage of a stand-alone system is that it provides an opportunity to design a first-best technological solution rather than adjusting to fit an existing platform. A drawback is the potentially higher cost and the need to define automated interfaces with other systems.

Examples of interfaces with external systems

Budget system

The PIM information system passes financing requests to the budget formulation system, and the budget system passes the corresponding approved appropriation to the PIM information system after the Budget Law has been adopted by the government. Budget changes that may occur during the year should be sent from the FMIS to the PIM information system. Functionality to support the budget allocation and negotiation process may be placed in either the budget system or the PIM information system.

FIGURE 12.3

Possible technical architecture of a stand-alone PIM information system

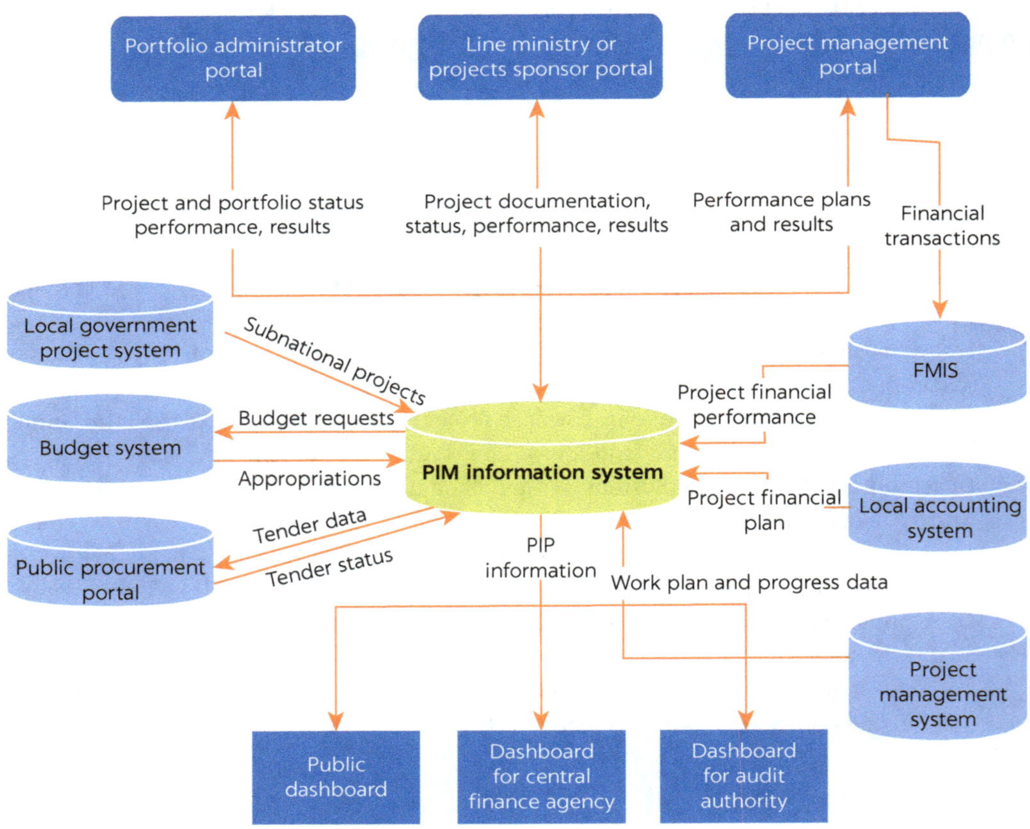

Sources: Adapted from World Bank 2016a, 2016b.
Note: FMIS = financial management information system. PIP = project investment portfolio.

FMIS

The basic nature of the exchange that should take place between the PIM information system and the FMIS is as follows:

- All project-related financial transactions carry a project code from the budget classification structure.
- Project managers submit project financial transactions: commitment requests, final commitments (signed contracts or purchase orders), and payment requests through the FMIS.
- The FMIS sends completed budget execution transactions back to the PIM information system after posting to the general ledger. These transactions should be stored cumulatively by the PIM information system over the lifetime of the projects and used for reporting on financial performance and calculating periodic financial performance indicators and rankings.

Procurement portal system

The current version of the procurement plan for each project should be entered by the project manager into the PIM information system, which will send the data to the public procurement portal to initiate a tender process. The public procurement portal will keep the PIM information system informed of the status of this process by sending updates every time the process advances one step.

Project accounting system

Full project accounting and financial reporting needs to be done outside the PIM information system and the FMIS by accrual accounting software. As this software may range from a sophisticated financial management system to simple, desktop accounting software, the most that can be expected is that the PIM information system will offer an appropriate application programming interface so that the project accounting system can feed financial planning data into it.

PLANNING FOR IMPLEMENTATION OF PIM INFORMATION SYSTEMS

As with other information and communication technology projects, implementing a PIM information system is a complex endeavor, the success of which is affected by many technical and nontechnical factors. A solid implementation process includes the following elements:

- Functional and technical requirements
- Detailed mapping of existing and future business processes
- System development strategy
- Change management strategy
- Project management and governance arrangements.

Functional and technical requirements

A critical initial step in implementation is to define functional and technical requirements.[2] As with other information systems, the definition of functional requirements should precede the technical requirements because the technical architecture and solutions often depend on the functional scope of the system.

Business process mapping

Identification of high-level functional and technical requirements should be followed by more detailed process mapping to ensure that requirements are formulated comprehensively. Process mapping typically starts with the existing ("as-is") processes before identifying needed changes and defining future ("to-be") processes. Process mapping can be helpful in making sure that all needed reforms of the current PIM system and processes have been identified and documented at a detailed level.

System development strategy

A fundamental decision to be made is whether the PIM information system will be built as bespoke software or on top of a commercial software package. If it is custom made, it is necessary to evaluate whether a systems integration approach would be a reasonable strategy for system development. Such an approach would involve taking software that is already available and integrating it with open-source or commercial software for authentication, single sign on, database, data warehousing, business intelligence, and so forth as a way to build the PIM information system. If this approach is taken, it will be necessary to conduct a market survey to identify existing software that can be acquired from either commercial suppliers or other governments. As a rule of thumb, to be considered, software packages should satisfy at least 80 percent of the functional and technical requirements of a PIM information system without requiring customization. If the software misses this mark, customization may be prohibitively costly.

Change management strategy

Effective and timely implementation of a PIM information system may be impeded by the uncertainty or resistance that it causes among affected staff and other stakeholders. A change management strategy for some of the root causes of such uncertainty or resistance is discussed below.

Informal procedures and "rent seeking"

Implementation of a PIM information system based on the reform of underlying processes is likely to formalize and systematize procedures and to increase transparency about how projects are reviewed, selected, and implemented. Implementation of a PIM information system reduces the opportunities for informal procedures and the flow of benefits emanating from an informal system. Public investments are particularly prone to such informal mechanisms because they involve very large transactions. In some countries, projects may be selected as a result of pressure from certain beneficiary groups rather than any measure of the socioeconomic merits of a project. For similar reasons, projects may be initiated in spite of forward financing requirements that exceed what is affordable. Faced with the prospect of reduced rents and increased scrutiny of decision making, some stakeholders may resist the adoption of a PIM information system. In some cases, systems either are not adopted or are subsequently abandoned even if technically sufficient. Box 12.6 summarizes the case of the National Investment Planning system in Serbia.

Countering such resistance requires strong ownership and leadership from top-level decision makers in government. A change management strategy should focus on activating senior management, selecting "champions" among political decision makers, and preparing them to push through system implementation.

Disincentives among primary data providers

A major challenge of PIM information systems is to ensure the receipt of timely and accurate data from project managers, particularly during project implementation. Balancing incentives is important for successful PIP system deployment. PIP systems are inherently burdensome for project-executing agencies, as they entail primarily bottom-up reporting obligations and perceptions of more detailed oversight and control. A PIM system designed to produce monitoring and control information will not generate much motivation among project managers. At a minimum, the system should be user-friendly and able to produce automatically all reports and data feeds required by project sponsors and portfolio administrators; data providers should not have to prepare ad hoc reports.

BOX 12.6

Learning from past failures: The National Investment Planning system in Serbia

A comprehensive PIM information system—the National Investment Planning (NIP) system—was developed in Serbia in 2007 but was eventually abandoned. The system was developed by the NIP Office, reporting directly to the prime minister and led by a NIP minister without portfolio. It was developed with financial and conceptual support from the World Bank and the European Union and followed extensive international consultation on good practices. By 2008, it reportedly had achieved almost 100 percent coverage of central, regional, and local investment projects and had some 17,000 projects in its database. The NIP system was underpinned by formal regulations and associated procedures for project selection and implementation.

The functional specifications of the NIP system reflected clear guidelines for project registration, prescreening, feasibility study, selection, implementation, progress reporting, and completion reporting. The NIP system also supported the NIP Office's centralized oversight of the PIP. The NIP system coopted the investment project screening procedures and forms of the Intersectoral Development Assistance Coordination Network system, which had been created to manage projects developed for European Union preaccession funds, and exchanged data electronically with that system. Similarly, the functionality of the NIP system aimed to be consistent with project formulation and implementation guidelines for World Bank–financed projects. A Serbian IT company developed the system as bespoke software.

While the exact reasons for discontinuing the NIP system are not known, the comprehensiveness of the system's functionality suggests that these reasons were mainly nontechnical. The institutional instability of the NIP Office and lack of coordination with the Ministry of Finance undoubtedly affected long-term institutionalization of the NIP system. The system is presumably still operational at the data center of the Administration for Joint Services of the Republic Bodies. Lessons should be drawn from this past failure to make the system sustainable—in particular, the government needs to commit to the obligatory use of a PIM information system as the official gateway for submitting and extracting project information.

Source: World Bank 2017b.

General uncertainty among affected staff

Staff working on various aspects of PIM may be uncertain about what the system might entail for them. Changes in processes may by themselves lead to discomfort among those affected. There may also be suspicions that any quoted objectives to increase efficiency could lead to lay-offs or changes in job conditions. However, the experience from the implementation of many information and communication technology projects worldwide indicates that well-designed communication campaigns can minimize such uncertainties.

Governance arrangements and project management

Sustained leadership and effective coordination and governance arrangements are indispensable for successful implementation of a PIM information system. Successful implementation requires a clear strategy, a political champion supported by a capable reform team, and well-established consultation and coordination mechanisms.

Starting and maintaining the implementation process requires the continuous proactive engagement of senior management in the involved ministries. The responsible central finance or planning agency should formally endorse an implementation plan and launch initial implementation activities. Continued political leadership is required to maintain the reform process and to guide stakeholders through critical junctures, including conflicting opinions on the details of reform as well as anxiety—and potentially even resistance—on the part of affected staff or other stakeholders.

A project steering committee can provide oversight and facilitate continuous and timely decision making. The committee could be chaired by a representative from the responsible central finance or planning agency and comprise senior officials from the main affected administrations. It should coordinate closely with bodies overseeing the implementation of related public financial management reforms; some overlap of key persons could be beneficial. Depending on country circumstances, development of a PIM information system may require mobilizing resources for technical assistance as well as some investment. The committee should therefore map out the corresponding financing needs, seek out funding options, and liaise with potential donors as necessary.

At the project management and technical level, roles and responsibilities need to be clearly designated. A full-time, experienced project manager typically needs to be assigned for the duration of the project; this manager would normally head up a project implementation team consisting of functional specialists and IT specialists to carry out all project activities.

NOTES

1. Different countries have used different approaches to distinguish projects and to ensure accounting at the project level. A typical program classification consists of programs, subprograms, and activities. Some countries use activity codes for projects, although activity codes will not by themselves distinguish between projects and other kinds of activities. Another option is to create spending units for projects and map them to the relevant programs.
2. Data and business needs of the main stakeholders.

REFERENCES

IMF (International Monetary Fund). 2011. "Manual de procedimientos del Banco Nacional de Programas y Proyectos, Departamento Nacional de Planeacion." IMF, Washington, DC.

USAID (U.S. Agency for International Development). 2015. "Main Features of an Integrated Database of Capital Projects." USAID, Washington, DC.

World Bank 2016a. "Public Investment Management in Serbia—Preliminary Requirements for a Public Investment Management Information System (PIMIS)." World Bank, Washington, DC.

——. 2016b. "Romania: Advisory Services Agreement on Support to Strengthening Public Investment Management—Output 2: Draft Report Identifying Potential Improvements to Information System for Monitoring the Public Investment Portfolio." World Bank, Washington, DC.

——. 2017a. "Public Investment Management Systems: Summary Note on PIM Systems." Report delivered to the Financial Management Information System Council of Parties, World Bank, Washington, DC.

——. 2017b. "Republic of Serbia: Strengthening Public Investment Management; Summary Assessment Report." World Bank, Washington DC.

A

References for International Guidance on Designing Appraisal Methodologies

When designing appraisal methodologies and estimating national parameter values, governments might find it useful to consult the following resources.

GENERAL GUIDANCE ON APPRAISAL METHODS

Commonwealth of Australia. 2006. *Handbook of Cost-Benefit Analysis* Canberra: Department of Finance and Administration. http://www.finance.gov.au/sites/default/files/Handbook_of_CB_analysis.pdf.

European Commission. 2014. *Guide to Cost-Benefit Analysis of Investment Projects: Economic Appraisal Tool for Cohesion Policy 2014–2020.* Brussels: Directorate General for Regional and Urban Policy. http://ec.europa.eu/regional_policy/sources/docgener/studies/pdf/cba_guide.pdf.

Government of Northern Ireland. n.d. "Guide to Economic Appraisal: Carrying out a Cost Benefit Analysis, Part D.03 of Public Spending Code." Central Expenditure and Evaluation Unit, Department of Public Expenditure and Reform, Belfast. http://publicspendingcode.per.gov.ie/d-standard-analytical-techniques/.

Government of Northern Ireland. n.d. "Northern Ireland Guide to Expenditure Appraisal and Evaluation." Department of Finance and Personnel, Belfast. http://www.dfpni.gov.uk/eag and https://www.finance-ni.gov.uk/topics/finance/northern-ireland-guide-expenditure-appraisal-and-evaluation-nigeae.

HM Treasury. 2003. *The Green Book: Appraisal and Evaluation in Central Government.* Updated in 2011. London: HM Treasury. https://www.gov.uk/government/publications/the-green-book-appraisal-and-evaluation-in-central-governent.

HM Treasury. 2013. *Public Sector Business Cases Using the Five Case Model, Supplementary Guidance to the Green Book* London: HM Treasury. https://www.gov.uk/government/publications/the-green-book-appraisal-and-evaluation-in-central-governent.

New Zealand Treasury. 2015. "Guide to Social Cost-Benefit Analysis." New Zealand Treasury, Wellington. http://www.treasury.govt.nz/publications/guidance/planning/costbenefitanalysis/guide.

World Bank data on transport, water, energy, and telecommunications. https://data.worldbank.org/topic/infrastructure.

World Bank road maintenance and planning data. http://siteresources.worldbank.org/INTROADSHIGHWAYS/Resources/338993-1115316562809/10-poor_rd_maint.pdf.

SECTOR-SPECIFIC GUIDANCE ON APPRAISAL METHODS

Multisector examples

Asian Development Bank. 2013. *Cost-Benefit Analysis for Development: A Practical Guide.* Manila: Asian Development Bank. Includes water and sanitation as well as power generation and transmission. http://www.adb.org/sites/default/files/institutional-document/33788/files/cost-benefit-analysis-development.pdf.

European Investment Bank. 2013. *Economic Appraisal of Investment Projects at the EIB.* Brussels: Projects Directorate. Includes water and sanitation, power generation and transmission, ports, and energy efficiency. http://www.eib.org/attachments/thematic/economic_appraisal_of_investment_projects_en.pdf.

Education

Woodhall, M. 2005 *Cost-Benefit Analysis in Educational Planning,* 4th ed. Paris: UNESCO, International Institute for Educational Planning. http://unesdoc.unesco.org/images/0013/001390/139042e.pdf.

Culture

Arts Council England. 2016. *Measuring the Economic Benefits of Arts and Culture: Practical Guidance on Research Methodologies for Arts and Cultural Organisations.* London: Arts Council England. http://www.artscouncil.org.uk/advice-and-guidance/browse-advice-and-guidance/measuring-economic-benefits-arts-culture.

Transport: Land transport

New Zealand Transport Agency. 2013. *Economic Evaluation Manual.* Wellington: NZ Transport Agency. http://www.nzta.govt.nz/resources/economicevaluation-manual/economic-evaluation-manual/eem/.

Transport: Roads

Transport Infrastructure Ireland, Ireland. Various years. *Project Appraisal Guidelines for National Roads.* Dublin: Transport Infrastructure Ireland. http://www.tii.ie/.

Transport: Airports

U.S. Federal Aviation Administration. 1999. *FAA Airport Benefit-Cost Analysis Guidance.* Washington, DC: Office of Aviation Policy and Plans. https://www.faa.gov/regulations_policies/policy_guidance/benefit_cost/media/1999_FAA_Airport_Benefit_Cost_Analysis_Guidance.pdf.

Transport: Railways

European Investment Bank, *RailPAG: Railway Project Appraisal Guidelines.* Luxembourg: European Investment Bank. http://www.eib.org/attachments/pj/railpag_en.pdf.

Environment

OECD (Organisation for Economic Co-operation and Development). 2007. *Handbook for Appraisal of Environmental Projects Financed from Public Funds.* Paris: OECD Publishing. http://www.oecd.org/env/outreach/handbookforappraisalofenvironmentalprojectsfinancedfrompublicfunds.htm.

Energy: Distribution

Giordano, V., and M. Sánchez Jiménez. 2012. *Guidelines for Conducting a Cost Benefit Analysis of Smart Grid Projects.* JRC Reference Report. Petten, the Netherlands: European Commission, Joint Research Centre. https://ses.jrc.ec.europa.eu/sites/ses/files/documents/guidelines_for_conducting_a_cost-benefit_analysis_of_smart_grid_projects.pdf.

Giordano, V., I. Onyeji, M. Sánchez Jiménez, and C. Filiou. *Guidelines for Cost Benefit Analysis of Smart Metering Deployment.* JRC Science and Technological Research. Petten, the Netherlands: European Commission, Joint Research Centre. https://ses.jrc.ec.europa.eu/sites/ses/files/documents/guidelines_for_cost_benefit_analysis_of_smart_metering_deployment.pdf.

Flood protection and coastal erosion

U.K. Environment Agency. 2018. *Flood and Coastal Erosion Risk Management: Appraisal Guidance.* Rotherham: U.K. Environment Agency. https://www.gov.uk/government/publications/flood-and-coastal-erosion-risk-management-appraisal-guidance. Other appraisal tools are available at https://www.gov.uk/flood-and-coastal-defence-appraisal-of-projects.

Information and communication technology

Australian Government, Information Management Office. 2019. "ICT Business Case Guide." Department of Finance, Canberra. https://www.finance.gov.au/sites/default/files/2019-11/ICT_Business_Case_Guide.pdf.

Sources of information on the value transfer approach to national parameter values

Where national values have not yet been calculated, values may potentially be derived from some European and international studies, particularly for the transport and environment sectors. This approach is generally known as the value transfer method. The following are examples of potential data sources:

Environment and Climate Change Canada and Department for Environment, Food, and Rural Affairs, Environmental Valuation Reference Inventory (EVRI), a searchable database of empirical studies on the economic value of environmental assets and human health effects. https://evri.ca/en/splashify-splash.

European Commission. 2005. "Developing Harmonised European Approaches for Transport Costing and Project Assessment (HEATCO): Current Practice in Project Appraisal in Europe: Analysis of Country Reports." European Commission, Brussels. https://trimis.ec.europa.eu/sites/default/files/project/documents/20130122_113558_74349_hd1final.pdf.

European Commission. 2013. *Update of the Handbook on External Costs of Transport: Final Report.* London: RICARDO-AEA. http://ec.europa.eu/transport/themes/sustainable/studies/doc/2014-handbook-external-costs-transport.pdf.

U.K. Department for Transport. 2013. *International Comparison of Transport Appraisal Practice: Overview Report,* specifically appendix B. London: Department for Transport. https://www.gov.uk/government/publications/international-comparisons-of-transport-appraisal-practice.

B

Further Issues in Developing an Economic Appraisal Methodology

This appendix deals with design issues where specific recommendations might be useful for governments in the process of preparing methodological guidance on economic appraisal. It covers the following topics in more detail than was possible in the main report:

- Setting of national parameter values and consideration of conversion factors
- Decisions regarding estimation of the social discount rate
- Treatment of labor market distortions
- Allowance for the deadweight cost of taxation
- Approaches to estimating values for nonmarket benefits and costs
- Decisions regarding the required degree of sophistication of risk analysis.

SETTING OF NATIONAL PARAMETER VALUES AND CONSIDERATION OF CONVERSION FACTORS

As well as providing general guidance on project appraisal methodology, governments should ensure that regularly updated, nationally applicable values for key parameters, especially nonmarket effects, are available for preparing feasibility studies. Having such information ensures that the valuation of costs and benefits is consistent across projects, eliminating the need to estimate and reestimate values on a case-by-case basis. Having consistent information improves comparability and delivers savings in analytical effort.

Box B.1 illustrates the parameter values provided as part of France's national methodological guidance. The United Kingdom takes a different approach, allowing line ministries to determine the values for key parameters for their sectors, subject to the finance ministry's approval. Only the discount rate is set centrally as part of the national methodological guidance and is updated when necessary.[1] The Republic of Korea has a similar system, with national parameter values updated annually in online guidance.

Where national values have not yet been calculated, it is possible to derive values from some European and international studies, particularly for the transport and environment sectors. This approach is known as the "value transfer" method of estimating parameters. When using such estimates, governments

BOX B.1

National parameter values for social cost-benefit analysis in France

The following values are provided in the central guidance on social cost-benefit analysis for France:

Transport-related values

- Value of a statistical life
- Values for severe and minor injuries
- Value of travel time by mode, purpose, location (Ile de France and elsewhere), and distance
- Value of freight time by type of cargo
- Value of passenger waiting time.

Environmental values

- Value per ton of carbon dioxide emitted
- Cost of atmospheric pollution by mode of transport and population density
- Values for noise emissions by mode of transport and population density.

In addition, guidance is given on how these values should change over time.

Source: Office of the Prime Minister, France 2013.

need to ensure that they are adjusted for the national context and updated to the relevant base year. Some examples of these data sources are given in appendix A of this guide.

Even where a market exists for project inputs and outputs, market prices may not represent the best basis for estimating the economic value of a project's costs and benefits. It may be necessary to adjust financial values to yield economic values ("social opportunity costs" or "shadow prices") because of substantial distortions in the economy. Such distortions can arise from taxes on trade, production subsidies, or inefficient labor markets, for example. Early guidance on cost-benefit analysis often recommended that the planning authorities estimate an elaborate set of national conversion factors, covering major sectors of the economy, to transform market prices to economic values for use in social cost-benefit analysis (SCBA). This guidance was developed when many economies were much more severely distorted than they are today. It was rarely followed, and, where it was followed, the factors were rarely employed in actual SCBA because few planners knew of their existence or understood how to use them.

For practical reasons and considering the generally more efficient markets now existing in many countries, it is not considered necessary to devote significant planning resources to developing economywide conversion factors. Good practice is to make adjustments for key inputs or outputs on a case-by-case basis when the adjustment is considered likely to make a significant difference to the findings of the SCBA.

Although it may not be necessary to estimate a full set of conversion factors for individual goods and services, a general factor may be estimated to reflect divergences in the relative economic values of internationally traded and nontraded goods. These divergences can be severe in countries with restrictive foreign exchange controls, which are rare nowadays; however, even when the official exchange rate is allowed to move more freely, import duties, quantitative restrictions, export subsidies, and export taxes impose their own distortions on the foreign exchange market (as well as on markets for the goods and services in question), affecting the relative prices of traded and nontraded goods.

The calculation of the relative price adjustment between traded and nontraded goods depends on the numeraire chosen for project appraisal. The numeraire is the unit of account used to measure all values in economic analysis. The choice of numeraire is immaterial for the final results of the economic analysis, but for the sake of consistency all costs and benefits must be expressed in terms of the same numeraire. There are other possibilities, but the choice of numeraire is often between the domestic currency expressed at the international price level and the domestic currency expressed at the domestic price level.[2] In the former case, a standard conversion factor (SCF) should be calculated to express the price of nontraded goods and services at the international price level. The value of the SCF will be less than 1. In the latter case, a shadow exchange rate factor (SERF) should be calculated to express the price of traded goods and services at the domestic price level. The value of the SERF will be more than 1.

Determining what is a traded good and what is a nontraded good is not always straightforward. The final price of traded goods usually includes local distribution costs, and the production of nontraded goods usually involves the use of some traded inputs—for example, chemicals to treat drinking water. For major project inputs and outputs, these components should be disaggregated and adjusted by the SCF or SERF accordingly, but the amount of effort applied needs to be balanced carefully against the likely effect on the final results of the economic analysis. It is sufficient to categorize most inputs and outputs as on-balance tradable or nontradable and to apply the appropriate factor accordingly.

Most countries with advanced systems do not estimate these standardized factors because their economies tend to be relatively open and undistorted and the required correction to prices would therefore be negligible. National financial and planning authorities need to decide whether it is worth making the implied adjustment, taking account of the relative openness of their economy.

One final area where a national parameter value may be specified is in relation to the deadweight cost of taxation. Using distortionary tax instruments to finance projects results in a generalized loss of social welfare. In effect, a part of general taxation is taken from consumers and transferred to no one; this situation is known as the deadweight economic cost from general taxation or the marginal cost of public funds. This issue is explored later in this appendix. Suffice it to say, practice across countries with advanced PIM systems is not consistent: some countries specify a factor to be applied to the project costs funded out of taxation, and others do not.

DECISIONS REGARDING ESTIMATION OF THE SOCIAL DISCOUNT RATE

Approach to the social discount rate

Social cost-benefit analysis involves discounting the estimated stream of net benefits generated by a project (and its alternatives) to yield net present values (NPVs) or net present costs (NPCs) in the case of cost-effective analysis. The social discount rate (SDR) is therefore a critical variable in appraisal, and governments need to decide how to determine a suitable value for their country, since different perspectives and corresponding methodological approaches are possible. Determining the SDR is not a purely technical matter;

depending on the perspective adopted, it involves a degree of value judgment, further complicating the decision.

Whichever theoretical approach is chosen, estimating the SDR is not technically straightforward; it requires capacity for economic analysis or access to it. One provisional option, therefore, is to benchmark against other comparable countries or to follow international guidance, where available.[3] As an example, box B.2 presents guidance from the European Union to beneficiaries of its European Regional Development Fund and Cohesion Fund. Whatever the case, it is always a good idea to carry out sensitivity tests of the robustness of the results of the quantified SCBA using a higher value for the SDR than the base case.[4]

A project's benefits and costs do not occur at the same point in time, and values occurring in different time periods must be adjusted to reflect society's preference for consuming goods and services sooner rather than later. The social discount rate is society's rate of time preference and is used as a basis for converting future values into present value equivalents. Expressing project benefits and costs occurring in different years in the future as present values puts them on a consistent basis and allows them to be added together and compared. In economic terms, simply adding benefits and costs occurring at different times without this adjustment would be as nonsensical as adding together values expressed in euros and dollars without converting them to a common basis using the exchange rate. Pursuing this analogy, the discount rate can be conceptualized as being the basis for an "exchange rate" between values today and values in the future.

There has been much debate among economists about which discount rate should be used as the SDR. The two main perspectives are the social rate of time preference (SRTP) and the social opportunity cost of capital (SOC):

- *Social rate of time preference.* The SRTP captures the way society values consumption at different points in time. This perspective relies on interpreting the discount rate as the minimum economic compensation per dollar invested required for a representative consumer to be willing to forgo present consumption in return for higher consumption one period later.

BOX B.2

European Commission guidance to member states on the social discount rate

"According to Annex III to the Implementing Regulation on application form and CBA [cost-benefit analysis] methodology, for the programming period 2014–2020 the European Commission recommends that for the social discount rate 5% is used for major projects in Cohesion countries and 3% for the other Member States [MSs]. Member States may establish a benchmark for the SDR [social discount rate], which is different from 5% or 3%, on the condition that i) justification is provided for this reference on the basis of an economic growth forecast and other parameters; ii) their consistent application is ensured across similar projects in the same country, region, or sector. The Commission encourages MSs to provide their own benchmarks for the SDR in their guidance documents, possibly at the start of the operational programmes, and then to apply it consistently in project appraisal at national level."

Source: European Commission 2014.

- *Social opportunity cost of capital.* The SOC reflects the rate of return on investment and derives from returns in financial markets. This perspective interprets the discount rate as a market-determined opportunity cost, which represents the additional consumption that would have been achieved one period later by investing a dollar in a financial instrument of equivalent risk to the project instead of consuming it now.

The SRTP and SOC perspectives are related and, in special circumstances, are equivalent. This relationship is illustrated in figure B.1, which shows, in simplified terms, the interaction between the supply of investible savings and the demand for investment capital in a representative financial market. The vertical axis represents the rate of return or interest, and the horizontal axis represents the volume of funds saved and invested. The "Savings" curve captures the time preference for consumption and shows people's preferences for trading today's consumption for future consumption. It can be used to determine the SRTP. The "Investment" curve captures the rate of return that capital must yield in order for investors to decide to invest. It can be used to determine the SOC.

In an idealized world with no market imperfections, only one market interest rate clears the market: this rate is defined as r_0 at the intersection of the savings supply and investment demand curves. At this rate, savings desires and investment demands are in balance and the SRTP and SOC are equivalent.

In the real world, where there are market distortions, a wedge is driven between the expectations of savers and investors. Such distortions include monopoly or oligopolistic power, positive or negative externalities, missing markets, asymmetric information, and risk and uncertainty. In the presence of market imperfections, the perspective of the individual as an investor and as a consumer does not equate. As a result, the discount rate reflecting people's preferences for consuming in different time periods ends up being different from the discount rate in the financial markets.

Table B.1 summarizes the perspectives taken by various governments in countries with advanced systems and the corresponding SDRs. The table indicates some variation between countries.

FIGURE B.1

Equilibrium and the impact of market imperfections

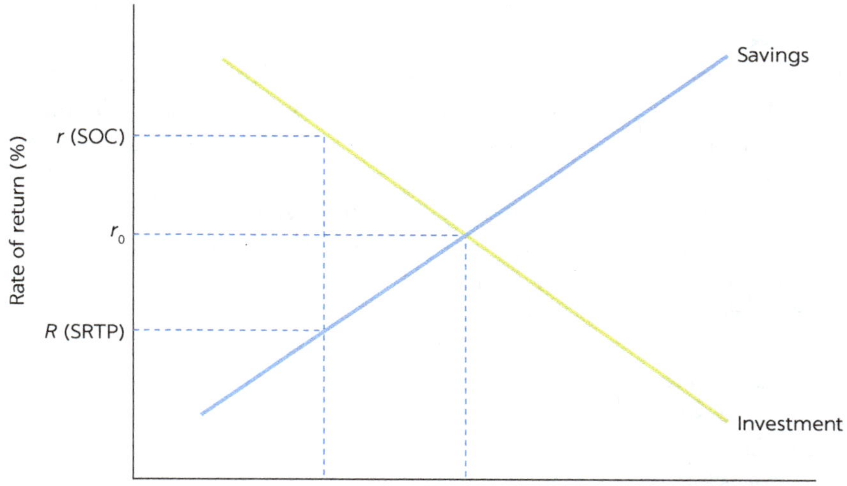

Source: Young 2002.

TABLE B.1 **Social discount rate (SDR) perspective and discount rate, by country**

COUNTRY	SDR PERSPECTIVE	DISCOUNT RATE
France	Risk-adjusted SRTP	4.5%
Germany[a]	SRTP	3.0% for analysis periods of 20 years or less
Japan	SOC	4.0%
Netherlands	Risk-adjusted SRTP	4.0% for climate change effects and 5.5% for other effects
New Zealand	SOC	8.0%
Norway[a]	Risk-adjusted SRTP	4.0% for analysis periods of less than 40 years
Sweden	SRTP	3.5%
United Kingdom[a]	SRTP	3.5% for analysis periods of 30 years or less

Source: OECD 2015.
Note: SOC = social opportunity cost of capital; SRTP = social rate of time preference.
a. These countries apply lower discount rates for long-term effects.

Declining social discount rates

When designing an appraisal methodology, governments should provide guidance on the length of the period of analysis for projects. Ideally, the analysis period should correspond to the useful life of the fixed asset created and should be the same for all alternatives. In reality, some major infrastructure assets have almost indefinite lives, if a program of planned routine and periodic maintenance is pursued. Until recently, it has been common practice internationally to curtail the analysis period and include a residual value as a benefit in the final year of the chosen analysis; however, this approach can be crude, depending on the extent to which future values are discounted.[5] Table B.2 presents the reference analysis periods by sector recommended by the European Commission. The longest analysis period in table B.2 is 30 years, with shorter periods specified for short-lived assets. European Commission guidance recommends applying a residual value for assets with useful lives exceeding 30 years.

In keeping with the approach now being adopted in some good-practice countries, there may be advantages in placing less weight on residual values and using an analysis period more closely reflecting the useful life of a long-lived asset. The analysis period for major infrastructure projects involving a large share of civil works—roads and ports, for example—may therefore be extended beyond 30 years to as much as 60 years. Projects with significant environmental benefits and costs that extend across generations may have even longer analysis periods.

A strong theoretical argument for declining discount rates over the long term can be made, and some countries have now adopted schedules of declining rates for infrastructure assets with long lives or projects with long-lived effects, particularly environmental externalities.[6]

The main reason for adopting declining discount rates is increasing uncertainty about future consumption and the consequent impact on the marginal utility of consumption (a component of the Ramsey equation). Because of the declining marginal utility of consumption, benefits that occur when future consumption is high are valued less than benefits that occur when future consumption is low, so that the benefits of "upside" risk are outweighed by the costs of

TABLE B.2 **Reference analysis periods for project, by sector**

SECTOR	ANALYSIS PERIOD (YEARS)
Railways	30
Roads	25–30
Ports and airports	25
Urban transport	25–30
Water supply and sanitation	30
Waste management	25–30
Energy	15–25
Broadband	15–20
Business infrastructure	10–15
Other sectors	10–15

Source: European Commission 2014.

TABLE B.3 **Schedule of declining discount rates in the United Kingdom**

DISCOUNT RATE (%)	PERIOD (YEARS)
3.5	0–30
3.0	31–75
2.5	76–125
2.0	126–300
1.5	201–300
1.0	300+

Source: HM Treasury 2003.

"downside" risk, implying a declining discount rate as uncertainty about the future increases.

France and the United Kingdom are among the countries that have adopted declining discount rates. In France the SDR is 4 percent for the first 30 years and then declines to a low of 2 percent over time. Table B.3 presents the schedule of declining discount rates adopted by the United Kingdom.

Estimating a schedule of declining discount rates requires developed analytical and research skills, and governments may wish to consider whether this work should be given priority in the early stages of improving their public investment management (PIM) systems and developing an appraisal methodology. It seems more sensible to focus on this refinement when PIM fundamentals are in place and functioning reasonably well.

TREATMENT OF LABOR MARKET DISTORTIONS

When labor markets work efficiently and there is no structural unemployment, the market wage rate is the best measure of the social opportunity cost of labor—that is, the marginal value to society of a unit of labor in its next best alternative use, the appropriate measure for SCBA purposes. Imperfections in the way labor markets are working, policy-induced rigidities—such as minimum wage legislation—or macroeconomic imbalances may result in the opportunity cost of labor being less than the market rate. In these cases, an adjustment factor can be applied to estimate what is usually referred to as a shadow wage rate. Box B.3 provides some examples of factors that could cause departures from an efficient market. Some of these factors may be region specific, requiring a case-by-case analysis (rather than the establishment of national parameters).

BOX B.3

Possible causes of labor market distortions

- Government subsidies to employment, which may cause the costs of labor for private companies to be less than the social opportunity cost
- Legislation establishing a minimum wage, even if people are willing to work for less
- Informal or illegal sectors with no formal wages, but with a positive opportunity cost of labor
- Fundamental macroeconomic imbalances and "stickiness" in wages.

Source: European Commission 2008.

The shadow wage rate may be obtained as the weighted average of the following:

- The shadow wage for skilled and unskilled workers previously employed in similar activities, which can be assumed to be equal or close to the market wage
- The shadow wage for unskilled workers drawn to the project from unemployment, which can be assumed to be equal to or less than the value of unemployment benefits
- The shadow wage for unskilled workers drawn to the project from informal activities, which should be equal to the value of the forgone output in these activities.

The weights applied should be proportional to the estimated amount of each labor resource employed in the project.

Governments need to decide how they are going to treat the social opportunity cost of labor. In making this decision, it is important to bear in mind that calculating a shadow wage rate is technically demanding and potentially costly. It is only worth considering if the resulting adjustment is likely to have a significant bearing on investment decisions. In this respect, countries with good PIM practices do not generally allow for the use of a shadow wage rate. An exception is in European Union guidance applicable to European Regional Fund and Cohesion Fund projects, which are directed toward regions and countries with structural problems, including in labor markets.

ALLOWANCE FOR THE DEADWEIGHT COST OF TAXATION

Using distortionary tax instruments to finance projects results in a generalized loss of social welfare. When the government raises revenues to pay for public services and associated capital investment through taxation,[7] it distorts price signals.[8] Market participants change their behavior when facing altered price incentives, consuming less of a taxed good than they otherwise would and, as a result, experiencing lower welfare.[9] In effect, a part of general taxation is taken from consumers and transferred to no one; this situation is known as the deadweight economic cost of general taxation or the marginal cost of public funds.

In practice, this situation means that the resources mobilized by the public sector are more costly in economic terms than in financial terms because of the

BOX B.4

International experience in adjusting for the deadweight economic losses from general taxation

The New Zealand Treasury suggests using a default adjustment factor of 1.2 to increase the value of public expenditures to reflect the deadweight loss from taxation. At the same time, the guidance draws attention to the weak evidence base, including estimates pointing to values in the range of 1.14–1.50.

France has also adopted a value of 1.2.

Ireland's Public Spending Code recommends applying a factor of 1.3 to public expenditures to reflect their true economic cost. A rule of thumb is that the distortionary costs of taxation vary roughly in line with the square of the marginal tax rate used to estimate this rate. The value previously stood at 1.5 but was under review in 2012 to reflect tax reforms.

The Australian federal government recognizes that the economic cost of public investment is greater than the actual amount of funds used because of the excess tax burden. It is therefore considered appropriate to adjust financial costs upward by a factor to ensure that the calculated net present value is not biased. Similarly, it is considered appropriate to adjust upward the financial value of any project revenue streams that will reduce the net financial cost of a project. An adjustment factor of 1.25 is suggested based on a study of the marginal excess tax burden for general taxation. However, in view of the uncertainty surrounding this estimate, it is not mandatory, but could be used as a sensitivity test.

Sources: For Australia, Commonwealth of Australia 2006. For France, Office of the Prime Minister, France 2013. For Ireland, http://publicspendingcode.per.gov.ie/technical-references/. For New Zealand, http://www.treasury.govt.nz/publications/guidance/planning/costbenefitanalysis/guide.

social welfare losses implied by a non-neutral taxation policy. To reflect this deadweight cost, costs incurred by the public sector should ideally be uplifted by a factor prior to discounting, so that public costs and private benefits are put on a comparable footing. This approach avoids an upward bias in the estimated economic performance of the project.[10] The other side of the coin is that the benefits from projects that result in direct public expenditure savings and hence lower taxation than would otherwise be the case should also be increased by the same factor to reflect their true economic cost.

The deadweight cost of taxation is easier to conceptualize than to measure. Box B.4 provides examples from Australia, France, Ireland, and New Zealand, countries that allow for an adjustment factor. The United Kingdom as well as Korea do not provide for this adjustment in their appraisal guidance, and the European Commission has taken a similar stance. Given the difficulties in estimating a factor to represent the deadweight cost of taxation, governments may prefer to adopt a position similar to those of the European Commission, Korea, and the United Kingdom, recognizing that this approach may lead to some overestimation of economic performance and taking this overestimation into account through sensitivity tests.

APPROACHES TO ESTIMATING VALUES FOR NONMARKET BENEFITS AND COSTS

Taking account of nonmarket effects is a critical part of SCBA, but their valuation is conceptually difficult for noneconomists to understand. Nonexperts in government often need to consult experts outside of government, if more sophisticated valuation techniques are employed, but in doing so they need to be able to specify the work and interpret the results. As such, it is very important to provide good guidance in this area.

Valuation of project costs and benefits should always be based on real or estimated market prices for the costs incurred or services produced by the project, where these prices are observable. By their nature, many public services are, however, free of charge, either because it is difficult or impossible to charge—for example, in the case of public goods[11]—or because of a policy choice driven by generally accepted equity or social concerns. Health, educational success, family and community stability, and environmental amenity are the kinds of intangible effects that fall into the category of benefits with no directly observable market values. By definition, positive and negative externalities have no market values.

In cases where no markets exist and therefore no market prices exist for valuation purposes, alternative, market-based means of estimating values for costs and benefits can be used, when doing so is feasible. These approaches hinge on estimating potential users' willingness to pay (WTP) for the project's benefits or willingness to accept (WTA) negative consequences. WTP is the maximum payment that a beneficiary would be willing to give up in order to receive a public service[12] and is therefore a measure of the "utility"[13] that a consumer expects to obtain. WTA is the minimum compensation that an affected party would require to be willing to tolerate a negative economic outcome, such as increased noise or pollution.

There are two approaches for estimating WTP:

- Revealed preference techniques
- Stated preference techniques.

Revealed preference techniques are generally considered to be more reliable and should be favored where the required data are available. To produce acceptable results, stated preference techniques need to be designed carefully using advanced research methods. They should be employed judiciously. Project promoters will need to make the choice of technique on a case-by-case basis, usually on the basis of advice from experts. Sometimes both techniques may be employed, and the results may be compared to check consistency.

Revealed preference techniques involve inferring willingness to pay by examining users' past behavior in similar or related markets. Information on past trade-offs made between costs and benefits in closely related contexts can be used to indicate the readiness to pay for the kind of benefits that the project will deliver. Three revealed preference methods are frequently used:

- *Hedonic pricing.* Involves deriving values by decomposing actual market prices into their constituent characteristics to obtain insights into willingness to pay for benefits for which there is no directly observable market. An example would be using the difference between residential property prices at varying distances from an environmental amenity—for example, a park or lake—to estimate the inherent utility of such amenities and hence to estimate the benefit of creating similar new amenities.[14] Another approach might be to look at wage rate differentials to infer the value that workers place on safety and, hence, to estimate the value of a statistical life. This estimated value can then be used to assess investments in improving transport safety, among other things.
- *Travel cost analysis.* Involves estimating the total costs that people are willing to incur to access free amenities as a minimum estimate of what they are willing to pay. For example, the generalized travel costs that

people bear in traveling to a park or recreation facility indicate the value they place on the amenities provided.[15] This value can then be used to construct a demand relationship for an amenity, which then can be used to value the potential welfare gain ("consumer surplus") from similar new amenities. Application of this technique requires the collection of good survey data on distance traveled, journey times, mode of transport, frequency of use, and income from a representative sample of users of existing facilities similar to the proposed project. It is therefore demanding in research effort.

- *Defensive expenditures.* Involves estimating the amount that households are prepared to spend on restoring assets as a result of negative environmental or other effects or on preventing these effects from occurring, which gives an indication of WTP. Examples would be medical costs incurred because of unsafe water or the costs of boiling the water to prevent disease.

Table B.4 provides some examples of appropriate revealed preference methods for various types of public goods or benefits.

Stated preference techniques simulate a market by using specially designed interviews or questionnaires to get users to state directly their willingness to pay for a service or to make hypothetical choices from which WTP can be inferred. Project promoters will almost certainly require specialized external expertise to advise them on stated preference techniques, especially for choice modeling, for which one of the following two general methods is potentially applicable:

- *Contingent valuation studies* ask open-ended questions concerning the maximum amount a potential user would be willing to pay for a given service through the project or offer a constrained choice of values from which the respondent is asked to choose.

TABLE B.4 **Use of revealed preference and stated preference methods, by the nature of the public good or benefit**

NATURE OF PUBLIC GOOD OR BENEFIT	REVEALED PREFERENCE METHOD	STATE PREFERENCE METHOD
Educational skills and training	Increased market earnings	
Public library services	Prices of substitutes	CV/CM
Value of life	Hedonic wage analysis Defensive expenditures	CV/CM
Value of health	Increased earnings Defensive expenditures Savings in expenditures	CV/CM
Police protection and safety	Hedonic property prices	CV/CM
Travel time savings (work)	Value of increased output	
Travel time savings (leisure)	Analysis of travel choices	CV/CM
Reductions in vehicle operating costs	Savings in expenditures	
Active recreational areas	Prices of substitutes	CV/CM
Parks and passive recreational areas	Travel cost analysis	CV/CM
Environmental inputs to production	Value of increased output Savings in expenditures	
Environmental amenities	Hedonic property price analysis	CV/CM
Flood and fire protection	Hedonic property price analysis Savings in expenditures	CV/CM

Source: Commonwealth of Australia 2006.
Note: CV/CM = contingent valuation / choice modeling.

TABLE B.5 **Strengths and weaknesses of willingness to pay valuation methods**

VALUATION METHOD	MAIN STRENGTHS	MAIN WEAKNESSES
Revealed preferences		
Market data	Is easily observable; provides important data on productivity impacts	Does not measure nonmarket goods such as quality of life
Hedonic wage method	Provides market-based method of valuing safety	Wages are not always a reliable indicator of risk
Hedonic property or land prices	Has many applications and is a reliable method	Requires extensive data
Travel cost analysis	Produces reliable answers if site is accessible and study is well done	Has to deal with multitrip purposes and the value of travel time
Defensive expenditures	Provides a useful lower bound to values	Requires caution when expenditures have several benefits
Stated preferences		
Contingent valuation	Has many applications	Respondents often find it difficult to express a monetary value for a nonmarket good; answers may be biased
Choice modeling	Respondents may give more accurate answers than contingent valuation surveys	Requires substantial professional resources

Source: Commonwealth of Australia 2006.

- *Choice modeling* presents potential users with a series of alternatives involving trade-offs between costs and benefits from which they are required to indicate a preference. This method is better for valuing specific attributes of a service than for valuing the service as a whole. It attempts to get around any biases that can arise from asking direct questions concerning hypothetical payments, but in doing so it adds more complexity.

Table B.3 indicates cases when stated preference methods might be applicable. Drawing on Australian guidance, table B.5 summarizes the strengths and weaknesses of the different valuation methods.

DEGREE OF SOPHISTICATION OF RISK ANALYSIS

Identification, analysis, and management of risks are critical for any project appraisal; however, risk analysis can be complex and demanding on scarce research and analytical capacities. Governments need to decide what degree of sophistication their national appraisal methodologies require. The European Commission has developed a stepped approach to risk analysis:

- Sensitivity analysis
- Qualitative risk analysis
- Quantitative risk analysis.

More complex quantitative risk analysis, the final step, is only required in certain defined circumstances. Governments may wish to consider adopting a similarly pragmatic approach.

Step 1: Sensitivity analysis

Sensitivity analysis aims to identify those variables that have the largest impact on the project's social profitability (as measured by the economic NPV). The European Commission defines "critical" variables as those for which a variation of +/−1 percent has more than a 1 percent impact on the value of the NPV. Sensitivity analysis is used to determine these critical variables. The analysis is carried out by varying one variable at a time, on both the benefit and cost sides, and calculating the resulting effect on the NPV. The calculation of switching values is a variation on sensitivity analysis and involves estimating the change in a particular variable required to reduce the NPV to 0.

Sensitivity analysis concludes with scenario analysis, by which combinations of optimistic and pessimistic values of the critical variables (as previously identified) are used to test the impact on the NPV. The values must be at the extreme of what is judged to be a realistic range. Clearly, the pessimistic scenario is the most interesting for testing the robustness of a project's social profitability. It is possible to draw conclusions about a project's riskiness after this step if social profitability remains strong in the face of the most adverse (realistic) scenario. Even so, step 2 should be completed for all projects. Quantified SCBA may not capture some important effects, and risks attaching to these effects should be captured through step 2.

Step 2: Qualitative risk analysis

Qualitative risk analysis consists of the following elements:

- Listing adverse events to which the project is exposed
- Preparing a risk matrix, indicating the following for each adverse event:
  - The possible causes of the occurrence
  - The link with the sensitivity analysis, where this applies—for example, where unexpected ground conditions lead to higher capital costs
  - The negative effects on the project that the adverse event would generate
  - The ranked levels of probability of occurrence[16] and severity of impact[17]
  - The risk level combining probability of occurrence and severity of impact[18]
- Interpreting the risk matrix, including assessment of the acceptable levels of risk. In the European Commission's four levels of risk, "high risk" is deemed unacceptable and requires a revision of the entire project design and preparation activities.
- Describing mitigation and prevention measures for the main risks and assessing their impacts on the robustness of the project's performance and the residual risk. If the remaining risk exposure is judged acceptable—that is, judged to be "low" or "moderate"—then the risk strategy based on qualitative analysis may be adopted and there is no requirement to move to quantitative risk assessment.

Step 3: Quantitative risk analysis

Probabilistic risk analysis is required where residual risk exposure remains significant after step 2.[19] This step involves establishing a probability distribution for each of the critical variables identified in the sensitivity test in order to estimate the expected value of the NPV.[20] Once the probability distribution is determined[21]—based on experience, experimentation, or expert guidance—a Monte Carlo simulation may be performed using appropriate software to establish a probability distribution for the NPV itself. A Monte Carlo simulation allows the expected NPV to be estimated and the probability of a negative NPV to be determined.

The advantage of the European Commission's guidance is that it does not require sophisticated risk analysis for all projects (although this analysis is not precluded). It only applies to major projects (greater than €50 million) seeking European Union funding. Governments may wish to consider limiting the application of quantitative risk analysis to their largest projects. Steps 1 and 2 of the European Commission's risk analysis process are valuable in all cases, and step 1 should be obligatory whenever SCBA is performed.

NOTES

1. See http://publicspendingcode.per.gov.ie/technical-references/.
2. This approach is proposed in the World Bank's *Handbook on Economic Analysis of Investment Operations* (World Bank 1998).
3. Even where a country-specific SDR is estimated, it is important to cross-check against other country experience.
4. A test using a lower value for the SDR is of dubious worth. If the NPV is already positive (the decision rule), it will still be positive at a lower rate. If the NPV is negative, using a lower SDR may turn it positive, but proceeding with a marginal project is not advisable, given the potential for optimism bias and other risks.
5. Reflecting the remaining service potential of a fixed asset that has not yet reached the end of its economic life.
6. This discussion comes from World Bank (2016).
7. Even if the government borrows, interest and eventually the principal will have to be paid through taxation.
8. In economic theory, nondistortionary lump-sum taxes with no impact on allocative efficiency can be used. In the real world, they rarely are, because they are often politically impractical or are incompatible with other distributional objectives that the government is pursuing through taxation.
9. In the case of income tax on earned income, workers may face a reduced incentive to work and therefore may consume more leisure than is socially optimal, resulting in an overall social welfare loss.
10. If public costs and private benefits are treated as having equal worth, the net present value of projects will be systematically overestimated.
11. A pure public good (or service) is one where it is not possible to exclude users from consuming the good (service) and consumption by one consumer does not diminish the amount of the good (service) available for the others. These characteristics mean that there is no incentive for the private sector to supply the good (service) because it is impossible to earn revenues and make a profit.
12. WTA is a closely related alternative measure used to value negative impacts. This is the minimum payment that a beneficiary would need to be compensated to forgo a benefit or accept a negative impact.
13. "Utility" is a concept used in welfare economics meaning the satisfaction or change in welfare that a person gets from consumption of a good or service.
14. Values would be expected to be higher the closer to the amenity.
15. Generalized travel costs include the value of personal time.
16. The European Commission proposes five categories of probability: A. Very unlikely (0–10 percent probability); B. Unlikely (10–33 percent); C. About as likely as not (33–66 percent); D. Likely (66–90 percent); and E. Very likely (90–100 percent)
17. The European Commission proposes five ratings of severity: I. No relevant effect on social welfare, even without remedial actions; II. Minor loss of social welfare, requiring remedial actions; III. Moderate social welfare losses, which may be corrected by remedial actions; IV. Critical social welfare losses, which are not avoidable through remedial actions; and V. Catastrophic, indicating project failure.
18. The European Commission proposes four levels of risk: low, moderate, high, and very high. Very high risk levels representing high-probability, high-severity events are deemed unacceptable and require action.

19. In effect, "significant" means that the project is at a "high" risk level, since "very high" requires redesign.
20. "Expected" in the strictly statistical sense of the word.
21. The simplest probability distribution is a triangular distribution. Estimating expected values using a triangular distribution is relatively straightforward and does not require a Monte Carlo simulation.

REFERENCES

Commonwealth of Australia. 2006. "Handbook of Cost-Benefit Analysis." Guidance Note, Commonwealth of Australia, Canberra.

European Commission. 2008. "Guide to Cost Benefit Analysis of Investment Projects." Directorate General for Regional Policy, Brussels.

———. 2014. "Guide to Cost-Benefit Analysis of Investment Projects: Economic Appraisal Tool for Cohesion Policy 2014–2020." Directorate General for Regional and Urban Policy, Brussels.

HM Treasury. 2003. *The Green Book: Appraisal and Evaluation in Central Government*. Updated in 2013. London: HM Treasury.

OECD (Organisation for Economic Co-operation and Development). 2015. "Adapting Transport Policy to Climate Change." International Transport Forum Research Report, OECD, Paris.

Office of the Prime Minister, France. 2013. "Socio-economic Evaluation of Public Investment." Commissariat Générale à la Stratégie et a la Prospective (CGSP), Office of the Prime Minister, Paris. http://www.strategie.gouv.fr/publications/levaluation-socioeconomique-investissements-publics-tome1.

World Bank. 1998. *Handbook on Economic Analysis of Investment Operations*. Washington, DC: World Bank. http://documents.worldbank.org/curated/en/749061468740206498WWandbook-on-economic-analysis-of-investment-operations.

———. 2016. "Discounting of Costs and Benefits in Economic Analysis of World Bank Projects." Draft technical note, World Bank, Washington, DC.

Young, L. 2002. "Determining the Discount Rate for Government Projects." Working Paper 02/21, New Zealand Treasury, Wellington.

C

Examples of Project- and Portfolio-Level Management Support Capabilities Provided by a PIM Information System

TABLE C.1 **Project- and portfolio-level support capabilities**

PROJECT STAGE	PROJECT-LEVEL CAPABILITY	PORTFOLIO-LEVEL CAPABILITY
PIM general portfolio administration	• Not applicable	• Provide extensive capabilities to the portfolio administrator to grant and revoke user access rights to the PIM information system
Project identification and preappraisal	• Exchange project data with local government systems in accordance with agreed-on protocols • Record preappraisal approvals and related documentation	• Keep a record of investment policy objectives and priorities • Produce programwide historical analyses of financial performance, nonfinancial performance, and economic impact against policy objectives and priorities
Design and appraisal	• Record project appraisal components and results of feasibility studies as well as related documentation	• Keep a record of feasibility study results and produce analyses on various dimensions
Review of appraisal	• Record independent review ratings, approvals, and related documentation	• Keep a record of independent review ratings and approvals
Selection and budgeting	• Calculate baseline financing requirements of each active investment project for the fiscal year and out years as a function of expected capital and operating expenses (and operational income, if any) • Receive and record project-level budget appropriations from the budget system • Record baseline implementation, financial, procurement, and performance plans; lock these baseline plans against modifications and provide on-demand comparison with corresponding appraisal stage plans	• Record and store prioritization criteria and results and project rankings • Pass to the budget system newly selected projects for inclusion in the Draft Budget Law • Calculate baseline public investment portfolio (PIP) funding requirements for the fiscal year and for the medium term for individual sector ministries and across sectors • Calculate fiscal space for individual sector ministries and in total as a function of overall PIP budget ceiling and baseline requirements

continued

TABLE C.1, *continued*

PROJECT STAGE	PROJECT-LEVEL CAPABILITY	PORTFOLIO-LEVEL CAPABILITY
Project implementation and monitoring	• Enforce submission of nonfinancial and work performance information by project managers at agreed-on time intervals and update current versions of implementation, procurement, and performance plans • Maintain current version of the procurement plan for each project through data exchanges with the public procurement portal and record all contracts signed • Maintain current and historic financial performance balances from completed financial transactions received from the financial management information system • Produce periodic and ad hoc project financial performance reports • Produce reports and answer ad hoc queries on physical implementation and procurement progress • Link to periodic project financial statements produced by a subsidiary project accounting system or financial management information system (FMIS)	• Develop PIP status and performance charts for sector or ministry (and other) groupings and produce analyses by various classifications and key performance indicators as part of system dashboards • Carry out scripted analyses of performance charts and advise interested parties of results and recommended actions • Allow authorized managers at direct budget beneficiary level or higher to drill down from PIP status or performance charts to individual projects • Provide online search functions to visualize the PIP according to various filters • Calculate cost-to-completion for all or parts of the PIP and produce filtered analyses by various criteria (ministry, investment type, policy objective or priority, funding adequacy) • Develop statistics of program implementation time and delay by project life-cycle stage to assess program management effectiveness • Calculate program implementation performance indicators as a function of budget appropriation or financial or physical performance trends; allow authorized users to drill down to affected individual projects
Project adjustment	• Allow reformulation of key project appraisal components and lock previous versions of such components for later comparison and assessment • Recalculate baseline financing requirements of projects as a function of needed project adjustments • Receive and record adjustments to project-level budget appropriations from the budget system	• Recalculate baseline public investment portfolio funding requirements for the fiscal year and for the medium term for individual sector ministries and across sectors • Recalculate fiscal space for individual sector ministries and in total as a function of overall PIP budget ceiling and baseline requirements
Operation	• Calculate indicators, targets, and results for monitoring service delivery	• Store indicators, targets, and results for service delivery from project facilities and produce analyses and monitoring
Evaluation	• Store ex post evaluation reports and assemble key indicators from ex post and ex ante studies for comparison • Develop project evaluation ratings based on above comparisons	• Calculate and store indicators, targets, and results for ex post evaluation of (samples of) projects

D

Types of Content for a PIM Information System Database

TABLE D.1 **Elements of a PIM system database, by project stage**

PROJECT STAGE[a]	DATA ELEMENT
Conceptualization and preliminary screening	• *Concept note or prescreening form data.* Unique project number and name; project objectives and outcomes, project cost, sector or subsector, sponsor(s); implementing agency(ies); project manager; key dates, project locations, cofinancing requirements • Link to concept note or prescreening document • *Eligibility.* National or sector strategy code(s); coding of the strategic policy elements allows filtering of public investment portfolio (PIP) statistics by eligibility criteria as part of analytical dashboards • *Approval.* Approval date; project score or ranking, if applicable
Design and appraisal	• Link to final versions of feasibility study documents • *Economic and financial cost-benefit justification.* Calculation parameters, net present value, financial internal rate of return, economic internal rate of return, payback time, switching values, or other, in accordance with sector-specific methodology; format should allow automatic comparison with corresponding values calculated at project evaluation time • *Preliminary work plan.* Time-bound list of major activities and milestones over project life cycle with their beginning and ending dates • *Cost tables.* Link to spreadsheet files of cost tables developed for project appraisal • *Preliminary financial plan.* Multiyear capital, operating expenses, and operating income (if any) • *Performance plan.* Time-bound progress, results, and impact indicators formulated according to programwide or sector-specific framework • *Risk management plan.* Risks, risk ratings, and mitigation measures formulated in accordance with programwide or sector-specific framework
Independent review	• Link to independent review document
Selection	• Project appraisal and project selection approvals and dates by project proponent, independent reviewers, and central finance agency representatives • *Project selection ratings.* Final priority or point ranking in accordance with agreed-on programwide standard or sector-specific methodology
Budgeting	• *Baseline budget request.* Multiyear capital, operating expenses, and operating income (if any); is also the baseline financial plan • *Baseline budget appropriation.* Multiyear capital and operating budget appropriation for initial project year that will be used to determine baseline funding adequacy for the project, by comparison with baseline budget request • *Baseline procurement plan.* Contract value and planned solicitation and award dates for investment contracts under the project; not a detailed procurement plan as needed for project management • *Baseline work plan.* A modification of the preliminary work plan used for appraisal • *Baseline performance plan.* May be the same or a modification of the performance plan used for the appraisal stage

continued

TABLE D.1, *continued*

PROJECT STAGE[a]	DATA ELEMENTS
Implementation	• Chronological links to project progress reports produced by project manager and to project progress evaluation reports produced by project reviewers • *Current work plan.* Current version of the baseline implementation plan with real dates for completed activities and projected dates for future ones; is used for reporting project progress and is not a detailed activity schedule as required for project management • *Current financial plan.* Projected capital, operating expenses, and operating income (if any) by year for current and medium terms; is also the budget request for the year • *Financial performance history.* Current year capital and operating budget appropriations against actual commitments and expenses and the same information for past years • *Nonfinancial performance.* Current, time-bound list of completed and pending nonfinancial performance indicators; completed indicator values and dates are locked upon entry and thereafter serve to assess performance variance with corresponding baseline indicators; pending indicators reflect currently estimated values and dates and are used for performance projections, including possible shortcomings • *Current procurement plan.* Contract value and actual solicitation and award dates of investment contracts to date
Monitoring[b]	*Project status indicators.* The following illustrates possible status indicators that could be calculated by the PIM information system. Many others can be considered, and each may be associated with more detailed conditions (for example, a "delayed" indicator may be associated with codes for more specific conditions, such as "procurement delay" or "effectiveness delay" or "implementation delay": • *Project stage.* Actual start and end dates for each investment project stage, along with authorized user responsible for closing of each stage; normally, all stage-related data are locked upon stage closing • *Implementation status.* Active, delayed, dormant • *Project risk.* Low, medium, high • *Performance rankings.* The following are examples of types of performance rankings that could be used in project monitoring dashboards. The derivation logic for each indicator needs to be worked out in detail. • *Budgeting performance.* Three-level project ranking as a function of project implementation delay induced by the average appropriation shortfall to date. This indicator and the next one ("funding performance") assess the efficiency of the treasury in releasing budgetary and cash resources for PIM • *Funding performance.* Three-level project ranking as a function of project implementation delay induced by average allocation shortfall to date • *Implementation performance.* Stages of implementation, for example, (a) start-up, < 10% of total project costs incurred; (b) stage 1, 10–29% of costs incurred; (c) stage 2, 30–49% of costs incurred; (d) stage 3, 50–69% of costs incurred; (e) stage 4, 70–89% of costs incurred; (f) completion, > 90% of project costs incurred • *Disbursement performance.* Three-level project ranking as a function of variance between planned (baseline) and completed disbursements to date • *Procurement performance.* Three-level, value-weighted project ranking as a function of delay to date between planned and actual solicitation and award dates, for investment contracts under the project
Adjustment	• Link to project adjustment documentation files • Adjusted versions of performance, financial, work, and risk management plans • Link to adjusted cost table files, if appropriate
Completion	• Current versions of work plan, financial plan, performance plan, procurement plan at completion date • Project performance rankings as of project completion date • Project performance evaluation ratings from completion report • Link to project completion report
Evaluation	• Economic and financial results: initial versus final net present value, financial internal rate of return, economic internal rate of return, payback time, or other, in accordance with sector-specific methodology • Baseline and final result and impact indicators • Link to project evaluation report

a. Project life-cycle stage at which data usually are first entered into PIM information system database.
b. Status indicators and performance rankings for project monitoring purposes calculated at predefined intervals, occurring after the corresponding deadline for project status reporting.

www.ingramcontent.com/pod-product-compliance
Lightning Source LLC
LaVergne TN
LVHW080038210926
848481LV00011B/3223